# "Fire from the Midst of You"

An artist named J. Dougherty prepared a pastel study intended for the publication of Stephen Vincent Benet's award-winning "John Brown's Body" (1928), but the sketch was apparently never used. The gravestone at the center of the eerie scene declares, "Here Lies John Brown." *West Virginia State Archives.*

# "Fire from the Midst of You"

*A Religious Life of John Brown*

Louis A. DeCaro, Jr.

NEW YORK UNIVERSITY PRESS
*New York and London*

NEW YORK UNIVERSITY PRESS
New York and London

Library of Congress Cataloging-in-Publication Data
DeCaro, Louis A., 1957–
Fire from the midst of you: a religious life of John Brown/
Louis A. DeCaro, Jr.
p. cm
Includes bibliographical references (p. ) and index.
ISBN 0-8147-1921-X (acid-free paper)
1. Brown, John, 1800–1859. 2. Brown, John, 1800–1859—Religion.
3. Brown, John, 1800–1859—Views on Christianity. 4. Abolitionists—
United States—Biography. 5. Antislavery movements—United States—
History—19th century. 6. Chrisitanity and politics—United States—
History—19th century. I. Title.
E451 .D43 2002
973.7'116'092—dc21    2002009590

082603 - 3080 D2

*To Michele*
*with all my love*

*By the multitude of your iniquities, in the unrighteousness of your trade, you profaned your sanctuaries. Therefore I have brought fire from the midst of you; it has consumed you, and I have turned you to ashes on the earth in the eyes of all who see you.*

—Ezekiel 28:18

# Contents

# Acknowledgments

I am most grateful to Niko Pfund, formerly director of NYU Press (now the academic publisher of Oxford University Press) for encouraging me to develop my interest in John Brown into a published work. This may not be the work Niko imagined, but I hope it is at least worthy of the kindness and vision he exerted in prompting my efforts. I am likewise thankful to Jennifer Hammer, editor of NYU Press, for her ongoing interest, helpful criticisms, and patience when I missed my deadline. This is my third effort with NYU Press, and so I could not fail to acknowledge also the labors of Despina Papazoglou Gimbel, managing editor, for her effective role in bringing this and many other works to publication.

I would like to honor several important individuals who are no longer living. Katherine Mayo, a writer and scholar, was the field researcher and interviewer who assisted Oswald Garrison Villard in the preparation of his 1910 biography of John Brown. With all due respect, it seems to me that Mayo's contributions—including an extensive number of interviews with Brown's children and associates as well as a myriad pages of notes and transcriptions—are just as important as Villard's work (if not more so). It was Mayo who reconstructed the valuable chronology and supplied the primary information so notable in his book. Indeed, having worked extensively in the Villard papers, I tend to think he failed to do justice to the meticulous, painstaking, and thoughtful research of Katherine Mayo. Later in the twentieth century, Boyd B. Stutler and the Reverend Clarence S. Gee found John Brown, and shared him throughout nearly four decades of friendly correspondence. Their expansive research and documentary work (especially that of Stutler) is indispensable, and their names are forever linked with the John Brown legacy itself. No biographer of John Brown can succeed without drawing on the wealth of their labors, or appreciating the nobility of their intentions. Likewise,

Edwin N. Cotter Jr., who died in 2001, was personally encouraging and helpful to me. Mr. Cotter was for many years the supervisor of the John Brown Farm at Lake Placid, New York, and did in-depth documentary work on the Browns in North Elba along with the black colonies. I will never forget the day he and his wife Alice showed us "John's Room"—the study where he kept his archives. The tour left no doubt in my mind why Edwin Cotter was on a first-name basis with "Old Brown." Mr. Cotter befriended me as he did many others. We will miss him, as we will also miss Marjory Blubaugh, a local historian from Chambersburg, Pennsylvania. Marjory was kindly interested in my work and particularly helpful when I was seeking information on John Brown's involvement in southeastern Pennsylvania.

In the land of the living, I am so grateful for the friendship and support of Jean Libby, an academic, photographer, and documentary scholar whose tireless and sacrificial labors to preserve and advance our understanding of John Brown and the black struggle are of inestimable value. Her generosity and assistance to me cannot be overstated, and her own contributions to the literature are vital. Thomas L. Vince, Historian and Archivist of the Western Reserve Academy in Hudson, Ohio, is another fine scholar who extended help and shared his time and rich insights during our meeting in 2000. At the Hudson Library and Historical Society, I was likewise kindly and patiently assisted by Archivist James Caccamo and Assistant Archivist Gwen Mayer, who endured my excited foray into their collections, giving hints and help throughout my research. I am also thankful to Gwendolyn Robinson from the WISH Center, Chatham, Ontario, Canada, and Cecilia Gross of the Springfield Technical College, Springfield, Massachusetts for their kind assistance. Also in Springfield, many thanks for the faithful correspondence of my friend, Sylvia Humphrey Spann, who has done all in her power to assist me in this work. Margaret Washington of Cornell University has been so kind, patiently sharing her rich insights into the nineteenth-century abolitionist context with me. Paul Lee of Best Efforts, Inc., and James Cone of the Union Theological Seminary, have offered criticism and encouragement during my scholarly transition from Malcolm X to John Brown.

I also received great assistance from the following individuals and the fine archives they supervise: Bernard Crystal and his staff at the Rare Books and Manuscripts Collection of Columbia University Library; Michele Plourde-Barker of the Connecticut Valley Historical Society, Springfield, Massachusetts; Debra Basham of the Boyd B. Stutler Papers at the West Virginia State Archives; and Leslie Fields at the Gilder Lehrman Collection, ably assisted by Inge Dupont, Sylvie Merian, and McKenna Lebens of the Morgan Library in New York City; Jerold Pepper of the Adirondack Museum; Howard Dodson, Chief at the Schomburg Center for Research in Black Culture in Harlem; and Elizabeth Braun of the Jersey City Public Library, who patiently and kindly processed many interlibrary loan requests on my behalf. Additional thanks go to Gregory Toledo, Peggy Russo, Arlene Hudson, Natalie and Richard Smith, Robert Carle, DeWitt Dykes, Sharon Sexton, Gerald McFarland, William Loren Katz, Karl Gridley, Eric Ledell Smith, Martha Swan, the Reverend Paulo Freire, the Reverend Charles Kenyatta, and my brother Frank DeCaro for their assistance and encouragement in the various phases of my work. Filial love and thanks always go to the Reverend Louis Sr. and Clara DeCaro, who continue to encourage me as only loving parents can. Above all, thanks and love go to my sweet singing and studious wife Michele, who "had my back" the whole time of writing. Perhaps her admiration for Sister Harriet Tubman has made her a doubly strong ally.

*Grace and Peace*

*With all the purifying and liberalizing power of the Christian religion, teaching as it does, meekness, gentleness, [and] brotherly kindness, those who profess it have not yet even approached the position of treating the black man as an equal man and a brother. The few who have thus far risen to this requirement, both of reason and religion, are stigmatized as fanatics and enthusiasts.*

—Frederick Douglass

# Introduction

## Reconfiguring Sainthood

I acknowledge no man in human form.
> —John Brown, under interrogation at
> Harper's Ferry, October 19, 1859[1]

Following the lead of biographers and journalists, John
Brown has often been portrayed in fiction and film as a white religious
fanatic who was obsessed with the violent destruction of slavery. He is
especially remembered for his failed raid at Harper's Ferry [West] Virginia, where he lead a small band of white and black men in seizing a
government armory in October 1859. Born in 1800, he spent most of his
fifty-nine years in pursuit of business success, though failing for the most
part to achieve his goals. In the decade prior to the Civil War, abolitionists intensified their attempts to aid and assist fugitive slaves and other
blacks resisting the long reach of slavery into the North. But whereas
most of them adhered to pacifism, Brown had steadily honed his belief in
the forceful overthrow of slavery until he himself determined to lead the
effort.

A deeply religious man and father of a large family, he believed that
slavery was not going to relent in the face of political compromise or
moral outcries from abolitionists. When pro-slavery and anti-slavery
forces clashed in the newly opened Kansas territory in 1856, Brown and
his family stood at the epicenter of the crisis as determined enemies of
slavery and—as a minority within a minority—passionate allies of the
black community. Though he and others fought fire with fire against pro-
slavery terrorists who had initiated the fighting and excelled in cruelty,
Brown's many detractors have increasingly emphasized his role in the violent Kansas conflict to the point of suggesting he was "the father of

1

modern terrorism." Yet he is best known in history for the raid on Harper's Ferry—though its underlying strategy and purpose are usually misunderstood and misrepresented in popular narratives.

After the failure of the raid, Brown and his surviving men were captured, tried, and hanged by the State of Virginia. Lionized in the North and hated in the South, he was a legend even before he climbed the gallows' steps on December 2, 1859. After the Civil War broke out in 1861, a playful soldier's song became associated with him, and "John Brown's Body" became the fighting anthem of the Union army. At the time, however, Abraham Lincoln described him as the kind of "enthusiast" who "broods over the oppression of a people till he fancies himself commissioned by Heaven to liberate them." But even Lincoln could not escape John Brown, whose spirit seems to have loomed over the country throughout the Civil War.[2]

John Brown has had zealous friends but far more enemies, many of whom deeply resent his militant role on behalf of black liberation. To this day, many white American scholars, writers, and clergymen overtly dismiss him for what they perceive as misguided zeal and religious fanaticism. But underlying their biased narratives is often the contempt of American racial scorn—the resentment that a *white man* would go to the point of killing other whites on behalf of black freedom. In the narratives of many scholars and journalists, terms like "fanatic," "insane," "violent," and "obsessed" are commonly used to describe John Brown.[3] These assessments have in turn informed standard history textbooks as well as popular films and novels, leaving the public with a hazy, sinister impression of the man who supposedly betrayed his race by going too far on behalf of black freedom. As one of my parishioners said when he heard about my interest in John Brown, *"Didn't he kill people?"*

Perhaps John Brown has been all but forgotten by most African Americans today, but until recently he has been viewed with great admiration and affection, even reverence, by many in the black community. African Americans have always understood the reason for the dismissal of John Brown by white society, knowing that their liberation struggle has never been a priority on our nation's agenda. Beginning with the founding fathers, freedom and justice for black people was never intrinsic to the American dream, nor was it even so for Abraham Lincoln, the so-called Great Emancipator. Brown, on the other hand, put black liberation first and foremost—not only as a political belief but as a personal ambition.

As black people have long realized, their famous ally is considered fanatical and insane largely because he presumed their humanity in a society North and South that categorically dehumanized them. White Americans have long glorified "violence" and "fanaticism" when it pertained to their nationalistic interests. For instance, the expansion of white settlers into Mexican territory and the establishment of Texas in the nineteenth century was largely premised upon the expansion of black enslavement. In contrast to Brown's efforts to liberate slaves at Harper's Ferry, the violent efforts of pro-slavery settlers culminating in the bloody Alamo incident of 1836 is commonly perceived as heroic and noble, even though the famous white insurgents were occupying land belonging to a government and nation that prohibited slavery.

Speaking to his organization after making the pilgrimage to Mecca in 1964, Malcolm X raised the issue of the white American perception and portrayal of John Brown. Speaking about potential white allies (which he now welcomed), the Muslim leader suggested that a good litmus test would be to ask them what they thought of the famous abolitionist. "You know what John Brown did? He went to war. He was a white man who went to war against white people to help free slaves." Malcolm continued:

> White people call John Brown a nut. Go read the history, go read what all of them say about John Brown. They're trying to make it look like he was a nut, a fanatic. They made a movie on it, I saw a movie on the screen one night. Why, I would be afraid to get near John Brown if I go by what other white folks say about him.

The movie that Malcolm saw "on the screen one night" was probably *Santa Fe Trail*, released in 1940 (six years before he was incarcerated). With an all-star cast including Raymond Massey, Olivia De Havilland, Errol Flynn, Van Heflin, and Ronald Reagan, *Santa Fe Trail* was based on a pro-Southern screenplay that minimized the evil of slavery while portraying Brown as a deluded religious bandit whose crimes far outweighed his fanatical devotion to black liberation. Malcolm went on to prison (and the prison library), and apparently read the prominent biographies of Brown too. As a "Black Muslim," he was neither free nor willing to acknowledge the positive contributions of certain whites, but as an independent leader, Malcolm could speak his mind on the common belief that John Brown was crazy.

But they depict him in this image because he was willing to shed blood to free the slaves. And any white man who is ready and willing to shed blood for your freedom—in the sight of other whites, he's nuts. . . . So when you want to know good white folks in history where black people are concerned, go read the history of John Brown. That was what I call a white liberal. But those other kind, they are questionable.[4]

But if Brown is misunderstood by modern scholars and writers, it is also because of his strong religious beliefs. However different their political and social views, even his nineteenth-century opponents had a better understanding of his religious world view than do many biographers and scholars today. That he considered himself "an instrument of Providence" smacks of delusion and fanaticism in modern and postmodern perceptions. That he likewise believed that all of the Christian scriptures reflect the same God at work in the history of redemption is likewise indigestible to most people in a post-Christian society. All the more reason, then, for a religiously oriented portrayal of the famous abolitionist. Indeed, such an approach suits him, as he might have put it, "midling well."

Brown was a man of faith, and well read in the Bible and Christian literature. Like many Christians, he was converted as a youth, and he grew up in a theologically conservative, evangelical, and Calvinist home. Though his early intention to study for the ministry did not work out, Brown was a founding church member, Bible teacher, and a devoted layman throughout his life. Even after he committed himself full time to the abolitionist struggle, he remained a church attender and faithful Bible student. Furthermore, he and his family represented a unique strand of the abolitionist movement. A devotedly Christian people who believed the Bible to be the inspired and infallible word of God, they were also biblical egalitarians—radical dissenters from the racialist beliefs of many white Christians. The Browns applied the biblical doctrine of *humanity the image of God* to the frontier as well as the slave market, and were thus righteously indignant at the social, political, and ecclesiastical realities of a society steeped in white supremacy. Like many Christian abolitionists, the Browns understood the Golden Rule as a mandate to fight slavery by undermining it in overt and covert political acts, such as antislavery groups, participation in the underground railroad, and support of candidates who held similar opinions regarding slavery. John Brown's war on slavery was undoubtedly an extension of the Christian legacy of his family.

As an evangelical Christian, he not only read the Bible as God's word, he read the Bible as *God's word to John Brown*. He believed that the scriptures continued to speak to life situations, radiating fresh truth and directives without obscuring its original and primary meaning. For him, God was speaking afresh on the enslavement of the African, and this was the ongoing theme of his devotional life. It guided his actions, guarded his values, and gave him strength. His piety was inseparable from his deeply felt call to destroy slavery. And though there is yet a need for studies of greater clarity and depth concerning his militant activities, my goal here is to present *the kind of man John Brown was* vis-à-vis his religious context and personal spirituality.

Though Brown's most successful biographer to date has recognized the centrality of religion in his narrative, he presents a negative interpretation of his Christianity—"the Calvinist tradition of an austere, implacable God who demanded the most exacting obedience from the sinful creatures He put on trial in this world." But this is a reading of Calvinistic Christianity from outside the theological and experiential boundaries in which Brown and many other Christians lived. Perceived as a Puritan "fanatic," his violent opposition to slavery is thus thought to be consistent with his belief in "the wrathful Jehovah of ancient Israel."[5] These assumptions reflect an inadequate understanding of the theology and spirituality of the Protestant Reformation, a deficiency that is easily overlooked in the post-Christian era academy. But they also lend themselves to skewed political portrayals of John Brown. In fact, his vision was premised upon a thoroughly biblical spirituality rooted theologically and ethically in the teachings of Jesus and the apostles *as much as* the Hebrew prophets and Old Testament accounts regarding the slaying of pagan tribes.

History is filled with stories of men and women who have felt compelled, guided, protected, and empowered by forces beyond themselves. In the name of objectivity historians may strip away the supposed myths, superstitions, and biases of the spiritual and supernatural from biography. However, in the end they may strip truth away from the story too. As E. Harris Harbison advised, we should be sensitive to "the unpredictable and sometimes unbelievable redemptive forces in history." Perhaps we will then sense an inscrutable purpose "behind both the personal decisions and the vast impersonal forces of history." At least, a religious analysis should allow us to ponder and wonder more than dogmatize or doubt.[6]

If we are to study John Brown from a religious perspective, then we cannot afford to ignore or stigmatize his religious faith as fanaticism and delusion. Neither should we apologize for acknowledging the still, small voice that he believed he heard, and the forces that he may have sensed flowing around and through him. Brown's first biographers are often charged with having written panegyrics lined with appeals to God's purpose.[7] The modern historian responds by saying that we are to strive for a neutral approach to the fiery abolitionist. We are also to reject any notion of sainthood.

In traditional religious terms, a saint is thought to be of an uncommonly holy character, virtually transcending the fallen human condition. This concept of sainthood evolved in the ancient church, originating with the Eucharistic veneration of martyred Christians. In time this veneration became cultic, forcing theologians to underscore the difference between worshiping God and honoring saints. Later, Protestant theologians pointed out that according to the Bible a saint was merely a believer—one set apart from the world through salvation in Jesus Christ. No longer seen as divine intercessors or holy models, saints were neither disrespected nor venerated by Protestants. Interestingly, this would have been the definition of sainthood employed by John Brown. Perhaps it is also a key to studying his life from a religious standpoint.

One would not claim John Brown to have been a saint in the popular sense of the term. He was clearly imperfect, as his story shows. As a husband, father, businessman, and soldier, he demonstrated his imperfections and would readily have acknowledged them in keeping with his belief in sinful human nature. But he was also a sincere and remarkably devout Christian. Of course, when it came to the subject of slavery, Brown could *burn*, and people who knew him saw the flame of hatred in his eyes, heard it in his voice, and felt it in his touch. Though he was hardly the only abolitionist to equate chattel slavery with sin, his struggle against slavery was far more personal and religious than it was for many abolitionists, just as his respect and affection for black people was far more personal and religious than it was for most enemies of slavery. Decades after his death, John Brown remained a bright light shining on a dark frontier of political betrayal and social rejection for many black people. Harriet Tubman, a leader whose spirituality has yet to be adequately considered, spoke of him in Christlike terms, so fond was his memory to her and her troubled people.[8]

All of this is to say that John Brown was very much a saint in his own way, if the term is understood in the Protestant sense. He was a sincere believer, however imperfect, also believing himself carried along by God's grace and mercy. By reconfiguring our notion of sainthood we find a fitting category for him. To study him as a Protestant saint we must weigh him in the balance of history, evaluating and criticizing him accordingly. Yet at the same time we should remember what William Roscoe Thayer once wrote, that we are "reporting from the heart of human life matters too sacred to be twisted in the narration to suit private opinion."

Upon his capture at Harper's Ferry, Brown was interviewed by a number of politicians and spectators, all of them curious to see and hear the bruised, bloodied, warrior who had opened the flood gates of tribulation upon the South. As he answered questions posed by his Southern captors, Congressman C. L. Vallandigham—the only Northern politician present—entered the room and interrupted the interview by asking, "Mr. Brown, who sent you here?" Being from Ohio, Vallandigham was probably just as determined to disassociate himself from the raid as he was to sniff out any hint of anti-slavery conspiracy among his bitter opponents at home. Like most Northern politicians in the antebellum period, Vallandigham was far more concerned about protecting Southern sensibilities and avoiding civil war than he was about liberating three million enslaved black people. "No man sent me here," Brown answered candidly. "It was my own prompting and that of my Maker, or that of the Devil—whichever you please to ascribe it to. I acknowledge no man in human form."[9]

John Brown gave his interrogators the prerogative to draw their own conclusions about him, but either way he assumed they would recognize the working of forces beyond himself. Whether those forces were supernatural is a question that cannot be answered by historical inquiry alone. However, recognizing the depth and value of Brown's religious life and the religious world around him may at least help us to better understand his story as a Protestant saint—a unique believer whose urgent, fiery devotion to human liberation in some sense counterbalanced the injustice and indifference of a whole generation of white Americans.

PART I

# A Power above Ourselves

It is a great mercy to us that we frequently are made to understand most thoroughly our absolute dependence on a power quite above ourselves. How blessed are all whose hearts and conduct do not set them at variance with that power!

—John Brown

# 1

# "And They Had No Comforter"

## John Brown and the "Everlasting Negro" Question

So I returned, and considered all the oppressions that are done under the sun: and behold the tears of such as were oppressed, and they had no comforter; and on the side of their oppressors there was power; but they had no comforter.

—Ecclesiastes 4:1*

In February 1859, the year of the Harper's Ferry raid, Jeremiah R. Brown, half-brother of John Brown, visited New Orleans, Louisiana. During his stay he saw notice of a slave auction to be held that weekend, and so found his way to the City Hotel. As slave flesh goes, this was an exceptional sale—featuring "Valuable Slaves, All from one Cotton Plantation in Carolina," representing ten distinct families. The eldest among those to be auctioned were apparently family heads, including field hands Nathan, age 57, Bellar, age 45, Charley, age 39, and Mathan, age 37. The youngest were Willson, age 1, Lucretia, age 2, Cornelia, age 2, and Daphne, age 3. All the slaves were noted as "field hands," except the children—though the youngest field hand, Chaney, was only ten years old. Other slaves were apparently sold on this occa-

---

* This and all other biblical epigraphs at chapter openings are passages John Brown marked in his Bible. All the texts marked by John Brown were made in the Authorized, or King James Version of the Bible, in an edition published by the American Bible Society, New York, N.Y., 1854. This was not the only Bible he owned, but it was the Bible that he read during his imprisonment and gave to one of the jailers, John H. Blessing, prior to his hanging. From Blessing's family the Bible eventually passed into the hands of a collector, and then into the possession of the Chicago Historical Society, Chicago, Illinois. See Harvey Rachlin, *Lucy's Bones, Sacred Stones, and Einstein's Brain* (New York: Henry Holt, 1996), 212–16.

sion, but it was this special plantation sale "without reserve" (in which slaves could be purchased on credit at 6 percent interest) that was the highlight of the auction.

Jeremiah Brown watched the ordeal, feeling desperate and helpless at the sight of human beings paraded before hungry eyes, blending business and bitter human sorrow. Unable to do anything else, Jeremiah pulled out his pencil and furiously scribbled the final sale prices on the face of an auction broadside, such as: "one Boy 12"—perhaps the young Edmon, torn away from his mother Clarisa and sold for $975; "Young woman 17"—probably the field hand called Sukey—sold for $1,570; "one man 35"—maybe Cusiler—sold for $1,400; "Girl handsom[e] 15"—possibly Evelina, sold for $1,490.[1] Jeremiah Brown's angry documentation would be displayed upon his return to Ohio, before family and friends.

By now Owen Brown, the patriarch of the family, was dead. But Jeremiah probably wished he could share his chronicle of rage with him. Owen's hatred of slavery exceeded that of any man Jeremiah had ever known—except perhaps for his elder half-brother, John Brown, whom he thought too extreme. At that moment, in fact, John was somewhere in Iowa, having liberated eleven Missouri slaves, moving them through the winter cold toward freedom in Canada. Heavily armed and unwilling to surrender his black friends without a fight to the death, he and his associates would see to it that this "stolen property" would find their way to Canada under the cold steel guardianship of their Sharp's rifles. But here in New Orleans there was no deliverance for the children of Africa. Here were forty-eight human beings (thirty-one of the forty-eight slaves were twenty years or younger), shipped from the cotton field to the slave block, destined to be torn from each other and sold away to the highest bidder—appointed once more for the exploitation and violations of the master's house and field.

To the Browns, chattel slavery was a revolting evil, a sin against God and man. Yet to a large segment of whites in the South it was considered an acceptable, even necessary, institution in line with the highest standards of civilization and Christian society. To an equally great number of whites in the North, chattel slavery was unattractive—but best left alone as long as it did not spread into the free states, carrying with it the accursed black-skinned sons and daughters of Ham. It was a wrong to be sure, but if kept confined and restricted, such a wrong was best tolerated for the good of the nation.

The realities associated with slavery in the United States are certainly more expansive than what has been taught in standard classroom history texts. The obvious issues—the injustices and horrors of slavery itself— were at the center of the conflict in John Brown's era, and despite the on- going debates between historians concerning various aspects of slavery in the United States, it cannot be questioned that it was a cruel and ex- ploitative institution. It is interesting that Brown's leading biographer thinks he was influenced by stylizations of slavery in abolitionist publica- tions, which portrayed planters as "beady-eyed, Heaven-flouting" vil- lains who not only "beat their slaves with savage glee but raped Negro girls in a frenzy of lust." Rather than having a realistic sense of slavery and slavemaster, he says Brown imagined the South to be full of "ogres" and . . . "devils trying to graft slavery forever on the tormented face of this Republic." "All slavemasters were not grotesque monsters like those described in the abolitionist literature," the biographer continues. "There were some very good slavemasters as there were some very evil ones." But the "vast majority of the South's 46,000 planters fell somewhere between the two extremes" of good and evil. This "vast majority" of slaveholders were the norm, characteristically using the whip only to enforce order, not for sadistic purposes. Indeed, this "vast majority" is to be sympa- thized with according to the biographer, for they are fraught with guilt— the offspring of Thomas Jefferson, reflecting his internal civil war, the rag- ing conflict between liberalism and human bondage. These planters, we are told further, held relentlessly to slavery for fear of what their world would become if slavery were abolished.[2]

It is more than doubtful that John Brown was so naïve as to the nature of slavery. To be sure, abolitionist literature highlighted only the most ex- treme cases of slavemaster violence and debauchery. "Sunday school sim- plicities had their place in anti-slavery literature," writes Bertram Wyatt- Brown, "because melodrama is the stuff of popular agitation."[3] One would expect this kind of treatment in any crusading literature, that the worst aspects would be highlighted. But this does not mean that aboli- tionists did not recognize gradations in the treatment of slaves by their masters, especially since pro-slavery advocates would naturally uplift what they considered upstanding examples of slavery in debates with abolitionists. Brown surely knew that slavemasters varied in their meth- ods of control, in their exercise of "discipline," even in their relationships to their human chattel. He was undoubtedly aware of "good Christian" slavemasters too, just as he was aware that there were Christian clergy protecting and defending slavery in principle and practice. In general, he opposed slavery on principle, not because it was believed that every slave-master was an ogre, rapist, or sadist. For Brown, slavery was a violation of human rights and biblical justice, and every part of the monster was equally guilty, whether the head or the tail, the ruthless stinger or the soft underbelly. It would have been ludicrous for him to pause in his zealous crusade to make such academic distinctions.

Slavery, in various forms and styles, existed throughout the world from antiquity. Christians knew that the biblical world was defined by slavery too, and that it could be found in various forms and styles throughout the Bible. Even the parables of Jesus demonstrate that ancient slavery was a hydra-headed creature—that slaves might be elevated to positions of great responsibility and influence, or treated with lowly contempt as secondary beings whose whole duty was to subordinate their interests in deference to the master. However, the overwhelming majority of slaves throughout history lived bitter, unpleasant lives as victims of an overpowering system of dehumanization and domination. Yet ancient servitude was not defined by the dubious conception of "race" that characterized slavery in the Americas. Furthermore, black enslavement in the United States was "regimented in a highly organized system that was geared to maximum production for a market economy." Above all else, "a slave life was one of toil"—labor continuously stolen on large plantations and small farms, in urban workplaces and private homes, systematically appropriated to enrich the southern economy.

It is true that only a segment of the South consisted of slaveholders, and an even smaller number of Southerners were planters with large plantations. But among the Confederate states that seceded from the Union, 31 percent of white families owned slaves. In South Carolina and Mississippi, nearly half the white families were slaveholders. "The ownership of slaves was spread among a remarkably broad proportion of the white population, and the extent of this investment was central to Southern white unity before, during, and after the Civil War."[4]

Like every other anti-slavery activist, John Brown viewed the South at the center of his abolitionist focus. Yet he was a Northerner, and most writers seem to place him in a stylized Northern context rather than as a man who was opposed to Northern racism too. Our conventional schoolroom lessons about North and South have all too often been based on self-serving political mythology—portraying the South as the land of enslavement and the North as the land of freedom. "The extent of prejudicial and discriminatory treatment of the Northern Negro is concealed or minimized," wrote Howard Mayer concerning the antebellum period. In correspondence with Andrew Hunter, state prosecutor in John Brown's trial, one Southern agent in Vermont (apparently conducting surveillance after the Harper's Ferry raid), assured Hunter that "the south extends farther north and nearer to the Blue Mountains than you have any idea of." Malcolm X's memorable observation, that anywhere below the Canadian border is "the South," was true in the nineteenth century as far as blacks were concerned.[5] Understanding that anti-black sentiment was a vital part of the North is essential to understanding John Brown's story too.

Brown grew to manhood in an era, not only when slavery was enjoying a renaissance in the South, but when hostility to blacks in the North grew more acute. Though many of the Northern states phased out slavery, the general experience of free blacks was that the North was a segregationist society. As one Quaker wrote in 1831, the "popular feeling" was against blacks, and the compassion that had brought about abolition in the North was now "exhausted." Alexis de Tocqueville affirmed this in 1831, when he commented: "The prejudice of race appears to be stronger in the states that have abolished slavery than in those where it still exists; and nowhere is it so intolerant as in these states where servitude has never been known." By the time Brown was forty years old, 93 percent of blacks living in the North were prohibited from voting, either by law or practice of white society. While many New England blacks could vote, those in New Jersey, Pennsylvania, and Connecticut could not vote in 1840, and those in New York could not vote until they met certain property and residence requirements. From 1819 through the end of the Civil War, every new state restricted the suffrage to whites by law.[6]

Throughout the 1840s and 1850s, conditions for blacks in the North were worsening, and the white enemies of blacks far outnumbered their friends. The abolitionists were blamed for destructive agitation, and blacks were seen as a perpetual problem to the country, largely because of their own supposed inferiority and inability to coexist in equality with whites. A *New York Quarterly* editorial stated that in "juxtaposition" to the superior Anglo-Saxon races, blacks could "only live apart by themselves, or be in a state of bondage, or worse than bondage, among the whites."

> Is history false that we expect the African to surmount every obstacle, of which his being enslaved is the least? What is he when free, at least so

far as regards becoming a peer of the Anglo-Saxon? . . . And there is much truth in the thought that he is continued in slavery not from the principles of slavery, but from the almost indelible circumstances of his condition.

Worse than slavery, concluded the author, blacks had to contend with natural limitations and substandard abilities. Appealing to readers in the North and South, *Harper's New Monthly Magazine* reflected this same matter-of-fact belief in black inferiority in a feature about the West African "Negroland." In a kind of upbeat, conciliatory introduction that made the black experience seem quite positive, the author states:

The negroes . . . have shown that they can live face to face with the whites. . . . We know how they have thriven, physically, intellectually, and morally among us. However much slaveholder and abolitionist may differ in theory and conclusion, they both insist upon the essential fact, that the colored race among us have made great advances, and are capable of and destined for still greater improvement.

The journalist's assumptions about benign white racial tutelage and black inferiority were shared by the majority of whites in the United States—though most often the "fact" of black inferiority was cited to justify what Leon Litwack calls the politics and economics of repression.[7]

In a sense, the whole experience of blacks in North America was defined by the fears and apprehensions of those who enslaved and oppressed them. In the South, fear was the spirit that energized slavery with tragic vitality. Black people were kept in bondage by fear of violence, murder, or separation. But whites were engulfed in fear as well—fear of slave insurrections, fear of competition in labor, and fear of what would become of the Southern way of life should slavery be abolished. In the North, whites were traumatized by the notion that their communities would be overrun by immigration of free blacks or, worse, former slaves. Though whites living in areas that bordered on slavery were the most traumatized, whites in Massachusetts and Connecticut also feared that they would gain unwanted black populations if slaves were turned away by other states. To prevent black migration, some states enacted laws that excluded blacks, or required that they post bonds from $500–$1,000 and show certification of their free status. Senator Stephen Douglas spoke in the spirit of whites in Illinois when he decried the notion that his state would become "an asylum for all the old and decrepit and broken-down negroes that may emigrate or be sent to it." In Southern Pennsylvania, whites often petitioned state government to put an end to black migration by law.

Though segregated from whites in nearly every phase of existence, Northern blacks were subjected to constant racial ridicule and caricature-making in print, public harassment and insult from adults and children, and the recurring threat of mob violence. Though racist Southern mobs might be distinguished for their sadistic violence, they were not outdone in sheer hatred and racial contempt in cities like New York and Philadelphia, where blacks were clubbed and stoned, and their homes and churches destroyed in numerous riots during the 1830s and 1840s. When the whites of Cincinnati mobbed the black community in 1829 because of their growing presence in that city, many blacks were driven out and forced to migrate to Canada and elsewhere. Less than twenty years later, whites in Cincinnati mobbed the black community again. When black men were jailed, ostensibly for their safety, the white mobs turned on black women and children.[8]

From the more "progressive" New England setting of John Brown's birth in Connecticut to the flagrantly racist northwest and western lands, whites demonstrated a vibrant opposition to the black presence. In Connecticut, an 1833 law was passed to prevent students from out of state from attending school there in order to stop the founding of a black college. Similarly, the efforts of Prudence Crandall to start a school for blacks in Canterbury were opposed with militance and violence. Crandall, a Quaker, was threatened to the point of abandoning her effort and leaving the state.

The Old Northwest Territory was heavily populated by Southerners and middle states folk who settled in Indiana, Illinois, and Ohio (with the exception of Ohio's Western Reserve and eastern section) in the 1830s. For the most part, these whites were unfriendly to blacks and had no moral objection to slavery as long as it remained in the South. Their hostility to slavery was due to the presumption that its castoffs and refugees would accumulate into a large free black population, "and their dread of free Negroes was aggravated by Negro migration into the region." One old settler recalled that "most people considered Negroes little more than sheep with wool on their heads."[9]

Knowing white people's obsession with the idea of race-mixing, politicians used the "threat" of miscegenation to fuel anti-slavery policies in the territory, while free blacks were excluded from service in the militia, denied the ballot, and proscribed from giving testimony in court against any white person. In Indiana, Illinois, Iowa, and Michigan, interracial marriages were forbidden and even nullified. One Illinois state senator warned that a black presence among whites would be "productive of moral and political evil," and in the Ohio State Convention of 1850–51, one representative declared the sentiment that essentially defined Northern white opinion prior to the Civil War: "The United States were designed by the God in Heaven to be governed and inhabited by the Anglo-Saxon race and by them alone." This became the northern dilemma. Blacks could be shuffled around, pressed down, and scattered, but they would not disappear. Whites could not avoid the "'everlasting negro' question."

Yet southern slavery remained foremost in the eyes of abolitionists. Thomas W. Higginson, who later became one of Brown's most important supporters, recalled visiting a slave market in St. Louis, Missouri, in the mid-1850s. Higginson entered at the moment three sisters were put up for sale—"nice little mulatto girls in neat pink calico frocks suggesting a careful mother"—the eldest being but twelve years old. The prospective buyer waived the opportunity to strip the girls for inspection, and seemed to want to befriend the human flesh he was about to purchase. "Don't you want to go with me?" the white man asked the sorrowful twelve-year-old. Bursting into tears, she replied, "I want to stay with my mother." At this point, Higginson recalled, the dealer sent the children away and completed the business deal with not the slightest sign of pity. It struck Higginson that the whole transaction was conducted in a "perfectly matter-of-fact" manner, and even with no apparent violence, rape, or cruelty, the whole scene seemed all the more terrible. "If these were the commonplaces of the institution," Higginson wondered, "what must its exceptional tragedies be?"[10]

Looking back over a century and a half, perhaps we have become more like John Brown than we realize. Few Americans today would tolerate the sight of whimpering little girls torn from their mothers and sold on an auction block. Yet we forget that these travesties "were the commonplaces" of slavery, and that the majority of Americans were content to let them occur for generations while only a small group of abolitionists cried out in protest. But unlike our more informed understanding of the holocaust in Europe, for instance, too many white Americans view black enslavement simplistically and remotely, failing to appreciate the extent of its depraved grip on our culture—probably because it was a monster created in the very laboratory of American freedom and sustained by many of our nation's ancestors and leaders. In contrast, John Brown had an intimate familiarity with blacks and recognized that slavery in any section was a cancerous danger to them as well as to the moral and political wellbeing of the nation. It was his particular grace that he saw black people as brethren and equals, and could not but see slavery as repugnant and worthy of destruction.

# 2

## John Brown's Heritage

Owen Brown was a greater character than history has recorded him.

—The Reverend Clarence S. Gee, Brown family scholar[1]

Given his controversial role in history, it is no surprise that John Brown's ancestral connection to the Mayflower Pilgrims of 1620 has been a point of contention among scholars for nearly a century. However, his descent from the Plymouth Rock Pilgrims is not as important as the fact that the "belief of Mayflower descent was well grounded in the Brown family—that the claim did not arise with John Brown, [n]or was [it] made to order for him."[2] Despite his strong identification with the Pilgrim founders of white America, John Brown was more a Puritan than a Pilgrim—the two often being confused despite their distinct roles in the founding of North American society. The Pilgrims were separatists whose flight from religious persecution ended in North America, while the Puritans came as holy pioneers on a mission to establish a model Christian society. Subsequent religious and political developments fused Pilgrim and Puritan children into a strong colonial people whose nation proved to be a strange, imperfect blend of Puritan model and Pilgrim refuge.

Numbered among this pale-skinned tribe of Bible-quoting colonists were the Browns of Connecticut, who at least could trace their lineage to "the early second wave of Puritan infiltration into the new world at Massachusetts Bay Colony." The Brown family boasted of their father, Captain John Brown, a regimental commander of "a Body of Minute-Men" during the American Revolution, who died of dysentery while in service on September 3, 1776. Beside his widow, Hannah, Captain John Brown left eleven children, one of whom was Owen, born in West Simsbury, Connecticut in 1771. One family history remembers the Browns for their thorough commitment to Calvinism, tenacity of opinion and principle, independence of thought, "pungency and pithiness of speech, remarkable power of sarcasm," and sometimes for their "excessive jealousy and un-yielding prejudices."

Without her husband, Hannah Brown struggled to maintain the farm-ing and herds, placing some of the children with relatives at periods of fi-nancial difficulty. Owen lived for a time with his grandfather, where he "was early brought under the influence of religious People." He later lived with an older married sister, who cared for his needs and taught him to read, though poverty and hard labor prevented any formal schooling for young Owen Brown. At this period a "great revival of religion" reached West Simsbury, which Owen later marked as the beginning of a mature understanding of Christian preaching, as well as a refreshing of his family's spiritual life and practice. The Browns attended the regular Bible "Conferences" and "singing meetings" that characterized the Sec-ond Great Awakening in Connecticut.[3]

When the Reverend Jeremiah Hallock became minister of the Congre-gational Church at West Simsbury, the teenage Owen became close to the clergyman, who took in the struggling youth and tutored him "a great deal." While staying with Hallock, Owen came "under some convictions of sin"—bothered by a sense of personal sinfulness, an experience un-doubtedly evoked by the preaching of his host. Owen later wandered about as a "bungling Shoe maker," returning home in the summer to work on his mother's farm. He seems not to have converted to Christian-ity, and moved to another town to work.[4]

After 1790, Owen's mother and family enjoyed some improvement in property, farming, and livestock, which he later attributed to the "kind providence of God." Another "kind providence" was his marriage to Ruth Mills ("the choice of my affections ever after"), a minister's daugh-ter, in March 1793. For Owen, marriage initiated a golden age of per-sonal satisfaction and growth that he remembered long after as "the be-ginning of days." Ruth's influence on him was great, and in autobio-graphical reflection he attributed to her a kind of "ascendance without usurpation" and credited her for whatever respect he gained in the world. Owen's tribute to Ruth suggests that her role in the marriage may have extended to being his teacher, business consultant, and perhaps the spiri-tual conscience of the home in the early days of his business pursuits. "A verry [*sic*] considerable part of my property was acquired in the lifetime and with the prudent assistance of my first wife," Owen wrote.

Taking counsel from Minister Hallock, the young couple began "with but very little property," building their home on spiritual fidelity as well as "industry and frugality." After a move to Norfolk, Connecticut in 1794, they began to establish themselves in the community. With a shoe shop and tannery businesses, Owen was becoming a responsible citizen. His personality was generally pleasing and friendly, and his wit was without guile. Perhaps his humble demeanor was shaped in part by his struggle with stuttering, a problem that plagued him throughout life. Stories of his stuttering remained part of the history of his family and community, including one account about Owen, much later in life, scolding and shaking a particularly naughty grandson: "Will you—will you—will you be a good boy?" The only time Owen did not stutter was in singing and public prayers.

Owen is also remembered by historians for his peculiar manner of writing, the tendency to spell words phonetically and inconsistently with almost no punctuation. "Owen was not educated in the schools," Clarence Gee wrote, "but he had a good mind and expressed himself well in writing, even if he used his own method of spelling and punctuation." Hacked and skewed, Owen's writing nevertheless reflects his interaction with educated people, such as ministers and abolitionists.

Before the end of 1796 the Browns lost their children, a two-year-old son and a newborn son, with Ruth herself nearly dying after childbirth. Later that year Owen and Ruth became foster parents to an infant boy, Levi Blakeslee, the son of the Reverend Matthew Blakeslee of Hartland, Connecticut. The arrangement to care for baby Levi was supposed to be temporary, perhaps to help his widowed mother. But the arrangement suited the Browns. Having lost both their sons, they may have been haunted with fears that they would never again be parents. When Levi's mother asked that they keep the child, the Browns agreed to take the infant as a member of the Brown family. Owen wrote of the arrangement as "addoption," but it does not appear that the child was ever legally adopted, nor did Levi ever take the Brown family name.[5]

In the next few years Owen and Ruth had more children, including a son born on May 9, 1800, whom Owen named John, after his father and grandfather. By this time, the Browns had moved to Torrington, Connecticut, which had recently been visited by another wave of "powerfull awakening" under the ministry of the Reverend Alexander Gillett. The Browns were so impressed with Gillett's ministry that they transferred their membership to the Torrington Congregational Church. Indeed, the

memory of this late eighteenth century movement became Owen's standard of evaluating religious revivals for the rest of his life.

Inseparable from Owen's hunger for revival was his zeal for the liberation of black people. According to his own recollection, his feelings of
sympathy toward blacks even predated his conversion to Christianity.
Owen recalled that his first involvement with a black person came in
1776, after his father had gone off to war and his mother was left to run
the farm by herself. A neighbor loaned the services of his Guinean-born
slave to help with the plowing. Each morning, five-year-old Owen would
escort Sam the African to the field, probably tailing him throughout the
day, and then riding on his back as he returned from the fields. "I fell in
love with him," Owen recalled of his boyish admiration. Unfortunately,
Sam became sick, probably with pneumonia, telling his little admirer that
he would soon depart for Guinea. Though Owen's father died from sickness on the battlefield of independence that year, the death of Guinean
Sam left an equally important mark on his life.

In the coming years Owen was attentive to the number and identity of
enslaved blacks in his vicinity, though there were few in West Simsbury.
At nineteen years of age, while living with the Reverend Hallock, Owen
began a serious consideration of the plight of black people. Hallock was
clearly an abolitionist, and was an associate of the notable theologian, the
Reverend Samuel Hopkins. A native of Connecticut, Hopkins also served
as a pastor in Rhode Island, where he gained a reputation denouncing
slavery as a great moral sin. Owen remembered a particular visit that
Hallock received from Hopkins in the summer of 1790, in which the two
abolitionist clergymen exchanged notes and ideas. Hopkins gave Hallock
an abolitionist pamphlet by the younger Jonathan Edwards, which he
then placed in Owen's hands. "I read it, and it denounced slavery as a
great sin. From this time I was anti-slavery, as much as I be now," Owen
wrote in later years.

While Owen and Ruth were in Norfolk, Connecticut, a Southern Presbyterian minister who had lived in the vicinity and purchased a small farm
during the war, returned to sell the property. Having brought a slave couple with him to care for the farm in his absence, the minister now intended
to reclaim his slaves too. But slavery had been abolished in Connecticut
by this time, and the former slave was determined not to return to the
South with the minister, hiding himself with the help of blacks in the vicinity. The community was soon embroiled in controversy, resulting in a
black-led protest that came to a heated exchange between the minister

and anti-slavery critics. Owen happily noted that the Southern minister "did not get away his 'property,' as he called it." Throughout his days Owen remembered this incident, for it was the first time he witnessed righteous indignation overcome injustice. "Ever since, I have been an Abolitionist," Owen wrote in 1850, "and I am so near the end of life I think I shall die an Abolitionist."[6]

"We did not come to a Land of idleness[,] neither did I expect it," Owen wrote concerning the family's move to Ohio in 1805. "I came with a determination to help build up and be a help in the [*support*] of religion and civil Order." The Connecticut founders of the Western Reserve in Ohio were devoted to "free schools, free churches, an open Bible . . . liberty of conscience, the Sabbath regarded and the pure worship of God maintained," wrote nephew Edward Brown in 1875. The westward advance was "both bold and conservative," since it took great stamina to establish a society in virgin wilderness. Yet it was a venture made with "certainty of safety from Indian attacks because of treaties and military success."

The State of Ohio had been admitted to the Union in 1803, including a portion of land earlier designated for settlement by Connecticut colonists. After the Revolutionary War, settlement lands outside state boundaries were to be claimed or lost, and the children of Connecticut soldiers set out to possess the reserve lands in northeastern Ohio. David Hudson of Goshen, Connecticut bought into a large part of these lands along with five others and began to personally recruit citizens, "concentrating on attracting migrants whose special skills were needed by the fledgling town." Owen Brown was the kind of citizen Hudson wanted for his new society. After a preliminary visit, he purchased land in the fledgling town and returned to his family in Connecticut to prepare for the move westward. On July 27, 1805, the Browns arrived in Hudson, along with the family of Benjamin Whedon, all their earthly possessions conveyed by an "ox Team."[7]

The early settlement at Hudson was more likely to be intruded upon by wolves and bears then it was to be attacked by Native Americans, though fear of Indian uprisings persisted in the minds of settlers. In contrast, Owen established a good rapport with the Native community, and when they "left [*their*] Tents," apparently being forced to abandon their settlement by the government, he expressed his disapproval to them and his Hudson neighbors. Unlike many whites, Owen believed the Indians were "very friendly," more "a benefit rather than an [injury]." Unfortunately, others on the Western Reserve typified the prevailing racism of white settlers. "[S]ome Persons . . . [*seemed*] disposed to [*quarrel*] with the Indians," Owen recalled, "but I never was." Brown and other friendly settlers traded bread and meal with the Natives in exchange for venison, turkey, fish, and other meats, and even extended them credit. It was this same rapport with the Indian community that brought Owen into conflict with many in Hudson during the early days. He firmly maintained that the Native population should be protected under the same laws that protected whites, and viewed their dispossession with contempt. The conflict with Hudson's whites occurred in 1806 after Owen, "with his customary independence of spirit," used his influence to have warrants issued for the arrest of two white men who had murdered an Indian. The case reflected the true nature of the expanding oppression of the frontier, as the white killers were ultimately freed and Owen became a target of resentment from all but a few of Hudson's early community.[8] Though this incident occurred when John Brown was only six years old, it indicates the kind of orientation he received from his father with respect to human rights issues.

Owen was not inclined to the routines and rigors of farm life, preferring to establish a tannery and land "speculation." Owen's tannery thrived and the financial surplus was invested in undeveloped land that he parceled into small lots, mostly for sale to farmers. Between 1805 and 1830, Owen prospered, though his real estate "speculations were always within his own means and under his own control" and in keeping with his preference to avoid making an appearance of wealth. At the height of his success in 1834, Owen became the third wealthiest man in town, and remained on the short list of Hudson's most prosperous citizens throughout his life. He also did well selling livestock and provisions to the U.S. Army during the War of 1812, though not all of his activities in war time were profit-oriented. Indeed, he was active in caring for "the sick and [*dying*]" in the midst of "a very sickly and [*dying*] time both in the Army and at home in Hudson."[9]

If Owen Brown had any regrets it was that his business and subsequent public service kept him away from home, filling his schedule with obligations. "I had many call[s] from home," Owen remembered. "I now [*believe*] it was an [*injury*] to my [*Family*]." Prosperity and community service detracted from family and church life, something that seems to have bothered his conscience. "The misimprovement [*sic*] of time is a great sin and one that lays heavy on my poor soul," Owen wrote to daughter Florilla in 1838. "Will God forgive me[?]" In his 1850 autobiographical sketch, Owen wrote further: "I will say my earthly cares were [*too*] many for the good of my [*Famely*] and for my own Comfort in religion[.] I do not look back on my life with but little [*satisfaction*] but must pray Lord forgive me for Christ[']s sake or I must perish." While Owen Brown could hardly be considered a driven man, he was determined to succeed, and in the father there was foreshadowed the stubborn determination of John Brown. Yet father and son were different in temperament. "Owen Brown, our grandfather, had a determined temper, but was cooler," recalled Salmon Brown. John Brown "had the Mills temper. He was hotheaded." Owen's "determined temper" was vivid, especially in matters of dishonesty and inequity. Once he went to great expense to track down a man who had passed him a counterfeit $5 bill. Another time he determinedly went to court over a stove pipe, losing the case at a cost of $1.60.[10] These trivial incidents reveal a stubborn temperament in Owen that was even more pronounced in his son John. The Browns would go to great lengths to fight for justice on behalf of blacks and Native Americans, but they might just as well go to war over a stove pipe or a plot of land if they believed inequity was involved.

With success in business came the call to public life. Besides serving as Justice of the Peace in Hudson's early years, Owen was asked to arbitrate in property disputes, a role that often kept him away from home. Besides serving on grand juries, Owen was also elected several times to serve as county commissioner—winning him the title of "Esquire" (which neighbors and associates shortened to "Squire"). "He was a friend to the poor, white or black," one local history recalls of Owen Brown. "There were many hidden ministries of love in which the left hand knew not what the right hand did." As a public figure, the stuttering squire was well-liked and respected. With renowned judgment, unpretentious charity, a keen sense of humor, and a liking for fine conversation, Owen Brown was not diminished by his speech impediment. His self-effacing humor, which mirrored his tendency to diminish himself as a Christian, tended to impress people as good-natured humility. When a traveler asked Owen for directions to another town, the Squire began, "You t-t-t—oh, go along. You'll get there before I can tell you."

Besides religion, "education was seen as an essential component" in Hudson. The townsmen had established a school in the center of the town in 1801, and David Hudson himself lobbied for a charter for the establishment of Western Reserve College in 1826. Like Harvard, Yale, and other leading colleges, Western Reserve College also included a prepara-

"Squire" Owen Brown of Hudson, as he looked in his prime as one of the leading citizens of Hudson, in the early decades of the nineteenth century. Though his famous son did not succeed his father as a successful business-man, he did inherit his unique evangelical aboli-tionist faith. *West Virginia State Archives.*

tory school to compensate for the generally inadequate public school ed-ucation young men received in the early nineteenth century. Owen Brown was involved with the founding of Western Reserve College too, serving on its board of agency, which made arrangements for the construction of the college building. One can only imagine what Owen must have been thinking as he joined the procession from the church to the new campus for the opening ceremony in April 1826. Taking his place in a solemn as-sembly with other community leaders, Owen Brown listened to the dedi-cation address delivered entirely in Latin.[11]

The pioneers of the Western Reserve "knew well that the three great forces which constitute the strength and glory of a free government are the family, the school, and the church." Perhaps the church was the place where Owen found the greatest fulfillment, though in later years his abo-litionist views made him a controversial figure in Hudson's Christian community. Owen and Ruth had made professions of faith and joined the Congregational Church in 1798, while still in Norfolk, Connecticut. But he characteristically diminished his faithfulness: "I have [*done*] many things to wound the cause of Religion and but very little to promote the cause of Christ[,] and if I am saved it will be by the mercy of God in Christ

Jesus for I am yet vile." However "it was characteristic of Owen Brown when speaking of himself, to deprecate his spiritual attainment," writes Clarence Gee. "This, however, was his own opinion, and not that of his children, nor his friends."[12]

Owen's self-deprecating comments reflect the Reformed conviction that mankind is sinful by nature and incapable of pleasing a righteous God. Like a true Puritan, Owen saw the gravest danger in the least of his sins and imputed no credit to himself for the best of his deeds. Man must be ever on guard because his heart is inclined to sin and self-deceit. Writing to his daughter Florilla in 1838, Owen lamented this tendency in his own life and the lives of his family:

> I have been fearing the [*righteous*] Judgments of God were about to fall on our Family as that were [*murmuring*] against God and we're not repenting of our sins[.] O the [*sinfulness*] of the human heart[.] [I]f God punishes us in proportion to our sins we must fall under his wrath. I hope you pray much for us that God would take away our sins.[13]

Yet fear was not the essence of Puritan religion, and Owen understood that the core of Christian doctrine is that God does not punish the Christian "in proportion" to his sins, since Christ was punished in the sinner's place. Indeed, Owen's letters have more references to God's mercies and kindness than to judgment. However, he was concerned for the quality of Christian life and the condition of the church, and he feared how human sinfulness—including slavery—corrupted the Christian witness. In a fascinating letter to his son John Brown in 1855, Owen wrote at length on religious and ethical matters, reflecting on an experience he had some years previous while in Boston, when he went to see an artistic rendering in wax of the Last Supper of Christ. As he studied the figurines, "the thought then struck me why Christ should [*choose*] and select such a company for his companionable Friends," none of them being men of renown.

> Since that day how many thousands have called themselves [*Ambassadors*] of Christ who have not [*imitated*] Christ or his [*apostles*][?] [C]an the Christian part of the World expect any thing but great Judgments[?] [B]ut the world and the Church are yet under the controls of Infinite wisdom, as well as the wrath of men.[14]

Gerald McFarland shows that the Browns came from a tradition in which the dissenting New England Puritans had concluded "precisely what they thought a pure church would be," and in so doing limited church membership to the "visible saints"—those who "could publicly testify to a direct experience of being one of God's chosen." With an emphasis on the individual's personal faith and salvation, Calvinists like Owen Brown thus looked to God's Sovereign will, not man's choice, as the great motivator behind revival and reformation. Owen's letters likewise demonstrate his Puritan hope, such as his concerns about the spiritual well-being at Hudson in the summer of 1837: "We very much need a revival of Religion[.] [W]e are truly [*cold*]," he wrote to Florilla. "We have not much [*spiritual*] life but . . . pray much for us."

A theology that uplifts the Sovereignty of God over against the free will of man seems indigestible to all but a minority of modern believers. Even in Owen's day, there was a growing move away from the tenets of Calvin and Luther, an increasing emphasis on the sinner's decision to follow the call of the cross. But true Puritans like Owen Brown believed the sinner can never come to salvation unless God first makes it so—that is, not unless he becomes the "subject of grace." Indeed, Owen looked back at his own life, wondering when it was that he himself had been a subject of God's grace. Was it when he was still a boy of eleven, in the midst of a "great revival" at West Simsbury? "I cannot say I was a subject of the work [of the Holy Spirit]," Owen wrote in 1850, "but this I can say[:] I then began to hear preaching," and even as an old man he could remember the preachers of 1782 and their sermon texts. It was not until he was a married man that Owen made a public profession of his faith, along with his beloved and influential Ruth.[15]

Owen Brown's story provides insight into the religious and social dimensions in which his controversial son came to manhood. But Owen's writings also testify to his own development as a "visible saint"—a humble, stuttering, stubborn Puritan whose salvation blended Reformation theology, personal piety, and a remarkable hatred of slavery and injustice into a unique family religion. John Brown shared his father's companionship for all but the last few years of his life, though historians tend to overlook Owen's ongoing involvement and influence. Yet the shared faith of father and son remains one of the strongest themes in the John Brown story.

# 3

## Revival, Resistance, and Abolition in the Time of John Brown

And he that stealeth a man, and selleth him, or if he be found in his hand, he shall surely be put to death.

—Exodus 21:16

Among the Brown family descendants a story survived into the twentieth century concerning Oliver Brown, one of John Brown's brothers. After donating a parcel of land for a new Congregational Church, Oliver fell into a conflict with the pastor, who would not allow him to use the church for anti-slavery meetings. The use of the church was part of their original agreement, and the fiery Oliver Brown was determined to have justice. After making demonstrations against the congregation's broken agreement and prejudice, Brown removed the pulpit, dragged it out into the yard, and set it on fire as neighbors looked on in amazement.[1]

While some considered John Brown a dangerous anti-slavery fanatic, it is often overlooked that he was part of an entire family that hated black enslavement and opposed it in many ways. Furthermore, the Browns shared the strong anti-slavery sentiments common in the Western Reserve. Perhaps the burning pulpit might also represent certain truths about the Christian church during this time. First, the church in large part was either pro-slavery or indifferent to the well-being of black people; second, the church ultimately proved a failure as a medium for the abolitionist cause; and finally, white believers who did oppose slavery were a zealous minority on the landscape of Christianity in the United States.

John Brown's alleged fanaticism and "monomania" was shared by other zealous white Christians opposed to slavery. These believers were not only professional abolitionist orators and editors like William Lloyd Garrison, but clergymen, "home missionaries," evangelists, seminary students, and laity who were as devoted to the abolition of slavery as to the advance of the Christian gospel. Of course, many of these Christian activists were involved in differing degrees with the underground railroad, as were three generations of the Brown family. Despite varying denominational affiliations and theological persuasions, anti-slavery Christians formed a lively, diverse evangelical movement in the antebellum period. However, to understand John Brown's religious context, one must begin with the Puritans of the colonial era, with whom he consciously identified, both politically and spiritually. Indeed, one of his admirers later described him as looking like an old-time Puritan awakened from the grave.[2]

By the time of the American Revolution, Puritanism provided "the moral and religious background of fully seventy-five percent of the people who declared their independence in 1776." Protesting the spiritual condition of England, the Puritans had come to the British American colonies with the intention of setting up a model society on three founding precepts: the elimination of Roman Catholic influence and establishment of "apostolic" principles; the advancement of the doctrines of the Reformation; and the revival of discipline and piety in clergy and laity. What they envisioned for their New England "city on a hill" was not a theocracy per se, but a society where church and state obeyed the Bible.

The Puritan mission gave to America the notion of God's sovereign rule and kingdom manifested, as H. Richard Niebuhr writes, "not only in human spirits but also in the world of nature and of human history." Puritan piety was based on God's unmerited favor and mercy extended through faith in Jesus Christ. However, rather than rejecting the Law of Moses, the Puritans emphasized it "as teacher and moral guide."

Inseparable from their theological world view was the belief in the sinfulness of humanity—the depravity of human nature. Human government, constitutions, and laws were seen as divinely ordained restraints on human depravity and were to be obeyed. Yet the Puritans were as comfortable in the Old Testament as they were in the New Testament. Puritan theology was covenantal, emphasizing God's dealing with mankind in both mercy and judgment from Genesis to Revelation, as a seamless garment. There was no tension between the testaments for the Puritans, no tug-of-war between the supposed "wrathful" God of the Old Testament and the "loving" God of the New Testament, as many historians assume. According to the Puritans, Christians were "visible saints," repentant sinners made aware of their sin by the Holy Spirit, then internally renewed by God's grace and called to live according to the demands of personal reformation.[3]

Puritan faith was exemplified by the Congregational Church in New England. The followers of the "Congregational Way" upheld the mandate to maintain the complete autonomy of every local gathering of Christians and emphasized "the way of salvation and its moral implications." Non-Congregational Churches formed too, some of them separating from the New England churches and others transplanted from Europe with new immigrations of Scots, Germans, Dutch, and Irish. The dominant religious groups prior to the Revolutionary war were the Congregationalists, Episcopalians, and Presbyterians. With the Great Awakening of the 1730s and 1740s, the first major revival movement in America, these Protestants worked across denominational lines, emphasizing religious experience rather than denomination.

After the Revolutionary war, other major Protestant denominations arose, especially the Baptists and Methodists, which were to become more popularly representative of American evangelicalism in the nineteenth century. In reaction to the excesses and abuses of the Great Awakening, some Congregationalists were less enthusiastic when the Second Great Awakening began in the late eighteenth century, continuing into the nineteenth century. In the Second Great Awakening, they emphasized spiritual sobriety and moral reformation over the emotion and zeal of the first wave of revivals. The Second Great Awakening continued in successive waves across New England for years, though it was hardly as expansive and influential as the revivals taking place among Baptists and Methodists. The "pietistic, evangelistic, low-church" revivals of the frontier swept across the nation, and became the standard for later religious revival movements.[4]

When John Brown was born in 1800, there were only about a dozen Christian denominations in the United States, the largest being Baptist, Congregational, Methodist, Lutheran (mostly comprised of recent immigrants), and Presbyterians. The smaller denominations were the German and Dutch Reformed churches, Quakers, Moravians, Mennonites, and Roman Catholics. However, as the nineteenth century progressed and the population increased (largely through immigration), new denominations were formed along with new sectarian movements that were entirely native to the United States, such as the Campbellites and the Adventists, as well as the Mormon cult. This was also the era of voluntary associations, the nineteenth-century version of today's para-church organizations. Voluntary associations were concerned with a good many moral and social causes, from temperance societies and Sabbath-keeping instruction to anti-slavery associations. Finally, his era was also notable for communitarian experiments, both religious and secular.

The age of revival was also the age of Christ's coming kingdom, and the era of millennial expectation ran the spectrum from mainline Congregationalists to sectarian Adventists. Although various groups had starkly different ideas about the nature and meaning of the biblical millennium, one of the common threads running through nineteenth-century American Protestantism was a sense of expectancy that excited Christians to engage society in socially and spiritually uplifting endeavors. At the same time, the Methodist movement was being carried into the western states by circuit-riding preachers. Methodism was distinguished by its success in reaching blacks and Native Americans, for selecting grassroots leaders, and for its Wesleyan Arminian alternative to Calvinism—a kind of "democratic" theology premised on human freedom and moral responsibility. The Baptists also enjoyed success as a grassroots religious movement, followed by the Presbyterians.[5]

Another important feature of the period in which Brown lived was the "Yankee exodus"—pioneer movements from Massachusetts to upstate New York, and from Connecticut to Northern Ohio, the latter including the family of Owen Brown, who moved from Connecticut to Ohio in 1805. In 1801, the Plan of Union was designed by Presbyterian and Congregational leaders to encourage the winning of the frontier without unnecessary duplication of labor. The Plan allowed local congregations to blend under either church government, and to call clergy from either denomination. In the long run, however, the Plan of Union worked to the advantage of the Presbyterians, who were more assertive and so absorbed more frontier congregations between the Hudson River and Chicago, Illinois. Although it failed to accomplished its purpose, the Plan of Union was a real part of John Brown's religious experience, beginning with his upbringing in the Western Reserve of Northern Ohio. His home church, the First Congregational Church of Hudson, Ohio, was for a time "received under the care" of the Grand River Presbytery in 1815—one year before the teenage John became a member of the church. In 1819, the Hudson church adopted the Covenant and Articles of Faith recommended by the same Presbytery, though apparently this was always a cause of dissatisfaction among many in the congregation. In 1835, the Presbytery dissolved the union by request of the Hudson church, and there is evidence that the Plan of Union, along with the slavery issue, was an ongoing source of division in the congregation.[6]

Along with revival was the growing issue of slavery and abolitionist protest. Though racist in orientation, New England society had no significant investment in slavery after the colonial period, and its Congregational Churches had almost no affiliates in the South. The South had been dominated by the Episcopal church from the beginning, but revivals brought growth and spiritual vitality to the Presbyterians as well as to Baptists and Methodists. However, while Northern evangelicals preached personal salvation *and* the abolition of slavery, the Southern churches became increasingly defensive, taking a theologically conservative stance that became far more rigorous and legalistic than that of their Northern counterparts. This conservative approach was as much a resistance to social change as to theological change, as Martin Marty observes of the Southern churches in the antebellum period: "The quest for holiness, however, came to take a very individualistic line. . . . The accent was on vices of persons, not evil in the forms of society. Reform meant change in the individual, not the tearing up or modification of a social contract that had been religiously approved."[7]

Denominations that spanned North and South were divided over slavery. For example, the Southern Presbyterians—like the rest of the Southern evangelical churches—functioned as a pro-slavery bulwark, while anti-slavery Northern Presbyterians sought to be a force for social change. Even with the mounting sectional crisis there remained a constant flow and exchange between Northern and Southern clergy for a while, until the situation became explosive.

Amidst the tensions between pro- and anti-slavery sentiment was the colonization movement, a "curious blend of piety and prejudice" that blamed "the sin of racial pride on the providence of God." Colonization advocates emphasized the preservation of national unity, and so hoped to deport the Negro "problem" to Africa in order to save the Union. Colonization was especially strong in the border states, where whites opposed any kind of black presence—slave or free—fearing either race-mixing or violent black revolts. Even after anti-slavery advocates of colonization split with their pro-slavery colleagues, their movement was only a "respectable racism under the cloak of benevolence."

Revival- and clergy-related abolitionism was also a vital feature of American religion during this period. John Rankin, a Presbyterian pastor who had organized anti-slavery societies in Tennessee and Kentucky, led a church in Ripley, Ohio, and became notable as an anti-slavery writer. Hugh Fullerton, a Presbyterian pastor whose father was a slavemaster, led Ohio's Chillicothe Presbytery, the vocal center of anti-slavery Presbyterians. The Chillicothe Presbytery banned slaveholders from communion, and many pastors from this presbytery worked cooperatively with Quakers on the underground railroad. However the most notable anti-slavery figure among clergyman was Charles G. Finney, a lawyer turned Presbyterian preacher. Finney's revivals were a major impetus both in the anti-slavery movement and in evangelism in the cities. Finney enjoyed his greatest prominence in western New York during the years 1825–32, afterward holding a pastorate in New York City.

Finney's role in the background of the John Brown story is real, particularly after the preacher became affiliated with Ohio's Oberlin College, where anti-slavery sentiment was rife. Through the endowment of abolitionist Arthur Tappan of New York, Finney was provided a seat as head of Oberlin's theology department. It was in Oberlin that Finney honed his doctrine of Perfectionism—the evangelical antithesis to Calvinism. Besides affirming the anti-slavery movement, Finney and his colleagues began to advocate the "second blessing" that enabled the Christian to live in "perfect obedience to the law of God"—a notion that became the mainstay of evangelical revivalism for decades to come.[8] While Brown was never in agreement with Finney's new theology, his family supported Oberlin, and its political and theological influence touched the Browns with inspiration and controversy.

Presbyterian clergyman Elijah Lovejoy also influenced John Brown, though mainly by his violent death in the abolitionist cause. Lovejoy had made his reputation as a writer and publisher more than a preacher, and was driven from St. Louis, Missouri, for publishing an abolitionist paper. Settling in Alton, Illinois, Lovejoy continued to draw the opposition of Northern Negrophobes. In November 1837, a swelling mob surrounded a private warehouse where his new printing press was stored (his old one had been dumped into the river after his arrival in Alton). Lovejoy refused to surrender his press to the mob, and was shot and killed while fighting off an attack.

Despite their sympathy, most abolitionists criticized Lovejoy because he died in an act of forceful self-defense. Years later, Wendell Phillips wrote that the killing of Lovejoy had "scattered a world of dreams."[9] But to John Brown, it was no shame that Lovejoy died with a gun in his hand. His death only reinforced a growing conviction that moral appeal to a depraved and violent system was vanity. Far more for the oppressed themselves, the realities of slavery increasingly outweighed the pet doctrine of the nonviolent abolition movement. While idealistic abolitionists formed societies, made speeches, and published newspapers, the real conflict with slavery was played out on the stage of black resistance. Brown never really participated in the institutional life of abolitionism, and eventually drove himself like a wedge between the idealism of white abolitionists and the hardcore reality of black experience.

Despite his later financial dependence on certain white abolitionists, Brown ultimately belonged to the realm of black realities. He was undoubtedly aware of the three most important slave revolts in the nation's history, all of which took place by the time he had reached his early thirties. They were not only models for his own militant plans later in life, but they instilled within him the certainty that black people would overthrow their oppressors and seize their freedom when given the support necessary to overcome slavery. Southerners shared this certainty too, though with fear and dread. "Wherever there was a black population, slave or emancipated," wrote Thomas W. Higginson, "[white] men's startled consciences made cowards of them all, and recognized the Negro as a dangerous man, because an injured one." Outgunned and outnumbered, most slave revolts were dwarfed by the militant giant of white supremacy, though even a general overview of antebellum slavery attests to the inevitable occurrences of slave rebellion.[10]

One important revolt, led by the brothers Gabriel, Solomon, and Martin (sometimes referred to by their master's surname, Prosser) took place in 1800, the year of John Brown's birth. Had it succeeded, Richmond would have fallen to a surprise attack by eleven hundred slaves and freemen divided into three columns, each targeting key points of the city, especially the weapons storage places. Only foreigners known to be sympathetic to the anti-slavery cause were to be spared. But heavy rains postponed the attack on the appointed day, and then informers betrayed the cause. Gabriel, his brothers, and thirty-five followers went to the gallows, though "making no confession that could implicate anyone else." An eyewitness later wrote of the fortitude of the condemned rebels, saying their human dignity, contempt for danger, and desire for retaliation portended "the most unhappy consequences" for slave society.

Just as Gabriel's leadership had been buttressed by preaching, a conspiracy in Charleston, South Carolina led by Denmark Vesey in 1822 was also premised on biblical teaching. On record as a Presbyterian, Vesey affiliated himself with Charleston's African Methodist Episcopal Church. The "African church" was the object of racist assault because the white community resented its prosperity, self-determination, religious education, and worship style. Repeatedly raided and assaulted, it was finally closed down by city authorities in early 1821. This formed the context of frustration and offense in which Vesey and others began to gather recruits for the assault on the slave capital.

By 1822, black Charleston had a complex network of rebels—what Vincent Harding calls "an all-class" movement, including English- and French-speaking blacks. But Charleston was also in the midst of a failing cotton economy with an expanding black population—blacks outnumbered whites by thirty thousand, something that gave blacks greater reason to fear. Desperation might lead whites to genocide in order eliminate "surplus black human beings." Vesey and his lieutenants planned a multifaceted attack on Charleston, South Carolina, in which the city would be set afire. All whites encountered would be immediately killed in order to prevent organized opposition or announcement of the attack to white Charleston. Besides the weapons his men could acquire on their own, Vesey paid a blacksmith to manufacture one hundred pikes—an idea that probably inspired John Brown to do the same thing in 1857. It appears there was some idea of taking refuge thereafter in the free black republic of Haiti.

Vesey would never see Charleston aflame. His plan was exposed by a loyal slave only weeks before the attack. The executions of Vesey and his lieutenants took place throughout July 1822, but none of them revealed the extent of the conspiracy. "Do not open your lips," one of Vesey's lieutenants advised his brethren. "Die silent, as you shall see me do."[11] Though thirty-five were eventually executed, the counsel to silence apparently frustrated further exposure, and saved many more lives from the wrath of white Charleston.

Unlike Gabriel and Denmark Vesey, Nat Turner succeeded in spilling the blood of slavemasters. Born the same year as John Brown, Turner was also an avid reader of the Bible and was recognized as both a religious leader and an intellectually superior figure in the slave community. Like Brown, Turner felt himself divinely appointed to the task of liberation, though his commission came by visions and voices. "The Serpent was loosened, and Christ had laid down the yoke he had borne for the sins of men," and Turner should "take it on and fight against the Serpent." This was revolutionary millennialism, the loosening of the Serpent being an idea drawn from Revelation chapter 20, where Satan is released only to be defeated by the consuming fire of God.

Unlike the two previous conspiracies, Turner did not target a major city, though his intention was to bring his army to Jerusalem, the seat of Southampton County, where they could raid arms storehouses. The purpose of the revolt was primarily to annihilate slavemasters and their heirs. John Brown would later study Turner too, probably fascinated by his strategy for retreat into the wilds where authorities would find it hard to reach him and his soldiers.

On August 22, 1831, Nat Turner and his men mowed down men, women, and children—even an infant asleep in his bassinet who was nevertheless a legal heir to slave property. The armed men continued cutting a bloody, flesh-torn trail through the county until whites organized themselves for a counterattack. At the height of the revolt, perhaps as many as eighty men had joined the march to Jerusalem. Approximately sixty whites were killed in the bloody advance, over a third of them children. Meeting armed opposition, however, Turner's army fragmented. Despite the determination of some of his warriors, they were overwhelmed by superior numbers and weapons. Turner escaped and evaded a manhunt for months, but was eventually captured, convicted, and hanged. In total, twenty-one of the captured fighters were executed and ten others were deported. Furthermore, immediately after Turner's advance was stopped, Southampton whites exploded in a vindictive rampage. Hundreds of blacks were massacred and mutilated, though most of the victims had nothing to do with Turner's attack. Even whites from neighboring counties came over to join the massacre.[12]

The leading white abolitionist, William Lloyd Garrison, was "horror-struck" by the news of Turner's bloody assault and the resulting carnage. As the editor and founder of the new publication, *The Liberator*, Garrison was an advocate of immediate emancipation and pacifism. He could not greet the news with approval even though he saw Turner's attack as a moral confirmation of the abolitionist message. "Garrison faced the pacifist's quandary about revolutionary social change. He did not want to condemn the ends because he disapproved of the means, and he especially wanted white Americans to realize that their own political experience sanctioned Turner's course." For decades to come, Garrison continued to reformulate the nation's spiritual identity by contrasting "a charitable Christian vision of society with that of the worldview of slaveholders," with the intention of shaming the nation into abolition. It was a noble intention that Garrison himself personified throughout the years, though he saw no inherent contradiction between his opposition to the use of force and his refusal to censure those who did. Garrison told a friend that he opposed any people's right "to *fight* for liberty," and did not justify slave rebellion, though he did not condemn the revolting black slaves, and applauded "similar conduct in *white men*." By 1832, *The Liberator* was being advanced by forty-seven agents, and editor Garrison was about the business of vanquishing the colonization movement. Indeed, not only did he defeat the American Colonization Society with his masterful book, *Thoughts on African Colonization*, but he went on to found the New England Anti-slavery Society, an organization committed to immediate abolition.

While John Brown undoubtedly read and appreciated *The Liberator* in his early years, he was never converted to Garrison's pacifism, which had evolved into a kind of "Christian anarchism" in the 1830s. To no surprise, Garrison's *Liberator* reflected a quiet contempt for abolitionist Elijah Lovejoy, who died fighting a racist mob in 1837. "Strictly speaking," Garrison wrote, "he was not . . . a Christian martyr." Brown would hardly have agreed. Garrisonians in the late 1830s abjured all manner of force and abstained from militia service or any role involving physical force. They were to "endure suffering for Christ's sake until righteousness and peace shall reign in all the earth"—a noble sentiment, and one that Mohandas Gandhi and Martin Luther King Jr. would later advance. But just as the threat of armed black resistance moved white society closer (alas, not close enough!) to King's dream in the twentieth century, it ultimately took John Brown to frame Garrison's idealism in a political and moral context that saved the latter from seeming absurd in historical retrospect. The notion that "non-violent resistance" and pacifist protest "draw out and expose the angry violence of a society and compel humanity to alleviate the suffering it caused" is really a myth.[13] *Any expression of anti-racism*, whether from a pacifist or an advocate of force, will draw out the bigotry and prejudice of society. Indeed, fear of escalating violence is a far greater catalyst for change within an indifferent majority than "moral suasion" or appeals to the conscience of a society.

In short, there would be little reason to celebrate William Lloyd Garrison without Elijah Lovejoy, Nat Turner, or David Walker.

David Walker was a free man living in Boston when he wrote his *Appeal to the Coloured Citizens of the World, but in particular, and very expressly, to those of the United States of America*, which was published in three editions between 1829 to 1830. Born to a free black woman in North Carolina, Walker came to adulthood with a hatred of slavery enhanced by observations made during a tour of the South. Of Methodist background, Walker eventually came north and cut his abolitionist teeth as an agent and supporter of moderate black publications. He was involved in the Massachusetts General Colored Association (founded in 1826), before which he declared in one speech that blacks ought to organize themselves in order to protect and aid each other "to the utmost of our power." However, it was Walker's *Appeal* that distinguished him as a radical voice in the black community.

Like Garrison, Walker approached his writing from a biblical and moral framework, and in opposition to the racist colonization movement. While criticizing the racist influence of Thomas Jefferson and Henry Clay, Walker's *Appeal* also burns with prophetic ire, calling upon a just God in condemnation of the whites, whom he interchangeably refers to as "Americans" and "Christians." The work, which Walker organized into four sections with a preamble, systematically examines the plight of blacks by considering slavery, the ignorance of blacks necessitated by slavery, the grievous double standard of white Christian religion, and the racism of the Colonization movement.

Walker made his living as a clothing store owner, but his life work was the advancement of his prophetic word to black people. He placed copies of his *Appeal* in black hands wherever possible, and even smuggled it into the South—most notably by stitching copies inside the jacket linings he sold to black seamen. Southern leaders were deeply disturbed by the *Appeal*, and in many cases blacks who were found holding or circulating the pamphlet were arrested. Indeed, word reached Walker that a reward of $1,000 had been placed on his head by some men in Georgia. As Benjamin Quarles wrote, while blacks considered the *Appeal* "an inspired work," Southern whites called it "the diabolical Boston Pamphlet."

But Walker did not live long enough to see the extent to which his pamphlet would electrify the black community. In August 1830, he "suddenly and mysteriously" fell dead in the doorway of his store. Many in the black community believed he was poisoned, but municipal death records and a published obituary show that Walker died of an apparent lung disease, similar to one that already had claimed the life of his baby daughter.[14] Resented by most white abolitionists and held at arm's length by the formidable William Lloyd Garrison, David Walker was now forever bound up in the very essence of black militance.

In the 1843 National Colored Convention in Buffalo, New York, the growing tide of black militance threatened to carry the convention. Garrison's nonpolitical philosophy was under attack as blacks were moving away from "moral suasion" and pacifism toward a more political conception of the struggle. The Garrisonians were dismayed that one black activist, Henry Highland Garnet, nearly carried away the convention with his militant cry. "Strike for your lives and liberties. Let every slave throughout the land do this, and the days of slavery are numbered," Garnet declared. "Rather die freemen than live to be slaves. . . . Let your motto be resistance! resistance! RESISTANCE!"

Perhaps it was a black colleague who first shared a copy of Walker's *Appeal* with John Brown, though there is no way of knowing when he obtained it or how long he pored over its blazing pages. Six years later, Brown had also read Garnet's address and recognized its kinship with the Walker pamphlet. When he obtained a pamphlet combining Walker's *Appeal* with Garnet's speech, he even authorized a new edition of the pamphlet at his own expense.

By the end of the 1840s, Garrison's principles no longer appeared "suitable or realistic weapons with which to abolish Southern bondage or Northern proscription." While Garrison continued as a major voice of abolition until the Civil War, a few blacks were more impressed by the stern but friendly businessman now becoming known as a most unusual white man. The leading black abolitionist, Frederick Douglass (who would shortly have a falling out with Garrison), thus wrote of meeting with John Brown in 1848.

> Though a white gentleman, [he] is in sympathy a black man, and is as deeply interested in our cause, as though his own soul had been pierced with the iron of slavery. . . . Mr. Brown said that for many years he had been standing by the great sea of American bondmen, and anxiously watching for some true men to rise above its dark level. . . . Mr. Brown is

one of the most earnest and interesting men that I have met in a long time.[15]

Douglass had seen fire in John Brown, fire that burned as brightly as that of Garrison—but with a flame that threatened to consume slavery in earnest. Even in shades of old age and distant memory almost a half century later, Frederick Douglass would remember his flame.

PART II

# A Good Cause and a Sovereign God

A good cause is sure to be safe in the hands of an all-good, all-wise, and all-powerful Director and Father.

—John Brown

# 4

## The Early Years
### *Autobiography and History*

That which is altogether just shalt thou follow, that thou mayest live, and inherit the land which the Lord Thy God giveth thee.
—Deuteronomy 16:20

In its day, the Torrington homestead where John Brown was born was "a typical New England house of the eighteenth century," with a country road running nearby, and a fence made of stones gathered from the fields and heightened by overlaid logs. In front of the house was the entrance to a New England-style cellar, and on the side of the house was a well. The house was built in 1776, the same year that Captain John Brown of the colonial army died from dysentery while serving in the struggle for independence. In 1799 his son Owen, a hopeful twenty-eight-year-old tanner, purchased the sturdy house for his young family. It was from the small window panes of this "clapboard house, well built and thoroughly finished," that the toddler John first viewed the world, sheltered under its sturdy pine ceiling. Little survives of the Brown family history from these early days in Connecticut. Much later in life, John Brown had few memories of those years, and writing to a young friend about his youth he found little "worth mentioning save that at that *early age*," he had been drawn to "Three Large Brass Pins belonging to a girl who lived in the family" until he succumbed to the temptation to steal them. "In this," Brown wrote of himself in the third person, "he was detected by his Mother; and after having a full day to think of the wrong: received from her a thorough whipping."[1]

He also wrote of himself that "John had been taught from earliest childhood to 'fear God and Keep his commandments,'" an ongoing course from infancy that shortly came to entail religious exercises and catechism as well as the rod of discipline. Both mother and father Brown administered the switch—that terrible instrument of chastisement that Owen dubbed "the limber persuader," as it was always freshly cut from the branch of a nearby tree. Even to his grandchildren, Owen had a reputation for reacting harshly to "any overreaching of dishonesty"—a trait he apparently passed down to John, who likewise practiced harsh and immediate reprisal when his sons and daughters lied or otherwise rebelled against the order of God and family established in holy scripture.

Modern readers may consider the use of switches and belts a barbaric method of discipline. Later in life, even John Brown learned to regret the parental harshness he exercised as a young parent. Yet the Browns and many other Christian families over generations considered the use of physical force in child-rearing a biblical mandate that not only instilled discipline and respect in young people, but also reflected the theological premise of divine fatherhood and spiritual discipline in the life of the Christian. The Puritans and many other conservative Christians followed the admonitions of the Old Testament, believing that "the rod and reproof give wisdom," and that "he that spareth the rod hateth his son" (Proverbs 13:24, 29:15). But they also saw, as did Owen Brown and his family, that the use of physical force reflected the New Testament teaching, "whom the Lord loveth he chaseneth and scourgeth every son whom he receiveth" (Hebrews 12:6). Chastisement was thus a living reminder and model of God's love for his children as well as proof of the imperfect but sincere and godly love of the human parent.

Along with the fear of God and the keeping of the commandments, John and his older sister, Anna Ruth, and Levi Blakeslee must have early heard the strong abolitionist sentiments that father Owen expressed at home. As children born in the wake of the greatest religious revival since the time of Whitefield, Anna, John, and Levi were steeped in the strong anti-slavery sentiments that often accompanied that work of grace in New England. The dual impact of Reformed revival and abolitionism was a vivid aspect of religious life in the Brown family, especially from the time of the great spiritual movement of 1799–1800 that had set Connecticut aflame. "My grandfather often said that preachers, who seemed inspired, denounced slavery in those meetings and predicted the wrath of God for our national sin," one of Owen Brown's grandsons recalled. "Abolition ideas were ever afterward more widely spread, more deeply rooted among New Englanders."[2]

Undoubtedly, John Brown was taught to hate slavery the way most Sunday School children are taught to hate the devil. Even before Brown understood the primary realities of human life he was undoubtedly aware of it as an evil institution. At nearly five years of age, while he studied the countryside from inside the colonial "clapboard" house—his little nose pressed against the window pane, his blue eyes tracing land and sky to the horizon—John's father Owen would have discussed slavery with guests and friends by the brick hearth of a great fireplace, warmed by its roaring flames and their own righteous indignation. However childish, little John Brown had some conception of slavery as a distant, evil monster shadowing the land. In time he would learn in earnest of slaves and slavemasters, of North and South, black and white, and of a white Christian people hopelessly divided over the nature and destiny of the Africans among them. But all these revelations awaited him just beyond the horizon, where New England Puritanism has already begun to encounter the hard realities of the white man's frontier.

The Browns' move to Ohio was sparked by a visit at their Torrington home by the Reverend David Bacon, a frontier missionary. Bacon and others regularly visited the Reserve to minister to the spiritual needs of "the homesick pioneers," who built their villages in reminiscence of their beloved New England. Bacon was the first to suggest to Owen that he might find a new and better life on the Western Reserve. He assured the young tanner that there were great opportunities in Ohio, especially the blossoming town of Hudson. They were among nearly five hundred families to migrate to the Western Reserve.[3]

The first family residence in Hudson was a cabin Owen built adjacent to the green at the center of town. In the early years, public school convened (when time and opportunity permitted) in another log structure near the town center. School was hardly mandatory, and John avoided it habitually. Until he was an adolescent, he was more likely to be working for his father, herding cattle, tanning hides, or plowing for his uncle, Gideon Mills. "Squire Mills" was apparently a fine shoemaker, and provided footwear for his sister's family in exchange for the labor of his strong, sprouting nephew. Of course, John played as hard as he worked, and would often be seen chasing wild turkeys and squirrels around Stow Corners, or battling it out with the sons of neighborhood Democrats in furious snowball warfare—boyish contests that reflected the sharp political divide in early Hudson between Federalists and Democrats. When John did study, his early education was sporadic, "fitful and scanty."

There were other reasons that he may have found it difficult to apply himself to study. On December 11, 1808, when John was nearly nine years old, his mother vainly travailed in childbirth, and then followed her newborn daughter to the grave a few hours later. The tragic deaths broke ground in the community's new cemetery barely four years after the Browns had arrived in town. Not surprisingly, the loss was bitter and difficult for husband and children alike. In his 1841 autobiographical sketch, Owen reflected on the devastating impact of Ruth's death upon him, writing of his bereavement as "the time when I tasted the wormwood and the [gall]." Years later, John Brown too acknowledged the pain of his mother's loss, writing that he not only "continued to pine after" her, but lost that "suitable connecting link between the sexes" that he believed young boys need to overcome their shyness toward girls. Given Owen's increasingly busy schedule, the home life of the Browns had centered around Ruth, who provided guidance, discipline, and probably saw to it that John got his primary education. With his mother gone and Owen busy at the tannery, perhaps John hung around the grave site, gazing hopelessly at the stone that marked it, and the verse inscribed: "She was a delightful child, A Sprightly youth, a Loving wife, A tender parent, a Kind neighbor, and an exemplary Christian."

Nor was John much consoled when his father remarried eleven months later, taking Sally Root of Southwick, Massachusetts, as his new wife. He remembered her as an "estimable woman" and grew to love and admire her in later years. But initially John, his brother Salmon, and foster brother Levi grappled with their new stepmother, who was eighteen years younger than their father and quite "snappish." John Brown's detractors later inflated stories about him playing cruel and dangerous pranks on Sally. But the stories are innovations that overlook the fact that resistance came from Owen's boys in general, and that seven-year-old Salmon gave her a worse time of it. Indeed, both John and Salmon were probably following the example of Levi Blakeslee, who was nearly sixteen and resented Sally's parental authority. If John played pranks on his stepmother it was probably because he saw Levi blatantly resisting her correction—once even provoking her so that when she tried to give him a kick, he grabbed her foot and refused to let go. Young John missed his mother and found it hard to warm to the parental advances of the younger woman now sharing his father's bed. Widowed fathers on the frontier were hard pressed to carry on without the support of a wife, as John himself would realize one day. At the time, he did not understand his father's loneliness and need of support, and he resented Sally's demands—especially when she made him stay inside to churn butter. It was not merely being kept indoors that John hated, but the butter itself. Throughout his life he expressed something of a contempt for dairy products, especially butter. "He never could bear the smell or taste of butter and cheese," his eldest son recalled. Once he even rejected a slice of bread because he thought it had been sliced by a knife with butter on it.

John Brown later wrote that when he was ten years old, a friend "induced him to read a little history" and offered him "the free use of a good library" as well. His growing interest in reading and new appreciation for the company of older people may reflect an adolescent awkwardness around other young people, especially young women. Though reading biographies and essays turned him against "vain and frivolous conversations," perhaps they were actually a kind of haven at an ungainly stage of life. Before he was sixteen John was already "very strong and large" for his age, and may have found comfort in the safety of solitude, reading, learning his father's craft, or tending to his own little collection of livestock.[4]

Owen Brown insisted upon the regular recitation of the *Westminster Catechism* as part of the family's home religious training. Liturgical Protestants used catechisms, or teaching materials, in preparation for confirmation and for confessional purposes. In order to distinguish themselves from Roman Catholics, Protestants prepared confessions representing the various branches of the Reformation in Europe. *The Westminster Confession* and catechisms (shorter and larger), and the *Savoy Declaration* were essential to the exposition and propagation of English Protestantism. *The Westminster Shorter Catechism* of 1647 was probably that which Owen Brown used in the religious training of his family. Comprised of 107 questions with brief answers and scripture references, the shorter catechism served well in teaching young people the essentials of the Reformed faith, including the biblical doctrines like predestination and limited atonement. The Westminster documents provide an expansive, systematic understanding of the entire Bible. As they grew from infancy into elementary years, the Brown children became familiar with the questions and answers of the *Catechism*, such as:

Question 1: What is the chief end of man?
Answer: Man's chief end is to glorify God, and to enjoy Him for ever.

Question 2: What rule hath God given to direct us how we may glorify God and enjoy Him?

Answer: The Word of God, which is contained in the Scriptures of the Old and New Testaments, is the only rule to direct us how we may glorify and enjoy Him.

Under the tutelage of Owen and Ruth, the Brown children thus learned the essentials of a theocentric world view—a view beginning and ending with the independent and sovereign will of God.

Question 3: What do the Scriptures principally teach?

Answer: The Scriptures principally teach what man is to believe concerning God, and what duty God requires of man.

Question 4: What is God?

Answer: God is a Spirit, infinite, eternal, and unchangeable, in His being, wisdom, power, holiness, justice, goodness, and truth.

The *Catechism* further explains the nature of God in explicitly Christian and Trinitarian terms (Questions 5–6), and then the "decrees of God"—the divine purpose by which God foreordains "whatsoever comes to pass" through the works of creation and providence, the latter being God's "preserving and governing all His creatures, and all their actions" (Questions 7–8, 11). The *Catechism* also provides an outline of the nature of mankind, redemption in Jesus Christ, the Decalogue, the Lord's Prayer, and other essentials of Christian faith according to the Reformed Protestant tradition.[5]

The *Westminster Catechism,* the *Savoy Declaration*, and other materials derived from the Reformed tradition in England were a vital part of the religious training of John Brown and his siblings, and these—inclined in the direction of an abolitionist perspective—provided him with the basis upon which he would come to understand himself and his role in the Providence and purpose of God. According to the *Savoy Declaration*, the official statement of the Congregational Church, the Creator

doth uphold, direct, dispose and govern all creatures, actions and things from the greatest even to the least by his most wise and holy providence, according to his infallible foreknowledge, and the free and immutable counsel of his own will, to the praise of the glory of his wisdom, power, justice, goodness and mercy.[6]

Human life and development is complex, and this hardly explains the whole of John Brown's increasing conviction that he was a chosen instrument of God, raised up by Providence for the purpose of destroying slavery. But without appreciating the Reformed view of vocation and Providence over against the claims of other supernatural callings (such as that of Joan of Arc or Nat Turner), one may have a skewed notion of what John Brown came to believe about himself.

In the Puritan mind, the idea of special vocation falls within the boundaries of Providence, not the supernatural. The governance of God is not discerned by extraordinary visions, revelations, or heavenly voices, but rather by the internal direction and leading of the Holy Spirit. For the Puritans this presupposed a life of prayer and Bible study (by which they both spoke to and heard from God), as a result of which one increasingly discerned himself being shaped and directed by events, circumstances, and the vibrant depths of heartfelt concern while yet involved in the normal pursuits of life.

For details on John Brown's early life in Hudson, we are largely dependent upon an autobiographical sketch he prepared in 1857 when he had become a public figure noted for his militant activities in the Kansas wars against pro-slavery forces. The writing was prompted by request of Henry Stearns, the young son of one of Brown's most important supporters, George L. Stearns. When he visited the Stearns in January 1857, Brown had become a controversial freedom-fighter, and his stories of war against pro-slavery forces had made a grand impression upon the Stearns family—especially young Henry, who even gave him some money. According to Mary Stearns, her son approached Brown at the moment he was preparing to leave, "as he was putting on his blue army overcoat in the hall," and asked him to write something about his own youth. Though busy, Brown agreed, and it must have crossed his mind that his benefactor would take an interest in whatever he wrote to young Henry. However, his critics have misinterpreted the resulting document as "a carefully constructed tactical device" intended to win confidence and financial support.[7]

If it was believed that he intended his personal sketch to be fund-raising propaganda, the facts seem otherwise. First, it was certainly not a priority for him, and he excused his belated efforts by pointing out his "constant care, and anxiety." Indeed, he had actually forgotten young Stearns for a time, and his father had written in April 1857, nudging him to fulfill his promise to young Henry. Enclosing a second gift from his son (thirty cents), the proud father wrote: "Will you at your leisure write a note to him, acknowledging the receipt of it for Kansas Relief. I want him to keep it. It was his own desire to give this money, not prompted by his parents. He is 12 years old." But he still did not write, waiting until July— suggesting that the document was not really about gaining financial support as much as it was a favor for young Stearns. Brown even wrote in the conclusion that if he was tempted at all, it was to exploit the opportunity to talk about later developments in order to gain an advantage. "I do not say that I will do it," Brown concluded—really foregoing the opportunity to turn his autobiographical sketch toward economic gain. Though aware of the importance of representing himself as a high-minded and assertive individual, Brown was primarily interested in crafting a story that would affect the life of a young man. His autobiographical sketch is really didactic more than strategic. Its purpose is to impress upon his reader that character, faith, and discipline are the real necessities of life and the real goals to be sought, even by a twelve-year-old boy. But Brown's sketch is nevertheless indispensable for the details it provides on his early life.

Brown wrote a tale to interest a twelve-year-old boy, with rattlesnakes, guns, and the chance to wear a buckskin suit while hob-knobbing with real Indians. Young John, now only six years old, learns to "dress" animal skins and wanders fearlessly in "the wild new country" in what at first seems a boy's paradise of adventure and fun. Yet all was not fun, Brown assured his reader as he wrote of himself in the third person:

> But about this period he was placed in the School of *adversity*: which[,] my young friend[,] was a most necessary part of his early training. . . . a severe but *much needed course* of discipline which he afterward was to pass through; and which it is to be hoped has learned him before this time that the Heavenly Father sees it best to take all the little things out of his hands which he has ever placed in them.

John Brown knows the "sore trials" that he mentions might seem laughable to a boy whose father could doubtless afford to buy him many fine toys and pets. But such was the pain and anguish of young John Brown when he lost a yellow marble, a pet squirrel called "Bob tail" which ran away, and a "little Ewe Lamb" which died.

As he became older and no longer fearful of Indians, John "learned a trifle of their talk," and besides rambling about in the woods, he began to enjoy rough play, wrestling, snowball fights—perhaps a bit of bullying, such as knocking off "old seedy Wool hats." Here Brown is a kind of preincarnate Huck Finn, mischievous, loathsome of school, and much more inclined to "be seen *bare footed and bare headed*" with only one leather suspender holding up his buckskin pants. At twelve years of age (which by no coincidence is the age of his young reader), John singlehandedly herds cattle for over a hundred miles and is perfectly delighted with this manly success. At this point, however, the author backtracked, for he pointed out to young Stearns that he was "left a Motherless boy which loss was complete and permanent," even though his father eventually remarried "a very estimable woman." The loss of precious things and pets had saddened him deeply, but his sorrow was perfected in this loss, the worst "mourning season" of all.

With his mother's death as the worst of young John's "sore trials," Brown continued with the narrative at age twelve, in the midst of the War of 1812. Preferring solitude while brooding over his mother's death, the buckskin John herds cattle for his father to an army camp (he does not provide a location, but it was probably Detroit). The camp becomes yet another setting for John's "School of *adversity*," this time bringing home to him the realities of violence and injustice in the world—something Brown very much wanted young Stearns to realize. There in the camp, young John observes the crude behaviors and immorality rampant in the military, which so disgusts him that later in life he opts out of military duty by paying exemption fines.

Far worse was the crisis that not only turned him into "a most *determined Abolitionist*, and led him to declare, *or Swear: Eternal war* with Slavery," but probably traumatized him for a long time to come. Brown wrote that during one of those herding expeditions for his father, the adolescent John was well-received by "a very gentlemanly land lord." The landlord made much of John's courage and skill, doting over him like a "great pet." The same man, however, owned a slave, a "*negro boy* (who was fully if not more than his equal)." The slave boy was subjected to blatant neglect, brutality, and the most cruel treatment. Rather than being parentally whipped with a "limber persuader" like young John, the black youth is battered and bruised by the master with an iron shovel or some other blunt object, and left to languish in the cold night.

Here is the point that Brown wanted to portray to the wealthy white heir. While affirming young Stearns's compassion for the Kansas struggle, he was inherently challenging him to look beyond the crisis of white Free

State boys and girls struggling against southern bullies in Kansas to the very heart of the issue—the oppression of the enslaved African: "This brought John to reflect on the wretched; hopeless condition of *Fatherless and Motherless* slave *children*: for such children have neither Fathers or Mothers; to protect, and provide for them. He sometimes would raise the question: *is God their Father?*" Here is the essential question, derived as much from the catechism and the scriptures as from the loving chastisement of Owen Brown. If such evil befalls a black child without even a loving parent to protect and provide for him, then where is the God of heaven and how can his righteousness be manifested?

Brown also exposed his youthful sins, especially the "[very] bad and foolish [habit]" of lying, as well as self-conceit, and the tendency "to speak in an imperious or dictating way." But after witnessing the traumatic abuse of the slave boy, Brown wrote, there was a change. He becomes sober about life and its disciplines, and acquires "some taste for reading," especially history. He avoids bad company and begins to hang around "old and [intelligent] persons" whose conversations please and educate him. Bashful and conservative, he avoids dances, eschews card games, and grows to detest "vain and frivolous conversation." Instead he pores over biographies and wisdom literature and begins to think seriously about life. Equally important, the writer continued, is John's conversion to Christianity and belief "in the divine authenticity of the Bible," which alleviates his apprehensions about the future.

Before he turns twenty years old, John seems wise beyond his years. He becomes proficient at tanning and preparing hides, studies common mathematics and surveying, and begins to formulate a "[definite] plan" in life—namely, to succeed in business in order to carry out "his greatest or principle object," the liberation of the slaves. At twenty years, he is an enthusiast for livestock, recognizing his vocation "*in early life*" was "to be a practical *Shepherd.*" Finally (and perhaps the least interesting to twelve-year-old Stearns), John takes a wife. He does not choose her according to looks (she is "remarkably plain"), but for her neatness, economy, character, practicality, and common sense, not to mention the prompting of his father.[8]

John Brown's autobiographical sketch fits into what Ross Miller calls the "classic line of autobiographical literature" because of its "self-reflective" quality. For Brown the writer, his life was "the stage upon which history, that is all the history he remembers, is played out." His record of life in Connecticut, the journey to Ohio with his family, his adjustment to frontier life, his encounter with the military and the cruelties of slavery, and his conversion to Christianity all recalled the past in order to possess it and "conceive of history as it was lived through an individual's senses." In short, the "silent proposition" of John Brown the autobiographer is that to know the world of which he speaks, "one must first know him." He also used personal language, metaphor, and a controlling narrative to create the impression that the particular facts of the story are also "valid indicators of a wider history just outside or parallel to the life of the writer." "Dressing" animal skins, making "Whip Lashes," and wearing "Buckskin Breeches" are terms that did not resonate with familiarity for young Stearns, and therefore lent authenticity to Brown's frontier story. Similarly, the losses of his prized yellow marble, favorite squirrel, and beloved lamb are all metaphors representing far greater losses in adulthood (by 1857 Brown had lost ten children, nine in early youth and one young adult). The losses also point to the human vulnerability to the intrusions of death and misfortune. Brown's controlling narrative is really that of Providence and the discipline of God in the life of his servant.

John's life is knowingly framed in Providence, for it is God the all-seeing Heavenly Father who places him in the "School of *adversity*," giving and taking good gifts from him in order to train him in the course of godliness. Ultimately it is not Owen Brown who brings young John to the Ohio frontier but God, and it is God who is working to guide and direct John Brown to realize his *raison d'etre*—to make of him a "practical *Shepherd*" whose work is only a means to his "greatest or principle object."

John Brown's sketch has its share of stylizations too. He did not tell young Stearns that his father Owen was a staunch abolitionist and that he may even have begun to help fugitive slaves back in Connecticut, not to mention later in Hudson. Nor did he write about the childhood experience he admitted elsewhere, of being excluded by "certain snobbish" boys in Hudson who rejected him from their "set"—a rejection that pained him for several years until he realized the shallowness of their claims. Neither did he mention any of his siblings besides an initial reference to an "adopted" brother, even though his elder sister, Anna Ruth, and his younger brothers Salmon, Oliver Owen, and Frederick were all a vital part of his early life and doubtless shared his strong convictions about slavery.[9]

The dominant stylization of Brown's autobiography is also the real climax of the narrative—John's firsthand encounter with the brutality of slavery in 1812. Many writers have accepted his record of meeting the young slave without taking a closer look at the account. Certainly the primary question to be raised is whether the abused black youth was really a slave. He did not record where the incident took place, though he mentioned that he had traveled more than a hundred miles in herding livestock. Since he was probably herding "beef cattle" to U.S. troops during the War of 1812, the visit could hardly have been to the South. Because the war was largely fought in Michigan and Canada, the question arises whether the black youth was a slave or an abused "employee." Did John Brown stylize the incident in order to bring his life story into harmony with the larger question of the slavery controversy as it existed in the 1850s? Perhaps the enslavement of the young man was a tragic exception, or he may have been an oppressed, abused worker—a wage slave who unfortunately depended on a cruel racist for his livelihood. If the latter is true, then Brown conflated the monstrous system of black enslavement in the South with the incidental, systemic, and often brutal racism that was part of everyday life for blacks in the North.[10]

Brown's autobiographical sketch was intended to enlighten and instruct a twelve-year-old boy in the things that mattered most *to John Brown*—such as the values of education, self-discipline, goal-setting, and belief "in the divine authenticity of the Bible." As a writer, he sought to bring young Henry, vicariously as it were, to the bloodstained threshold of the house of bondage. In so doing, the writer framed the entire story in the transcendent theme of a Heavenly Father who wisely guides and directs a young boy through the "School of *adversity*" and loving chastisement to the point of realizing his preordained calling as a shepherd-liberator. For a moment the process is frozen, the journey becomes a still life, and the hand of God is visible. "With an honest desire" for the "best good" of young Henry Stearns, Brown committed the story into his hands—perhaps hoping he was also placing it into the hands of history.

# 5

# Millennial Hopes, Abolitionist Awakenings

> Thus saith the Lord, Keep ye judgment, and do justice: for my salvation is near to come, and my righteousness to be revealed.
>
> —Isaiah 56:1

By the 1840s, Hudson began to be considered a center of abolitionist sentiment even though it was actually a community divided over the anti-slavery issue. After a student activist from Western Reserve College narrowly escaped being tarred and feathered for presenting an anti-slavery lecture, he was trailed back to the town by a racist mob. Failing to lay hold of him, they satisfied their contempt by returning with a sign which they posted along the road leading to town that pictured a grinning black man and read: "Dis be de rode to Husson." The sign was left standing, and in time it became a symbol of pride to the young town as it evolved into an anti-slavery stronghold in the decade prior to the Civil War. The Western Reserve area was generally despised by the South because of its growing sympathy for the slave, as illustrated by a Richmond, Virginia, newspaper in 1848 which declared the inhabitants of the Reserve a "hypocritical, canting, whining, totally depraved and utterly irredeemable set of rascals." By the 1850s, Hudson reached the point of being "congenitally hospitable to runaways" and contemptuous of slavecatchers. Contempt for slavery was perfected largely with the passing of the Fugitive Slave Law in 1850. Northern Ohio increasingly became hostile toward the pro-slavery policies of the federal government, and by 1860 the black population of the Western Reserve increased 100 percent. As a strong underground railroad region, the Reserve became a thorn in the side of the Slave Power. One slave-catcher noted that he had never seen so many blacks and abolitionists in one place. "Might as well try to hunt the *devil* there as hunt a nigger."

Despite the stark contrast with other sections of the country where racism was overwhelming and blatant, the Reserve was still conservative, maintaining the social and political views carried from New England by its founders—including an inherently condescending view of blacks. When Boyd Stutler wrote that Hudson was "in all respects a New England village pulled up by its roots and transplanted in Ohio," his words could apply as much to its prejudices as its virtues. In the first three decades of Hudson's community life only a small number of families formed an active minority of abolitionists who opposed slavery and believed in the equality of blacks and Native peoples. Though generally opposed to slavery, most people in Hudson supported the idea of colonizing blacks as the best solution. But abolitionists opposed to the colonization scheme were growing more outspoken, and a fierce debate between the two groups was "raging in small towns like Hudson when John Brown grew to young manhood."[1]

As a teenager, Brown began to seriously consider the Christian religion and the Bible. He wrote that when he was around fifteen years old he "became to some extent a convert to Christianity," which probably suggests that despite other thoughts or questions he might have entertained, he was strongly inclined toward Christianity prior to his public confession of faith. Given his devout parents and home life, his early religious training, and the strong spiritual community that supported him, John Brown's "conversion" was hardly a dramatic event.

Probably because his interest in church membership had waned in later years, he did not mention that his affiliation with the Congregational Church in Hudson began when he was sixteen years old. Owen, Ruth, and the children had probably attended Sunday services at the church since their arrival at Hudson in the summer of 1805, but for some reason the couple did not join the congregation until 1808—only a few months before Ruth died. Why the Browns hesitated to transfer their membership from Connecticut to Hudson is unclear, except that perhaps the Hudson church was a mission effort until 1815, when the congregation called their first pastor, the Reverend William Hanford. As a Congregational Church, the Hudson society had no denominational association with which to affiliate at first. As Clarence Gee observed, the Congregationalists "needed, for discipline and other advantages, the help of the presbyteries," and this apparently required some measure of compromise. Perhaps Hanford was a Presbyterian minister, for he introduced the *Westminster Confession* instead of the *Savoy Declaration* of the Congregational Churches, the first church covenant requiring members to affirm their belief in "the Confession of Faith of the Presbyterian Church in America." As has been discussed, the dependence of Congregationalism upon Presbyterianism became officially pronounced when the Plan of Union joined the two denominations in 1815, bringing the Hudson congregation—somewhat unhappily—under the ecclesiastical jurisdiction of the Grand River Presbytery.

While the Hudson church covenant designated the *Westminster Confession*, it maintained other Congregational earmarks, such as this post-millennial statement: "You believe it to be the revealed purpose of God hereafter to raise his church from its present depressed state and to give his people rest and prosperity for a thousand years, when the Jews shall own the Messiah and all nations shall know the Lord."[2] Post-millennialism is the belief that the millennium spoken of in the twentieth chapter of Revelation refers to a coming golden age of Christian predominance in the world *before* the second coming of Jesus Christ. In contrast to pre-millennialism, the belief that Christ will return and enforce a 1,000-year reign, the optimistic post-millennialists hold that a great spiritual renewal will precede Christ's return. Congregational post-millennialists believed that a great move of Christian conversion was going to sweep over Muslims, Buddhists, Hindus, and others. Similarly, they anticipated a great harvest of the Jewish people, with many (if not all) of the descendants of Abraham proclaiming Jesus the Messiah. While the Presbyterians did not specify a millennial interpretation, the Congregationalist *Savoy Declaration* included a post-millennial statement very similar to what is expressed in the Hudson church covenant.[3]

The optimism of Puritan post-millennialism was typified by Jonathan Edwards, the leading theologian of the Great Awakening, whose writings were part of John Brown's library. Edwards predicted the millennium would take place "through the ordinary processes of propagating the gospel in the power of the Holy Spirit." Besides holding to the conventional Protestant belief that the Roman papacy was the antichrist, Edwards believed that the revivals of his era would transform the colonies. Religious conditions would increasingly improve until finally the millennial era would ensue in North America by the year 2000. Edwards and fellow believers were "awaiting the golden age, definitely not the Judgement." As he surveyed the spreading revivals of Europe and North

America, he saw them as "the ongoing work of the Holy Spirit preparing the way for the coming of Christ."

Post-millennialism also informed and empowered reform movements ranging from abolition to temperance. However, we cannot be certain that because Hudson's Congregationalists were post-millennial, they were necessarily more vigorous than social-minded pre-millennialists in their era. Yet insofar as post-millennial thought was part of the Congregational heritage transplanted to the Western Reserve, it cannot be discounted. With such strong convictions about the imminent golden age of pervasive Christian virtues, and that the rule of righteousness would precede the return of Christ, something of post-millennialism probably informed the anti-slavery sentiments of Owen Brown, his family, and the few other early abolitionists in Hudson. John Brown was hardly a millennial fanatic, nor did he ever advance the notion that his anti-slavery campaign would open the golden door to the millennium. But very likely he held deep, often unspoken post-millennial convictions about the role of Christians in the world—perhaps that an active opposition to the evil of slavery could help usher in the millennial kingdom. Before his execution in 1859, Brown wrote to the Reverend H. L. Vaill:

> I was enabled to discover the secret of [happiness]; somewhat early. It has been in making the prosperity, and the happiness of others *my own*: so that really I have had a great deal of prosperity. I am very prosperous still; and looking forward to a time when "peace on Earth and good will to *men* shall every where prevail."[4]

In the closing days of life, Brown referred to the millennium, a time of pervasive peace and justice to come. That he wrote so assuredly suggests that post-millennial expectation was woven into the fabric of his religious and political thought. This hardly makes him exceptional by any means, but it may at least suggest that post-millennialism was one kind of leaven in the rising loaf of abolition in Hudson and the Western Reserve.

Brown's acquaintance with Vaill went back many years to his youth, when for a brief time he studied in preparation for the ministry. After being examined by the Hudson congregation on March 6, 1816, teenage John was approved for membership in the church, and officially recognized on March 31 after the Sunday worship service. As a son of believing parents, he had undoubtedly been baptized as an infant in the Congregational Church in Connecticut in keeping with the teaching of the

*Savoy Declaration*, that "[n]ot only those that do actually profess faith in and obedience unto Christ, but also the infants of one or both believing parents are to be baptised, and those only." Far from the Roman Catholic idea of baptism as a washing from sin, the English Reformers agreed with the other Confessional Protestants that baptism was a sign of salvation and inclusion in the church. The greater number of Reformed people also baptized their children as a "sign and seal of the covenant" similar to circumcision in the Hebrew scriptures.

His conversion to Christianity was thus an affirmation and fulfillment of his status as a child of the covenant—a happy outcome, since the church must be comprised of "visible saints, who by a profession of their faith in Christ and a life agreeable to the presept [*sic*] of the gospel, give reasonable evidence in the judgement of charity of being real saints." The tenet of "visible saints" was the key distinctive of the Congregational movement, and one that somewhat distinguished them from the prevalent theology of the English Reformation. Baptizing one's infant only to watch him grow to adulthood and reject orthodoxy (which happened to John Brown as a parent) was always an awkward problem to the Puritans. Since the Congregational movement was premised on the church being a "gathered" company of believers, it was especially a relief when a "child of the covenant" proved to be a "visible saint" too.[5]

At seventeen, John Brown went back East to attend preparatory school in New England with the objective of entering Amherst College, accompanied by fifteen-year-old Salmon. (Brown's cousin on his mother's side, Heman Humphrey, was president and head professor at Amherst at the time.) With no preparatory school or college yet established in the Western Reserve, prosperous Owen Brown saw an opportunity to have his sons properly educated. Owen undoubtedly recognized John's zeal for the Bible (John wrote that he had become "very familiar and possessed a most unusual memory of its entire contents"), and hoped that his sons would surpass his own stunted education. John was not completely ill-prepared for this endeavor since he had studied at nearby Tallmadge Academy during the academic year 1815–16, the same year he became a member of the Hudson church. The Tallmadge academy was run by the Reverend Simeon Woodruff, whose instruction offered him "something near the high school level" of study, and who may also have encouraged him to pursue schooling further.

"The Browns were among the few families in the Western Reserve area at the time who could afford to send their son back to New England to seek an education," notes Thomas Vince. If they lacked anything, it was access to good roads and transportation routes. The canals and railroads that John Brown later used in his abolitionist adventures were not yet constructed, and travel was necessarily a slow, tedious experience. In the summer of 1816, John and Salmon, along with another neighbor, Orson Oviatt, left for Connecticut. With one horse to ride and carry their baggage, the boys took turns on the mount. After it had served the purpose of transportation, the horse was sold and its profits applied toward tuition and living expenses. The weary travelers finally reached Canton, Connecticut, where they were received by the Reverend Hallock, Owen and Ruth's first pastor. After ascertaining their educational needs, Hallock advised the boys to go to the private academy led by his brother, the Reverend Moses Hallock, of Plainfield, Massachusetts.

The course of study at the Plainfield academy was perhaps too rigorous for John Brown, despite his bright mind and strong familiarity with the Bible. Preparatory study, especially as it was largely designed to provide a pre-ministerial and liberal arts training, probably included biblical and classical languages and this may not have come easily to him. Perhaps the setting of the academy itself disagreed with him too. He had distanced himself from snobbish boys back in Hudson, possibly because his father was not as well off initially as other Connecticut settlers. It may be that John likewise found life in New England stuffy and stifling. Despite his appearance as a "tall, sedate, dignified young man," older in appearance than in years, he was a tanner and a frontiersman. It may have been efficient and thoughtful for him to bring his own sole-leather for boot-mending, and to give out strips of tanned sheepskin for his classmates to stretch and pull for fun, but it also may have made him appear quaint to his classmates. Despite the "kind, immovableness" of his expressions, John was probably unhappy. By the winter term, he and Salmon had transferred to an academy at Morris, Connecticut.

John and Salmon always tangled, the younger accusing the elder of being a kind of dictator, calling him "a king against whom there is no rising up." Though brotherly conflicts are normal, John Brown himself acknowledged this trait as an adult, and his imperious tendencies characterized his relationships with others throughout life. At the Morris academy, John thrashed Salmon for some misdeed even though his teacher, H. L. Vaill, did not feel discipline was required. "If Salmon had done the thing at home, father would have punished him," he told Vaill. "I know he would expect you to punish him now for doing this—and if you don't, I shall." Vaill, who wrote to Brown years later when he was awaiting execution, remembered this incident as an example of his forcefulness when it came to anything he considered a duty. Vaill also recalled Brown as "a godly youth," but one overwhelmed while "laboring to recover from his disadvantages of early education."

Providence seemed to be working against his ministerial plans. He was not only fighting an uphill battle on academic terms, but developed an inflammation of the eyes that created great discomfort. He may have been further discouraged when "crossed in love affairs." What seems to have been the determining factor in terminating his studies was the same problem that he would face years later as an anti-slavery warrior. In the spring, John and Salmon found themselves with a shortage of finances, not only due to "money stringency but of general crop failures and great lack of provisions."[6] Years later, Brown alluded to this episode in a letter to one of his sons at a time when scarcity of money had again become a point of concern:

> I would not be afraid of spoiling myself by working hard on such conditions for a few days. *I* and three others were in exactly *such a fix* in the Spring of 1817, between the Sea-Side and Ohio, in a time of *extreme scarcity* of not *only money*, but of the greater distress for want of provisions, known during the nineteenth century. It was the next year after the "*cold summer*," as it has ever since been called.[7]

The "cold summer" of 1816, as Edwin Cotter Jr. has noted, was an unfortunate meteorological phenomenon that was especially damaging to the northeastern United States. In 1815, a powerful volcanic eruption at Tambora on the island of Sumbawa, Indonesia, not only devastated thousands of lives in the vicinity, but deposited volcanic ash over everything lying within five hundred miles. The outcome was destruction, famine, and health crises which ultimately claimed over 75,000 lives. The Tambora eruption reached to the shores of North America with a cold and devastating touch. As a result of the volcanic debris blasted into the stratosphere, one-fifth of the sun's light and heat was blocked, and the spring and summer of 1816 were overshadowed by a frightening period of global cooling. In Connecticut, drying laundry was found frozen stiff in early June, and snowfalls were reported in the northeast as late as July. Agriculture in the United States was devastated, and farmers thereafter referred to that memorably traumatic year as "eighteen-hundred-and-froze-to-death." By 1817, most of the country was feeling the economic aftermath of this ruin, including Owen Brown back in Hudson. During his temporary setback, Owen could not send money to his sons. Broke, discouraged, and frustrated, John and Salmon both quit school. Bidding farewell to New England, they set off for Ohio, depending entirely on hard work to finance the journey back home.[8]

When John returned home, his experience of independence and his need to find a place in the world necessitated change. Furthermore, Sally had already begun to bear children for Owen, and a second set of Browns were now filling the house in Hudson. Between 1811 and 1816, Sally Marian, Watson Hugh, and Florilla were born and brought under the "sign and seal" of baptism. Sally was now mothering Ruth's children, Anna, Salmon, Oliver Owen, and Frederick, and would give birth to five more of her own—making a total of twelve, not counting John or Levi Blakeslee. Still jesting, stuttering, and praying, Owen sired his last child at sixty-one years. Owen Brown fathered a total of sixteen children, but buried eight of them before his own death in 1856.

Beyond the aberration of 1816, Owen's tannery continued to make money, enabling him to invest in land—an enterprise that provided him "with extensive land holdings in both the village and the township." John immediately went to work for his father upon returning to Hudson, moving into the tannery with Levi Blakeslee, who was nearly twenty-five and ready for independence too. John himself was nearly a man, and there were moments when the father and son chafed each other. He began to resent his father's blunt corrections, such as the time he was talked into buying an old cow by a man pleading poverty. Taking one look at the purchase, Owen said, "I see you do not know old cows" and then walked away from his son. Considering John's admitted self-conceit and his fondness for livestock, the words probably cut him deeply. In turn, he savored the opportunity to embarrass his father, such as in the tannery, when he was able to sharpen and use a "curring knife" that Owen had insisted was useless. Perhaps Owen was somewhat relieved when John and Levi moved out and built their own tannery in Hudson in 1819. Along with the tannery, John also built his first home, a log cabin where he and Levi stayed until marriage divided the brothers, and Levi moved away to start his own family.

Another profession shared by father and son was a far more passionate endeavor, and one somewhat controversial in the community. Owen's pro-Native attitude had early distinguished him as a peculiar white man, and his friendship and assistance to blacks raised the eyebrows of some Hudson residents. Neighbors like John Whedon, whose family traveled to Ohio with the Browns, thought Owen a "real nice man," but also knew him to be quite rigorous in his abolitionist views. Owen's step-daughter recalled that "Owen was a great friend to Negroes and used to take in every one that came along." Not to be rivaled in zeal or good works, bachelor John immediately turned his home and tannery into an underground railroad stop. One account of a fugitive visitation survived in the family history, doubtless because of the impact it made on John Brown himself. One night, while John and Levi were feeding a fugitive and preparing to send him on his way refreshed, they suddenly heard the gallop of horses. Thinking the riders were slave-catchers, John rushed the fugitive through the window at the back of the cabin and told him to hide in the woods. When it turned out to be a false alarm, he went to assure the fugitive that he was safe. As Brown often told the story in years to come, he did not have to search for the man. "I heard his heart thumping before I reached him."[9]

He also returned to the Congregational Church, by now working on their first church building, which they finally occupied in 1820. Continuing under the spiritual guidance of Rev. Hanford, the Hudson congregation produced and adopted a more Presbyterian-styled church covenant on March 9, 1819. The document was clearly reflective of the actual alliance between Congregationalists and Presbyterians that had become official in 1815. The covenant itself, though a local church document, reflects the spirit of compromise necessary to forge such an alliance between two traditions. Certainly, the Congregational distinctive of "visible saints" was maintained, and no reference is made to the Presbyterian confession. However, the 1819 church covenant is silent insofar as post-millennialism is concerned. Instead, the covenant presents a kind of minimalist evangelical statement concerning the "last things": "You believe that the soul is immortal and that [on] the last day, Christ will raise the dead and judge the world in righteousness." Perhaps the post-millennial doctrine was deemphasized as part of the compromise with the Presbyterian church.

The Browns had become vital members of the Hudson church, Owen being elected to serve on the membership committee in 1818. He remained a prominent member for two more decades, until finally coming into conflict with the conservative colonization advocates in 1842. These tensions were already present, but the conflict in Hudson over slavery did not begin to heat up until abolitionists became nationally controversial in the 1830s. For the present, compromise seems to have been the prevailing theme. The Browns and a few other families assisted fugitive slaves while exchanging arguments with colonization advocates in town, as all of Hudson and the Western Reserve watched events taking shape on the national scene. The year 1820 was also one of compromise regarding slavery, for both Maine and Missouri were brought into the Union. The former came in as a free state, and the latter as a slave state, while all of the Louisiana Purchase territories north of the 36° 30' were restricted to the advance of slavery.

Yet Owen Brown pulled no punches. His "native wit, combined with stuttering, made him one of the drollest" defenders of abolition in the Western Reserve. In one exchange—perhaps with a colonization advocate—Owen proved he could handle himself despite his famous speech impediment. When the combatant grew so frustrated with Owen's stuttering that he tried to finish his sentences for him, the tanner rebuffed him with a biblical illustration: "I am as well provided for as B-B-Balaam. For when he could not speak, the ass spoke for him."

Meanwhile John Brown became interested in marriage, clearly through the prompting of his father. Her name was Dianthe Lusk, whose family had come to Hudson from Bloomfield, New York in 1801, the year of her birth. Remembered as tall people who claimed some kinship to the patriot leaders John and Samuel Adams, the Lusks found sorrow in the move to Hudson. Amos Lusk, who became a member of the Hudson Congregational Church in 1802, died during the war with England. His widow had found work keeping house and cooking for John and Levi, and Dianthe came along to help her mother. John took to Dianthe, recognizing that her assets were more of excellent character and spiritual commitment than outward appearance. Known to retreat into the woods to pray, Dianthe had an excellent reputation in the community and the church, and a lovely singing voice. Owen clearly liked Dianthe for his son too. Always one to formulate a plan and push it through to his satisfaction, John saw to it that she applied for membership in the Hudson church. After this was accomplished, in August 1819, he proposed to her, and they were married on June 21, 1820.

Years later John Brown wrote of Dianthe with affection, suggesting that what she lacked in physical beauty was more than compensated for in piety, kindness, and her "powerful; and good influence." He always remembered the day he came upon her, perhaps while she was working in the cabin, and found her singing his favorite hymn, the lyrics of which were written by Charles Wesley:

> Blow ye the trumpet, blow
> The gladly solemn sound;
> Let all the nations know,
> To earth's remotest bound.
> The year of jubilee is come;
> The year of jubilee is come;
> Return ye ransomed sinners, home.

He loved this hymn above all others, and hearing it sung in the angelic tones of Dianthe's golden voice seemed to beautify her, grace more than glamor drawing him to her side. Wesley's hymn celebrated the Old Testament theme of jubilee in Leviticus 25, in which trumpets signal the liberation of slaves and the forgiveness of debts at the fiftieth year, or jubilee. In the years to come, "Blow ye the trumpet" became John Brown's personal anthem, a song he carried with him into battle, and one which he sang aloud as he bounced children and grandchildren on his knee or tucked them into bed. "He sang us all to sleep, one after another, with that same hymn," John Brown Jr. remembered in later years. "It was his 'call' to duty and sacrifice." In his own inimitable way, Brown claimed Wesley's song for himself, a song to serenade the awakening call that increasingly haunted his life, beckoning him—or so he felt—closer and closer to "carrying out his greatest or principle object":

> Ye slaves of sin and hell,
> Your liberty receive,
> And safe in Jesus dwell,
> And blessed in Jesus live.
> The year of jubilee is come;
> The year of jubilee is come;
> Return ye ransomed sinners, home.[10]

# 6

## "This Path of Life"
### From Ohio to Pennsylvania

And I have also established my covenant with them, to give them the land of Canaan, the land of their pilgrimage, wherein they were strangers.

—Exodus 6:4

The first few years of married life in Hudson were prosperous for John and Dianthe Brown. The tannery business and farming went well, and between 1821 and 1824, John Jr., Jason, and Owen Brown were born. With a growing family, the log house was no longer sufficient, and was replaced by a large frame home in 1824. The same year, John became a member of the new Masonic Lodge No. 68, probably at the urging of his uncle Gideon Mills, who was Worshipful Master. However, his father Owen had misgivings about joining any society other than the church, though friends and associates like city father David Hudson and neighbor Heman Oviatt were members. John was soon promoted, and during 1824–26 passed from the Entered Apprentice to the Fellow Craft degree, and then to Master Mason.

John Jr. remembered that their Hudson home had a garden and orchard. Through the woods just behind the house was a downhill path leading to a bubbling brook, from which the elder John drew water for his tan pits. John Jr. also recalled the night when his parents took in a desperate couple fleeing from slavery. Not much more than a toddler, young John had never seen dark-skinned people and was quite amazed when the grateful woman fugitive picked him up and kissed him—he thought her blackness would rub off on him.

Like his father, John Brown obtained animal skins from frontier hunters or traders. These skins were first "cured," either by drying or salt, then soaked and washed in pure water, and then scraped to remove impurities and flesh. Then he soaked the skins in various solutions, especially tannin, extracted from the bark of oak, hemlock, or chestnut trees. In gradually increasing amounts, he applied the tannin to the skins to the point of saturation. Various treatments and procedures were used for finishing depending on the skin and its intended use, and he was extremely particular about his product. He was known to withdraw goods in the midst of a sale if even the slightest detail dissatisfied him.

Meanwhile, Owen Brown's family began to outgrow their home, and he put up a new frame structure on an acre and three-quarters of land to house them more comfortably. He was prospering too, though he felt himself too busy to spend time with his children. Owen and Ruth's children—John's siblings—were now young adults, and Sally's first four were of elementary school age, while toddler Edward was running about and baby Martha slept in the cradle. The younger part of Owen's brood were now the same age as his son's children, and there was still enough twinkle in the old man's eyes to give John Brown two more half-siblings by 1832.[1]

But all was not right in the world. John was beginning to worry about his wife. After the children were born, Dianthe's behaviors became peculiar at times, suggesting moments of disorientation. While her quiet and peaceable personality never changed, even relatives began to notice her "strangeness" in "small ways." Once as they walked from church, Dianthe's cloak slipped off her shoulders, though she seemed not to notice it even after John picked it up and put it back on her.

Brown also began to quarrel with brother-in-law Milton Lusk, which probably cast some shadows over the marriage. Two years younger than Dianthe, Milton adored his sister as his "guiding star" and "guardian angel," and thought her a guileless woman locked in a harsh and abusive marital yoke. At least this is the substance of the Lusk family history, though the truth lies somewhere amidst the testimonies and countercharges that came later from the Browns. Dianthe probably suffered from some degree of mental illness, though the nature and extent of it is unclear. There was a history of mental illness in the Lusk family and two of Dianthe's sisters also suffered from it. But it is also likely that Brown had harsh tendencies in marriage as he did in parenting during these years. Though Milton Lusk was unfair to attribute his sister's poor health to a "broken heart," probably she was often wounded by the severe manner in which her husband ruled the house and disciplined the children.

Milton Lusk had other gripes with John Brown which seemed both to precede and supercede real concern for his sister. Lusk and Brown were youthful peers with a shared conviction about the evil of slavery. One Lusk family member recalled that both men came to be first-class underground railroad operators in Hudson. But Lusk may have been intimidated by the Brown family's growing reputation and his widowed mother's need to work for John Brown. He may also have been threatened by Brown's drive to succeed. Lusk was not impressive by any account, and some thought him "lazy and thriftless." Furthermore, the two men clashed even before the marriage, which Lusk underscored by not attending his sister's wedding. One witness even recalled his mother scolding him for making negative remarks about John Brown in public. Brown and Lusk had begun as friends but ended antagonists, especially over religious issues.

Lusk took offense to Brown's objection to his visiting on the Sunday Sabbath, and probably resented the strong religious opinions espoused by his brother-in-law. But Brown's objection to Lusk's Sabbath visitation was probably principled more than mean-spirited. It reflected a religious debate between the men in which Lusk disdained the observance of the Sabbath. When his sons got older, Brown was very disturbed to find out that they had gone to visit their Uncle Milton. Afterward, he charged his brother-in-law hotly: "It is through you that I have lost influence over my boys." When Lusk questioned how that could happen, Brown concluded, "It makes no difference. They refer to *you*." Milton Lusk thought Brown a pushy, arrogant man who doted on being "top of the heap," though he could not deny his brother-in-law's natural influence over people. John Brown probably saw Lusk as an unproductive man with aberrant religious ideas, and feared that he might mislead his sons. Despite their common hatred of slavery, the two mixed like water and oil. Years later, when Brown was hanged, Lusk would not attend a memorial service for him, even though he acknowledged Brown's noble effort to liberate slaves.[2]

John Brown's dreams of success seemed to be panning out. At the core of his plans, however, was the intention of achieving the kind of financial strength that would allow him to come to the aid of the oppressed. Merely becoming wealthy was not his focus. "I don't think he ever really cared for business success," Thomas Vince concludes. "What was important to him was that it gave him facility to be active in the anti-slavery cause. That was always his underlying commitment, and most important to him."

Brown's decision to move to western Pennsylvania not only presented a substantial business opportunity, but also enabled him to continue underground railroad work. But he may have been spurred into moving during a time of financial difficulty in Hudson. When the aftershock of the Panic of 1819 finally reached Hudson, his father Owen experienced a painful setback. Money became scarce in mid-1823, property values declined sharply, and several of his expensive and promising real estate investments were ruined. Salmon, John's younger brother, was studying law in Pittsburgh, Pennsylvania, and Owen was worried over whether he could afford to keep his son in school and support his family too. John Brown considered his options, finding one in a proposed business relationship with Seth Thompson of Hartford, Ohio, who would provide him with animal skins from the Western Reserve. With a new tannery in northwestern Pennsylvania, Brown would process the skins while drawing from a rich resource of tannin barks in the virgin forest.

After visiting Crawford County, Pennsylvania in 1825, John bought a 200-acre tract of land at seventy-five cents an acre. It was a good investment for a young man with a wife and several children to support. The land was rich with an ample supply of water, fish, and wild game, and dense with hemlock, maple, and beech trees—though "the task of clearing it was heartbreaking." But in a short time Brown had cleared five acres of forest, erected a log home and barn, and installed a functional, two-story tannery with eighteen vats. The new tannery was an amazing accomplishment, with an upper level made of wood and lower level of cut stone with walls two feet thick, the whole structure measuring about 26 x 50 feet. By the fall of 1826—about five months after arriving, the twenty-six-year-old pioneer had made quite an impression on the area. The blossoming community (with about twenty-five families), situated only twelve miles east of Meadville, Pennsylvania, quickly labeled John Brown an influential citizen. Having studied enough of *Flint's Survey* to have made himself "tolerably well acquainted" with surveying, he put his study to good use. Brown became involved in town planning and helped with the layout of new roads.[3]

With his family situated in a double-log house, he made sure that his other priority was secure. In the hay mow of his new barn he built a ventilated secret room for housing fugitive slaves. Many nights, while hungry wolves howled at the scent of packed hides, Brown would sit near a large, radiant fireplace speaking of slavery with his family and tannery employees. "I often heard him say he would do anything to abolish slavery," one visitor recalled. But he was far from the point of doing just *anything*. Boyd Stutler suggested that John Brown was still "a peace man and believed at that time in settling the slavery question by peaceable methods . . . moral forces—by ballots instead of bullets." Brown was certainly exposed to the writings of the pacifist Garrison, but it is more likely that his early preference for peaceful methods was an expression of his own conservative Christian tradition. In contrast to Garrison, he believed the use of force was undesirable but not immoral. When evil left the righteous no alternative but to fight, then the sword should be wielded with an eye toward justice, not vengeance. "He was even then an advocate of force. He saw more clearly than his neighbors that the slave would be freed through bloodshed." Yet Brown hoped that bloodshed could be averted. Who knew what God's Providence had in store? Could not slavery itself fall by the sheer weight of its immorality, or the hand of the Almighty bring it tumbling down like the walls of Jericho? When the news broke about Nat Turner's attack in Virginia in 1831, he probably saw the event as a sign of things to come—the slaves themselves might rise up and seize their freedom. Unlike Garrison, Brown would not be torn between lauding black liberation and condemning the use of force to achieve it. "Without the shedding of blood," he would often quote from the New Testament, "there is no remission for sin."

Several years into his Pennsylvania venture, Brown thought he had an opportunity to uplift black people. In a letter to his brother Frederick in late 1834, he shared an idea about helping "my poor fellow-men who are in bondage." Having discussed the matter with his family, he wrote, they had agreed "to get at least one" black youth and rear him "as we do our own," providing him with a "good English education"—including history, business, general studies, and religious training ("teach him the fear of God"). Brown believed a black youth might be obtained from a cooperative "Christian slaveholder." If not, they would either adopt a free black or even buy one from his master, even if it meant great sacrifice on their part. All of his family were in support of this scheme, he assured Frederick, because they believed that God was about to bring black people "out of the house of bondage." Brown claimed it had been a long-held desire to start a black school, and now he believed that Pennsylvania was the ideal place for it. He also expressed hope that "first-rate abolitionist families" would move to Pennsylvania to unite their "exertions" on behalf of God and humanity in this effort.

Some think that Brown got the idea for the proposed black school from Prudence Crandall's ill-fated experiment in Connecticut. But Connecticut Puritans in Ohio were all about planting schools and education. Having worked with fugitives, it was probably clear to Brown that education was an issue of great concern to the oppressed. Educating blacks was intrinsic to John Brown's earliest thoughts on subverting slavery, part of what he called his "greatest or principle object." Neither was the idea of a black school the passing fancy of a "peace" phase; over a decade later, John Brown was still trying to find a qualified headmaster for another such endeavor.

That he believed he might find a "Christian slaveholder" suggests another aspect of his conservative orientation. Later John Brown would conclude that Christianity and slaveholding were so incompatible that there was no such thing as a "Christian slaveholder." Indeed, to ask a slaveholder to give up his chattel was an implicit recognition of the master's right to own slaves. As Brown emerged from a conservative orientation and began to view slavery from a black perspective, he began to recognize that chattel slavery was really a state of war conducted by one people against another. The time would come when John Brown would seize slaves at gunpoint, without the slightest concern for the rights of "Christian" masters. In the meantime, his zeal for underground railroad work continued and he became one of the most adept and committed in his work. Each passing fugitive hardened his fortitude—walking testimonies to the brutality and villainy of slavery. One frigid winter night, a fugitive arrived at the Brown settlement after traveling for days in the dead of winter. The Browns never forgot how the man's feet were frozen so badly that he had lost his toes, and "the front ends of his feet were just as smooth as his heels."[4]

Another example of Brown's early ideas about the use of force involves an incident of white hostility toward Native Americans who crossed their lands to hunt and camp on a branch of French Creek, east of Meadville. The Browns and Brittains and a few other neighbors did not mind when the Natives, yet quite visible in this part of the country, stopped by their cabins in the winter to warm themselves or ask for food. But other whites resented their presence and sought an opportunity to drive them out. This frontier racism became unbridled one Sunday when a group of whites got together an armed band to go after the Indians. "Get your gun and powder flask," they shouted to John Brown from the road. Thinking that he and his hired men would eagerly join them, they were shocked when he came out and said, "I will have nothing to do with so mean an act. I would sooner take my gun and help drive you out of the country." The whites were highly offended by Brown's remarks, his son Jason recalled, "but father stood his ground, and the result was that the expedition was abandoned."

John Brown's growing reputation and moral determination enabled him to interrupt the inclinations of the mob, and his settlement brought a measure of social uplift to the young community. The tannery not only provided employment to as many as fifteen people, but also introduced employees and friends to the values of education and religious discipline. "He took great pains to circulate general information among the people, good moral books and papers and to establish a reading community," one associate recalled. Brown especially loved history and religious literature, and among the favorite titles he strongly recommended were Puritan devotional books. Chief among his favorites was Richard Baxter's *The Saints' Everlasting Rest*. Written in the mid-seventeenth century, Baxter was one of the leading Puritan pastors of the English Reformation. A Protestant classic by the nineteenth century, the work presumed a Protestant view of sainthood—not "super Christians" and spiritual intercessors, but believers following Christ on "this path of life." Baxter's main theme was the "perfect endless enjoyment of God by the perfected saints." This happened when believers reached "the measure of their capacity to which their souls arrive at death . . . after the resurrection and final judgment." *The Saints' Everlasting Rest* was thus a methodical discourse on the Christian life and the goal of walking the pilgrim's path with spiritual awareness and diligence and the necessity of "heavenly contemplation." It was also the Puritan call to active involvement in the world, "helping others to discern their title to the saints' rest," teaching them their "need of a Redeemer; how Christ did mercifully interpose, and bear the penalty; what the new covenant is; how men are drawn to Christ; and what are the riches and privileges which believers have in him." *The Saints' Everlasting Rest* resonates in John Brown's story, especially in its call to take responsibility for the spiritual admonition and guidance of those over whom one has charge, especially one's children. "Consider, it is a duty you owe your children in point of justice. From you they received the defilement and misery of their natures; and therefore you owe them all possible help for their recovery."[5]

Brown maintained a kind of parental theocracy in the home, a biblically based lifestyle that shaped values, rules, and discipline, and that was exemplified and enforced by him. To him, knowledge of the Bible was paramount, and his conversation was naturally filled with biblical quotations reflective of his personal devotion to reading and memorizing scriptures. John Jr. recalled of his father that "his oft repeated scripture was 'Buy the Truth and sell it not.'" His daughter Ruth likewise remembered a long list of Bible verses that laced her father's conversation and directed the values of the children. As to lifestyle, Brown often reminded his children and employees that "a good name is rather to be chosen than great riches, and loving favor rather than silver or gold"; and "except the Lord build the house, they labor in vain that build it; except the Lord keepeth the city, the watchman walketh in vain." As to concern for the underprivileged, he would repeat: "Whoso mocketh the poor, reproachesth his Maker; and he that is glad at calamities, shall not be unpunished"; and "Whoso stoppeth his ear at the cry of the poor, he also shall cry himself, but shall not be heard." Of course, as John Brown taught his children to hate slavery, he often repeated the biblical command to "remember them that are in bonds as bound with them."

Discipline continued to be a significant theme in John Brown's home as it had been in the home of his childhood. As an employer, he was stern and unyielding when his workers proved dishonest. A close associate in this era remembered his suspicion of an employee at the tannery, whom he eventually caught stealing a valuable calf skin. Brown lectured him so sternly that the man was reduced to tears, also threatening to have him arrested if he left the job. As punishment, he required the other employees to snub the thief until he was evidently reformed. Brown showed the same firm conviction in his community, as exemplified when a poor man stole a neighbor's cow. When the thief was apprehended and the cow returned, the neighbor felt sorry for him and so did not press charges. This disturbed Brown, who "always laid great emphasis on justice." Intervening, he pressed charges and had the man arrested and jailed, but then made it his responsibility to provide for the family of the thief throughout the time of his incarceration. He believed justice required that the crime be punished, but held that "his innocent family should not suffer for the man's guilt." Some felt John Brown was too extreme in his devotion to justice, and like his father Owen, he would go to great lengths to rectify inequities even if the offense was minor and the circumstances impractical. When Dianthe's declining health required him to go for a doctor, Brown happened to see some thieves in a neighbor's orchard and detained himself to stop them. In later years, he showed the same willingness to set aside personal interest in order to pursue justice for others. But his wife and family had to endure frustration and difficulty as a result.

"His government of family was strict and his chastisements for disobedience or misconduct, while perhaps not seriously severe, were impressive," recalled George Delamater, a classmate of John Jr. Witnesses from the Pennsylvania period agree that John Brown was intensely religious. "He would never come to the house but that he would have prayers," recalled a woman whose father was a friendly neighbor of the Browns. "He always insisted upon that. His religious fervor was the characteristic that made the deepest impression upon my childish mind." Brown insisted that his employees and family attend church every Sunday, and also held morning worship to start every work day. "I do not believe he ever ate a meal of even potatoes and salt but he asked a blessing and returned thanks," recalled James Foreman, another family associate.

But the other side of Brown's piety and love for justice was strict discipline. If he chastened strangers according to an exact sense of justice, he certainly did not spare his children. "John Brown was a peculiar character—obstinate—but a good man for all that," remembered Dianthe's nephew, Charles Lusk. "He was absolutely truthful [and] religious. Very strict with the boys." John Jr. long recalled how his father kept a written record of instances of his disobedience at home and at the tannery. When he began to neglect his work of grinding tree bark for tannin, Brown warned him repeatedly before confronting him with his record. When it was apparent that the list of sins and misdemeanors was far too long to spare him, Brown called John Jr. to follow him into the woods behind the tannery, as Jason, Owen, and Ruth trailed behind. After explaining the importance of faithfulness even in small matters, Brown cut a "limber persuader" from a birch tree. Aware of the judgment about to fall on John Jr., the younger children became frightened, little Ruth ducking behind a tree stump as the lash came down on her brother's backside. Suddenly their father stopped, and the wide-eyed children wondered why. "And now, my son," the father said as he handed the switch to young John and stripped off his own shirt and knelt before the children. "There are twenty-five lashes due you, and I will take them in your stead. When you know that I suffer in body as well as in mind for your faults, perhaps you will learn to be more careful." John Jr. and the other children were weeping, now more traumatized by their father's behavior than by fear of the switch. The children shrieked as the "limber persuader" snapped against their father's back, young John begging to stop. Insisting he strike all the harder, the father did not relent until the full account of blows was given. With beads of blood on his back, the stern father gently gathered his weeping children around him, explaining how Christ had similarly suffered for their sins.[6]

Unsympathetic writers and novelists have distorted this episode as a vignette of sadism and aberration. But given Brown's temperament and forceful way of going about his designs in any matter, it is no surprise that he would use a dramatic—even traumatic—illustration in teaching his children the central tenet of the Christian faith. Brown believed Christ's death was more than a bloody cosmic tragedy, but rather a vicarious act of atonement by which God's elect were spared divine judgment. He clearly intended to show his children that God's holiness required justice and that God's love had substituted Jesus in their place. Years later John Jr. recounted this incident, telling a journalist that he afterward came to realize "how much his father loved him, and thereafter he never doubted his father, nor believed him a wrong-doer."

There were other occasions, however, when his determination to serve justice seemed more ruthless than redemptive, enough to move Dianthe to tears. "Father believed every word of the Bible and acted on that saying in his harsh way," Jason remembered. When he was barely five years old, Jason was caught telling a lie to his mother. Another "limber persuader" was cut, Jason recalled, as his back-end was bared to the switch. Holding him up by his hands, John Brown thrashed. "How I danced! How it cut!" Jason recalled. "But father had tears in his eyes while he did it, and mother was crying." Even little Ruth was not spared the "limber persuader" after wading in a wintry brook in pursuit of pussy-willows. After Ruth lied to her father to explain her wet, muddy shoes, Brown put her over his knee, "talked kindly and tenderly" about her fault, "and then switched me with the willow that had caused my sin." John Jr. recalled that the "traits of the Brown family were all exaggerated in my father. . . . I can understand that he may not always have been a comfortable neighbor. But his integrity was never doubted."

In his discipline and hatred of slavery, Brown was seen as "eccentric, even feared somewhat." Of course, harsh chastisements in the family were still quite common in Brown's era. This was an age when community norms excused blunt, even brutal treatment of children at home and school and blatant inequity and sexism reigned in society. In the Brown home sternness was seasoned with consideration and the switch was not always administered, though the threat of it loomed at all times. Once, John Jr., Owen, and Jason slipped out the second story window to play on the Sabbath. Following his brothers down the protruding log-end corners of the house, Jason missed a step and fell, breaking his arm. His howls brought John Brown from the house. "Well, Jason," he said. "I think I will not punish you for this. You have had punishment enough."

Most of the thrashing accounts of the Brown children pertained to lying, the sin that John Brown said he struggled with as a child—"a [very] bad and foolish [habit]" to which he had been "somewhat addicted," as he recalled in his autobiographical sketch. One can almost imagine his concern, then, as he pondered Baxter's urgent appeal in *Saints' Rest*: "Consider what work there is for you in their dispositions and lives. Theirs is not one sin, but thousands." As a Christian father, Brown would have to teach them godliness even though it be "contrary to the interests and desires of their flesh." For if he did not teach them godliness while they "were tender and flexible," they would grow from disobedient "twigs" into sinful oaks. They would be "thorns" of his own planting, bearing the worst aspects of their "temper and inclinations." Despite the controversy of Brown's methods, one writer concluded, "it must be admitted that they were the legitimate outgrowth of his faith."[7]

Of greater concern to the family was Dianthe's worsening condition. By 1832, her declining health had become acute, perhaps physiological. Neither prayer nor Providence intervened, and John Brown went to work each morning burdened by the failing condition of his wife, who was also pregnant with their seventh child. Following John Jr., Jason, Owen, and Ruth was Frederick, born in 1827. But death made its first, cruel visitation to the Brown household in 1831, snatching little Frederick away. The child had probably become deathly sick several months prior to 1831. Three months before he died, Dianthe gave birth to another male child on December 21, 1830, also named Frederick—apparently in expectation of the death of the sickly four-year-old Frederick.

Hard life on the frontier, childbirth, and infant mortality added to the anguish of her troubled mental state, and took a heavy toll on Dianthe's health. When she became pregnant again, John and the children tried to help by doing the cooking and housework while she rested, but Dianthe never fully recovered. Jason later recalled how, at nine years of age, he accompanied his mother into the field while she planted peach pits. Suddenly he heard sobs and realized she was weeping. When he asked his mother why she was crying, Dianthe replied, "I am most sure that I shall never eat any of the peaches from these trees." Looking up into his little face, she said, "I hope you will live. But if neither of us does, the peaches will do someone some good." Her pregnancy brought little joy to the worried household and when the time for her delivery came, Dianthe withdrew to her bed. Having called in a "good physician," Brown later wrote his father, the doctor found the baby's position wrong and impossible to correct; he determined to "take the child" in surgery, but for some unfortunate reason did not have his instruments. When finally able, the doctor delivered the infant stillborn, and it was now apparent that Dianthe was in danger. She rallied for a time, temporarily reviving the hopes of her grieving family. But the recovery was short-lived and she slipped back into the valley of shadows. "I thought I might go to rest on God's Sabbath," she whispered to her husband, who could say nothing in response. It seemed to John Brown that Dianthe's "reason was unimpaired and her mind composed with the Peace of God." When night fell and she felt life ebbing away, Dianthe asked him to gather the children to her bedside. "Your mother is dying," Brown called, his voice fractured with grief. "Come and see her." One by one, he took the children in to see Dianthe, beginning with the oldest. "Remember now thy Creator in the days of thy youth," Dianthe recited to John Jr. in a weak, pathetic voice. "While the evil days come not, nor the years draw night." Without stopping, she recited the 12th chapter of Ecclesiastes. "Then shall the dust return to the earth as it was: and the spirit shall return unto God, who gave it." When it was Jason's turn, Dianthe took his hands into hers and whispered her final admonitions. She lived three days longer than her stillborn son, and on August 10, 1832 the "affectionate, dutiful and faithful Dianthe" breathed her last. "Farewell to Earth," she whispered as her hand became weak and lifeless, releasing John Brown into a new wilderness of loneliness. He buried his wife in her wedding dress, laying her with their stillborn child alongside the body of Frederick, "our dear little son." The gravestone inscription he prepared read: "In memory of Dianthe, wife of John Brown. She died Aug. 10, 1832, aged 31 years. Farewell Earth."

The day after her death, Brown painfully inscribed details about Dianthe's last days in a letter to his father. "We are again smarting under the rod of our Heavenly Father," he wrote. Owen fully understood the sting of such a rod. He had already lost a wife and children himself, and before the year was out would lose his nineteen-year-old son, Watson Hugh. (Indeed, the following year Owen lost another son, thirty-one-year-old newspaper editor Salmon Brown, who died in the state of Louisiana.) Owen and John struggled hopelessly with the angel of death time and time again, repeatedly feeling the sting of God's "limber persuader" upon their backs. As for John Brown, he struggled through the initial months of separation, finding slight comfort in the peaceful manner of Dianthe's last hours. Not given to showing his emotions, Brown turned his pain inward, leaving himself in a kind of "dead calm" and numbness that he confessed was quite a surprise even to himself. He really had loved his wife, Brown wrote to associate Seth Thompson. "I supposed, and have always supposed my feelings to be as warm and tender as those of other men towards my family." But his numbness disturbed him, and his "old difficulty" had reoccurred too—perhaps the inflammation of the eyes that had overcome him in earlier days. Strong remedies did not help, and he simply felt too weak and emotionally drained to work. Thompson should come out, he wrote, as soon as possible to help him settle their business affairs because he felt himself slipping, "getting more and more unfit for everything." He would eventually find his way back on Baxter's "path of life" and saintly devotion. In the meantime, he would wait until day's end and steal away to the quiet place where Dianthe rested. Lying there alone, he would study her gravestone or bury his face in the ground and weep.[8]

# PART III

# Providence and Principle

I would rather have the small-pox, yellow-fever and cholera, all together in my camp, than a man without principle.

—John Brown

# 7

# Citizen Brown's Calvinist Community

Ye shall do no unrighteousness in judgment: thou shalt not respect the person of the poor, nor honour the person of the mighty: but in righteousness shalt thou judge thy neighbor.
—Leviticus 19:15

Even before Dianthe's death, John Brown had become quite active in various aspects of community building. His most notable role was as postmaster in Randolph township, an appointment he received by commission from the administration of John Quincy Adams in January 1828. Though it yielded little remuneration, Brown made the most of the opportunity, taking on the twenty-two mile mail route himself as a subcontractor, then subletting portions to others. Later reformulation of township lines changed Randolph to Richmond township, but did not erase his contributions in the eyes of his fellow citizens. Brown brought quality livestock into northwestern Pennsylvania in 1828, and even in the early twentieth century he was still appreciated for having introduced "superior breeds of cattle, sheep and horses" into the area. "He was a man who always was highly respected," recalled one neighbor. "His standing was very high. He was considered a good man," recalled another. Boyd Stutler noted that in the mid-twentieth century the phrase, "honest as old John Brown" was still in use in certain parts of the country.[1]

For a time the grieving widower and his five children (now between three and twelve years old) boarded with a friend named James Foreman, who was newly married. It was hardly a practical arrangement, but Foreman's wife put up with the pitiable, motherless brood until Brown was ready to return home. After processing his grief for the first few months,

Brown finally returned to the tannery operation and began to awaken from the melancholy numbness that had overtaken him at Dianthe's death. In early 1833 it appeared that he was ready to get on with life, the first order of business being the need for domestic assistance. Help came from the home of Charles Day, a blacksmith from Troy township and a relative of Brown's neighbors, the Delamaters. Day's eldest daughter was sent to cook and clean for the Browns, and eventually brought her younger sister Mary Ann to assist as "spinstress." A teenager of seventeen, Mary Ann was not any more attractive than the plain but sweet-tempered Dianthe. Large-boned and quiet by nature, Mary knew that her elder sister had fancied herself the next Mrs. Brown, and went about her work without realizing that John Brown was watching her with interest. When he could no longer refrain from making an advance, the thirty-three-year-old with "extraordinary self-confidence and tenacity of purpose" found that he could not approach Mary in person to propose marriage. Perhaps he was embarrassed by the age difference between them (she was only five years older than John Jr.), or maybe he was trying to handle the matter discretely to spare her sister's feelings. Brown wrote out his proposal to Mary and slipped it into her apron as she worked. Overwhelmed, she could not answer until she went out to the spring for water, Brown following on her heels. When Mary agreed, he made plans for her in preparation for their union. "He sent her to school for a time but she was apparently not attuned to study, and 'she could not think of anything but John Brown.'" To no surprise, the lonely widower did not press her; instead they were married on July 11, 1833. Not quite a year had passed since Dianthe's death.[2]

It is unclear whether the Brown children responded to their stepmother the way John and his brothers had responded to their father's second wife. If tensions existed between Mary and Dianthe's children, they appear to have developed over time rather than at the onset of the marriage. As Dianthe's children grew to young adulthood, they seem to have had differences with Mary and her children. In one incident, Ruth resented a remark she overheard when her stepmother said she was "just like her mother"—a remark that Ruth immediately reported to her brothers. Their reaction became so bitter that Brown had to call a family meeting to smooth things out. Ruth felt that her stepmother "was not one who drew the children to her though she was just and good." With the passing of years, John Jr. expressed similar feelings about Mary's children, whom he found to be "coarse." Friends in Ohio later said that Dianthe's sons held their father in high esteem, but "none of them liked the second wife much." When John Jr. was grown, his father wrote to him referring to Mary as "my wife"—perhaps indicating that he and Dianthe's children had some difficulty accepting Mary as a mother figure. Family relations between the stepmother and Dianthe's children probably reached the lowest point in later years, when Mary clashed with John Jr.'s new wife, Wealthy. Ruth had become close to her new sister-in-law and felt her stepmother was trying to sabotage their friendship. "Mother has said more to make me think that you almost hate me than ever before," Ruth wrote to Wealthy. However, Wealthy recalled that even though Mary Brown found it difficult to express tenderness, she softened in later life.

If John Brown clashed with people, it was either because they did not observe the Sabbath, or they were not anti-slavery, or they did not support common schools. Besides being anti-slavery, Brown took education very seriously. Since there was no state law authorizing public schools in Pennsylvania until 1834, he saw to it that his own children received schooling at home. His neighbor Thomas Delamater also had a growing family, and the two fathers worked out a cooperative educational program for their children. The effort entailed a live-in arrangement on a seasonal basis, the Browns hosting the Delamater children during the cold months, and the Delamaters taking the Brown children during the warm months. Until Brown could hire a teacher, he taught them himself. George, the eldest of the Delamater children, recalled afterward that Brown "was a kindly but firm teacher and insisted upon strict attention from his pupils." If they failed to attend to his words, he might rap them on the forehead with his fingers—though with his own boys he might just as well use the handle of his pocket knife, a disciplinary procedure that he referred to as "ringing the bell." Brown was determined that John Jr. and George Delamater receive an adequate education, and so hired a single woman named Sabrina Wright to come and teach the children. Wright gave the boys good preparatory training, and both went on to attend collegiate institutes as young men.[3]

Brown also presided over an informal educational and religious program for his tannery employees, who lived on site and shared meals with the Brown family. George Delamater always remembered the communal over which John Brown presided, and the various activities he instituted in the large, spacious first floor of the Brown home. After work in the evenings, Brown's concern for "physical and mental culture" was expressed in organized "contests of strength and skill" among the workers and young people, events ranging from debates to well-controlled sport and gymnastic competitions. As a "magnificent fire" roared in the large fireplace, this community of workers, students, and family sat nearby on chairs and benches, Brown leading discussions on religion, politics, and scientific topics. He "always had a decided opinion" in a discussion, but was equally decided in his dislike of "anyone without their own opinions." The spacious home was well-suited for this kind of unofficial Christian community. With two large rooms on the first floor and a large fireplace on either end, the lower level provided dining, recreation, and library space, with ample sleeping space in the upper floors of the house and tannery.

Delamater recalled early breakfasts in the winter months, after which Bibles were distributed and verses assigned for reading. Brown presided over these daily morning worship exercises, and none of the workers or students dared to refuse to participate. Delamater says there was no coercion or browbeating, and John Brown's influence seemed natural and "fixed as fate" by his "inspiring presence." Of course, he made sure to guide the discussions and events in such a way as to "enforce conformity to his ideas." This tendency, which had early annoyed his younger brother, was one of his signature characteristics. To his enemies it seemed like hubris and self-centeredness, while those who knew and appreciated him thought Brown a worthy and "inspired paternal ruler." Throughout his life he exerted this kind of influence on those he encountered, from employees and colleagues in business to collaborators and comrades in the war against slavery, and did so with the apparent assumption that he was correct and that people should follow him. "He expected to succeed in everything he undertook," said John Jr., "and failure daunted him not at all. He was stiff-necked in his independence, [and] people's opinions never turned him a hair's breadth." No wonder that his family, employees, and associates followed him in strict observance of the Sunday Sabbath, prohibitions of alcohol and tobacco, and even abstinence from the leisure activities that *he* considered spoiling and lazy, such as hunting and fishing. Instead, Brown encouraged the members of his community to read the Bible, devotional and theological writings, history, and the wit and wisdom of writers like Aesop and Benjamin Franklin. He always felt that truly successful men were those with their own libraries.

Though Brown disdained coffee and loathed the use of butter, they were not kept from the table. However eccentric he may have appeared at times, Brown did not make prohibitions or demands of his employees without some rationale behind them. As far as temperance goes, he was probably never a militant teetotaler, though he seems to have come to the conclusion that hard liquor was "poison." Salmon Brown wrote that his father swore off whiskey after dabbling in another man's barrel while transporting it for a local tavern-keeper. A more believable account says that Brown smashed a man's whiskey barrel after storing it in his cellar as a favor. When the cellar flooded, Brown was appalled by the man's desperation to recover the barrel. Believing him enslaved to the whiskey, Brown forced the man to dispose of it. While not a temperance man by profession, Owen Brown was clearly inclined to condemn alcohol abuse and had probably reared John with strong sentiments against hard liquors. Some years after his son's venture in Pennsylvania, Owen wrote a sketch of whiskey abuse in Hudson's early days. According to Owen, settlers brought home-made distilleries, using whiskey to trade with the Indians for furs and skins, which corrupted the Natives and the Western Reserve itself. Soon taverns and bars spread like "[whirlpools] of [destruction]," and the sickening fumes of whiskey and tobacco almost consumed the early Ohio settlements. Unlike the Pietistic sects and the later holiness movement, the Reformed tradition did not proscribe alcohol per se—which explains why John Brown felt free to make wine for exhibit and sale, and even gave cherry wine as a gift in the early 1850s. Although he later moved away from wine production, Brown's attitude toward alcohol was not so much shaped by the temperance movement but rather by conservative Calvinist values, suggesting avoidance of abuse without abstinence.[4]

When the Browns first came to Crawford County in 1826, they worshiped at the Guys Mills Church, about six miles from their home. However, they eventually changed affiliation to the Meadville Bible Society, because it was closer to home and gave Brown better opportunity to associate with an abolitionist in town named Harm Jan Huidekoper. The Browns seem to have transferred to the Meadville Bible Society in 1827, which was a house-church hosting regular meetings at the residence of Andrew Wilson. The Meadville Bible Society was probably the same "neighbor's house" that Ruth vaguely remembered attending on a Sunday morning, in what she considered her earliest childhood memory. She recalled that she and another sibling, probably Frederick (2nd), were baptized—which perhaps sets the year at 1832, before her mother Dianthe's death. Later the same year, however, Brown began to pull away from the Meadville Bible Society, while enjoying some sort of fellowship with members of another congregation, the Independent Congregational Society in Meadville, founded by Huidekoper in 1825.

After Dianthe's death in 1832, Brown may have begun to have conflicts with the Meadville Bible Society over the issue of blacks in Christian fellowship. Richard Hinton, one of Brown's earliest biographers, wrote that it "was at Meadville, near by, that John Brown was practically refused church fellowship because he insisted on breaking sacramental bread with the fugitive, and held the brother in bronze the equal before God of him whose hue was lighter." George Delamater remembered John Brown at this period as "a Calvinist . . . anti-slavery in sentiment," and a "Christian of high tone." James Foreman also recalled that John Brown "looked upon [slavery] as a great sin against God and [a] menace to the morals of the country," and considered it as much his duty to help a black man as it was to catch a horse thief.

The population of Meadville and its vicinity was relatively small in Brown's era, and there was an even smaller number of free blacks, many of them living in town. Prior to the organization of Meadville's first African Methodist Episcopal Church in 1850, there was no black church per se (though there was probably a house-church among blacks in the Meadville area). Some blacks probably found their way into Meadville's Independent Congregational Church, whose abolitionist leadership would have been open to their presence. Still others might have wanted to visit the Meadville Bible Society where Brown and family attended. If Hinton was referring to the Meadville Bible Society, then perhaps Brown became involved in a conflict with the white minister's refusal to accept blacks in the house-church. This may explain why he left the Meadville Bible Society.

Perhaps Brown was attracted to the Independent Congregational Church in Meadville. Organized and driven by a significant number of abolitionists in the community, especially Harm Jan Huidekoper, he probably found it an appealing fellowship. But the problem with the Independent Congregational Church was that it was Unitarian in doctrine, and thus opposed to historic Trinitarian orthodoxy and other tenets of the Reformed confessions. Huidekoper was not only an active abolitionist but "a fierce Unitarian" known for publishing anti-Trinitarian statements. Not only did Unitarians reject Trinitarian orthodoxy, they also denied the doctrine of man's sinful nature and distanced themselves from creeds and confessions. Though Brown might have enjoyed fellowship and collaboration with abolitionists in Meadville's Independent Congregational Church, it is doubtful that he would ever have joined the church, even if he could squeeze himself past its diplomatically worded "fundamental principle" of belief. Thus began a problem he would face for the rest of his life. On one hand, his radical anti-slavery views were unacceptable to conservative Calvinists, while on the other his evangelical convictions made him religiously incompatible with liberal Protestants and other unorthodox abolitionists. Caught between evangelical racism and theological liberalism, John Brown ran out of churches to join. It was perhaps in early 1833 that he began to formulate the "articles of faith" for his own Congregational Church in Richmond township. They were undoubtedly Trinitarian, Reformed, and evangelical in content.[5]

Even though a later Unitarian pastor from the Congregational Church in Meadville saluted John Brown for holding "cardinal virtues and eternal truths" above "denominational distinctions or written creeds," the remark was self-serving. Actually, Brown cared a great deal about confessions and the divine inspiration of Scripture. He may have transcended the racism of evangelical society, but he at no time threw out the baby of Confessional faith with the dirty bath water of white racist religion. His own Congregational Church effort was not only a response to racism in the evangelical church, but a statement about the necessity of theological orthodoxy. Both Delamater and Foreman remembered him as a thoroughgoing Calvinist, the latter writing that "Brown was always a strong predestinarian and firm believer in foreordination." Delamater said that he "had great reverence for the Deity," and was often "shocked" at the familiar and irreverent manner in which people used the name of God. In moments of anger or frustration, the worst he could shriek was, "God bless the Duke of Argyle!"

Brown likely relied on the *Westminster Confession* and catechisms in the new church, its meetings being held either in his house, barn, or tannery. He enlisted ordained ministers to preach when possible, but often had to undertake preaching and teaching himself. Though he would allow no pro-slavery or racist preacher into the pulpit, neither would he have permitted a "free will" preaching Arminian to preside. The teachings of the Arminians (named for Jacobus Arminius, the chief gadfly of Reformation theology in the sixteenth century) contrasted with the Calvinists. Arminians believe Jesus died for every individual, man cooperates with divine election, sinners can resist God's grace, and true believers can lose their salvation and "backslide." Since these teachings were increasingly popularized in the age of revivals, John Brown probably encountered a good many Arminians. Brown apparently mellowed toward them in later life, showing a greater degree of toleration toward theological differences—at least among anti-slavery men. But in these early days, he was argumentative when confronting advocates of "free will."

James Foreman recalled an incident when Brown tangled with a somewhat pompous Methodist minister over the predestination issue. Apparently the preacher got the best of him in their first discussion, and word spread quickly that "Brown was used up on his favorite doctrine." No doubt, his expansive pride was hurt, especially because the minister had outdone him by a quick tongue rather than a sound argument. Aching for a rematch, Brown put out the word that the Methodist "was no gentleman, let alone a clergyman." When the preacher returned to defend his reputation, Brown flared: "I said, sir, that it would take as many men like you to make a gentleman as it would wrens to make a cock turkey." The Methodist minister had embarrassed the "inspired paternal ruler" in the midst of his own Calvinist community, and now Brown was challenging him to a contest to reclaim his honor. At their next meeting, Brown was armed with twenty-four questions that seem to have been based on the *Westminster Catechism*. Brown's arsenal of Calvinist missiles were devastating, and soon the "flippant" Methodist fell silent. One can imagine John Brown firing off questions, wearing the same determined expression he always showed in contests since childhood. "He did not seem to be angry, but there was such force and mastery in what he did, that everything gave way before him." The mouthy preacher could no longer endure, and so "confused himself so much that he gave up the debate." Brown claimed victory for Reformed theology and the scriptures, but inwardly he probably felt the vindication of his role as the "leading spirit" in his settlement.[6]

Over in Meadville, Harm Jan Huidekoper and the Unitarians were not so fortunate in facing their opponents. Eric Smith writes that "the early history of Unitarians in Meadville was one of turmoil for they were without a building for many years and in disagreement with one another over theology and social issues." So while Huidekoper and many of his brethren were abolitionists, other congregants may not have been open to receiving blacks, or to the idea of helping fugitives. As in Hudson, the Plan of Union was operative in this period and, as usual, the Presbyterians had the upper hand on the Congregationalists. Overlaying this tension was an apparent split within the Meadville Congregational Church, as liberals contended with conservatives. On Thanksgiving Day, the orthodox Presbyterians went so far as to lock out the Unitarians, even hiding the candles so they could not light the church. Of course, this was not Brown's conflict. He was neither a Presbyterian nor a Unitarian, and the only thing that might have interested him about the goings on in the Independent Congregational Church of Meadville was its relevance to abolition activities.

While the underground railroad did not come to full strength until the Fugitive Slave Law of 1850, those fleeing slavery had long found help in their northward flight. Northwestern Pennsylvania was hardly an antislavery hotbed, but at least state laws did not lend much strength to slave owners' attempts to recover runaways, and this inadvertently strengthened abolitionism. Unlike other parts of the state, northwestern Pennsylvania only had a small free black population, corresponding with the sparse population in general. Meadville had slightly over one thousand people when Brown lived in the vicinity, and the several free black families there had businesses. The most notable black citizen of Meadville in the era of slavery was Richard Henderson, who settled there about two years before John Brown arrived, later becoming one of the leading underground railroad operators.

Though Brown's later experience with the black community of Springfield, Massachusetts represented a deeper, more intimate relationship, it was in Meadville that he first interacted with the black community. Little record of Brown's interactions has survived, but in later years Ruth recalled that her first childhood experience of recognizing a black person was with her father in Meadville. Her childish mind was already educated as to the plight of the slave children, and when her father struck up a conversation with a black man, little Ruth—probably about five years old—asked him to come home with them. According to another source, the man was named Jasper, and Brown was conversing with him about starting a school for black children. Jasper greeted the suggestion with mixed feelings, appreciating the sentiment but fearful of reaction from whites. Brown was seriously considering taking one or more black children into the family, just as he wrote to his brother Frederick in 1834. He seems to have been preparing the younger children by stimulating their sympathies and talking about making sacrifices in order to adopt a black child. Local legend suggests that his notion of rearing and schooling black children was prompted by a report that a Southern slaveholder had offered to release a group of slaves into the hands of Northerners if they would care for them. Brown began organizing families in his vicinity to join in the project, but the plan was stifled by local authorities, who feared introducing poor and dependent blacks into the community.

Nevertheless, John Brown was active in opposing slavery through the underground railroad movement, his settlement becoming a leading station along with other prominent homes in Crawford County. The son of a Meadville doctor recalled when a badly wounded fugitive arrived in town, and his father was called "on a secret errand" to help the mangled ex-slave. After receiving medical treatment, the fugitive was taken home with the Browns to remain sequestered until he was well enough to proceed to Canada. Fugitives generally came eastward from Ohio to Meadville en route to Lake Erie and Buffalo, or in a northwestern direction from Pittsburgh to Meadville and northward. Local folklore has it that Owen Brown funneled slaves from Hudson to his son in western Pennsylvania, and it may be that John Brown's presence accelerated underground railroad activity by drawing fugitives over from Ohio. John Jr. remembered the passionate feelings his father expressed about the plight of the slaves, and how he was moved by an old song called "The Slave Mother's Lament":

> Ye've gone from me, my gentle ones,
> With all your shouts of mirth;
> A silence is within my walls,
> A darkness around my hearth.[7]

Brown had been an active Mason in Ohio, but the rituals and the mind set of the secret order were bothering him before he moved to Pennsylvania. Given their close relationship, it likely concerned him that his father Owen had refrained from joining the Masons. Brown's daughter Sarah—probably repeating what her mother told her—once said that her father was irritated by the pomp and ceremony of Masonic meetings and initiations, increasingly finding them silly and disgusting. But when news of the murder of a former Mason named William Morgan reached Pennsylvania in 1826, these tensions came to the surface. Before his death, Morgan published an expose entitled *Illustrations of Masonry*, claiming the order was subversive to democracy. The Masons reacted violently to the poorly written work, and if Masons did kill Morgan, they lived to regret it. Morgan's death gave rise to an anti-Mason movement "based on principle, prejudice, and hysteria." John Jr. recalled that news of the murder caused his father to denounce the crime "in the hottest kind of terms." The Morgan murder thus became the occasion for Brown to make a 180-degree turn against the Lodge—probably the excuse he needed to justify breaking with the secret order.

While Brown's zealous turnabout was unusually synchronized with a popular movement, he was certainly not being led by the crowd. The anti-Mason movement was strongly political in nature, giving birth to the first "third party" in U.S. history. But Brown's revulsion toward the Masons was personal and individualistic, like his evolving anti-slavery efforts. Writing to his father in 1830, Brown reflected that he had even been observing the Masons back in Hudson with a critical eye:

> Some of them have said to me that courts of justice have no right to compel a mason to testify any thing about masonry, of course they are above the laws of the land. Some of them I suppose intend pleading to the Jurisdiction of the great Supreme, at least their actions say who is Lord over us.[8]

Calling them "distinguished professors of religion at Hudson" (perhaps a reference to his own Uncle Gideon Mills and others from the Hudson Congregational Church), Brown seemed to believe the Masons were indeed contrary to a democratic state since they secretly expressed a condescending attitude toward the laws of the land. For the egalitarian Calvinist, Masonry was at worst a subversive society, and at best an elitist movement fraught with vain ceremonies that bound men in quasi-religious obligations that watered down the unity of the church. Brown thus expressed hope that the Hudson church would take a "mild but persevering [sic] and firm course" in dealing with the Masons.

John Brown had set to undermine the Masons in an independent fashion, such as buying and circulating copies of *Giddin's Anti-Masonic Almanac* in the Meadville area. Of course, Brown could hardly have hurt the Meadville Masons by himself, since the Lodge had been inactive since 1828. It seems the most he could do was to rub salt in the wounds of the secret brotherhood.

In the letter to his father, Brown also referred to the published affidavit of another ex-Mason named Anderton, who claimed another Masonic murder had taken place. Though Anderton's statement was thoroughly refuted shortly after its publication in April 1830, he persisted in using it in his own anti-Mason campaign. As a result, Brown wrote to his father,

"I have aroused such feeling towards me in Meadville . . . as leads me for the present to avoid going about the streets at [evening] and alone. I have discovered that my movements are narrowly watched by some of the worthy brotherhood." Perhaps the animosity that Brown met (or imagined) was due to the fact that he had offended a few die-hards in the Lodge by advancing the questionable Anderton document. One family anecdote says Brown was hounded in the streets of Meadville, and in one case narrowly escaped an attack by the Masons. Brown was able to retreat into the *Gilded Lion*, an inn he liked because it was also an underground railroad station. The proprietor was a friend from the Unitarian Congregational Church, and so helped him escape through a back window. Boyd Stutler believed that the hostility Brown faced from the Meadville Masons was "largely magnified" in the telling and retelling of the story by family members. Whether or not the incident at the *Gilded Lion* took place, Brown probably did have problems with individuals from the Lodge.

His trouble with the Masons certainly showcased his belief in the use of just force in self-defense. As Brown's family attested, concern over possible attacks by the Masons became the first occasion for him to arm himself with a pistol and knives. At the same time that he was learning how to shoot his pistol, Brown was also practicing his theory about life, death, and service to a cause. Young Delamater remembered him discussing the necessity of having "an object in life, and sometimes in death." Seated by a bright, yawning fireplace and surrounded by his small community of family, friends, and employees, John Brown declared that "life was short at its longest," and *how* one died was far more important than when one died. Was not an early death for a good cause better than inactively "rusting out" life for no purpose? "Death . . . was not the worst of evils," Delamater remembered him saying. "As to death, it was only a question of time—of a very short time."[9]

# 8

## The Pursuit of Success and the Disappointments of Providence

Vanity of vanities, saith the Preacher, vanity of vanities; all is vanity. What profit hath a man of all his labour which he taketh under the sun?

—Ecclesiastes 1:2–3

By 1835, business had declined to the point that John Brown chose to leave Pennsylvania and return to Ohio. He wanted badly to be like Harm Jan Huidekoper, the Unitarian abolitionist whom Boyd Stutler calls "a Meadville tycoon." Ultimately Brown would come to depend upon men whose stature he once desired for himself, men like Huidekoper or Gerrit Smith, who bankrolled abolitionists and gave land grants to free blacks. Throughout his frustrating business history, a decline into financial misfortune, failure, and embarrassment, his "spirit was constantly struggling with the problems of the National life." Brown was not only "a born dogooder," he was also a visionary in the modern and the archaic sense of the word. He was a visionary in modern terms since his view of humanity was well in advance of his time. His determination to oppose injustice may look fanatical to those with no idea what it means to be black in society formatted by white supremacy. Flawed and eccentric though he was at times, Brown's genius was his ability to identify with an oppressed people. No wonder black people have never thought him fanatical or extreme. "John Brown's business luck ran out when he left his Pennsylvania farm," wrote Boyd Stutler.[1] But Brown did not believe in luck. He believed in Providence. Even misfortune was thought to be an outworking of Sovereign design. Yet understanding this thought style does not justify his visionary tendencies, in the archaic sense of the word. Marvin Kent, a business associate, said that had Brown continued at his trade, which was that of a tanner, he would doubtless have met with success. But when he stepped outside of his legitimate business and engaged in other enterprises, I think he was a failure. I don't think he would wilfully overstate his business, but he would likely build some air castles and thereupon through his enthusiasm set things up fully as high as they would stand.[2]

Heman Oviatt, a friend and business partner, admired Brown and was never shaken by his financial failures, but "thought him a visionary—a dreamer." His errors in business were largely done "honestly and in good faith, expecting successful results," concluded Marvin Kent. But his errors and mistakes sometimes proved that he could be "a man of fast, stubborn and strenuous convictions that nothing short of a mental birth would ever alter." Sometimes this stubbornness led him to take chances that ended up causing him more trouble. Other times he simply had to do things *his* way, and in so doing ran his business affairs aground, sometimes stranding others with him. Yet behind it all was his overarching belief that Providence was at work, and that he was being guided by a sovereign and loving hand to fulfill the calling of his life.[3]

By the end of 1834, the tannery operation in Pennsylvania had declined to the point that Brown was running short of money. In the spring of 1835 he was already corresponding with Zenas Kent of Franklin Mills (now Kent), Ohio, about operating a tannery and wool carding operation. But Brown had another reason to move his family, a frustration that may have hastened their departure from Pennsylvania. According to Salmon Brown, his father was vexed when Mary's sister and her husband opened a saloon in Richmond township. Brown's brother-in-law was said to be "a smart, fiery fighting man," and rather than have conflicts with him, he preferred to leave the community.

From the time John Brown returned to Ohio in 1836 until about 1842, the story of his business pursuits is complicated and at times very difficult to follow. His foremost biographer writes that after 1836, "he plunged into a vortex of business ventures that defy clear description." His first venture, the partnership with Zenas Kent of Franklin Mills, was short-lived. Kent had constructed a new tannery in 1835 and wanted Brown to run the operation. But by the time the tannery was completed, his son Marvin Kent had rented the building, putting Brown out of business. The sudden change in plans did not end all business association between Brown and Kent, nor does it seem to have ruined their friendship. But

Kent's grandson believed that his grandfather had changed plans because he came to see that Brown was inflexible and wanted to direct the business. "John Brown saw everything large; felt himself equal to anything; had little understanding of business obligations or responsibility in debts, and would accept no suggestion, advice or directions from anyone," the grandson concluded. Perhaps, as Marvin Kent believed, if Brown had remained in tannery work, he might have done well in time.

Nevertheless the blossoming community of Franklin Mills was seductive to someone looking for business opportunities. Lying between Akron and Ravenna, the "scattered village" of Franklin Mills was happily located on the line of the new Pennsylvania and Ohio Canal, then under construction from Akron to the Ohio River. As an extension of the Ohio Canal from Cleveland, the new canal would provide an inland waterway from the Great Lakes to the Ohio River. It also promised prosperity to investors and businessmen with imagination and means. John Brown had plenty of imagination, but not means. Believing that Providence had closed one door to open another, he felt certain that Franklin Mills real estate would soon become valuable to manufacturers and other businesses thriving off the new waterway. Borrowing money from his father and Heman Oviatt back in Hudson, Brown purchased an expansive farm, sold half of it to his old partner, Seth Thompson, and began to parcel the land for sale. Using borrowed capital, Brown and Thompson made further purchases of land and even put up buildings that they expected to become profitable business centers. At the height of this ill-fated expedition it was reported that John Brown was worth at least $20,000.

But it was paper-and-credit wealth, as vulnerable as a house of cards before the threat of a strong wind. The wind came in the Panic of 1837, and the "wealth" that Brown and other credit hounds had accumulated in real estate speculation suddenly collapsed. Writing to Harm Jan Huidekoper, his Unitarian friend in Meadville, Brown admitted in 1838 that he had "made money rather fast" during his first year back in Ohio, but was holding his own in hopes that things would get better. But he was only telling part of the truth. In fact, he was not holding his own, not to mention the losses shared by his father, Heman Oviatt, and Seth Thompson. In fact, Brown and Thompson's real estate dream took a gasping last breath when the flow of the canal was suddenly diverted away from Franklin Mills to nearby Akron. Franklin Mills would have to wait for prosperity, and it would not come in John Brown's time.

Quickly turning to another open door, Brown began to focus his attention on breeding race horses. Always at his best with livestock, he seemed to do well; some of his stallions even became winners on the track in Warren, Ohio. Brown broke the horses himself—one place where being stubborn was actually helpful. "Father is a hard man to throw," noted one of his sons. But he eventually abandoned the venture when his sons became unrestful with their clientele. "At first he argued that if he did not breed them, somebody else would," but when John Jr. pointed out that some of the best buyers were Kentucky slaveholders, Brown decided to quit.

As to his land speculation debacle in Franklin Mills, John Brown's losses were partially due to circumstances out of his control. In the 1920s, a writer pointed out that Brown's land speculation in Franklin Mills was ahead of its time, and he "would probably have made a fortune for him[self] and those who invested with him" if he had come along later in history. As Thomas Vince notes, it was "utterly commonplace" in Brown's era for people to go bankrupt or have financial ups and downs. "We have various safety nets that they didn't have in the nineteenth century. You faced the possibility of economic ruin if things didn't work out. But it was not a reflection on character." Furthermore, what happened in northeastern Ohio was a reflection on the troubled character of the nation in 1836–37, President Andrew Jackson having undermined the Bank of the United States. Without the national bank, small, financially unsound banks issued notes without sufficient gold and silver backing. Prior to the Panic there was twelve dollars of paper money in circulation for every dollar of gold or silver in banks across the nation, especially in the West. Land speculators were running roughshod over government lands, buying huge tracts with impotent paper money and selling small parcels to settlers at great profit. Such was the time, and though John Brown might have conducted his business more conservatively, he was hardly alone in his dilemma amidst the credit fever sweeping the country.[4]

In 1837–38, Brown took his family back to Hudson to recuperate from a heavy-handed Providence. His membership in the Hudson Congregational Church was still intact, and he fell into place right away as a Sunday School teacher. One woman recalled seeing John Brown walking from his farm to the Hudson church with Dianthe's boys, sixteen-year-old John Jr., thirteen-year-old Jason, twelve-year-old Owen, and six-year-old Frederick—the latter probably carried in his father's arms for part of the two-mile stretch. "He was rather a leader in the church," one of his students remembered. "He was looked upon as an honest man—with nothing particularly wrong with him." However, Brown was "considered very eccentric—more eccentric than any other of Owen's sons." This was probably because of his pronounced hatred of slavery and his defensiveness on behalf of black people—always close to the surface of his conversation. Brown never missed an opportunity to discuss the sinfulness of slavery in his Bible lessons. His student also remembered that he was an excellent Bible teacher. He "was a pretty good talker" though he "didn't want anyone to explain the Scriptures to *him*." Brown seemed to be sensitive to the possibility that there were theologians in the church who were better equipped to be Sunday School teachers. "One man's opinion is just as good as another's on the interpretation of the Scriptures," he told his students, "provided he is naturally as smart." Perhaps when it came to Bible teaching, old regrets arose about his failed pre-ministerial studies. Despite the fact that everyone knew John Brown was extremely well read in the Bible, he was likely mindful that a professor from the Western Reserve College was also on the teaching staff and was well liked by Sunday School students too. Brown may have hoped that even though he could not parse a Greek verb, he was at least as smart as the esteemed theology professor when it came to plain old Bible knowledge.

But more critical issues than Bible knowledge were being discussed at the Hudson church. Indeed, Hudson itself was becoming embroiled in a growing controversy that would first inflame the college and then spread into the church. Toward the end of his stay in Pennsylvania, Brown was probably apprised of Hudson's brewing conflict between the dominant colonization advocates and the minority of determined abolitionists, including his father. In the letter to his brother Frederick about starting a black school several years before, he had diminished Hudson "with all its conflicting interests and feelings" because he knew that many in town had a very limited, racist approach to ending slavery. The idea of free blacks living and working among them was not their idea of being anti-slavery. Community leaders like David Hudson reportedly rejoiced to hear of Nat Turner's revolt in 1831, but probably would not have wanted Nat and company to come and live in Hudson. The once glorious Plan of Union between Presbyterians and Congregationalists was also collapsing under the stress of denominational incompatibility and the debate over slavery. The battleground of the debate in Hudson was Western Reserve College.

Until John Brown became prominent for his militant activities in the 1850s, his father Owen was a far more influential and controversial figure in Hudson. He had long supported Native rights and was an outspoken abolitionist. No one mistook Owen's speech impediment for weakness, or his lack of schooling for ignorance. As Gerald McFarland observes, if nothing else, Owen Brown's ledger proved "he had no difficulties with business arithmetic." His neighbors thought him "a real nice man" but also marveled at his ferocity toward slavery. He was an upstanding spiritual figure in the Hudson church, known to participate in the watchful care of the saints by visiting their homes. Rather than browbeat one member who had absented himself from church services, Owen approached him diplomatically: "We need your help." He had also served the Portage Presbytery under the Plan of Union, sitting as an officer of the education society.[5]

Owen Brown had also gone to war against the Masons. Probably through his influence, Owen's sons Frederick and Oliver had turned against the Lodge, following their father's belief that secret societies undermine the unity of the church. Along with many other evangelicals, the Browns had come to believe that "Masonry was a heathenish substitute for the church and Bible." Owen became a subscription agent for the leading anti-Mason publication, the *Ohio Star*, a publication that echoed Garrison's call for immediate emancipation. Owen's ardent anti-Masonic stance did not split the church, even though city and church founder David Hudson remained in the "worthy brotherhood," and some Masons even presided over the cornerstone ceremony at the founding of Western Reserve College in 1826. However, the Hudson Masons were eventually shamed into a corner, surrendering their charter to the Grand Lodge in 1841. It would be decades before the Lodge reopened in Hudson.

Owen had also been involved with Western Reserve College from its founding, though he was never a trustee. Serving on the committee overseeing construction, Owen also gained from the endeavor, securing building contracts that turned him a fine profit. He was an enthusiastic supporter of the college and its faculty, though his abolitionist views put him in a minority among the school's backers. An overwhelming number of the college's trustees were colonization advocates and believed in a gradual approach to ending slavery. Around 1830, the debate between colonization advocates and abolitionists became inflamed when three faculty members, persuaded by the writings of Garrison, openly published calls for immediate emancipation. By 1833 the conflict became acute, pitting

The campus of Western Reserve College (today, Western Reserve Academy), which Owen Brown helped to construct. He later pulled away from the institution because of its prevalent anti-abolition sentiment. *Author's photograph, 2000.*

student against student and most of the small faculty against the trustees. However, the abolitionist faculty leader (who was also the school's president), died in the spring of 1833. With this loss, the remaining abolitionist teachers resigned. Before they left, however, they thumbed their noses at Hudson's colonization advocates by bringing a local black barber onto the commencement stage with the faculty and trustees. Though Western Reserve College regrouped with a conservative president and faculty, the debate was hardly at an end, and now extended across the Reserve to the newly founded Oberlin Collegiate Institute. Owen was very disappointed by the outcome at Western Reserve College, and was bothered by the reactionary stance of the trustees who made it clear they opposed the idea of immediate emancipation. Pulling his support from Western Reserve College, he turned in the direction of the Oberlin Institute. As the third wealthiest Hudsonite in the 1830s, Owen's departure was a significant loss to the college and a great gain to the fledgling evangelical institute at Oberlin.

Backed by the influential New York abolitionists, Arthur and Lewis Tappan, and stocked with student and faculty refugees from Cincinnati's

Lane Theological Seminary, Oberlin was an academic powder keg for abolitionism. Topped by the dissenting Presbyterian evangelist, Charles Finney, the school was the matrix of a dynamic new anti-slavery spirituality, including its controversial Perfectionist theology. Oberlin was also on the cutting edge for admitting female students, like Owen's daughter Florilla, who was twenty years old when her half-brother John returned from Pennsylvania in 1836. Oberlin's first offense to the leadership of Western Reserve College was in aspiring to the status of a "collegiate institute" instead of a manual labor school. Some were also offended after Oberlin welcomed its first black preparatory school student and then waved the acceptance in the face of Western Reserve College. But it was a smug, baseless gesture, especially since a black student had already been admitted to Western Reserve College in 1832. Perhaps competition was inevitable. Oberlin folks doted on an avant garde curriculum which emphasized biblical Hebrew instead of Latin and classical Greek. The offering of student-friendly courses reinforced the claim that Western Reserve College was too inflexible and antiquated. In response, voices at Western Reserve College charged that Oberlin had lower academic standards. While Oberlin was probably academically inferior in this early phase, the quarrel was really over politics—the background always being the larger debate over immediate abolition and colonization.[6]

John Brown was no doubt concerned over the debate and although he did not immediately become involved, it may have fueled his fire to gain the kind of success that would enable him to support abolition endeavors. After spending some time recovering in Hudson, Brown moved his family back to Franklin Mills in the summer of 1838, embarking on a tour de force of business ventures that brought him no success and ensnared him in greater debt and financial anxiety. While subcontracting to build and install lock gates for a section of the new canal, he turned his attention to cattle, which "were cheap in Ohio." Finding he could sell them in Connecticut, Brown allied himself with two partners in New England who entrusted him with $5,000 to buy more cattle out west. But lawsuits stemming from his land speculation failure in Ohio were pressing upon him, and cattle sales did not go well. Somehow he decided it necessary to spend a large part of the money advanced by his partners in the cattle business, Wadsworth and Wells; perhaps to make a partial payment on back property taxes he owed, and the rest of the appropriated funds went to support Mary and his nine children. Desperate to replace the money he now owed his partners, Brown sought a loan in Boston and prepared to return to Ohio. While apprehensively awaiting the manifestation of God's design, he wrote to his wife: "I am now somewhat in fear that I shall fail of getting the money I expected on the loan. Should that be the will of Providence, I know of no other way but we must consider ourselves very poor." Still, he was certain that even the disappointments of Providence would not overrule divine mercy. He wrote to Mary that they would somehow "conform to our circumstances with cheerfulness and true resignation." There was always this sense that Providence was working for his good, and that God's calling leads ever upward no matter how far downward the road falls. "Tomorrow may be a much brighter day. Cease not to ask God's blessing on yourselves and me." Like every true believer, as Boyd Stutler says, "John Brown was ever a pensioner of hope."

The next day was brighter indeed. While awaiting word on the loan, Brown encountered George Kellogg, the agent of a wool company in Connecticut. Kellogg was evidently taken by his familiarity with livestock and his knowledgeable access to the abundant herds of eastern Ohio and western Pennsylvania. Enlisting him to obtain wool from the west, Kellogg advanced Brown $2,800. Here was a smiling Providence indeed. Believing that God had thrown him a golden lifeline, John Brown promptly handed over Kellogg's money to Wadsworth and Wells, satisfying the debt but creating another problem that Providence would have to solve. While traveling home, Brown read a book that, he wrote to Mary, "afforded me great support and comfort during my long absence." He did not say which book it was, but it may well have been Philip Doddridge's *Rise and Progress of Religion in the Soul*, a text his family later cited as one of his most beloved readings. Doddridge was an eighteenth-century English Calvinist somewhat influenced by the Methodist revivalists of his time, his work being perhaps "the last great Puritan spiritual autobiography . . . shot through with evangelical fervor." In the midst of his anxiety and frustration over his financial dilemma, Brown may have complemented his prayer and Bible reading with Doddridge, whose discourse in chapter 25, entitled "The Christian struggling under great and heavy affliction," must have run across him like a stream in the desert.

As he read Doddridge's work, he owned every admonition and counsel as if the Puritan had meant it for him. First, John Brown was to realize that "the hand of God" was in his affliction; then he was to consider that he was a sinner, ever standing in need of God's discipline—the merciful "corrections he sends upon his children." Brown should even praise

God in the midst of his trials, practicing the biblical admonition to "give thanks" since even tribulation was working patience and hope within him. He should then consider any words of correction from wise friends and then follow them (something he generally found hard to do). Above all, he should retreat to a prayerful salutation of God's Providence, such as one suggested by Doddridge:

> O thou supreme, yet all-righteous and gracious Governor of the whole universe, mean and inconsiderable as this little province of thy spacious empire may appear. . . . I believe thy universal providence and care; and I firmly believe thy wise, holy, and kind interposition in every thing which relates to me and to the circumstances of my abode in this world.

The prayer goes on a few more pages, chock full of scripture, and one can imagine Brown reading every line, his thin lips moving while he prays every line in silence:

> I would bear thy strokes, not merely because I cannot resist them, but because I love and trust in thee. . . . I have no objection against being afflicted—against being afflicted in this particular way. . . . Only be pleased, O Lord, to stand by me, and sometimes to grant me a favorable look in the midst of my sufferings.[7]

It is quite conceivable that he believed the Kellogg loan was indeed "a favorable look" from Providence, and his step lightened as he returned to Ohio expecting God to finish his work of deliverance.

Instead, "the limber persuader" once more fell upon him. The loan he expected from Boston was refused, and now he was left to face George Kellogg of the New England Wool Company, not only owing a debt he could not pay, but hard pressed to explain why Kellogg should not consider John Brown a dishonest man. Stutler wrote that "this was the most doubtful transaction in all his business life," and in truth his juggling of other people's money to pay his own expenses "seriously compromised his reputation as a straightforward business man and the honesty and integrity of his character." Whether Brown talked himself into this inappropriate and dishonorable behavior with a Bible in one hand and Doddridge's book in the other is unclear. But it is certain that Brown must have known he was taking a risky course—which is probably why he made no mention of it when he wrote to his partner Seth

Thompson the following month, saying the prospect for final success "is rather dark."

Brown put off responding to Kellogg's inquiry about the money owed, the letter setting on his desk for almost a month before he finally gave up hope in Providential deliverance. "I flattered myself till now," he finally wrote to Kellogg, "with the hope that I might be able to render a more favorable account of myself, but the truth, and the whole truth, shall be told." Brown then unfolded his story of anticipating a much needed $5,000 loan, and upon being refused he expected to be jailed on charges by Wadsworth and Wells. In his desperation the only alternative seemed the use of Kellogg's money. Since that time he had waited vainly "in painful anxiety" for the loan to come through, and was now prepared to sell his "real and personal property" to repay his debt. Unfortunately, Brown owed money to many people, and the worth of his property was hardly enough to meet the other demands let alone his debt to Kellogg's firm. But Providence was at least merciful to John Brown. Though Kellog's firm did not forgive him his debt, they did not press charges. "I hope we shall all feel disposed to acquiesce in the will of Providence in regard to all our concerns," Brown had written earlier in the year to his wife. "He knows what is best, and may his holy will be done." Even after his exposure and embarrassment before the New England Wool Company, he was still hoping "for final success after all."

Through the influence of Owen Brown, who had now become a trustee of the Oberlin Institute, John thought Providence was looking his way once more. As it turned out, the wealthy magnate and abolitionist, Gerrit Smith, had gifted Oberlin with twenty thousand acres of land in western Virginia's Tyler County. Oberlin's administrators wanted the land surveyed, and Owen directed them to his son. John Brown responded to the opportunity with less interest in a surveyor's wage than in the possibility of cutting out a portion of the land for himself. Oberlin gave tentative approval and advanced him some money, but when he arrived in Virginia he found the land was filled with squatters on almost every tract. Observing the culture of the region, Brown found people backward in farming and livestock, and their work sloppy and unproductive. In comparison to the neat, efficient farms of the Western Reserve, Brown wrote home, the lackluster farms of western Virginia reminded him "that knowledge is power." He liked the land nevertheless, particularly the rich, watered, hilly tract that he marked off for himself and imagined settling upon with his family, "if it be the will of Providence."

However, Brown's reports and the outcome of the episode suggest that he found the overall experience "frustrating and unproductive." Perhaps he developed second thoughts as he encountered the squatters, most of whom were indifferent to his official notice that they had no right to be there. Second thoughts may explain somewhat why he dragged his feet in making a decision, and in early 1841 he finally admitted he had pretty much given up on the idea. Besides, Providence had provided another possibility of entering into a remunerative partnership in a tannery and wool business in Ohio. Meanwhile, Oberlin's leadership were no more decisive, for it took much of the summer for them to approve the well-watered 1,000-acre tract Brown had requested. At the same time, they were strongly considering the surrender of a good portion of the land in payment of a debt to Arthur Tappan, their wealthy friend and benefactor in New York. By the time Owen told his son about the Tappan concern, the deal was done and John Brown could only write letters of protest—though admitting his own lack of promptness had contributed to the disappointing outcome. "He bowed to Providence, concluding that 'there is no doubt the best of reasons for it, and we will rejoice that he who directs the steps of men knows perfectly well how to direct them; and will most assuredly make his counsel to stand.'" Eventually Oberlin paid him the balance of $29 owed him for his labors.[8]

Along with the story of Brown's ongoing business frustrations—the wrong turns, dead ends, failed attempts, lawsuits, and grinding debts—that characterize his adult years in Ohio, he was still compelled by the unfolding drama of slavery. He read the papers and studied the signs of the times while "standing by the great sea of American bondmen . . . anxiously watching for some true men to rise above its dark level." While he waited for another Nat Turner to appear, Brown continued to keep the faith. No matter how small the contest, the concern of the black man was prominent in his thinking. In those days he was already nurturing within him the belief that he was God's instrument for the deliverance of the slaves. "Many a night he had lain awake and prayed concerning it." (Was this why he once reminded his wife to have his sons copy his letters, instructing her "to have them all preserved with care"?) "It was always difficult for him to fit himself to circumstances," his son Salmon remembered. "He wanted conditions to change for him—and he usually brought about the things he most desired. . . . His persistence was as strongly developed as his firmness." This persistence in wanting things to change *for John Brown* was perhaps why he fumbled, bumbled, and nearly drowned trying to wade through the deep pool of debt and financial controversy he had largely made for himself. But persistence also enabled him to burn with righteous indignation while other men were content to close their eyes to other people's pain.

After the Browns affiliated themselves with the Congregational Church in Franklin Mills, the church cooperated in a widely advertised revival series. John Jr. and Ruth remembered their family attending the evangelistic meetings featuring a guest preacher from Cleveland. At the first service, the Browns sat in their family pew, which was rented according to the custom of the day. During the service, Brown noticed that black people—some of whom he knew—had been seated at the very back of the church near the door. At the next meeting, he noticed that the same discrimination had taken place. Indignant, he stood up and announced to the church that an inequity had been committed in the seating of the "colored portion of the audience." Ruth, who was nearly ten years old when this occurred, always remembered the facial expressions in the church: "The whole congregation were shocked; the minister looked angry," she said. "But I remember father's firm, determined look." Brown then invited the blacks to switch seats—they taking the Brown family pew, and the Browns taking their seats in the back by the door. The next day two deacons came to the house to scold him for his actions, but he would have none of it. For the rest of the revival series, black people sat in the Brown pew and the Browns sat around the wood stove near the door.[9]

# 9

## Of Vows and Tears

Oh that my head were waters, and mine eyes a fountain of tears, that I might weep day and night for the slain of the daughter of my people!

—Jeremiah 9:1–9

According to John Jr., his father repelled a scolding visit from some of the deacons in the church, sending them on their way "with new views of Christian duty." The incident probably prompted serious conversation around the large fireplace that night, especially among Brown's teenage sons who were old enough to understand the issue of racism and their father's strong feelings against slavery. Though John Jr. apparently exaggerated the outcome of the incident, it did help the younger Browns to realize the gross contradiction existing between biblical faith and white religion when it came to racism. "This was my first taste of the proslavery diabolicalism that had intrenched itself in the Church, and I shed a few uncalled for tears in the matter, for instead I should have rejoiced in my emancipation," wrote John Jr. The people of the Franklin Mills church were probably not "proslavery," but advocates of gradual emancipation and colonization. The Browns rightly perceived that the prevailing racism of the Congregational Churches was on a continuum with slavery itself. "The segregated pew," observes Robert Handy, "was the symbol of the acceptance by many Christians, North and South, of belief in the inferior status of the Negro." This was a problem for the entire Brown family, though John Brown eventually responded by weaning himself from church membership while his sons reacted by rejecting the evangelical faith. The incident made it easier for the family to relocate to Hudson, though the move back to Brown's hometown was an economic expedient. "In the reverses of 1836–37, Father made an assignment of all his property for the benefit of his creditors," John Jr. remembered. "His farm in South Kent, then called Franklin . . . went with the rest." The farm itself was not sold by 1838, enabling the Browns to return to Franklin Mills for a time. But in 1837 it looked as if they were leaving the farm for good.[1]

The Browns returned to Hudson, and to the heightening controversy between the colonization majority and abolitionist minority. Perhaps the presence of Southern students at the Western Reserve College helped to sustain an anti-abolitionist sentiment in the community. Owen Brown had shifted his support to the Oberlin Collegiate Institute and became a target of criticism throughout Hudson as a result. John Brown undoubtedly stood with his father and the other abolitionists in Hudson, though there is no record of any prominent role on his part in conflict with colonization advocates.

However, Brown seems to have rekindled his old "friendship" with Milton Lusk, his late wife's brother. From the late 1830s, Milton was among the leading underground railroad activists in Hudson, including Owen Brown, Oliver Brown, Jesse Dickinson, Sylvester Thompson, Lora Case, George Kilborn, Garry Sanford, Frederick Brown (whose station was in the woods), and John Brown. Lusk had come into conflict with first citizen David Hudson (his former employer) and other church leaders. While in Pennsylvania, Brown had reached out to Lusk, whose conflict was probably reflective of a move toward the Perfectionist movement. Lusk recalled that John Brown rode in from Pennsylvania and "prayed with me, and shed tears, and said perhaps I was nearer right than he had thought." This passing, tender moment between the two rivals was not only due to John's sympathy for Lusk's position, but was probably due also to the loss they shared after Dianthe's death. The two men continued in their love-hate relationship throughout the years, bound by a mutual opposition to slavery and the memory of godly Dianthe, but otherwise locked in a conflict over personality and religious differences.

By the time Brown moved back to Hudson in 1837, Lusk seems to have fallen out with the Congregational Church in full commitment to Perfectionism. While Perfectionism digressed from Reformed theology in a number of significant ways, its core doctrine was that Christians could attain a state of sinless grace in this life through a kind of second conversion experience. This was the prominent teaching of revivalist Charles Finney and the basis of Oberlin's theology. The Browns seem to have sympathized with the "Oberlin doctrine" at first, but reconsidered when they saw its unorthodox inclinations.

Hudson was officially introduced to Perfectionism about 1834, when a preacher came from New York state teaching that Christians could attain a "state of sinlessness." The Perfectionist inroad followed an ill-fated attempt on the part of the Millerite sect to gain a foothold in Hudson. Not surprisingly, Milton Lusk had been swept from Perfectionism to the Millerite sect for a time, which undoubtedly brought him into further conflict with John Brown. The Millerites followed the teachings of William Miller, an evangelical revivalist who made a number of failed predictions about the return of Christ, the last one in 1844. Miller was a pre-millennialist, believing that Christ would return to initiate the millennium on earth. His failure marked a "short-run victory for the Post-millennialist churches," who believed the return of Christ would follow the millennium. However, pre-millennialism would make a startling comeback later in the nineteenth century to become the predominant evangelical viewpoint. Probably to Brown's disgust, Milton Lusk then went from the Millerite sect to Spiritualism, another unorthodox religious fad of the nineteenth century.[2]

As it concerned the Oberlin Institute, Owen Brown had no choice but to confront the upstart Perfectionist movement. The presence of his daughter Florilla as a student, and the animosity toward Oberlin back in Hudson, served to heighten his concern for the abolitionist school. To "prepare herself for usefulness" in the Lord's work, Florilla had enrolled in Oberlin's women's program in 1836 (she was among Oberlin's second group of female graduates in 1839). As a trustee, Owen sometimes used his correspondence with Florilla to obtain information or send messages to the school's leadership, such as in 1836 when he wrote to her, prompted by harsh criticism of Oberlin in Hudson. Filled with anxiety over Oberlin's fate, Owen asked her to get one of the administrators to write to him, adding that "things go bad at Hudson at present but God is on the throne." As opposition in Hudson heightened, his concern increased. "We hope things go well at Oberlin," Owen wrote a year later, in June 1837. "I have had some anxiety about Oberlin but trust God will take care of her. She has friends and Enemies and but few mutuals among her acquaintance." Like her parents, Florilla was serious about abolition. Her mother wrote to her that she had narrowly missed being drafted to serve on an anti-slavery fund-raising committee. But Florilla served an important role as the eyes and voice of Owen Brown at Oberlin. During a trip east in June 1837, Owen again wrote to Florilla, being "anxious to know the state of the Institution." The following month he reiterated his concern, asking her to get a school representative to write to him with details.[3]

However, in 1837, Owen began to question whether all the criticisms of Oberlin were undeserved. In an interesting letter to Florilla that October, the old man wrote:

My mind has been somewhat tried with the subject of [Perfectionism]. I did not [formerly] care but very little about it[.] I was not afraid of [anybody] being [too] good as I thought nothing more can be [meant] than a high state of sanctification, which we all should pray for.

Owen began to realize that he had accepted Perfectionism uncritically, thinking it was merely an enthusiastic approach to Christian piety—something he probably associated with the glory days of the Second Great Awakening. But now he heard rumors that ministers at Oberlin were diminishing the Sunday Sabbath and the ordinances of the church in the name of Christian love. "I state partly from the conversation I have had with them and partly from hear-say [*that*] these things are dangerous," Owen concluded. He urged Florilla to read his letter to a faculty member, hoping that these reports from Oberlin were just distorted bits of news.[4]

One year later Owen had come to the conclusion that Perfectionism was a problem to the church. "I do not believe any body in these parts is made better by it," he wrote. His Calvinism had finally overcome his sentimental acceptance of the teachings of Finney and his associates. Yet for the sake of Oberlin's strong anti-slavery position, he clearly did not wish to withdraw his support, and still hoped that an Oberlin representative would come over to Hudson.

During the year of John Brown's retreat to Hudson, the chill of death twice swept over the Browns, once from a distance and the other within the very bosom of the family. On November 7, 1837, the abolitionist pastor and journalist, Elijah Lovejoy, was mortally wounded while defending his printing press in Alton, Illinois. The news of Lovejoy's death reached Hudson the next day, and Laurens Hickock, a professor at Western Reserve College, was particularly outraged. Hickok was sympathetic to the abolitionist cause, but others knew him as a conservative. Canceling his classes for the day, Hickok personally spoke to the students and faculty, inviting them to a special meeting in the college chapel that afternoon. In the chapel meeting it was decided to hold a mass prayer meeting at the Hudson Congregational Church the next day. Burning with indignation, Hickok then mounted his horse and rode throughout the town and its vicinity, informing people of Lovejoy's death, and inviting them to attend the special prayer meeting the next evening.

The turnout for the prayer meeting was strong, and Owen and John Brown were both in attendance. After giving a detailed account of Lovejoy's killing and the destruction of his printing press by a racist mob, Hickok declared:

> The crisis has come. The question now before the American citizens is no longer alone, "Can the slaves be made free?" but, "Are we free, or are we slaves under Southern mob law?" I propose that we take measures to procure another press and another editor. If a like fate attends them, send another, till the whole country is aroused; and if you can find no fitter man for the first victim, send me.

The meeting was filled with holy indignation, speeches, and resolutions. After sitting quietly throughout the meeting, John Brown arose from his seat in the back of the room. Raising his right hand, his voice carried throughout the church as he declared: "I pledge myself, with God's help, that I will devote my life to increasing hostility toward slavery." Before anyone else could respond, his father Owen stood up. Stuttering badly, he reminded the congregation about the story of John the Baptist, the prophet beheaded for his righteous rebuke of an evil king. The followers of the martyred prophet told the bad news to Jesus, Owen declared, and so should they. "Then, in a very fervent prayer, weeping," the elder began (his stuttering always relenting while he prayed), closing out the meeting with an earnest and fervent invocation.[5]

Six months after death struck a martyr in Alton, Illinois, it overcame a saint in Ohio. In June 1838, Owen wrote to Florilla that her older half-sister Anna Ruth was dead. Thirty-five years of age, Anna Ruth had gone to church three times on the fateful Sunday, afterward becoming deathly sick. When word reached Hudson of her worsening condition, Owen and John went out to her house, finding her weeping husband standing at the bedside, and her grown son kneeling close to his dying mother. For both Owen and John, the scene must have invoked terrible memories of loss. She lingered several days, rallying for a time so that Owen was encouraged of her recovery and departed for home. Instead, she took a turn for the worst and expired the next day. Her dying words in prayer were, "May I be released?"

"And now what shall we do," grief-stricken Owen wrote to Florilla, "shall we not go and tell Jesus. She was dear to me but not more than my other Children. God has given me a very large [family] and I have been very [unfaithful] to them. Do pray to God to pardon my [unfaithfulness] and make me more [faithful] in the future." Owen would always tell Jesus of these sorrows, believing the same God who chastised was also a God who loved and forgave. Yet chastisement was hard, and the stinging loss of loved ones was an anguish both Owen and John Brown would experience often in life. Just two years later, Owen's second wife Sally died of dysentery, and in all he would live to see eight of his children buried. John Brown, soon to receive a visit from death at his home, lost twenty-two close family members in his life, including a wife and eleven children. In most of these losses the Browns were in no way unique, their world lacking the medical knowledge that we take for granted today. Life was indeed a veil of tears, and "telling it to Jesus" would always be an anchor for the Browns.[6]

Both father and son were contemplating death. Owen wrote to Florilla: "I think [']what would be my case were I [to] cast off for Eternity [to][*enjoy*] an other [*sic*] friendly interview with my friends'?" He was becoming frail and vulnerable in old age, such as the time he could not move fast enough through the snow and was knocked down by a horse and sleigh. But as John Brown tucked his old father lovingly into bed "as a mother would do with her children," he too was nursing within himself "a steady, strong desire to *die*," as he later wrote. Intermittent thoughts of death increased during the years of vows and tears. He was deeply wounded by the deaths of loved ones, and increasingly frustrated by the inability to attain success. Instead, debts and lawsuits hounded him, and the rest of his Ohio years were scarred by further disappointments. The time would come when he finally found a way to become a "'reaper' in the *great* harvest." When that time came, Brown wrote, he was not only "quite willing to *live*," but happy in life and "rather anxious to live for a *few* years more." But in the meantime, he continued to struggle with Providence.

After the Browns returned to the farmhouse in Franklin Mills in 1838, they became members of the Congregational Church, though the Browns would hardly have lessened in vocal opposition to slavery and racial segregation, and opened their home to black friends too. One frequent guest of the Browns was a black theology student at Western Reserve College named John Sykes Fayette. Fayette was from New York City, having been referred to Western Reserve College in 1832 by letter of his pastor, the Reverend James H. Cox of the Laight Street Presbyterian Church. Cox referred to Fayette as a "worthy member" and a "young man (of color) whose principles appear fixed and sound." At the time of his stay in Hudson, Fayette was in his early twenties, and was probably on good terms with Owen and John Brown. Fayette eventually completed the bachelor of arts and the pastoral degrees at Western Reserve by 1837, perhaps enduring the heated debate in Hudson by staying close to abolitionist allies in the community. Indeed, Fayette found a particularly pleasant ally in one of Hudson's first families, marrying her before leaving for Canada to resume a Presbyterian pastorate. Sometime in 1838 or 1839, John, Mary, the elder Brown boys, and Fayette, "the colored theological student," were seated around the fireplace in the Franklin Mills home. After a lengthy discussion about the evils of slavery, Brown declared that "he had long entertained" the purpose of opposing slavery, though not in the manner proposed by Garrison and his kind.

He was ready to make a forward step, but only a small one—hardly to the point of plotting a raid on the South, but away from his earlier dream of becoming an abolitionist "tycoon." He "would never again be engaged in any business that he could not leave on two weeks' notice," Brown told his family. Mindful of the martyred Lovejoy as well as the many anti-abolition incidents in the North, Brown was reconsidering his role in the struggle. Though mob violence against abolitionists sharply declined in the late 1830s, many had turned to political abolition while adhering to nonviolence. Not so with John Brown, who was clearly reevaluating conservative standards and considering the necessities of force in opposing slavery. "It might be years before opportunity offered to strike the blow, but he meant to prepare for it," John Jr. recalled. "When the 'call' came, his wife was to consider herself a widow, his children committed to the care of Him who fed the ravens." One by one, Brown asked his wife and sons if they would agree to join him in a family effort. When they agreed, Brown knelt and prayed, asking all present to raise their hands and seal their commitment with a vow. They must promise, he told them, that they would never tell of their determination to "break the jaws of the wicked and pluck the spoil out of his teeth." John Jr. recalled his surprise when his father knelt to pray. More than one family member testified that Brown always prayed standing up, invariably leaning forward on a tilted chair. To his family, the unusual kneeling posture was significant.[7]

These events transpired at the same time that Brown "was walking a financial tight rope and trying desperately to save his property and his credit." Whatever opportunities he found for financial advance, like breeding race horses or subcontracting for work on the new canal, were greatly offset by his credit blunders and unskillful manipulation of money, which landed him in debt and legal problems. From time to time Brown attempted to repay his debts, such as the $57 he paid to George Kellogg of the New England Woolen Company—though "small as it was," he knew the payment was little more than a token of his sincerity. Brown had likewise fumbled in his attempt to segue into a thousand verdant acres of Oberlin's land in western Virginia, and the new decade of the 1840s greeted him with more disappointments. Having done business by "drawing against future expectations," Brown found himself involved in numerous lawsuits, such as one by the Bank of Wooster, Ohio, which won a judgment of about $917 against him.

The worst case, from the time of the Panic of 1837, pertained to some valued property that Brown had bought with a loan from the Western Reserve Bank in Warren, Ohio. A number of associates, including his friend Heman Oviatt and his brother Frederick, became Brown's sureties for the loan. When things went badly and he could not repay it, the full brunt of responsibility finally fell back on Oviatt, who was obligated to pay the bank $6,000. Besides his other debts and lawsuits, now Brown owed Oviatt a large sum, but had nothing to give him except a penal bond of conveyance on some property called Westlands that he had purchased on credit. Brown had no intention of surrendering Westlands to Oviatt, but used the penal bond of conveyance in a kind of sleight of hand arrangement. If things went well, Oviatt would be content to hold the bond of conveyance for a time, believing he had security in case Brown did not repay him. This would give Brown time to come up with money to settle his debt to Oviatt, who would then return the bond of conveyance. Following this strategy, as soon as he received the actual deed to Westlands, Brown registered the property under his name without telling Oviatt. Oviatt continued to believe the bond of conveyance gave him the right to Westlands, while in fact Brown not only possessed the property according to law, but then mortgaged it. If things had gone as Brown hoped, he could have paid Oviatt without him ever knowing what he had done with the property.

Providence did not smile upon John Brown, for at this time another lawsuit concluded in judgment against him. Believing his opponent in this case was dishonest, Brown feared he would have legal claim to Westlands, which now hung by the thread of a mortgage. To subvert the possibility of losing Westlands to him, Brown headed off the court decision by making an assignment of his property. As a result, Westlands was sold in a sheriff's sale, and the only hope Brown had was in persuading a friend named Amos Chamberlain to purchase the property on his behalf so that he could buy back the deed from him. Instead, Chamberlain began to savor the sweetness of paying barely $1,600 for a $6,000 property, and decided to keep it for himself.

Chamberlain was legally entitled to keep the land, and in the end neither strong words from Brown nor a lawsuit by Oviatt could salvage it, the latter being left with a worthless bond of conveyance. Without legal means to recover the $6,000 he lost as security, neither could Oviatt require it of Brown, who was legally safe from litigation. When it became clear that Chamberlain intended to keep Westlands, Brown's lawyer advised him to try to keep possession, which he did by taking teenagers John Jr. and Owen and holing up inside a shack on the property. When Chamberlain sent for a constable to remove them, they intimidated the official with old-fashioned muskets pointing through the cracks of the shanty. Eventually a sheriff was sent who recognized that Brown's bluff was all barrel and no bullets, and there was no resistance when he hauled John and the boys off to the Akron jail. However, they were soon released on their own recognizance, and since Chamberlain had what he wanted, all charges were dropped against the Browns. Oviatt brought countersuits against Chamberlain to the highest court in the state, but ultimately Chamberlain's right to the land was upheld.

Brown was embittered by what he felt was a betrayal by Chamberlain, and wrote an appeal to him that suggests he really believed his neighbor had redeemed the land on his behalf. His letter was a work of Christian diplomacy, in which Brown informed Chamberlain that he still thought him a friend, was happy for all his successes, and was writing in a friendly spirit with peaceful intentions.

And now I ask you why will you trample on the rights of your friend and of his numerous family? Is it because he is poor? Why will you kneedlessly [*sic*] make yourself the means of depriveing [*sic*] all my honest creditors of their Just due?

Brown wrote further that he was aware that Chamberlain had been "circulating evil reports" about him, and believed he was doing so in order to cover his own unfaithful behavior. Citing a biblical story about an Israelite king who brought false charges against a poor man in order to steal his small but desirable property, he crafted his appeal to strike at his neighbor's conscience. "I ask my old friend again[:] is your path a path of peace?" Unfortunately for Brown, Chamberlain not only ignored his appeal, but denied that they had ever made an agreement regarding the property. The unfaithful neighbor made no reply, entrenched as he was in his own lie. Chamberlain probably bad-mouthed Brown for years to come. In the early twentieth century an interviewer noted that descendants of Amos Chamberlain still resented Brown's claim and "nourished [an] inherited ill will" toward him.

Four years before the Westlands case came to a final, disappointing conclusion in 1846, John Brown had hit rock bottom. In 1842, Brown's former partners in the cattle business, Wadsworth and Wells, brought suit against him in order to collect the balance of what he owed them. With nothing left to lose, Brown's only way out was to take advantage of a new state law, based on an act of Congress passed the year before to "establish a uniform system of bankruptcy throughout the United States." In September 1842, an inventory was conducted on his estate, leaving nothing to the Browns except kitchenware, furniture, foods, field and household tools, assorted men's and women's clothes, a small number of livestock and fowl, and Brown's surveyor's compass. The man conducting the inventory also noted books remaining in the Brown library, including eleven Bibles—undoubtedly those used in daily family worship—and a few theological texts, as well as grammar and miscellaneous texts.

He had explored the depths of defeat as a businessman. His dream of making a fortune in land speculation had crashed down upon him, and a few other ventures in business had proven failures. He had run aground, as he later acknowledged, by fueling his ventures on credit in an unstable economy. But he also failed because he made mistakes in judgment, sometimes acting in selfish desperation or stubborn determination to make things work. By the mid-1840s he was the object of a handful of successful lawsuits intended to recover money loaned on promissory notes (executed by him individually or jointly with others), and finally was bankrupt.

Yet "John Brown had a way with him," Boyd Stutler wrote. Despite all these embarrassing defeats, his reputation emerged relatively unscathed—

partly because his overall conduct and operations were impeccably honest, and also because he did at least acknowledge his errors and made attempts to compensate those who had been harmed because of him. These attempts were appreciable more for sentiment than financial worth. After his bankruptcy was made official, Brown wrote to George Kellogg of the New England Woolen Company, binding himself to the "moral obligation" to repay what he owed the firm plus interest, "from time to time, as Divine Providence shall enable me to do." He made a similar promise to repay his associate, Heman Oviatt, likewise invoking the help of "Divine Providence" in fulfilling his "ever binding moral obligation." When the inventory for his bankruptcy claim was made, nineteen sheep were noted as "pledged to H. Oviatt." Another time, Brown encountered one of his disappointed creditors as he rode home on horseback with a new saddle and bridle. "'Will you take this horse and saddle for the debt?' asked Brown. A moment later the creditor was astride the animal, while Brown, thanking him, started for home on foot."[8]

Interestingly, Heman Oviatt maintained trust in John Brown and continued to work with him. Unlike him, Oviatt was a successful client of Providence, though with a reputation for being far more interested in business than the things of God—it once having been remarked that the best way to awaken him during church service was to toss a coin on the floor. According to his own grandson, Oviatt "regarded John Brown as thoroughly honest," and despite the heavy losses he sustained in Brown's venture, "never charged [him] with moral turpitude." Oviatt's high regard for Brown is illustrated by the fact that he went so far as to partner with him in a tannery venture prior to the bankruptcy proceedings. According to their agreement, Brown was to tan hides purchased by Oviatt and apply Brown's share of the profits to his debt. As these arrangements developed, the Browns moved to nearby Richfield, Ohio, hoping to start over again with Oviatt's help. At last there was a happy Providence smiling upon the loss-weary Browns. Of course, Oviatt was astute enough to realize that Brown's strengths in tannery work and livestock, as well as his honesty, far outweighed his failures as an entrepreneur. Furthermore, Brown's humbled state perhaps made him more compliant—less likely to try to force matters to suit his wishes, at least for a time.

But Providence was not satisfied with such humility. In September 1843, a plague of dysentery swept through Richfield, invading the Brown household. At first the children were generally sick. Sandy-haired Charles, barely six years of age but "swift and strong" with "legs and arms straight as broomsticks," died on September 11th. Ten days later, baby Austin perished—just past his first birthday, as his sickly parents looked on helplessly. The following day, little Peter, not yet three years old but stout and good looking, was taken away. Still unsated, death waited one more day to seize beloved and faithful Sarah—the first child of John and Mary, nearly ten years old. Sarah amazed her parents, for she seemed to want death, and on her sick bed displayed a "great composure of mind, and patience, together with strong assureance [*sic*] at times of meeting God in Paradise." John Brown could do nothing but bury them in "a little row together." In a note attached to the bad news Brown sent to John Jr., now away at school, his brother Jason expressed the sentiments of the family: "These days are days of rebuke and severe trial with us. . . . let us not murmur, The Judge of all the Earth, has done, and will do right. But let us give glory and honor and power and thanks unto him that sitteth on the throne forever and ever." They had drunk deeply from the bitter cup of sorrows, John Brown wrote to his namesake. "But still the Lord reigneth and blessed be his great and holy name forever. In our sore affliction there is still some comfort." The Browns understood that until the time swords are finally beaten into plowshares, the grieving saint must beat his murmurs into praises, for every decision made by the Judge of all the Earth *must* be right.

The disappointed tanner was approaching his mid-forties. Despite his wiry, muscular vitality, his five-foot ten-inch frame, he was beginning to bend as if the cares, burdens, and losses of Providence were acting upon him like gravity—so pulling him down that he began to appear stoop-shouldered. His dark brown hair was tinged with slight streaks of gray. One might see him walking along, lost in thought, with hands clasped behind him and eyes fixed downward as if plowing a straight row of solitude on the ground before him. His settling profile was peculiar, with a "hawked" nose that one of his sons said made him resemble a "meat-ax." Always dressed in carefully polished boots, his apparel was neat but a bit old-fashioned for his time, especially his brown broadcloth suit and white shirt, a kind of Puritan uniform.

In 1843, John Brown was very much like the abolitionist Arthur Tappan, of whom his brother Lewis wrote: "He has made some great mistakes in money matters, yet his many valuable qualities should induce us to show him all the substantial marks of affection we can." But Brown had no wealthy brother to excuse his errors or intercede in his losses. His all too human misjudgments and business blunders would not only ride on his bending shoulders throughout the rest of his days, but be forced upon him by scholars and novelists for generations to come—often in order to dismiss him or negate his accomplishments. Of course, the grieving, stoop-shouldered Puritan was oblivious to such things in 1843. The road he studied so intently as he walked along was his own inner life. Life was a road marked with the signposts of Divine Providence, leading onward through the sorrows and comforts that precede one's final, welcomed rest.[9]

# PART IV

# In Times of Difficulty

It is in times of difficulty that men show what they are. It is in such times that men mark themselves.

—John Brown

# 10

## Belted Knights and
## Practical Shepherds

But as an hired servant, and as a sojourner, he shall be with thee,
and shall serve thee unto the year of jubilee.

—Leviticus 25:40

Salmon Brown long remembered an incident from early childhood, probably at the family home in Richfield, Ohio. While a large brass kettle of water was heating in the kitchen, he and his brother playfully traced lines on a steam-clouded window. But Salmon became rowdy and blurted out an offensive word. Their father heard Salmon's "smutty" language from the next room and came rushing in with such ferocity that the little boy became frightened. When Brown demanded that he repeat the word, Salmon was so afraid that he said every bad word except the one his father had heard. Thinking Salmon was lying, Brown sent for a "limber persuader," which so disturbed Mary that she ran from the house. But his mother's grief did not win a reprieve for the boy, and Salmon got a "tremendous whipping." His younger sister Sarah remembered her father's harsh whippings too, recalling that John Brown was "terribly severe" in punishing the elder children, and though they loved him, they greatly feared him too. He was especially harsh when the children told fanciful stories, Sarah recalled, and Salmon seems to have been the most frequent transgressor of the great law against lying. Sarah said that in later years, after he had traveled and observed other people disciplining their children, Brown softened considerably and "even expressed regrets for his earlier fashion." But even she did not escape his harsh measures. Sarah recalled an incident from early childhood when she "made a blunder" during Bible reading. Thinking she was lying to cover up her mistake, Brown took the Bible out of her hands and boxed her ears with it.

"That was the only time I can remember him ever striking me a blow with anything."

Despite the warm and admiring words of Brown's children in later life, there is no doubt that he was harsh, and that his heavy-handed manner with the children was in part due to his strong, excitable temperament. Yet he shared his family's values, seeing the world from a standpoint of moral laws and principles. Salmon, who resented his father's discipline and short temper, also thought his father's piety was "cranky" because he had no tolerance for men whose piety was blended with pacifism. Knowing how it galled their father, perhaps there was a measure of revenge in the apostasy of Brown's sons when they became young men. As Richard Boyer wrote, they laughed, "perhaps a little painfully" in recalling the harsh disciplines of youth, though acknowledging their own misbehavior as well. His sons also recognized the religious conviction underlying his discipline. "In administering such punishment," Salmon said, "my father believed he was living up to the last analysis of Scriptural injunction." Jason likewise recalled: "Father believed every word of the Bible and acted on that saying in his harsh way." But in later years, Watson (who died at Harper's Ferry) expressed how the boys really felt. "The trouble is, you want your boys to be brave as tigers, and still afraid of you."[1] Still, John Brown lived in an era before "a good spanking" was the final measure of discipline. Rather, it was a time when "the birch and the rule swished stingingly against bottoms and hands for the slightest infraction."

However, in all fairness to John Brown, his sons were also devout in disobedience. Salmon often lead his siblings in mischief, such as stealing fruit or playing practical jokes on neighbors. The daughter of his employer in Akron said that even though Brown was a "terrible tyrant," it was perhaps "to rule all those swarming children, all of whom were rebellious, [and] demanded a firm hand." When Salmon was a few years older, he so disturbed his mother that she dragged him out to the woodshed. But unruly Salmon dodged her blows and grabbed the switch out of her hand, until the incident became something of a brawl. Another time Salmon and Oliver were caught stealing fruit from a neighbor's orchard. Both fled from Brown's "limber persuader," but Salmon could not match the bounding steps of his father, who caught him and beat him terribly. But Brown was exasperated with Salmon's rebellion. "You are a very bad boy," he told Salmon. It was the last time his father ever hit him.

Yet these "painful climaxes in family life" were not the only defining moments at home. John Jr. observed that although his father "was not especially demonstrative in his affectional nature," he was very earnest as a parent, few fathers holding "deeper or warmer sympathies" for children in general, especially his own. "But for his strong *paternal sympathies* joined with his sense of *justice*, his mind would not, in my opinion, ever have become absorbed in [abolitionism]." Another family member observed that John Brown "was very tender" to his children in times of illness, taking great pains to nurse them back to health. Though he was generally "undemonstrative of his affections it did not betoken coldness." Even Salmon acknowledged that he and his siblings recognized "a strain of intense tenderness" in their father's nature, and that in turn Brown put great confidence in his children, which promoted strong bonds of affection in the family. Salmon and the other children even spoke of their father as displaying maternal instincts at times—in singing his children to sleep by an open fireplace, pacing the floor with a "collicky child," or hovering over wife and children throughout the night as a nurse in times of sickness. The tears he sometimes had shed when thrashing his children were genuine. "Every fiber of his being was wrung by the suffering of others," Salmon concluded. Suffering "brought out the woman in him, the John Brown little known to history."

The most important moments in the Brown family were centered around the table, where both physical and spiritual feeding took place in great portions. In a family that at one point reached fourteen persons, an orderly meal time was an imperative, as was economy, and teaching the older children how to cook in order to assist their mother. During the family's residence at Richfield, the children would sit around a large table, quiet only when their father was present. A favorite meal of the family was corn meal mush, cooked for hours in a huge iron cauldron, and served with milk or fresh cream—neither of which their father liked. After breakfast, Bibles were distributed to the children, John and Mary reading several passages of scripture before the children read their assigned verses. When it was time to pray, everyone stood as Brown led the family in devotions. Praying with his face toward the wall, Brown typically stood behind a chair, leaning on it while slightly tipping it forward. On Sunday evenings the Browns would read through a portion of the *Westminster Shorter Catechism*, including the recital of the Ten Commandments, after which he would preach a sermon.

Throughout their lives, John Brown's sons and daughters recalled how sincerely and unrelentingly he sought to see them committed to the Christian faith. One Sunday when he was troubled by his sons' lack of interest, Brown took them to a depressed area of Akron "where the roughest class of men stayed," "and then told us that such would be our descendants if we broke away from the faith of the fathers." Yet the only pronouncedly evangelical children seem to have been Ruth and Sarah, the latter doing mission work with Japanese children in California in her later years. As his children grew to adulthood, Brown "was greatly concerned over their spiritual welfare," especially his sons. "He constantly expostulated with us, and in letters when away," Salmon wrote. "His expressed hope was 'that ye sin not, that you form no foolish attachments, that you be not a companion of fools.'"[2]

Back in Hudson, Owen Brown was breaking old attachments and finding few companions in the ongoing debate raging over colonization and abolition. But tensions between Western Reserve College and the Oberlin Institute had now spread to the Hudson Congregational Church. Hard feelings ensued when an endowment to Western Reserve College was redirected to Oberlin. The matter even went to court, but Oberlin won, further embittering the Hudson congregation against the abolitionists.

In fact, the debate within the Hudson Congregational Church was layered, the slavery issue being only the most prominent. There were also tensions over the Plan of Union, co-ed education, and curriculum, all reflecting the contest between the college in Hudson and the Oberlin Institute.    Owen Brown's involvement in anti-slavery organizations probably grated on some of his Congregational brethren too. He was an outspoken advocate of equal education, and in 1837 he wrote a letter to the Ohio Anti-Slavery Society admonishing them to form a "State Anti-Slavery Education Society" in order to provide schooling for "black and mulatto youth and children." He impugned the "common schools" in Ohio for not serving black people, concluding that without proper education black people would be deprived of the information necessary to participate in society as "useful and happy neighbors."

Interestingly, the breaking point in the Hudson Congregational Church came after Owen had reconsidered Oberlin's theology. By the time he and the other abolitionists seceded from the Hudson church in 1842, he was gradually pulling away from active association with Oberlin. When he broke with his church over Oberlin, it seems it was more a matter of principle than politics. Writing to his new son-in-law, the Reverend Samuel Adair (who had married Florilla in 1841), Owen revealed that the Congregational pastor in Hudson had snubbed a visit from Oberlin's president, Asa Mahan. As a result, twelve abolitionist members had withdrawn their membership and decided to form their own congregation. Other abolitionists, including Owen, were hanging on, but even they were preparing to leave if no compromise could be reached. "We hope God will overcome all things for his Glory," Owen concluded. When the pastor and church leadership remained firm, Owen felt he had no choice but to secede with the rest of the abolitionists. The secessionist church was formed on October 6, 1842, with twenty-one people, eleven women and ten men—all but two of them refugees from the Congregational Church in Hudson.[3]

Despite its association with the Oberlin Institute, the new "Free Congregational Church" showed no significant confessional dissent from the traditional Congregational viewpoint. Despite an openness to preachers from Oberlin, its "Articles of Faith and Covenant" showed no obvious inclination toward Oberlin's theology. The only hint of dissent is in repeated references to the Hudson Congregational Church as the "Calvinistic Congregational Church"—which suggests that the Hudson abolitionists had begun to use the term "Calvinist" synonymously with "colonizationist." The document reflects an abolitionist commitment in several ways, the most obvious being the name, *"Free* Congregational Church of Hudson." "Free Church" members would hold a monthly anti-slavery prayer meeting, and stand firmly for the contention that "a great portion of the Church of nearly all denominations are withholding their testimony and influence against the Sin of Slavery and oppression." It would be their duty to call other Christians to "a right procedure" as "Christ's representatives on earth." They would "receive no one into our communion who is a slave holder or an advocate of slavery nor will we invite a Slave holding Minister or one who advocates the system of slavery to preach or officiate in our pulpit." Finally, the Free Church document strongly implied a post-millennial expectation, in speaking of the church's work in removing "all sin from the face of all the earth."

Having settled into a new building by 1843, the Free Church (also referred to as the "Oberlin church") stood in contrast to the Congregational Church in Hudson, but was by no means a satellite of Oberlin College. In August 1844, Owen resigned from the trustee board of the college. Although he left on good terms, his decision to step away from Oberlin probably reflected his disenchantment with Finney's theology,

This structure was originally the "Free Congregational Church" of Hudson, founded by Owen Brown and other abolitionists in 1842. The lower floor was added later. *Author's photograph, 2000.*

and his disappointment in the evangelical panacea prescribed by the Perfectionists in lieu of real political action.[4]

John Brown's name had never officially been removed from the membership roster of the Congregational Church in Hudson. Throughout his adventure in Pennsylvania and his involvement in other churches, he remained a member of the Hudson church from March 31, 1816 through September 1, 1842, after which his membership was transferred to the Richfield Congregational Church. Brown probably requested the transfer of his membership to underscore his dissatisfaction with the prejudiced Franklin Mills congregation, but it was likely also an act of solidarity with his father and the abolitionists of Hudson.

Other things were changing for John Brown too. In the spring of 1842, John Jr., nearly twenty-one years old, left Richfield, traveling on foot to study at the Grand River Institute at Austinburg, Ohio. He had already tried teaching in a country school in 1841, but found it frustrating and difficult to deal with what his father called "ill behaved, ill governed, snotty" children. Despite his father's encouragement, John Jr. left the teaching position after one year. Meanwhile, Brown was laboring to repay his debts, his expertise in the tannery and livestock proving a great boon to Heman Oviatt. Indeed, Oviatt's business grew almost beyond its capacity, as Brown also busied himself breeding and tending to Oviatt's flock until it gained local prominence. Typically, he worked long hours and late nights during "lambing season," which involved nursing newborns, even taking the lambs inside from the cold, rolling them in blankets near the fire, and feeding them warm milk. "In the morning there might be a half-dozen such wooly babies, staggering and skipping about the kitchen in the most comical manner," his son recalled. Brown was exhausted, but he loved this work, and liked to remind his family that the life of the shepherd was "favorable to religious meditation." Meanwhile, Brown was breeding cattle and sheep (he was fond of Saxony sheep and Devon cattle), and his reputation as a breeder of fine livestock began to spread in the region.

Brown was not only rebuilding his reputation and career, but gradually working off his debts and clearing away the clouds that overshadowed him for so long. Though great success in business would continue to elude him, Brown would never again suffer the personal losses and setbacks that he did in the late 1830s and early 1840s. Perhaps Providence would now be kind to him and his family. After all, he reasoned to himself, despite their hardships, misfortunes, and embarrassment, they had kept their faith, upheld the family's dignity, and worked hard without relenting. They had no reason to be ashamed. Before God, at least, they were like a "company of Belted Knights."[5] But someone else beside God had taken notice of John Brown's little company of belted knights and practical shepherds.

Sometime in late 1843 Brown was contacted by Simon Perkins Jr., a wealthy Akron magnate with land, industry, farms, and flocks. Perkins had heard about his expertise with the Oviatt flock and wanted to recruit him for his own interests in the wool industry. Salmon Brown remembered that Perkins had "in some way . . . caught the fine wool craze," and so wanted to enlist his father to advance his interests. Salmon may have been too young to recall that during the time of the Perkins-Brown partnership that ensued, the wealthy Akronite had entered into another partnership with four other leading citizens in opening a wool manufacturing operation. Five years after the Perkins-Brown partnership began, the Akron *Summit-Beacon* noted that the factory was "one of the best conducted establishments of the kind in this section of the country." Perkins inherited his land and wealth as the son of Akron's founder, and married

Grace Tod, whose brother David Tod served as the governor of Ohio during the Civil War. "This I think will be considered no mean alliance," Brown wrote to John Jr.

In January 1844, when the business aspects of the partnership were solidified, John Brown wrote to his namesake, explaining the arrangements. Perkins was to furnish all the feed and shelters for his flock of 1,500 sheep, and the two would share the rest of the expenses for maintenance. The older boys would continue working the Oviatt farm in Richfield "for pasturing," while Mary and the younger children would prepare to move to Akron. It is not clear if Oviatt pressed any requirements upon him, but it seems he was satisfied that Brown's contributions had reimbursed him for his losses; neither did Brown make mention of Perkins compensating Oviatt. With the help of the older boys, Brown was able to spread himself between Perkins and Oviatt during the transition, while taking over the management of the Perkins farm. Salmon also remembered that his father employed men for haying and harvesting on the farm. Brown was quite strict about employee conduct. If he heard any of his workers speaking with vulgarity or irreverence, he promptly drew their pay and fired them. As Perkins expected, the first year of the partnership went quite well, Brown himself taking home more than $1,500. In 1844, Perkins and Brown sheep earned gold medals at exhibitions in New York City and Boston, which won John Brown such acclaim in his home state and vicinity that he began to be called upon as a consultant, or to certify the quality of flocks and wool.

The family also benefited. Brown wrote happily to his son about the new living arrangements that awaited them in Akron. The family would move "into a verry [sic] good House belonging to Mr. Perkins . . . the most comfortable and the most favourable [sic] arrangement [sic] of my worldly concerns that I ever had, and calculated to afford us more leisure for improvement by day, and by night than any other." Remembering what they had undergone in recent years, Brown wanted to remain cautious about the windfall of blessing: "I do hope that God has enabled us to make it in mercy to us, and not that he should send leanness into our Souls." He also expressed the concern that his family would have the wisdom to "make the most of the arrangement," especially since Perkins had done a great favor for all of them—a "poor Bankrupt and his family." Perkins even knew about their foray against the traitorous Chamberlain which had landed them in the Akron jail. God had not overlooked them, and Perkins was firm about his commitment even knowing of "our poverty, and that times have passed over us."[6] Mary and the children moved into the simple two-room frame house on the Perkins estate in April 1844, which Brown rented for $30 a year. It was the temporary residence of Simon and Grace Perkins after they got married, while their impressive stone mansion was being constructed. The property, known at the time as Mutton Hill, was a country residence about a mile outside Akron, with grazing sheep and a charming view over the valley and the flats below.

Grace Perkins regularly spied on her new neighbors, but despite some passing disagreements, the Brown and Perkins families were awkward but friendly neighbors. But Grace Perkins was annoyed by the behavior of the younger Brown boys—invariably led by mischievous Salmon. The Browns were inveterate teasers who preyed on her children, and were capable of worse crimes. Once, Salmon, Oliver, and Watson raided Perkins' cherry orchard, but did not escape being seen by some female workers, who reported them. Seeking "suitable revenge," the boys decided to put some "cow-itch" (a root that is extremely irritating to the skin) in the outhouse, hoping the young ladies would contact it. Perkins was outraged when she learned of the prank, and brought accusation to Mary Brown, who deftly handed the boys over to their father. Probably because he was up to his eyes in wool, Brown only interviewed the boys—who denied knowing anything about the prank—and let them off without a whipping. This only reinforced Perkins' belief that Brown was responsible for his sons' "rebellious" nature. Believing the boys belonged in school instead of working with their father, Grace Perkins privately criticized Brown for letting his sons "grow up wild." A child of privilege herself, Perkins did not appreciate that Brown had not sent his sons off to school because he could not pay their tuition.

Perkins watched her neighbors critically, noting how "wild" the Brown children seemed, especially on Sunday evenings. Since the Browns were strict Sunday Sabbatarians, the children were generally kept indoors throughout the holy day. Even when the children were permitted to go outside on Sunday afternoon, they were watched closely lest they slip into play and break the Fourth Commandment. The Perkins children probably thought it unfortunate that Sarah Brown could only "pretend play" if she came outside on Sunday, though more often they would see her sitting quietly inside by the window, watching them play as she waited through the dismal restraints of the Sabbath. Salmon hated his father's "strict control and Sunday rules" too, and cut loose on Sunday evening at sundown. "We used to carry on pretty high," Salmon said. Anna Perkins remembered, too, that every Sunday at sunset the doors of the Brown house flew open and the children "came rushing out perfectly wild"—desperate for some fresh, fun-filled air.

Despite the prejudices of their reminiscences, the Perkinses did have an ongoing opportunity to make close observation of the Browns. Perkins's son George remembered Brown as always being "dressed as a gentleman—a *farmer* gentleman," taking great care as to appearance and personal cleanliness. Perhaps Brown was also typical of the pioneering gentlemen observed in that era by Alexis de Tocqueville, which he wrote about a decade earlier in *Democracy in America*: "He wears the dress and speaks the language of the cities; he is acquainted with the past, curious about the future, and ready for argument about the present. . . . [He] penetrates into the wilds of the New World with the Bible, an axe, and some newspapers." Yet if John Brown was a pioneer gentleman, he was also a Puritan, and his restrained lifestyle was not simply an expression of his anemic finances but also conservative values. Anna Perkins recalled that her mother and Mary Brown were assisted by a seamstress in making clothes for their children. The seamstress observed that Brown would not allow his children to wear any bright-colored clothes and, "were it possible, would have clothed the birds in the trees in black." In fact, Brown loathed any striking colors in apparel, especially in women's clothing. Probably the only one to violate his ban on red was a doll belonging to Sarah, for which she requested a piece of worsted scarlet cloth to make a little dress. Brown bought the knitted fabric for his daughter but not without showing displeasure. With a peculiar pun—his expression probably closer to a grimace than a smile, Brown told his daughter: "I have heard of *crewel*. I think *this* must be *murder*." His jokes were more cutting than cute, and Sarah agreed that this was generally true of her father. His sense of humor was usually harmless, but John Brown "was inclined to sarcasm." When displeased, his words could become "as sharp as his eyes," and "his displeasure expressed itself in cutting, terse sentences."

Grace Perkins observed something else about the Browns that disturbed her. From time to time, she and her children began to see black people about the Brown house, and eventually learned of Brown's efforts on behalf of fugitives. Though he may have been discrete about his underground railroad work, Brown probably never concealed his sentiments, and his anti-slavery opinions were no secret in Akron. The Perkins family were uncomfortable with blacks coming and going in the night, and it seemed unconscionable to Grace Perkins that Brown would give so much time and attention to fugitive slaves and other blacks while neglecting the proper training of his sons. "He did not send them to school nor look after their rearing and education," her daughter recalled, "yet was always concerning himself with Negroes, after having several hidden at once above his place." A woman like Grace Perkins could never understand John Brown's values and convictions, let alone the family's united commitment to help bring about the destruction of slavery. As "wild" as Salmon and his brothers could be, they were being schooled for a work that the Perkinses would never understand, not even after it was accomplished. "The tannery business, farming, wool buying and the raising of blooded stock were my father's life occupations," Salmon said. "Though all of them were subordinated to his one consuming passion— freeing the slaves."[7]

Brown had no need to worry about what Grace Perkins thought as long as her husband was well pleased with his work. After the Civil War, Simon Perkins was highly sensitive regarding his former business partnership with Brown, probably because he feared being associated politically with the controversial Harper's Ferry raid and his "extreme" views on black equality. In later years Perkins displayed cynicism regarding Brown, probably in self-defense (such as his tendency to diminish John Brown's style as a shepherd), and this resentment seems to have informed his children's cynical recollections. Perkins was generally truthful about Brown's hard-headed ways and his business failures, though he made sure to tell his interviewer that he classed his old partner among "the biggest set of fools in the world" with regard to the raid on Harper's Ferry. Yet, over thirty years after their association, Simon Perkins remembered John Brown's excellent abilities as a judge of wool, saying also that he had an unusual knowledge of the flock, to the point that he could "distinguish every sheep from every other." Brown believed that sheep "looked about as much alike as men do," the grumpy Perkins concluded. Salmon Brown agreed: "Father was a natural stockman. To most people all sheep look alike, but to Father each sheep had as marked an individuality as the human race." Salmon claimed that if sheep from another flock became mixed with his band, such as might happen when going to market, his father "could instantly pick out his own." But as Brown was getting to know sheep, he was also getting to know sheep farmers.

As an expert whose opinion and advice were increasingly in demand from sheep men, John Brown began to travel around to observe various herds and farms. His many years of interest in livestock and his more recent obligations to Oviatt and Perkins had made him a specialist. "The flock of Mr. Wm. or Samuel Brownlee exceeds any other that I have seen in [Washington] County," Brown declared in a document in 1844. In late 1845, his recommendations were even more reflective of how he was flexing the muscles of his expertise, with references to having "spent much of my life in the examination and care of sheep; [(] and haveing [*sic*] traveled Tens of Thousands of miles in the search after the best flocks)." If the so-called experts, he declared, would only use "a little plain common sence [*sic*]," they would begin to pay attention to the fine flocks of Northern Ohio. John Brown had his own opinions about fine sheep and wool, just as he had about abolition.

As his travels increased from one section of the country to another, "sometimes with team and light wagon, at other times with teams and heavily loaded wagon bearing wool, he became acquainted with thousands of people." In the first years of the Perkins and Brown partnership, he came to know many sheep men across the Western Reserve in Ohio, in the Northern panhandle of western Virginia, and western Pennsylvania. As he traveled, he might notice a flock, stop in to meet the owner, and perhaps even become a guest for dinner. Invariably Brown scouted for fine sheep and wool for Perkins, while also studying the wool market from the standpoint of the growers. Sometimes these visits involved times of prayer and Christian fellowship, and even lead to invitations to speak in churches.

This period of growth and exploration opened up new interests and concerns to him. Based on his personal survey of the wool farmers in the tri-state area, he observed that the wool growers did not properly prepare their wool to get the best prices on the market. He also came to the conclusion that even well-prepared wools "were at the mercy of itinerant buyers and representatives of the eastern manufacturers." If the eastern markets were not interested, the farmers had no recourse—which inevitably meant the market controlled the prices. One of these wool manufacturers had extensive dealings with Perkins and Brown and was quite favorable toward Brown's work with sheep and fine wools. Indeed, the manufacturer, Samuel Lawrence of Lowell, Massachusetts, wrote an exuberant letter to Simon Perkins in 1844, in which he praised the Perkins and Brown sheep and wools. Brown himself probably passed the same letter to the editor of a new agricultural journal, the *Ohio Cultivator*, who published it in 1846:

Mr. Brown's wool has ever been of the highest character . . . but this year it has amazed us. . . . The show in our wool house, of this parcel of wool, I never saw equaled. I have said to Mr. Brown, what I sincerely believe, that if he will go on a few years more, he will have a better breed of sheep than are now in existence.

Though Perkins and Brown could wear such praise like a feather in the cap, Brown was beginning to think of Samuel Lawrence in a different light. There was much for him to do in order to advance the product and the cause of the wool men, though he would inevitably alienate the manufacturers in the process.[8]

# 11

## "We Are Tossing Up and Down"

... and wheat and beasts, and sheep, and horses, and chariots, and slaves, and souls of men.

—Revelation 18:13

For one who believed in the depravity of man, John Brown seemed a bit naïve in his first effort to resolve the problem of reforming the wool industry. Perhaps because his own interaction with wool manufacturers had been so positive, Brown mistook their appreciation of his fine wool for a willingness to cooperate for the greater good of wool men. Using the network of wool growers he had cultivated in his work with Perkins, he convened a meeting of wool growers at the office of the Middlesex Company in Lowell, Massachusetts on July 1, 1846. With the reins of the meeting in the hands of the hosting wool manufacturer, it is no surprise that nothing pertaining to reform in the wool industry was accomplished. Brown did not help the cause, instead getting caught up in a debate among the wool men in defending the superiority of Saxony sheep. Lawrence and other wool manufacturers were probably pleased with the distraction the debate provided, for nothing else was accomplished. In fact, the wool manufacturers must have chuckled when they read in the Lowell *Journal* that Lawrence was asked to be the judge in a contest between the wool growers. However, Brown's ability to rally wool men from eight different states suggests he had become an influential figure, a fact that even the manufacturers could not have missed. Furthermore, with new journals like the *Ohio Cultivator* conveying the activities and ideas of wool men in the mid-1840s, farmers had begun to see themselves in a unified manner, something inconvenient to the wool manufacturers.

Brown was clearly prone to involve himself in other kinds of activity when he felt it necessary to promote economic and political equity. He had been a nuisance to a Pennsylvania land company in the late 1820s by involving himself in the case of some settlers evicted from their claims in Erie and Crawford counties. Believing them to have been wronged, Brown tried to organize them to resist eviction. How he got involved in the case is unclear, but officials viewed him as "evil and unprincipled" because of his aggressive organizing efforts. Now he had uncovered another inequity, this time in the case of the wool farmers. On the other hand, Brown did not spare criticism of those he supported either. He felt that wool men undermined their own cause by sloppy and disingenuous methods, and insisted that the reputation of American wools was diminished by the deplorable condition in which they were delivered to manufacturers in the United States and abroad.

Brown's leadership in reform is evident in a convention of wool men in Steubenville, Ohio, facilitated by Perkins and Brown in February 1847. Announcing the meeting in the *Ohio Cultivator*, he promised that attendees would be informed as to "the best manner of preparing wool for the market" as well as "the state of manufacturing in the country generally, and the machinery *by which prices are manufactured yearly."* This time, Brown concluded, there would be no self-defeating "*Saxony or Merino disputes to settle."*[1]

By this time, Perkins and Brown had already established a presence in Springfield, Massachusetts, representing the wool growers in the manufacturers' region. Input from New England and from western wool men made for a different convention, and Brown himself enjoyed a platform to lecture his colleagues, especially on the necessity of preparing their product with integrity and care.

Brown used the *Ohio Cultivator* to provide advice and information to sheep farmers, such as his successful research in treating sheep infested with maggots, also known as "Bots" or "Grubs." He found that when these pests infested the membranes of the head and eyes of sheep, a tobacco water remedy was quite successful in both relieving and preventing infestation. During these experiments, he promised his younger sons ten cents for every fly they caught amidst the flock. But instead of paying Salmon and his brothers for their catch, Brown decided to "invest" their pay in Christian literature. He presented ten-year-old Salmon with a copy of Doddridge's *Rise and Progress of Religion in the Soul,* and another son with Baxter's *Saints' Everlasting Rest.* As an elderly man, Salmon recalled that his "father was looking toward the ultimate good, as he saw it, of his children, thinking what he cared for they must of necessity be made to care for, because it represented the highest and best he knew."

Brown had also provided the sheep farmers a detailed procedure for the vigorous washing of the sheep prior to shearing, likewise published in the *Ohio Cultivator*. At the Steubenville convention, he not only reiterated his method of washing sheep, but chided farmers for not removing burrs from the wool, and otherwise neglecting to properly prepare wools for market. Some farmers had even used dishonest methods, Brown said. "Our farmers generally have no idea of the injury they suffer by the neglect of these matters." He lectured to the farmers that if the wool growers took care of their product the way other farmers treated their products, the interest of the European market would work to their advantage. Instead, their "slovenly, dishonest habits" deprived them of foreign competition, leaving them "entirely at the mercy of our large manufacturing companies—bodies without souls." Finally, the convention voted to consider organizing themselves, and to support wool depots acting in their interest.[2]

Throughout his wool travels John Brown never forgot his vow against slavery. Though his time and attention were absorbed by his work with Perkins and his zealous efforts on behalf of the sheep farmers, his vehemence toward slavery was actually increasing during these years. He was a member of the Richfield Congregational Church but had no real presence there after the mid-1840s. As Boyd Stutler noted, Brown "left the Congregational Church in the 1840s and for the rest of his life was, apparently, without church ties of any character but without 'backsliding' or losing any part of his deep and abiding Christian faith." By the time of his involvement with Perkins, he was clearly beginning to refine his religious interests to exclude Christians and Christian churches that were not patently anti-slavery. Consequently, Brown leaned more heavily on family worship, relationships with other Christians, visitation at various evangelical churches and revival meetings, and certainly his own biblical study and readings in the Reformed tradition. He continued to read and advance books like the popular *Pilgrim's Progress* by John Bunyon, the sermons and writings of Puritan theologians like Jonathan Edwards, and his perennial favorites, Baxter's *Saints' Everlasting Rest* and Doddridge's *Rise and Progress of Religion in the Soul*. One can imagine John Brown's impassioned blue eyes, intent and focused, as Doddridge's words touched the depths of a soul burdened for the slave:

He is a barbarian, and deserves not to be called a man, who can look upon the sorrows of his fellow-creatures without drawing out his soul unto them, and wishing, at least, that it were in the power of his hand to help them. Surely earth would be a heaven to that man who could go about from place to place scattering happiness wheresoever he came, though it were only the body that he were capable of relieving, and though he could impart nothing better than the happiness of a mortal life.

The early church had its apostles who could heal the sick and give sight to the blind, but "in every age . . . there still are those whom [God] has condescended to make his instruments in conveying nobler and more lasting blessings than these to their fellow-creatures." Doddridge was primarily referring to preachers of the Gospel, but the lesson of chosen instruments could not have been lost on Brown, who pored over the pages of *Rise and Progress of Religion* time and time again. He understood the biblical doctrine of Providence to allow for the Sovereign God to raise up mortal instruments of his purpose, and he would like nothing more than to "go about place to place scattering happiness," especially among his downcast black brethren.

"He was a red hot abolitionist and we were radical antislavery and this gave us additional interest in each other," wrote James Ladd, a wool grower in Richmond, Ohio. Ladd had met Brown when he came into the area on behalf of Perkins in 1845–46, speaking to shepherd families about starting a wool depot. Brown got to know Ladd, a Quaker, and his associate, Elisha Cook, another Quaker abolitionist. "For some years thereafter he was frequently at our house and we at his," Ladd wrote. Cook's wife found Brown laughably odd at times, as did his own sons. "Father had a peculiarity of insisting on *order*," Salmon Brown remembered. "He was [finicky] about all matters connected with his own methods and had a horror of departing from the *order* that he fixed in his own mind." The boys sometimes played jokes to exploit this, like asking people to help their father pack his goods. "It was a family joke . . . to see how it stirred him up." Cook's wife probably also got a kick out of Brown's sons teasing him with nicknames like "Old Defiance."

His Quaker associates did not think his excitable hatred of slavery was peculiar, though they differed with him as to method. Ladd recalled one of many conversations with Brown about slavery, during which they differed regarding the use of force. "Well, Benjamin, you Quakers are admirable in many ways and your theory of resisting evil by doing good is a beautiful one," Brown said in sincerity. "But I believe in fighting the devil with fire, trusting in God, and keeping the powder dry." Ladd also recalled an incident that took place when an associate went with Brown to Buffalo, New York, on sheep business. While they were unloading, a "big, burly Irish drayman" drove his horse and low cart almost into the sheep, and Brown "sprang to the horse's head and jerked him back so suddenly that it threw the driver onto the dray." As he continued to pull the horse backward, the driver grabbed his whip and came toward him. Brown shouted, "Stop! Don't you take another step." The man halted and Brown commanded, "Now go back; get on your dray and go about your business. If you had struck me, you would have got so badly hurt you would not have been able to do any business for some time."[3]

An important abolitionist he came to know at this time was Alexander Campbell of Bethany, [West] Virginia. Campbell was a wool man too, and he and Brown established a rapport based on wool and anti-slavery. Campbell served as chairman of the Steubenville convention in 1847, making the convocation that much more impressive since he was well on his way as a significant figure on the landscape of American religion. Of Scot-Irish background, Campbell came to the United States in 1810 to join his father, Thomas Campbell, who had already established an association of churches in Ohio and Kentucky. Nicknamed the "Campbellites," his followers preferred to call themselves "Disciples," reflecting their belief that the church needed to return to primitive unity and doctrinal simplicity. Campbell became a prominent preacher and a writer, especially known for his 1835 publication, *The Christian System*. Brown differed with him on certain theological points, though he would probably have applauded Campbell's debates against secularists and Roman Catholics, and likewise appreciated his avoidance of revivalistic extremes. Furthermore, Brown was becoming more flexible in his relationships across denominational lines, probably because of his growing conviction that anti-slavery conviction was integral to orthodoxy.

In March and April 1846, the Perkins and Brown operation at Springfield, Massachusetts was officially unveiled in the *Ohio Cultivator*, and in a special circular prepared by Brown for "Wool Growers." The announcement stated that the Perkins and Brown wool commission house (P&B) had been formed in order to "class the fleeces into the different grades," to "offer it to the different manufacturers and purchasers for exportation," and to enable wool growers "the advantage which the quality and condition of their wool deserve." P&B offered its clients wool storage for a maximum of six months, and charged them two cents per pound to cover sorting and sales fees. The firm required wool growers to submit wool properly cleaned and tied, and would pay the shipping fee on receipt of the wool. P&B's ad reminded prospective clients that their Springfield operation would provide them a "central place of deposit" where their wool could be stored without great expense while a market was sought on their behalf. "Our location will be one of the most central and convenient for that purpose in New England."[4]

John Brown had ventured into deep waters. Though boasting in the press that he had "traveled many thousand miles, spending from one to four months at a time, in examining flocks, visiting factories, and large wool dealers," Brown was not a skilled businessman, especially not the type to lead a sales commission operation like P&B. It was not merely that he lacked a business head, but that he was obstinate and invariably refused counsel from any direction. Simon Perkins later said that his partner "was solicitous to go into the business of selling wool, and I allowed him to do it; but he had little judgment, always followed his own will, and lost much money." Brown was not like his father Owen, whom Perkins said "had more judgment and less will." Yet Perkins had the money and the final word, and in the 1840s he was actually more inclined to follow Brown's lead than he admitted in retrospect. In March 1846, Brown reported to John Jr. that Perkins was "full in the faith of our plan, having completed our arrangements," clearly referring to the P&B enterprise. Despite the first rising wave of difficulties, the wealthy partner still gave Brown a nod of approval. Writing to Perkins in December 1846, Brown declared: "Nothing could be more grateful to my feelings after the anxiety I have experienced in managing the business of our customers, than to learn from you that you do not disapprove of the course I have taken to relieve them."

Neither should we assume that Perkins, though wealthy, was necessarily the most adroit merchant. Because Brown has been so harshly judged by historians as being a poor businessman, Perkins should not be exempt from sharing in the eventual failure of P&B. Indeed, Perkins did far worse for himself later on, when he lost a great deal of money investing in an unsuccessful railroad enterprise. On the other hand, Brown's inability to navigate the depths of his challenge to the wool manufacturers cannot be overlooked. "Whether he knew it or not, Brown was facing conditions and forces that he was ill-prepared to meet; his was a job of tact and diplomacy to bring the producers and consumers together to raise quality and price." But the Practical Shepherd was no politician,

The Practical Shepherd. Perhaps the earliest photograph of John Brown, made around the time he came
to Springfield in 1846 to lead the firm of Perkins &
Brown. *West Virginia State Archives.*

nor was he skilled enough to counter the inevitable machinations of the
manufacturers, who played some part in the eventual failure of P&B.[5]

When P&B was opened in Springfield in June 1846, Brown, his sons
Jason and John Jr., and his hired men went about sorting, grading, and
setting prices for the wools. Brown "made his gradings, fixed his prices—
and that was it; the buyer could take the wool or leave it." In 1846,
P&B's initial year of operation, their clients did well. But even though
wool growers were eager to enjoy profits from P&B's fixed prices, they
were not prepared to act in an organized, cooperative fashion to check
the manufacturers. Because a surplus in wool existed the following year,

sales declined and P&B's operation slowed down too. Despite the principled war that P&B was waging on their behalf against the dominant manufacturers, their clients began to clamor for payment. "Their calls are incessant," a frustrated Brown wrote to Perkins, "and how to avoid sacrificeing [*sic*] their wool, and yet relieve them, calls for all the tact I am master of." But he was intent on selling the wools at the prices he had fixed, and despite the cries for some return on their product, he told Perkins, he would seek other routes to "help the wool growers without putting down any of our prices."[6]

Though Brown evidently lacked the flexibility needed to steer P&B through rough waters, the lack of organization among the wool men proved a serious detriment to the efforts of the firm. Making frequent trips to the sheep farms of his clients, Brown tried to get them to see the need to organize while promising sales or offering advances from whatever he could obtain from bank loans. But it was all he could do to get the wool men to understand that what was at stake was about more than fast returns on fixed prices. "No sacrifice kneed [*sic*] be made," he wrote, "the only thing wanted is to get the broad shouldered, and hard handed farmers to understand how they have been imposed upon, and the whole matter will be cured effectually."

Over the next year or two P&B would have its ups and downs, but with each wave of difficulty the firm was pulled deeper into debt—Brown finding it increasingly difficult to stay afloat. In April 1847, he wrote a somewhat defensive letter to his seventy-six-year-old father. Apparently Owen Brown had written his son a spiritually minded letter about the fleeting days of life and the vanity of wealth. The son wrote back that he "felt unconcious [*sic*] of a desire to become rich," and hoped that "my motive for exerting myself is higher." He felt no inclination, he wrote, "to move my family to Springfield on account of any change that I am itching for." His only reason for moving Mary and the children to Massachusetts would be to have them with him.

John Brown deeply missed his wife and children, and was still grieving over the tragic death of their one-year-old daughter, Amelia (nicknamed "Kitty") in late October 1846. He had gotten the bad news from Akron in two shocking letters, from Simon Perkins and his son Owen, informing him that his seventeen-year-old daughter Ruth had accidentally scalded little Amelia in a household accident. Brown felt dumbstruck and helpless, being hundreds of miles away and unable to leave the business to attend his grieving wife and family. "One more dear little feeble child I am to meet no more till the dead small and great shall stand before God," he wrote to Mary.

> This is a bitter cup indeed, but blessed be God: a brighter day shall dawn; and let us not sorrow as those that have no hope. Oh that we that remain, had wisdom wisely to consider; and to keep in view our latter end. Divine Providence seems to lay a heavy burden; and responsibility on you *my dear Mary*; but I trust you will be enabled to bear it in some measure as you ought.

He urged the family not "to cast an unreasonable blame on my dear Ruth on account of the dreadful trial we are called [to] suffer," pointing out how they all had made mistakes, and if they were without "fatal consequences it is no thanks to us." Rather, "this dreadful, afflicted Providence" might remind them all of how even the smallest action or word might have "vast results for good, or for evil."

In another letter written several weeks later, Brown expressed his deep longing to see his family, and could only imagine being with Mary to mourn and comfort her in the wake of "Kitty's" death.

> I feel assured that notwithstanding God has chastised us *often, and sore*; yet he has not himself entirely withdrawn from us, nor forsaken us *utterly*. The sudden, and dreadful manner in which he has seen fit to call *our dear little Kitty* to take her leave of us, is I kneed [*sic*] not tell you how much on my mind; but before *Him*; I will bow my head in submission, and hold my peace.

For nearly fifty years, Brown wrote, he had "sailed over a somewhat stormy sea," his experiences teaching him that the best thing to do was to brace himself for the storm. "Mary let us try to maintain a cheerful self command while we are tossing up and down," Brown concluded, "and let our motto still be Action, Action; as we have but one life to live."

If he thought of himself as a storm-tossed soul, braced for even worse tempests in the Providence of God, he was probably also speaking out of a deep dissatisfaction welling up within. In a letter to his father in Ohio, Brown said he was constrained to stay in Springfield, but if he could return to his family the following day, he would "feel like one out of prison." P&B had promised so much, but now he felt like a prisoner locked in a cell or a captive in the hull of a storm-tossed ship.

> When I think how very little influence I have even tried to use with my numerous acquaintances and friends, in turning their minds toward God and heaven, I feel justly condemned as a most wicked and slothful servant; and the more so, as I have very seldom had any one refuse to listen when I earnestly called him to hear. I sometimes have dreadful reflections about having fled to go down to Tarshish.[7]

What message was John Brown sending to his discerning father? Was he expressing regret that his pursuits in business had left little time for evangelical service? Was he lamenting his failed plans for ministry so many years before? His reference to "having fled to go down to Tarshish" pertained to the biblical story of the prophet Jonah, who fled from God's command to preach to the Gentiles of Nineveh. Instead, Jonah chose to hide himself on a boat going the opposite direction, to the ancient trading center of Tarshish. But God did not permit Jonah to evade his calling. The little ship in which he traveled was tossed in a terrible storm, and the sailors cried out to their gods until they realized that Jonah's disobedience had put them in peril. Their only recourse was to throw him into the sea, after which the prophet was swallowed by a great fish that held him captive in its belly until finally vomiting him back onto dry land. Jonah thereafter obeyed God and became a great revival leader in the pagan city of Nineveh.

Apparently Brown feared that he had turned out to be a kind of Jonah, fleeing his real calling by going in the wrong direction—a stowaway on a trading ship instead of a servant of God in a wicked land. Perhaps he wondered whether the crashing of Providential waves against P&B's weakening hull was God's way of arresting him and setting him on the right course. Had God called John Brown to tend to beasts or the souls of men—to sell fine wool or liberate slaves? The longer he remained in Springfield, the more the answer became as obvious to him as it was irresistible.

# 12

# The Practical Shepherd in Springfield

Verily I say unto you, Inasmuch as ye did it not to one of the least of these, ye did it not to me.

—Matthew 25:45

When John Brown moved to Springfield in 1846, it was a traditional community on the brink of change. The established social order was not yet challenged by the influx of immigrants and minorities, and many features like traditional celebrations and volunteer fire companies suggested an older Springfield. But there was a new Springfield too, the commercial center of Hampden County connected by railroad to cities like Boston, Albany, and Hartford. The population was rapidly increasing, including Irish and French Canadians, both Roman Catholic groups. The small free black community was also a new presence, largely centered in two neighborhoods in the hill area known as "Hayti" and "Jamaica." With the opening of the Hartford-Springfield railroad, the black community began to grow as well, and in Brown's era only about a tenth of Springfield's blacks were fugitives from slavery. Some blacks also settled downtown to be closer to their work; not long afterward the first African American church in Springfield, the Zion Methodist Church, was established downtown on Sanford Street.

It was not uncommon for Springfield's business leaders to be of out-of-town people, like John Brown, who blended in with older families in the community. The Congregationalists had an established presence under the leadership of the Reverend Samuel Osgood, pastor of the First Congregational Church for nearly forty years by the time Brown arrived. There were also Baptist and Methodist churches in the hill area of Springfield, where many armory workers lived. A significant feature of the

Springfield community was the presence of a U.S. armory—the only other government armory in the country apart from the one in Harper's Ferry, Virginia.

According to Frederick Douglass, who visited Springfield periodically in his abolitionist efforts, the armory's military influence was strong in the community—too strong for the nonresistant abolitionist philosophy to overcome. His experiences in Springfield were dismal and unrewarding, bringing "little satisfaction to myself or advantage to the cause." Douglass believed the military industry and the white evangelicals in Springfield promoted a spirit of conservative indifference toward slavery. "I am told that of all the churches in this town, there is not one that says aught against the 'Arsenal,'" he wrote in *The North Star* in 1848. But Douglass, who fought in self-defense against racists in Indiana several years before, was playing to the crowd. Springfield's indifference to abolition had nothing to do with the armory, nor was embracing pacifism a prerequisite to abolitionist belief. Typical of the North, most whites simply had no concern for black liberation until opposition to the spread of slavery (read: keeping the black presence from spreading) became commonplace in the 1850s. Springfield only had a small but active number of citizens who engaged in anti-slavery efforts. Otherwise, the community was a "curious blend of aristocracy and egalitarianism" that paid little attention to abolitionist concerns.[1]

John Brown was never a predominant leader in Springfield's circle of abolitionists. The underground railroad was already operative there before his arrival, though it was not extensive in western Massachusetts. Fugitives generally came up through Connecticut using the Connecticut River as a concourse, and then proceeded on land to Massachusetts. Brown soon became acquainted with the leading underground railroad station operators, especially the influential Congregational minister Samuel Osgood. Osgood's influence was so beneficial that some fugitives even chose to remain in Springfield. One such fugitive was William Green, who made a harrowing escape from Maryland, finally reaching Osgood's house in Springfield. Green remained in town, opened a barber shop, became involved in the first black church in Springfield, and was later an associate of John Brown. Some other prominent abolitionists were Jefferson Church (a renowned physician and friend of Brown), George H. White (a dentist), Rufus Elmer (a local shoe store owner and spiritualist), John Holland, and John Woods. Other important figures in Springfield's underground railroad effort were the Chapin brothers,

Ethan and Marvin, who owned the *Massasoit House*, a fine hotel that was also used for underground railroad activities. Last but not least were Jeremy and Phoebe Werriner, who kept the *United States Hotel*, known also as "Uncle Jerry Werriner's Tavern." Werriner employed blacks who also assisted in sequestering fugitives. Brown established a friendly rapport with these white abolitionists of Springfield.

He initially attended the First Congregational Church where Osgood was pastor, and was "greatly esteemed" by the abolitionist minister. However, Brown apparently refrained from joining the church, probably because he was already intent on maintaining an independence that allowed him flexibility in church associations and anti-slavery activity. Similarly, although Brown participated in underground railroad work, he endeavored to establish an operation that bore *his* unique signature and values instead of the pacifist abolition movement. He "stood aside from the organized railroad he found in Springfield" because of his growing sense of identification with black people. This is not to discount the passionate devotion of men like Osgood, who was known to fill his home with fugitive guests. But the Springfield years marked a time when John Brown "came to know blacks in a more personal way and in a more sustaining relationship" that not only benefited the African American community but influenced his evolving militancy in a manner uncommon to most white abolitionists.

Brown first came to know blacks in Springfield by hiring them at P&B when he moved the company into the larger Chapin facility on North Main Street. His first abolition associates were white merchants like George Graves, who was employed in a nearby hardware store. Graves recalled Brown as "a man of one idea," incapable of attending to more than one thing at a time. "If the negro had his attention it was negro for the time and nothing else." Brown's frugality was admirable, Graves said, but he lacked business discipline and ability, which is why he often had to submit his books to the bank for auditing. As an abolitionist, Brown was "but one of a party," though he quickly assumed a leading place among those assisting fugitives. Graves remembered him—always known for repeating pithy sayings and Bible verses—often repeating a favorite slogan: "Not one cent for purchasing a slave, but millions for abetting escapes."

Almost from the beginning of his time in Springfield, John Brown's interest in the P&B endeavor began to decline, largely because his passion for social action and anti-slavery efforts were developing beyond his earlier, conservative style. Although prejudiced, one Springfield writer noted that Brown's "hobby had grown upon him so that during the years he resided here it had reached a passion, if not a mania." The political situation regarding slavery was intensifying in the 1840s, while at the same time Brown was living within an evolving urban center with a small but increasingly politicized black community. The surviving records of P&B document the difficulties of the firm, and his failure to manage it properly. But P&B also declined because Brown was increasingly distracted and drawn down new paths of interaction and activity in abolition. Salmon Brown may have been exaggerating when he said that P&B was "sacrificed on the altar of freedom for the black man," but there was a slender truth in the claim.[2]

Brown's most famous local contact was Thomas Thomas, later a friend of Abraham Lincoln and a popular restauranteur in Springfield. They met after Jason Brown encouraged Thomas to come to the P&B office for an interview with his father. After he was hired as a porter, Thomas asked Brown what time he should report for work. Brown told him that work began at 7:00 A.M., but that he should come in earlier to talk. Thomas came at 5:30 A.M. and Brown began to unfold his plan to liberate slaves, asking Thomas to join him in the effort. Eventually, P&B's "downstairs, low-ceilinged office" became the place where Thomas and other black employees regularly engaged in anti-slavery conversations, early in the morning prior to work or "into the night after work was over." But Brown's passionate interest in abolition began to consume his attention, so much so that his bookkeeper remembered him and his sons talking "on the slavery question by the hour, in the counting room of the wool depot." The bookkeeper also remembered Brown saying that it was right for slaves to kill their masters and escape.[3]

Though enslaved from the time of his birth in 1817, Thomas Thomas did not arrive in Springfield as a fugitive. Born in Oxford, Maryland, he was able to purchase his freedom, afterward making money by speculating in provisions. Coming east to join family members in Springfield, Thomas became involved in the Zion Methodist Church, a black congregation with a new building in Springfield. The Zion Methodist Church also became known as the "Free Church" because of its strong anti-slavery sentiment. Zion Methodist was founded in 1844, only two years before Brown arrived in Springfield, with the assistance of the Pynchon Street Church, a breakaway from the white Methodist Church. However, most African Americans preferred the Free Church, which quickly became a religious, cultural, and political center in the black community.

Zion Methodist "created opportunity for black leadership and created a forum for the free exchange of ideas among blacks in Springfield while also serving as a rallying point for anti-slavery activity." Jason Brown may have first been attracted to the Free Church because its name was reminiscent of his grandfather's "Free Congregational Church" back in Hudson. Once John Brown came to know Thomas and other Free Church members, he switched from the Congregational Church to Zion Methodist.[4]

Brown's attendance at the Free Church became so frequent that some think he may have become a member. Certainly, Brown felt at home at Zion Methodist and was accepted by the congregation—sometimes he was even asked to preach. "He was not a great orator, his voice being high-pitched and his delivery nervous and irregular," one writer concluded. "But his heart and soul were in what he said." He became known for his religious sincerity and his political devotion to the anti-slavery cause. Indeed, Brown became "independent and so ready to express his views at any and all times that he made many enemies, especially among the more conservative citizens, or those who openly disagreed with him on the subject of slavery." Nor did he show concern for what whites might say about his involvement in a black church. "No other white face was seen in the congregation, but he took a stern pride in lending his presence to the cause which he had espoused." He also took a strong interest in the welfare of the black community and their fugitive brethren residing in Springfield. "John Brown and his family became known for their extraordinary concern and generosity," Thomas remembered. "The Brown boys often could be seen carrying things to families that Brown knew were in need."

He was also known as a quiet, modest man "of strict integrity and honorable purposes" in Springfield. However, some considered him peculiar, especially when he was stubborn to his own detriment. Brown once challenged a hypnotist in a Springfield theater, openly accusing him of fraud after he appeared to have rendered a young woman insensitive to pain. As a challenge, he subjected himself to the same tests, having his skin rubbed with cowhage (the irritating plant also referred to as "cow itch") and ammonia thrust under his nose. Brown suffered while the young woman under hypnosis felt no discomfort. Afterward, he probably found it even more painful to have to admit to the hypnotist that he had been wrong. Apparently convinced of the power of the mind, Brown later came out of his house in the dead of winter, "clad in short trousers and with shirt open at the neck." Seeing him so underdressed, a neighbor warned that he could freeze to death. Brown replied assuredly, "Freeze to death, no. Keeping warm is a mere act of the will." According to a cashier at Springfield's Agwam Bank, he displayed a peculiar stubbornness when P&B was paid a draft for $2,500. Even though the draft was cleared, Brown did not want to sign it, probably remembering the tribulations he experienced back in Ohio after endorsing bank notes. No matter how much the bank's officers pleaded with him, he "could not be induced to do it, in spite of a two-hours' argument." The bank draft had to be returned, rewritten, and sent to the bank president, who then endorsed it for P&B.[5]

In early 1848, Watson Brown, now about thirteen-years-old, wrote to his grandfather Owen in Hudson that Springfield was a "very busy, stiring [sic] place and very pleasant," though he preferred Ohio. He and Salmon were not attending school that winter, he wrote, because they were helping their mother at home by cutting wood and doing other chores. Jason had returned to Ohio in 1847 to carry on the work at the Perkins farm with his brother Owen. John Jr., who had also returned to Ohio, married a young woman of abolitionist sympathies named Wealthy Hotchkiss and then returned to Springfield to assist his father. When John Brown brought Mary and the children to live with him, they finally settled into a house on Hastings Street. Located near Armory Hill, Hastings Street had only a few houses. John Jr. recalled the home was located on a "mean street," and that "not an unnecessary penny was spent, except for education"—referring to the fact that eighteen-year-old Ruth was now studying at the Grand River Institute in Ohio. "But that bare old house, sparsely furnished, was saturated with religious feeling, like the home of a Puritan family." Actually, the house was fairly new when the Browns moved in, and it was a nice structure though modest. The front was ornamented with a piazza supported by four fluted columns, with a one-story addition connected to a small shed in the rear that could be used to sequester fugitives or thrash a bad boy.

Frederick Douglass had a similar recollection of John Brown's home. Douglass met with Brown on February 1, 1848, after speaking at Town Hall in Springfield. When Douglass saw him, it was "during the course of some casual remarks to a group of colored men," especially abolitionists Thomas Van Rennselaer, a New York restaurant owner, and Augustus Washington, a teacher and photographer from Hartford. When he returned to town later that year, he was invited to the Browns for dinner.

Douglass remembered his surprise at finding that his host lived in modest circumstances. "It was a small wooden building, on a back street, in a neighborhood chiefly occupied by laboring men and mechanics." The house on Hastings Street was plain but not poor—"no disguises, no illusions, no make believes. Everything implied stern truth, solid purpose, and rigid economy," Douglass wrote. The Brown household was striking for its simplicity as well as its godliness. "Certainly I never felt myself in the presence of a stronger religious influence than while in this man's house," Douglass recalled.

According to Douglass, after a hearty but simple dinner Brown began to unfold his plan for a raid into the South. He countered every objection from Douglass, and pointed out that the "simple manner" in which he and his family lived was an economic expedient to save money for his plan. Even the dinner table, Douglass wrote, had neither finish nor tablecloth—though one of Brown's daughters later questioned Douglass's testimony. If there was a Spartan appearance in the home, it was also because P&B was not doing well and the Browns were paying for Ruth's schooling in Ohio. Furthermore, they were simply not given to style and "ostentatious display." Like his father Owen, John Brown shunned expensive and bright-colored clothing, and eschewed jewelry and other lavish accouterments of fashion. Money was only useful to provide essentials, finance the spread of the Gospel, and come to the aid of the needy and the oppressed. Whatever one spent otherwise should beautify the mind and the soul—like Puritan devotionals and subscriptions to abolitionist newspapers. Brown held an inflexible standard in this regard and believed it applied to all people, especially those locked in the struggle for liberation.[6]

Brown's association with Augustus Washington in Springfield is significant. Primarily an educator, Washington made a living from an early form of photography named for the French inventor, Louis Jacques Daguerre, in which images were made on light-sensitive silver-coated metallic plates. At sixteen, Washington had organized a black school for children in Trenton, New Jersey, and later taught at black schools in Brooklyn, New York, and Hartford, Connecticut. His pursuit of further education was always overshadowed by financial hardship, which interrupted his studies at the Oneida Institute in New York and Dartmouth College in New Hampshire. Washington eventually left teaching to open a daguerreotype studio, and probably visited various black communities for business and political reasons. Brown may have been introduced to Washington by

Brown posed with the "Subterranean Pass Way" banner for black photographer Augustus Washington (ca. 1848). *West Virginia State Archives.*

Thomas Thomas, with whom he posed in a daguerreotype. The picture (described by writers though unfortunately lost to history) featured the two in a brotherly pose, Brown's hand resting on Thomas's shoulder, while the latter held a small banner bearing the letters "SPW"—"Subterranean Pass Way," an alternate reference to the underground railroad. Another picture was taken during the same session featuring Brown alone—his right hand raised as if making a solemn vow, his left hand holding the "SPW" banner, its letters all but obscured. It is not clear whether "Subterranean Pass Way" was a term he invented, or if it was already in use in the black community and among underground railroad associates. Certainly, Brown had his own distinct plan, and "SPW" shows his inflexible tendency to work independently for the anti-slavery effort.

Perhaps Brown thought the Washington daguerreotypes a kind of declaration of his improved role in Springfield—a visual portfolio of the real intentions he had made known to black associates. Douglass wrote that he first heard of John Brown from eminent colleagues like Henry Highland Garnet and J. W. Loguen. When they spoke of Brown, their voices dropped to a whisper. Perhaps they thought him volatile, an untried weapon that could explode upon their enemies at any moment.

Brown valued Washington, probably for his experience in setting up schools, especially since his idea of starting a school for blacks had not faded since the 1830s. In May 1847, Brown wrote to his son: "I would like to know if George Delamater would feel disposed to go to Canada in order to commence an Affrican [*sic*] high school provided he can be properly supported." Although Delamater was not interested, it is clear that Brown had not abandoned the idea. In April 1848, he wrote to John Jr. telling him to look up Delamater again, and inquire if he was interested in visiting Essex County, New York, where Gerrit Smith had donated an expansive amount of land for black settlement. The idea of a black colony in the Adirondack mountains excited Brown and animated his dream of an "African high school" once more. If Delamater would visit the new colony, Brown wrote, he might "see to making some beginnings." Nothing more came of his plan for a black school, but it was probably still an issue at the time Brown met Washington in 1848.[7]

Brown's association with Thomas Van Rensselaer is even more significant. Prior to starting *The North Star*, Frederick Douglass lent his name and assistance to Van Rensselaer's journalistic venture, *The Ram's Horn*. Based in New York City, *The Ram's Horn* was the brainchild of Willis Hodges, a free black residing in Williamsburg, Brooklyn. Though *The Ram's Horn* was a response to the racism of city newspapers, Hodges found no support from blacks until he met Van Rensselaer, whose investment brought the paper to press at the beginning of 1847. The biblically styled name and manly spirit of the publication had a magnetic effect upon John Brown, such as the editors' promise to trumpet its message "until the walls of slavery and injustice fall." Combining biblical sentiment with a strong pronouncement of black manhood (the masthead declared, "We are Men—and therefore interested in whatever concerns Men"), *The Ram's Horn* was exactly the kind of black voice that Brown wanted to hear. Though Douglass went on to begin his own publishing venture in late 1847, Brown remained devoted to *The Ram's Horn* and established a good relationship with editor Hodges.

Brown and Hodges were both fed up with the talk-only approach of abolitionists, which Hodges called "speechifying." Born free in Virginia, Willis Hodges migrated to New York in the 1830s, becoming involved in the anti-slavery and black suffrage movements. Like Brown, Hodges was more comfortable in the country than in the city. Hodges thought farming life presented the best possible foundation for blacks to build upon, and that blacks faced less restrictions in rural, agrarian settings than in the cities. He probably shared Brown's discomfort with the spending habits of Northern blacks too. But he was especially frustrated by the lack of support he had found among "colored men of note, influence, education, and money," many of whom had discouraged his dream rather than back it. Given his disappointment with "successful" blacks and his disgust with talk-only abolitionism, Willis Hodges was a ready ally for John Brown. According to his autobiography, a complementary copy of *The Ram's Horn* had found its way "into the house of a good and noble-hearted Christian gentleman," whom he identified as John Brown of Springfield. Brown "has always been a friend to the poor and oppressed, and particular[ly] the friend of the poor slave," Hodges wrote in 1849. Brown responded to Van Rensselaer and Hodges by sending money and a list of prospective subscribers. Brown also felt confident enough to submit an essay for publication in *The Ram's Horn,* which not only reveals the extent of his interest in the black community, but also the degree of acceptance he attained.

Written in the voice of an experienced black man, "Sambo's Mistakes" was John Brown's way of expressing his constructive criticism of the free black community. By presenting these criticisms as confessions, "Sambo" speaks of reading "silly novels and other miserable trash," instead of cultivating a taste for "sober truth, useful knowledge or practical wisdom." Trying to emulate whites, he also spent a lot of money on tobacco products instead of good books, and joined "secret societies" rather than seeking the company of wise and spiritually minded people. "Sambo" had also been waylaid by trivial issues of human pride instead of taking "measures calculated to promote the general welfare" of black people. He was likewise guilty of opposing a brother's attempts to succeed, instead being determined to "injure his influence, oppose his measures, and even glory in his defeats while his intentions were good, and his plans well laid." In attire and leisure, "Sambo" never denied himself of decorations and pleasures, like "gay clothing," jewelry, watches, expensive parties, and other "fashionable amusements." Now he had come to realize that he might have spent his money for his "suffering Brethren" instead. He also confessed to political weakness.

> I have always expected to secure the favor of the whites by tamely submitting to every species of indignity, contempt and wrong, instead of nobly resisting their brutal aggressions from principle and taking my place as a man and assuming the responsibilities of a man, a citizen, a husband, a father, a brother, a neighbor, a friend as God required of every one.

Like Northern politicians who cow-towed to the demands of the pro-slavery faction, "Sambo" came to believe that blacks who did not resist racists were weak and unworthy of respect. Finally, he realized that he had been too partisan and doctrinaire, allowing differences in theology, religious denomination, and political affiliation to keep him "constantly at war with my friends" rather than joining them in a common struggle against slavery.

Obviously, the confessions of "Sambo" were John Brown's personal convictions. He thought little of those who neglected the inner life of spirit and mind for the entertainment of selfish desires and shallow things. He "had a rabid contempt" for any kind of tobacco usage, and thought "secret" organizations subversive to the best interests of a Christian society. He was contemptuous of anyone who bowed to Southern demands, and believed their Northern allies were nothing more than spit-licking imps. Brown's "Sambo" even reflects his growing regret for the theological and denominational dogmaticism of his earlier days. He had come to believe that he should cooperate with people of differing political and religious viewpoints for the sake of the struggle against slavery, and that he could do so without sacrificing his Christian beliefs. Finally, Brown was clearly irritated by the passive manner in which many blacks responded to racist abuse in the Northern states. Unlike Garrison, he did not want "Sambo" to turn the other cheek.

Still, the essay by "Colored Sambo" was a blunt criticism of free blacks, and probably reflected the thoughts and opinions of many black leaders too. Hodges undoubtedly approved, for instance, when "Sambo" confessed how he had opposed good efforts (like *The Ram's Horn*) of a brother for petty reasons. Brown was not alone in his belief that free blacks needed to pull in the reins and tighten their belts.

There is really nothing revelatory about "Sambo's Mistakes," especially since there was already an ongoing discussion among black leaders as to the uplift of free blacks in the North. Frederick Douglass reflected this early on in *The North Star*, calling for suggestions from readers on improving the "wretched condition" of free Northern blacks. A prominent critic whose ideas were similar was Mary Ann Shadd, later a leader among blacks in Canada, who wrote a pamphlet called, *Hints to the Colored People of the North*. Shadd denounced "'Processions, expensive entertainments, excursions, public dinners and suppers, a display of costly apparel, and churches on churches, to minister to our vanity.'. . . 'How does that better our condition as a people?'" Shadd was particularly critical of low-brow fashion and ostentation among people of color: "Negroes and Indians set more value on the outside of their heads than on what the inside needs," she wrote. No wonder that Benjamin Quarles considered "Sambo's Mistakes" an "unburdening of confidences within the family circle." A half century later, W. E. B. Du Bois called Brown's essay "quaint," but recognized that it was written "not in condemnation but in faith." John Brown approached black people "on a plane of perfect equality," wrote Du Bois, and "neither descended upon them from above nor wallowed with their lowest." Van Rensselaer and Hodges undoubtedly recognized the same concerned spirit in Brown's essay. "Captain Brown had a higher notion of the capacity of the negro race than most white men," one of his associates later recalled.[8]

Increasingly interested in the Gerrit Smith land grant program in the Adirondacks, Brown wrote to John Jr. in April 1848, mentioning that he might "make the acquaintance of some colored men of the right stamp for colonists" in New York. Meanwhile Brown was also trying to persuade an Ohio congressman, Joshua Giddings, to sponsor a contest for the best American wools in the name of the anti-slavery cause. He hoped that an emphasis on American quality would silence the charge that antislavery people were not patriotic, and that the contest would also encourage "American tallent [sic], and industry." Whether or not Giddings thought the contest a good idea, nothing came of it. Brown seems to have missed following up, and then abandoned the contest idea altogether.

Brown and others from Ohio's Western Reserve held Giddings in high regard. As congressman from Ohio's sixteenth district, he was the strongest opponent of slavery in Washington since John Quincy Adams.

Having taken every measure to counter the efforts of pro-slavery politicians, Giddings paid the price of being treated like a social outcast in the nation's capitol. When a group of blacks forcefully liberated themselves on the American slave ship, *Creole*, in late 1841, Giddings jeopardized his political career by speaking in favor of the coup. After the *Creole* was seized and forced into British waters in the Bahamas, pro-slavery forces in the United States could not regain control over their victims. But because of his strong support of the *Creole* warriors, Giddings was forced out of Congress by pro-slavery forces in 1842. After welcoming him like a war hero, his Ohio constituents promptly returned him to Congress by an overwhelming majority in a special election.

In 1848, another controversy surrounding a ship ensued after the *Pearl*, a small coastal vessel, was apprehended and found to be harboring seventy-seven black men, women, and children seeking to escape slavery. The *Pearl* was leased by a white man named Daniel Drayton and launched from Washington with the intention of escaping to the North. Detained by bad weather and betrayed by a black informant, the *Pearl* fugitives were sold deeper into the South, and both Drayton and the ship's owner were tried, convicted, and sent to prison. The city of Washington was inflamed and racist mobs turned their outrage on abolitionists. Giddings was once more on the firing line, arguing that blacks should hardly be penalized for struggling for liberation when all of Europe was aflame with wars of independence. When teeth-clenched Southerners argued back, fearful moderates in Congress thought it best to quell the war of words, believing themselves cautious rather than cowardly. Among those seeking to compromise was a new congressman from Illinois named Abraham Lincoln.

"The prospect of a general war all over Europe everyday increses [*sic*]," Brown wrote to John Jr. after the *Pearl* incident. "The slave case at Was[h]ington seems likely to get the Pot a boiling again in Congress." Like many others, Brown felt the pulse of the times, and understood that slavery was writhing in anxiety despite the bed of comfort provided by Northern politicians. White racists could riot and mob, but the signs of the times seemed to color the skies red with judgment, and change was imminent. Europe too was convulsing with wars and rumors of wars, and abolitionists could not help but presume that their struggle was part of a larger movement toward a dawning republican era.

Meanwhile, P&B continued its own troubled voyage, with John Brown stubbornly clinging to the helm. But much like the unfaithful plowman in the parable of Christ, he was too distracted to follow a straight course. "We feel a good deal of spirit about the oppressions, and cruelties that are done in the land," he wrote to his father in early 1849. "But in regard to other verry [*sic*] important interests we are quite too indifferent. I suppose it may well be questioned whether any one duty can be acceptably performed; while most others are neglected."[9] In his early days, the business failures were piercing and painful, especially because Brown had believed success was vital to his role in abolition. But P&B was no longer as vital as he had once thought, and new visions were quickly replacing old dreams.

PART V

# Big Difficulties and Firm Footholds

Allow me to say that a man can hardly get into difficulties too big to be surmounted if he has a firm foothold at home. Remember that.

—John Brown

# 13

## A Cold and Snowy Canaan Land

Now therefore fear yet not: I will nourish you, and your little ones.
And he comforted them, and spake kindly unto them.

—Genesis 50:21

Nearing fifty years of age, John Brown might be seen walking the streets of Springfield alone, distracted by thoughts of slavery—his thick hair combed back from his forehead and his blue, deep-set eyes fixed downward as he strolled with his hands clasped behind his back. Or he might be seen walking and talking intently with his friend Thomas Thomas. They had become warm associates over his three-year stay in Springfield. However different, they shared a common faith and Thomas undoubtedly found John Brown's hatred of slavery unusually sharp for one who had never known it himself. Both men also knew deep loss, since Thomas too had been widowed and had lost his only two children. Even after his return to Ohio, Brown visited Springfield and the two friends got together, attending a new theatrical version of Harriet Beecher Stowe's popular novel, *Uncle Tom's Cabin*. As a token of their friendship, he gave Thomas a solid mahogany walking stick with an ivory head and a silver band inscribed: "John Brown to Thomas Thomas." Thomas went on to adventure in California, and then worked in a restaurant in Springfield, Illinois, where he became acquainted with Abraham Lincoln. After Lincoln's election, Thomas was supposedly offered a job on the White House domestic staff, but family obligations forced him to return to Massachusetts instead. Thomas ran a popular eatery in Springfield from 1862 until his death in 1894. Brown and Lincoln never came so close as they did in friendship with Thomas Thomas, and the black man could speak with some authority about both leaders.

Thomas recalled that it "was the custom of the manufacturers to buy the wool in bulk from the farmers, without any sorting. The farmers

Thomas Thomas was perhaps John Brown's closest associate while in Springfield. An employee of Perkins & Brown, he quickly became an ally in matters pertaining to the black struggle, serving as the leader of Brown's "League of Gileadites." In later years Thomas started a successful restaurant, becoming a public figure in Springfield. *Sketch from the* Springfield Republican *(March 10, 1894), courtesy of the Connecticut Valley Historical Museum, Springfield, Mass.*

could not judge the quality, and the manufacturers bought the wool for less than it was really worth." He said further that the manufacturers had combined to crush P&B, forcing Brown to quit. On the other hand, there is strong evidence that P&B was undermined as much if not more so by Brown's lack of business skills and inflexible manner of pricing wool. Certainly he "was no *trader*," recalled businessman E. C. Leonard. P&B was clearly hurt by Brown's questionable price setting and his refusal to negotiate the values he attached to the sorted wools. "Brown was in a position to make a fortune, and a regular-bred merchant would have done so," Leonard concluded. Another critic claimed that he undersold lower quality wools and over-priced the fine wools.[1] Still, P&B was a real threat to the manufacturers, who dominated an "open, free-lance market," as Boyd Stutler wrote. The wool manufacturers were not only accustomed to buying wool in bulk and sorting it afterward, they also "could fix any price they chose." When Brown and his associates tried to grade the wool and fix a fair market price in advance, they were branded as a threat and labeled by the manufacturers as being "crazy."[2]

Beyond P&B's growing indebtedness and the lack of unity among wool growers, Brown "would have had more worries had he known at that time just what the manufacturers were doing, and how much interest they were taking in the affairs of the firm." He had become suspicious of the Burlington Mills Company in particular, and later it was revealed that one of their agents had infiltrated P&B's operations and tampered with the wool gradings. "For several years father had hopes of becoming a capitalist, intending to devote his wealth to his mission," John Jr. recalled. But his plans were thwarted because "the manufacturers were better organized than the farmers."[3]

But the Practical Shepherd already had other plans. In the spring of 1848, Brown had gone to see Gerrit Smith in Peterboro, New York about the black colonies he was sponsoring in the Adirondacks. Smith and Brown were devout Christians and ardent anti-slavery men, but Smith had the kind of wealth that Brown desired in order to conduct his campaign against slavery. "Father had given up the idea of getting rich—meant to accomplish his purpose without money; and he wanted to know how best to help the free negro," recalled John Jr. Indeed, Brown's first meeting with Smith about the Adirondack land grant program foreshadowed a future relationship in which he would often prevail upon the Peterboro mogul for support. Of course, Smith had other reasons for making the land grants, though his enemies were quick to impute selfish reasons, as a critic did in the *Plattsburgh Republican*. Mocking his "liberality," the writer charged that Smith had merely rid himself of a tremendous tax burden—especially since the land would require "gigantic labor and indomitable perseverance" to make it productive. But Smith was more positively motivated, perhaps hoping that the land grant would empower black suffrage by helping men attain the state's $250 property qualification. Though he de-emphasized the suffrage issue, "his offer came in the wake of the defeat of equal franchise for blacks in 1846 and would presumably have enabled some to meet the special suffrage requirement."

Explaining to Smith that he was of pioneer background, Brown offered to settle, clear, and establish a farm on the land in order to "show my colored neighbors how such work should be done." He knew that most of the black colonists were city folk and would need help in adapting to the wilderness. Brown would then "give them work as I have occasion, look after them in all needful ways, and be a kind of father to them." Like Brown, Smith had an excellent rapport with blacks too, demonstrating "little of the fear of social intimacy that many white abolitionists revealed to blacks." They also shared a common friend in Frederick Douglass, who was increasingly aligning himself with Smith, finally breaking with Garrison in the early 1850s. Smith understandably approved Brown's proposal, though the Practical Shepherd had to purchase his tract of Adirondack land.

Brown could hardly have missed Willis Hodges's articles about the land grant program in *The Ram's Horn*, such as one appearing in November 1847 noting how the New York Emigration Association was gathering blacks from the state for the move to the Smith lands: "You must agree with me that the lands given to our people by Mr. Smith, must eventually prove a blessing or a curse to the people of the State of New York, and we may add to our whole people as a class in this country." Hodges's appeal was that the best hope for black economic advancement lay in farm settlements. Agricultural employment, mills, forges, and factories could be developed in such a rich and well-watered wilderness, and young people would escape the "vice and idleness" of the cities. The month before, Hodges appeared prominently at the Colored National Convention in Troy, New York, as a state delegate, along with Thomas Van Rensselaer, his partner in *The Ram's Horn*. The New York delegates were many, including abolitionist leaders Henry Highland Garnet, Charles B. Ray, and James McCune Smith. Massachusetts had the next largest representation, including Frederick Douglass, writer William Wells Brown, and Thomas Thomas.

Among the topics of the convention was a national black press and the theme of agricultural life, which featured Gerrit Smith's donation of over one hundred thousand acres of raw wilderness. The debate over a national black press reflected a dynamic conflict of interests among the black leaders. Proponents cited the fragile nature of present black papers, and also argued that a black-run press would be a powerful weapon against slavery. To no surprise, Willis Hodges declared that "a National Press was not needed" in light of *The Ram's Horn* and other publications. Since he was about to begin publication of *The North Star*, Frederick Douglass straddled the fence. While favoring the idea, he said, a national press "could not well be sustained" and would "dwindle down to be the organ of a clique." Douglass maintained that active black newspapers like *The Ram's Horn* and his own rising *North Star* ought to be sustained instead. The convention finally voted in favor of a national black press, but the vote proved more about sentiment than action. Douglass seems to have abstained from the vote, probably because he hoped to benefit regardless of the outcome—either by maneuvering *The North Star* into position as the national black paper or by winning support from those who opposed the idea.

*The Ram's Horn* survived for another two years, though its editors began to clash over the future of the paper, and Hodges's move to the Adirondacks marked the paper's decline. Douglass thus became the leading black publisher by default, though even he struggled to keep the presses running over the coming decade. Forced to travel and lecture to raise support, he even mortgaged his home to keep *The North Star* viable.[4]

In 1848–49, Brown was once more in correspondence with Hodges, who had relocated to Franklin County, New York to lead the colony he called "Blacksville." Brown visited the Adirondacks in October 1848, and stopped off in Troy, New York on his way back to purchase supplies for the settlers. Writing to Hodges, he noted that he was sending five barrels of pork and flour to him, to be shared with the black settlers at North Elba in Essex County, in a settlement he referred to as "Timbucto." Brown was aware that whites in these vicinities were not happy with the presence of the black colonists, whom they called "Smith niggers." He also learned of opportunists working to take advantage of the unseasoned grantees by overcharging them for goods, or by blatantly misleading them. In late summer 1847, the abolitionist Jermaine W. Loguen made a seven-week tour of Franklin and Essex counties, making a careful report afterward. Loguen felt the donated land was "first-rate," though he admitted that some of it might not be as good for farming as for timber. Loguen also warned about the chicanery of opportunists playing "a high-handed game . . . upon many of our colored brethren, who had gone there, to visit the lands of which they had received the deeds." Loguen advised black settlers to "procure a guide or pilot, to enable him to find the object of his pursuit," and to avoid dishonest guides by reporting to the county clerk at the onset. False guides were either taking the new colonists on extended tours at great expense, or showing them desolate, undesirable land in the hope of discouraging them, and buying off their tracts at a low price. Loguen urged the colonists not to sell their land "for a song" since "in the course of a few years, they must rise in value, and may hereafter furnish them or their children with comfortable homes."

John Brown had an optimistic view of the Smith lands too. When a meeting was held in Troy, New York for land grantees in that city, the program featured a letter from Brown, who was called "the distinguished friend and firm supporter of the colored man." Citing his authority as an "experienced Surveyor," Brown wrote that he had "explored to some extent" the Smith lands and approved of them highly:

> [T]hey possess many very superior natural advantages. I would therefore recommend to all those that have received lands, or who may hereafter receive lands, to hold on to them as their most valuable earthly treasure and sooner suffer nakedness and hunger than part with them.

The Troy meeting resolved that grantees should do everything possible to reach their tracts, wherein they could attain a "respectable position in society" rather than remain "lounging about these crowded cities." The sentiments at the Troy meeting clearly echoed the pronouncements of the national convention in the same city the previous year, which culminated with Charles Ray and Willis Hodges's call for black people to "forsake the cities and towns" for the country and the farm, "and hereby build a tower of strength for themselves."[5]

"You must try and make your money reach untill [*sic*] Spring as I have now paid out quite a sum," Brown had written to Hodges prior to the winter of 1848. With his country background, Hodges had no trouble building a cabin for himself atop "Hodge Hill." But few of the colonists were prepared for the long, cold winter ahead and the hard work involved in establishing the settlements. However, the difficulties at Blacksville and Timbucto were not only due to the inexperience of the settlers and the racist exploitation of local whites. The Smith lands were simply not the place to start an agrarian movement.

It is not clear to what extent Smith knew that the land he was giving away was substandard for farming, though he had already been unable to sell the Essex County lands at auction in 1846. Brown had gotten caught up in the excitement to the point that even after surveying the lands on behalf of the settlers, he overestimated the value of the Smith lands to prospective farmers. Another meeting was held for grantees in late 1848 in Rochester, New York, presided over by Frederick Douglass. It featured the official surveyor of the Smith lands, who declared that

Willis Hodges was a publisher, activist, and leader of the black colony experiment in the Adirondacks. Despite his camaraderie with John Brown, however, Hodges did not support the Harper's Ferry raid in 1859. *Sketch from* The Afro-American Press and Its Editors *(1891)*.

"none of the lots were worthless, but the greater portion excellent." Douglass also repeated John Brown's glowing report. But years later, Salmon Brown contended that the Smith lands project was "the wildest scheme" that his father got involved in, "considering that all the colored people were all from the big cities and knew nothing of making homes in a dense forest in that cold region where there was frost almost every month in the year."

In fact, a great deal of the Smith lands were rocky, "on steep mountain slopes, or too wet to farm, and some of the land [Smith] gave away before he had legal title to it," notes Edwin Cotter. Most of the lots were designated in 40-acre parcels, but some were larger because they covered water, such as the case of one settler whose 160-acre lot included a portion of Lake Placid, and another, whose lot was on a range 2,500 feet high—hardly worth owning, let alone cultivating. "Smith meant well, but he had never seen the lots and knew little of the hardships and struggles involved in trying to live on the land." One disenchanted settler put it best when he concluded that "the grasshopper has to get down on his knees to smell the clover."[6]

Unfortunately, the promised lands of Gerrit Smith were largely a disappointment, and only the heartiest and most determined settlers persevered in the first few years. By September 1846, Smith had made out 2,000 deeds across eight counties, but mostly in Essex County, where 22,000 acres had been deeded to Timbucto settlers. But when James McCune Smith visited the colony in 1850, he estimated about sixty settlers remained. By the time of the 1855 census, there were only twelve black families left—about forty men, women, and children remaining from over four hundred grantees and their families. Of course, successful settlers emphasized the other benefits besides farming, as did Brown's close friend, Lyman Eppes. A native of New England, Eppes wrote to Frederick Douglass in 1854 saying that the lands in the vicinity of Saranac lake had rich forests that would be valuable as the need for lumber increased. Eppes advised the grantees not to sell their lands, as some had done, in order to pay their taxes. But the great majority of New York's black settlers found "the backwardness of the season" in the chilly Canaan quite discouraging, and the effort seemed hopeless.

"I have not forgotten you; but have had so many things to do that I could not well write you before," explained John Brown to Willis Hodges in another letter shortly before Christmas 1848. Brown was eager to know how the settlers of Blacksville and Timbucto were holding up in the winter season. "I hope you are all full of courage and good feeling, and going in earnest," Brown closed, adding a scriptural admonition: "'To him that overcometh'—remember." Writing about a month later, Brown informed Hodges that he had arranged to rent a farm in North Elba to be close by the Timbucto settlers. Encouraging the settlers to cut plenty of wood and busy themselves with any available work, Brown concluded:

> Do not let anyone forget the vast importance of sustaining the verry [*sic*] best character for honesty, truth, industry, and faithfulness. I hope every one will be determined to not merely conduct *as well* as the whites; but to set them an example in all things.

Throughout the spring months of 1849, Brown wrote to Hodges intermittently, telling him of gradual preparations as well as setbacks, until finally announcing in early May that he would soon leave for Timbucto. By mid-May 1849, Brown and family were on their way, but things were not going smoothly. When they reached the vicinity, Mary Brown was sick and Brown's arrangements for a wagon had not worked out. Besides these difficulties, Brown informed Hodges that he had to return to Springfield almost immediately to tend to business concerns.[7]

The Browns' first visit to North Elba in early 1848 had not ended well either. Though Brown had returned from the Adirondacks charmed "by the grand mountain scenery" and convinced of his vital role among the black settlers, his baby daughter Ellen got sick on the journey, and developed consumption after their return to Springfield. John and Mary nursed little Ellen, but they could see her health declining until one morning, when Brown sensed the nearing shadow of death and hurried home to find Ellen waiting for him, with her little arms outstretched and "a pleading look for him to take her." Brown carried her until she died, then closed her eyes and folded her hands, and laid her in her cradle. After baby Ellen was buried, daughter Ruth remembered, John Brown "broke down completely and sobbed like a child."

Mary Brown was already a sick woman when the Browns moved to North Elba, though it is unclear what ailed her. Mary was more than a survivor, despite the many hardships she endured throughout twenty-six years of marriage to John Brown. By the time the Browns moved to North Elba in 1849, she had given birth to eleven children and lost six of them to fatal illness. She shared her husband's faith, values, and abolitionist convictions, and though one observer found her homely and somewhat masculine in appearance, even he thought her gracious and hospitable. A kinder assessment, by Brown's supporter Thomas Wentworth Higginson, describes Mary as "dignified and noble," a "Roman matron touched with the finer element of Christianity." In the initial months of her stay at North Elba, Mary may have tried various home remedies, like herb teas, castor oil blends, or charcoal and brandy. There were patent medicines too, supposedly good for colds, coughs, asthma, influenza, and consumption. But most of these cures were of little medicinal value, or only medicated consumers with enough opium to make them feel better. American medicine was taking great strides in the 1840s, but it would be another two decades before doctors began to understand and apply pathology in treatments.

Though life in North Elba was hard compared to Springfield, it was not entirely a wilderness. The small community of about two hundred, not counting the new settlers, had a school building (also used as a church), post office, and tavern. Even in John Brown's time, Lakes Placid and Saranac attracted tourists, and hikers enjoyed the vast mountain scenery. The Browns brought as much of their possessions and furniture as they could (Brown gave his favorite rocking chair to Thomas Thomas's mother), leaving Springfield just as a smallpox epidemic was raging. As they approached the wilderness community, Ruth Brown remembered her father's efforts to cheer up the family, stopping periodically so they could drink fresh water from mountain streams, or pointing out the fragrances arising from abundant spruce, hemlock, and balsam trees. When they reached the rented farm house, Brown surmised that his family was disappointed. "It is small. But the main thing is, *all* keep good-natured," he urged. They immediately hired a widow from the black colony to assist Mary in housekeeping, and a fugitive as farm help. However, the presence of fugitives in Timbucto was exceptional since the overwhelming number of colonists were free people. From time to time fugitives or associates from Springfield might find their way to the Brown household, such as Cyrus, whom the Browns hired the day after they arrived in May 1849. He had been enslaved in Virginia and Florida but escaped northward to Springfield, where he met the Browns and then seems to have followed them to North Elba. "Cyrus was hired for farm work, and made as one of the family," and was remembered by Ruth Brown as "a bright, pleasant colored boy." Other black youths were taken in by the Browns too. "My father employed as many of them as he could, fed the rest, and helped them on to better fortune," John Jr. recalled.

The Browns rented a farm house from Caroline and Champin Flanders for about $50 a year during their first stay in North Elba (1849–51). The property Brown had purchased from Gerrit Smith was located on Lot 95 (Brown called it "Old 95"), a 244-acre tract on which the family house was later built. Though sparse, there were neighbors in the vicinity, such as the family of Alexis Tender, whose name Brown mistook for "Lextender" when he was first settling into the area.[8]

Far more important to John Brown was Timbucto. Brown was clearly excited about the prospects of moving onto the Smith lands with his black neighbors, as shown in a letter to his father Owen written several months before the move:

There are a number of good Colored families on the ground; most of whom I visited. I can think of no place where I think I would sooner go; all things considered than to live with those poor despised Africans to try, and encourage them; and show them a little so far as I am capable how to manage.

Upon arrival, Brown immediately "engaged himself . . . in providing for the wants of the colored settlers," recalled an admiring narrator in 1859. Learning that one of the settlers had been swindled out of his land, "Brown sought out the offender and made him surrender the deed, threatening him with a lawsuit to the end of his means. Again, finding the people in destitution and out of employment, he hired them to cut cord wood, paid them for their work, and afterward presented them with the wood."

But there was a cooperative effort between the Practical Shepherd and the blacks of Timbucto. Brown needed assistance too, as his daughter Ruth recalled, and "some of the colored colony began at once to clear up our own purchased land." At other times, when away from North Elba, Brown depended on his black neighbors to assist him in similar matters. Nevertheless, if he had promised Gerrit Smith to "be a father" to the black colony, he kept his word. "Father felt deeply over the way so many of them had been treated, and tried to encourage and help them in every way he could," Ruth recalled. Brown recognized that the settlers were intelligent, industrious people, "glad to do with best they could," and his concern extended even to their spiritual well-being. On Sunday he regularly gathered them together for worship and Bible study.

When the Browns arrived in North Elba in 1849, neither whites nor blacks had built a church, and worship took place in private homes and later in the school building. Salmon Brown, then about thirteen years old, recalled that his family regularly attended services in the home of Deacon Osgood, who was known as the leading religious figure in the area. "Father, when he was there, used to help Deacon Osgood by reading a chapter from the Bible, singing and praying. There were some 25 or 30 people who came from all the roads in that region," Salmon recalled. Some walked, or rode ox carts, or even sleds. The church people brought their dinner and feed for their animals, and ate their dinners in the house and outside. Since no pastor was yet called to serve, ministry was conducted by Deacon Osgood, John Brown, or guest speakers. Brown became quite involved in this informal spiritual community, and it probably gave him great satisfaction that the congregation was racially blended, worshiped very informally, and had no specific denominational commitment. One resident recalled being a child in the church at the time Brown served as

This huge rock outside the Brown house is notable today as marking the place of John Brown's grave. For Brown, however, it was a natural platform from which to observe the beauty of the Adirondacks, and a place where he read his Bible and practiced religious contemplation. *Jean Libby, Photographer, October 2000.*

Sunday School superintendent—perhaps a bit intimidating to the smaller Sunday School students who remembered him as "tall and serious-looking." He kept tight reins on the young people in church, including playful Salmon, who was always a mischievous thorn in his father's side. Of course, Brown's sermons and Sunday School lessons always included references to the "extinction of slavery."[9]

Only one of John Brown's sermons survived in the form of some incomplete notes, but it provides a clear sense of his approach as a preacher. Taking his text from the Prophet Micah (6:8), one can imagine him reading, his voice somewhat nervous, high-pitched, and nasal: "He hath shewed thee, O man, what is good; and what doth the Lord require of thee, but to do justly, and to love mercy, and to walk humbly with thy God?"

Who that understands those requirements and does not live in thoughtless disregard of the course they pursue, like "beasts that perish," can possibly avoid mentally saying "Amen"? . . . Nothing but an incomprehensible stupidity on our part, can keep us from breaking out at once in strains of the most exalted praise when we reflect that God is ever reasonable. His language to erring man *is*; "Come and let us reason together" [Isaiah 1:18].

Brown continued by asking his listeners to imagine the man who follows God's requirements—would not even this much "awaken in us the most powerful 'hungering, and thirsting after righteousness'?"

But *alas* is it not *too true*, that such a character has but poor if any attraction for us? Let each one enquire of their own heart. . . . But how shall unjust, unmerciful, proud feeling man, with all his guilt, and sin upon him, bring his mind to dwell on him who is Infinitely Just? . . . What can so properly become poor, dependent, sinning, and self-condemned mortals like *us* as humility?[10]

The view from Brown's grave site today gives a sense of his pleasure at viewing the vast sky and mountains from his own yard. "I like to live in a country where everything you see reminds one of Omnipotence," Brown declared. *Author's photograph, 1999.*

Brown probably felt more inspiration in his sacred studies since he moved to North Elba, largely because the lifestyle and work were close to his heart and appealed to his justice-oriented evangelical beliefs. But he simply loved the panoramic beauty of snow-capped peaks, lush forests, and fresh mountain streams too. "I like to live in a country where everything you see reminds one of Omnipotence," he would tell his family. "Where if you do get your crops cut off once in a while, you will feel your dependence." In 1855, after the family built a home on "Old 95," Brown's neighbor remembered seeing him seated on the huge boulder that still sets near the house, "reading his Bible and looking at the mountains."[11] Although he had come to the Adirondacks to help others, John Brown instead had found a cold, snowy Canaan land where something of heaven could be found on earth.

But there was a sound of war in the camp, and he would soon return to the world of masters and slaves below. "*Nothing* but the strong sence [sic] of duty, Obligation, and propriety, would keep me from laying my bones to rest there," he wrote of his beloved North Elba homestead. Someday he would finally rest beside that boulder on "Old 95," but not until he had traveled many miles, wept many more tears, and discovered a life yet to be born.

# 14

## "So We Go"

### Failed Ventures and Disappointing Outcomes

Woe is me for my hurt! My wound is grievous; but I said, Truly this is a grief, and I must bear it.

—Jeremiah 10:19

In the summer of 1849, Richard Dana Jr. and two companions went hiking in the Adirondacks. Wandering for a whole day, they found themselves lost until coming upon a path and finally "a log-house and half-cleared farm." With their faces and arms marked and swollen by insect bites, the frustrated tourists were weary, sore, and extremely hungry. Over two decades later Dana, a Boston attorney and author of *Two Years Before the Mast*, would remember this day. Using his journal notes from 1849, he wrote a piece for *The Atlantic Monthly* recalling how he and his weary companions were taken into the home of John Brown—"a small log-house of one story in height," filled "with a great many sons and daughters." Dana and his friends were served by daughter Ruth, because Mary Brown was "rather an invalid" and did not meet them at first. He noted details of the newly settled farm, such as Brown's fine livestock and freshly planted fields—and Ruth too, whom he described as "a bonny, buxom young woman of some twenty summers, with fair skin and red hair." Ruth cheered them up with her good humor while rationing water, milk, and bread in small servings so they would be able to eat the meal she was preparing. Later in the afternoon, Brown himself arrived on a long buckboard wagon, and seated next to him were a black couple with baggage. Dana recalled that he had surveying instruments with him, a detail consistent with the fact that Brown had regularly undertaken the survey of deeded lands for the Timbucto settlers. He welcomed Dana and the others "with kindness" and "natural dignity." At mealtime, Dana and his companions, Brown's black friends, and the family were seated at a long table but did not eat until the head of the household prayed over the food. As they dined, Dana noticed the natural manner Brown showed to his black guests, and was even a bit put off by the way he addressed the blacks "using their surnames," such as "Mr. Jefferson." Dana assumed these guests had "not been so treated or spoken to often before," and that "they had all the awkwardness of field hands on a plantation; and what to do, on the introduction, was quite beyond their experience." Of course, Dana could only describe what he perceived. Being immersed in the racism of his culture, he assumed these black people were not used to being called "Mr. Jefferson" or "Mrs. Wait," when in fact this courtesy was part of everyday life in the black community. In fact, Dana imputed his own discomfort to the "awkward" black guests at his table, even though they were probably city-dwellers like him, and had probably never been on a plantation. Dana was so impressed by his hosts that he made note of the accidental visit with the Browns in his diary. Sometime after the raid on Harper's Ferry in 1859, Dana was reading reports and profiles describing John Brown and suddenly realized this was the same farmer Brown he had met a decade before in North Elba.

Like the black guests at Brown's table, Lyman Eppes was never a slave. Born in Connecticut and educated in the North, Eppes brought his family to the hopeful black Canaan in 1849, and never left Timbucto despite its cold disappointments. Being the son of a Native American father and African American mother, he was considered "mulatto" in nineteenth-century terms. A widower like Brown, Eppes brought his wife, mother, and growing family to Timbucto around the time the Browns arrived, and thereafter held a high reputation among blacks and whites in the vicinity. Educated and trained in music, Eppes also had a knack for country life, and in the 1855 census had the best valued cabin among the black settlers.

As devout evangelical Christians, Eppes and Brown developed a close rapport in the first years of settlement. "He'd walk up to our house on the Table Lands and come in and play with us children and talk to father," a misty-eyed Lyman Jr. recalled in the 1920s. "Many's the time I've sat on John Brown's knee. He was a kind and friendly man with children." The two fathers often talked of slavery and scripture, and at times collaborated to help black neighbors or an occasional fugitive—such as one whom Brown brought to the Eppes' home to stay overnight before continuing his flight to Canada. Eppes remembered that Brown never rode horseback, nor dressed in the typical farmer's flannel shirt. Instead, he always wore linen and a brown frock coat—too dressed for the country but never formal enough for a city gentleman. Neither did Brown fish or hunt, nor think highly of men who did.

If whites perceived Eppes as a man of "gentle dignity and benevolence," his companionship with John Brown nevertheless reflected an agreement of mind and heart over the slavery issue. Like Brown, Eppes was a strongly independent man, willing to live out his days in a rural farming area largely removed from the black mainstream. At one point Eppes even considered joining the Congregational Church, perhaps because of his association with Brown. But for reasons both social and theological, he finally joined a Methodist Episcopal Church in the vicinity, becoming the choir director. According to the pastor, Eppes was esteemed as "an educated and cultured gentleman of the purest water . . . companionable and honorable." As he did with Thomas in Springfield, Brown eventually disclosed his anti-slavery plans to Eppes, who likewise chose not to participate in the raid.[1]

With John Jr. back in Springfield to oversee business, Brown neglected P&B's interests in the first months of his stay. Yet his letters to Perkins show that he did so based on an understanding about closing P&B in the near future. In April 1849, he wrote that he was overwhelmed by letters from wool growers calling for payment, and found it so increasingly difficult to deal with their demands that he felt the need to have his "face hardened over every morning." He complained that the manufacturers were holding off on orders to force P&B's prices down. The following month he wrote that despite all his efforts, things looked dark. The manufacturers were going elsewhere and paying more "rather than buy ours (!) *in order to get back the full controll [sic] of the market.*"

Brown had made a sale to the French firm, Thirion Maillard and Company, and now hoped he could introduce fine American wool and sheep abroad. "Nothing short of that will ever give stability in any measure to the business," he concluded. Thus far, he had been able to keep a good face on P&B in the business community, and commercial reports from that period list the firm as "safe and good for all its contracts." But resistance from manufacturers continued, and the low ebbs of the market due to the Mexican war and the reduction of import duties had intensified P&B's problems. The façade was crumbling, and Brown hoped for salvation in the European market.

Lyman Eppes was the foremost of the Timbucto settlers. Having been informed of Brown's plan to raid Harper's Ferry, he chose not to join the raiders. A native of Connecticut like Brown, Eppes was also a devout Christian. He remained a life-long friend of the Brown family and was still in contact with them in the 1880s. *West Virginia State Archives.*

Brown left for Europe on August 15, 1849 with the approval of Simon Perkins and the participant agreement of many P&B clients. Sailing from Boston on the steamship *Cambria*, he reached Liverpool, England on August 26 and traveled to London the following day. Finding that he would not be able to conduct sales until mid-September, he embarked on a tour of the continent, passing through France, Germany, and Belgium before returning to London. Contrary to legend, Brown's visits to famous battlefields and other military sites were no more than tourist visits—not the careful study of military strategy and fortifications that has been portrayed. Of course he enjoyed seeing the battlefields he had read about from the time of his youth. But the foray into Europe was a diversion, a kind of working holiday for a man who had never taken a vacation in his life. Brown toured Paris, and stayed in Calais at the *House Meurice,* sipping wine with his meals and enjoying the markets and farms, which he wrote to his son were "most magnificent . . . equal to that of a most perfect garden." Perhaps he slept leisurely and enjoyed a meal at the *House de l'Europe* in Hamburg, Germany. Back in London, Brown enjoyed ale and English cooking, declaring that the tasty roast beef and mutton prepared in English restaurants was "not to be exceeded."

Unfortunately, whatever enjoyment he experienced as a tourist was dashed upon the hard rocks of the "stupid, obstinate prejudice" of the English market as well as conflicting interests between European and U.S. markets. Little wool was sold, and what was sold Brown believed to have been undersold. The finer wools were not selling, and nothing came of his hopes for the European redemption of P&B despite the supposed interest of the French market. The prejudice Brown faced was directed against American wools in general, which he knew had a bad reputation on the foreign market because of poor and dishonest presentation by wool growers. To his embarrassment, some of the wools he had brought with him proved to be filthy and improperly prepared for market.

Furthermore, Brown was still dealing with an industry that did not like having wools graded in advance of the sale, and European manufacturers were no less disturbed by the method and presentation of the self-assured American shepherd. Once a group of London merchants banded together in a practical joke intended to belittle Brown and his wool grading expertise. During a conversation about fine wools, one of them produced a sample, asking him to evaluate it. Brown—who could identify wool fibers by touch—rubbed the sample between his fingers a few times, finding no evidence that it was sheep's wool. "Gentlemen, if you have any machinery that will work up dog's hair, I would advise you to put this into it," he responded, putting them to silence. But personal vindication did nothing for P&B. Though Brown would even take a bronze medal for Perkins's Saxony sheep at a London fair, the trophy would have to serve as a consolation prize for his wealthy partner. He tried to find market interest in other English cities to no avail, and almost all of his wools were shipped back to the United States—finally being sold in Boston for even less than he was offered prior to leaving for Europe. Brown's venture abroad proved a "stark disaster," a debacle that incurred a loss of nearly $40,000. When he arrived in Boston on October 26, 1849, P&B's last gasp had already been heard across the Atlantic. Thomas Thomas, who was undergoing therapy in a Massachusetts "Water Cure" establishment, wrote to John Jr. in late August to inform him that a Boston newspaper had picked up the story of P&B's troubles in England, the article stating that unsold wool was being returned, having failed to attract buyers even at thirty cents per pound. Though a bit premature, the newspaper article ultimately proved to be a valid report of P&B's failure in Europe.[2]

Mary Brown's health problems worsened throughout the spring and early summer of 1849 until she became desperate for some kind of medical relief. In fact, she showed up at Springfield the day after her husband's departure for Europe, taking John Jr. and Wealthy completely by surprise. She had packed her bag and traveled alone from upstate New York to Springfield, supposedly in the hope of catching her husband before he left—but her "principal design" was really to check herself into the "Water Cure" establishment of David Ruggles, a self-trained doctor of hydrotherapy residing at Northampton, Massachusetts. Mary was disturbed by her husband's tendency to minimize her ailments, and was "*bent* upon" the hydrotherapy retreat "as her only salvation," according to John Jr. Whether or not John and Mary Brown had argued about her receiving hydrotherapy is not clear, though apparently he did not think much of the treatment. Initially, Mary asked her stepson not to inform his father about her going to Northampton. She told him that she did not want to worry her husband while he was away, but she probably wished to avoid telling Brown as long as possible—perhaps not until she could find a degree of relief in defense of her independent decision.

The Water Cure retreat of David Ruggles was interesting for a number of reasons, including Ruggles himself. Ruggles was a free-born black man from Connecticut, known for his underground railroad activity, anti-slavery writings, and bold approach toward Northern racism—such as a lawsuit he lodged against a Massachusetts railroad after being forced off a train for refusing to sit in the "dirty car" reserved for blacks. Though he lost that case, Ruggles distinguished himself in the eyes of Garrisonians and other abolitionists as "militant" (in pacifist terms). With their financial support, he was able to set up the hydrotherapy establishment in Northampton. Ruggles himself had suffered far too much abuse at the hands of violent racists, and his own interest in establishing a Water Cure was in part a reflection of his own need for therapy. Having observed the hydrotherapeutic treatment of German-born Dr. Robert Wesselhoeft of Cambridge, Ruggles opened his establishment on Mill River, near town. It occupied a three-story building equipped with various baths and water treatments, as well as lodgings that could be rented for $5–$8 per week.

Given the Garrisonian influence and support undergirding the Water Cure, Ruggles's center was also a kind of abolitionist retreat. Garrison himself had received treatment from Ruggles to some success. Other abolitionists and their associates patronized the Water Cure, including many leading women abolitionists. During Mary Brown's stay (August until November 1849), she soaked, strolled, and conversed with a variety of abolitionists, including Lucy Stone, who was there as a guest and lecturer in early November, and Sojourner Truth, who stayed at the Water Cure during the same period. In such a community, Mary finally had an opportunity to escape the lonely, demanding routine at North Elba and enjoy the company of like-minded people in a therapeutic context. Ruggles listened attentively to Mary's complaints and diagnosed her as having "Neuralgia" and a "Scrofulous humour" on her glands. She lost weight too, but perhaps because she was eating a healthful diet, exercising regularly, and enjoying a different kind of lifestyle.

When John Jr. finally wrote to his father to report that his stepmother was in Northampton, she had improved—though only after narrowly surviving an outbreak of dysentery that had swept through the Water Cure. At one point Thomas Thomas had written to John Jr., asking that he send Wealthy up to Northampton to assist Mary through her sickness. John Jr. wrote that although he could not say if the Water Cure would actually help Mary, he hoped it would. "Ruggles firmly believes that he can benefit her," John Jr. concluded. Brown was probably annoyed to receive news that Mary had gone to Northampton—not only because he was not convinced that his wife was seriously ill, but also because he probably thought of the Water Cure as a Garrisonian fad. The very idea of associating too closely with high-profile abolitionists may have irritated Brown as well. He had likely met Ruggles while living in Massachusetts, and probably thought it unfortunate that such a fine man would allow himself to take physical abuse from racists because of pacifist principles. By the late 1840s, Ruggles was very sick. According to the observations of Frederick Douglass, he was "blind and measurably helpless, but a man of sterling sense and worth."

Mary Brown with two of her daughters, Anne (left) and Sarah, around 1851, at the end of the Browns' first stay in North Elba, where they had moved to be near Timbucto, a fledgling black colony in the Adirondacks. *West Virginia State Archives.*

Mary seemed relieved when she learned that her stepson had later informed Brown of her stay at Northampton. "I am glad you told him. [H]e has never believed there was any dissease [*sic*] about me, but I think if *he* was here now he would change his mind. Say to him I would like a letter from him," she wrote to John Jr. When Brown finally returned to the United States, he stopped in to see Mary and Thomas Thomas at Northampton before proceeding back to North Elba and Timbucto. He may have expected his wife to pack her bags and return with him, but she did not. Instead, he returned to the Adirondacks alone. Finding the family well, Brown wrote to John Jr., instructing him to let Mary know he had reached home—perhaps being too perturbed to write for himself.

It is impossible to determine what was actually wrong with Mary Brown and to what degree, if any, Ruggles's diagnosis had any validity. (She lived for nearly thirty more years, dying of cancer in 1884.) If nothing else, Mary enjoyed the Water Cure treatment and the time it afforded her away from the cold and demanding Adirondacks. And unlike her husband's desperate venture in Europe, at least Mary could return home claiming a degree of success. By mid-December 1849, John Brown was in Springfield on business and Mary had returned to North Elba. When news reached him that Ruggles had finally succumbed in his sick and broken state, Brown sent word to his wife. "Dr. Ruggles died about one week since," he wrote flatly. "So we go."[3]

If Brown had seen an important venture end in failure, so had his seventy-eight-year-old father. He had written faithfully to Owen Brown during the European tour, and in return had probably received news of the demise of the Free Congregational Church at Hudson. From the beginning it seems that the breakaway church had never realized the promise it proposed of its mission. Despite the presence of sincere men like Owen, the church's seven-year existence (1842–49) saw little more accomplished than the building it left behind in Hudson. In the initial years, records of the congregational meetings are filled with the business of church life— new members, letters of transfer, building committee matters, and references to attendance at religious and anti-slavery conventions. But in 1847 the church began to decline, with deep rifts appearing in the small congregation as key members either left or openly opposed its leadership. When the church secretary and others resigned in preparation to move westward, elderly Owen was left to record the final days of the abolitionist church venture. Appropriately enough, the last page of the church records is written in Owen's shaky, septuagenarian scrawl. One can almost see his hand trembling, the ink blotching here and there as he notes that a meeting was proposed for July 19, "to take into consideration wheather [sic] it would not be more for the glory of God and our future usefullness [sic] to give up our present organization as a Church." On the appointed day, the remaining members opened with prayer and then agreed it was time to dissolve the Free Congregational Church of Hudson. Recommending each other to "any evangelical Church where God in his providence may place them," the tired, disappointed abolitionists went their separate ways.

Owen returned to the First Congregational Church, though it is not clear when or if he reapplied for membership. It is not difficult to imagine that the respected elder would be accepted back into the fold of the faithful, especially since the general attitude toward abolition had already begun to change. The old conflict between abolitionists and colonization advocates had become too dated to matter. However, the pastor of the First Congregational Church could not resist chiding those who returned from the wreck of the Free Church. During the fiftieth anniversary of the Hudson church in 1852, he made sure to comment on the presence of Free Church seceders who had returned to the fold. "This church has been an inheritance of sorrow to its pastors. God has held you up in your wanderings, but not for any goodness He found in you." If he was present, Owen probably took the pill with grace and humility. But the old saint had kept the faith until the last trembling page was turned, and would keep it still. Later that year, Owen wrote to his grandson John Jr.: "I am in the full beleaf [*sic*] that slavery is sinfull [*sic*] and should never be connected with christianity."[4]

Meanwhile, Brown could only make dismal reports to P&B's clients. Not only were the manufacturers still resistant, he wrote in a circular, but their wools were generally ill-prepared for market—something he felt a disgraceful proof of the low character of "people in the United States." Though they had charged otherwise, he contended that P&B had tried its best and should receive "at least a candid consideration of the difficulties, which have attended the effort."

John Brown was entering his last decade with another failure to explain, but this time not all the fault was his own. Nor were the debts incurred to be borne by him alone in impoverished humility. Indeed, to his pleasant surprise, Simon Perkins faced the failure without a "frown on his countenance or one sylable [*sic*] of reflection, but on the contrary with words of comfort, and encouragement," Brown reported to his family. "He is wholly averse to any seperation [*sic*] of our business or interests, and gave me the fullest assurance of his undiminished confidence and personal regard." Contrary to what might have been expected, P&B's failure did not ruin the association of Perkins and Brown. "Such a meeting I had not dared to expect, and I most heartily wish each of my family could have shared in the comfort of it. Mr Perkins has in this whole business from first to last set an example worthy of a Philosopher or of a *Christian*," he concluded.

Between 1850 and 1851, Brown closed down P&B's operations and began to prepare for the move back to Ohio, where he would resume his previous role in keeping the Perkins flock and farm in Akron. His letters throughout 1850 reflect several trips between North Elba and Springfield and other trips west on business. Sending instructions to Mary on various farm issues, Brown was distracted and wearied by the task of contacting wool growers, paying off debts, and trying to close the business with decent sales. "The settling up of the wool business is what I am still detained about, and it is a very tedious business" he wrote to his wife from Akron in September 1850. "I shall escape like a bird out of a cage the first moment I can get clear."

Timbucto was also facing imminent decline. In the first quarter of 1850, Ruth wrote to her father that many of their black associates had stopped working and were leaving the settlement. "Mr. Rice has moved away and Smith is going as [soon as] he gets his pay." Their housekeeper had also gone, and young Owen had to pay her out of the family's farm money. Funds were becoming scarce for the Browns, and scarcity of money would ultimately finish off most of the black settlers too. The most meaningful loss to the black colony experiment was the departure of Brown's friend, Willis Hodges. Though it is not clear when he quit the Adirondacks, Hodges had abandoned Blacksville and returned to Brooklyn by 1853. But the failure of the Smith lands venture was hardly noticeable compared to new developments in the nation's capitol that would shortly spread a blanket of gloom over the entire black community in the North.

In the fall of 1850, while Brown was still dealing with the unpleasant aftermath of P&B's demise and his family was in North Elba, news came of the passing of the Fugitive Slave Bill. The bill provided for the power of district and circuit courts to enforce by law the work of marshals and their deputies in seizing fugitives and returning them "to the State or territory from which such persons may have escaped or fled." Marshals were threatened with fines if they did not participate in the return of fugitives. Those claiming to be masters could pursue fugitives and seize them, either on their own or with the assistance of marshals, and bring them to court. Fugitive testimonies would not be admitted in evidence, and the rights of the alleged master would be upheld over all. Those found hindering or opposing the exercise of the Fugitive Slave Law would be subject to fines and imprisonment. To assure the success of the Law, marshals and their deputies were to be awarded ten dollars for every fugitive they returned to slavery, and only five dollars for those not returned to slavery after the court hearing.

"It now seems the fugitive slave law was to be the means of making more abolitionists than all the lectures we have had for years," Brown wrote to his wife from Springfield. "It really looks as if God had his hand in this wickedness also." Brown had apparently gone to Springfield's

Zion Methodist Church on Thanksgiving Day, where he stood up to encourage the brethren with his favorite quote, "Trust in God and keep your powder dry." Like his black friends, he knew the Fugitive Slave Law was part of a larger compromise package passed by Congress and signed into law by President Millard Fillmore. It brought immediate and dramatic changes to the nation. As a result, black people began to stream by the thousands from Northern cities into Canada. Furthermore, black abolitionists were driven forward to militancy, while pacifism and "moral suasion" seemed impotent, if not obsolete. Rather than be upset at the bad news, John Brown saw the handwriting on the wall and believed it was Providential script. After returning to North Elba to spend Christmas in the snowy Canaan with family and friends, Brown packed his suitcase and took a sleigh to Elizabethtown, making his way from there to Albany, and then to Springfield once more. He was not back in town for wool business.[5]

# 15

## "All the Encouragement in My Power"

When the ear heard me, then it blessed me; and when the eye saw me, it gave witness to me: Because I delivered the poor that cried, and the fatherless, and him that had none to help him.
—Job 29:11–12

"Mr. Brown believed American slavery to be wrong, and that no man made laws would make it right," remembered one who knew John Brown in North Elba. He also "believed that in all ages of the world God had created certain men to perform special work in some direction far in advance of the rest of their countrymen," even at the cost of their lives. "He believed that among his earthly missions was to free the American slaves. . . . and it *must be performed*. He was very strict in his religious duties and he regarded *this as sacred*." When the Fugitive Slave Law was enacted, many people responded in a similar manner, but given Brown's unusually close connection with the black community, his commitment put him on the front line of struggle. The first Fugitive Slave Law was rooted in the Fugitive Slave Act of 1793. But that Act was increasingly defied until southern politicians feared for the survival of slavery. The Fugitive Slave Law of 1850 thus revitalized slavery for a new decade. Newly empowered, the monster's reach was now even more stunning and merciless.

Lecturing at Corinthian Hall in Rochester, New York, Frederick Douglass noted that one victim had been "arrested and delivered up in a most secret and hasty manner, without the legal and friendly aid which might have been rendered." Worse was the case of Henry Long, a fugitive living in New York City. According to Douglass, Long was tracked down by his former captor in Virginia, arrested in public, and held over for a hearing that was well publicized. He pointed out that there was not even "a sign of disturbance" from New York's abolitionist community. Douglass declared it a scandal that the black community in particular had done nothing between the time of Long's capture and deportation. To add insult to injury, a group of New York City businessmen and merchants had raised money to hire a lawyer to represent Long's "master." The trauma of Henry Long's return to slavery was felt all over the North, including Springfield.

The sympathetic *Springfield Republican* observed the anxiety of the black community: "Our colored friends are getting considerably excited in regard to the new Fugitive Slave Law." One young woman working as a housekeeper was reported to have taken a sharp knife with her on an errand for her employer. Hiding it in the folds of her apron, she was determined to fight back if seized by an agent or marshal. "We understand that most of them have armed themselves against any emergency that may arise and are determined to do valiant battle for their rights," concluded the *Republican*'s commentator in October 1850. Black people had responded to the Fugitive Slave Law either by fleeing or digging in for a fight. Clearly John Brown did not first instruct black people to arm themselves, though it seems he recognized a need to encourage better organization and training to repel invasions in the community by agents of the Fugitive Slave Law.

Like his activities in Timbucto, Brown saw his role in Springfield as a facilitator and ally. He was already secure in the personal acceptance and friendship he enjoyed in Springfield's black community, and their openness to his support was evident. Working with the Zion Methodist Church, Brown and the Reverend John Mars recognized the need to prepare the black community to make aggressive resistance. Mars was only a few years younger than Brown and was likewise born in Connecticut. His parents had been held as slaves by a Presbyterian minister, and upon his conversion and ordination for ministry he understandably chose the Methodist Church for affiliation. One Sunday morning Mars preached a sermon based on the words of Christ in the Gospel of Luke, "and he that hath no sword, let him sell his garments and buy one." Perhaps it was after that same sermon that John Brown stood in the back of the sanctuary, distributing Bowie knives to congregants.

"Since the sending off to slavery of Long from New York," he wrote home to Mary, "I have improved my leisure hours quite busily with colored people here, in advising them how to act, and in giving them all the encouragement in my power." Brown's letter reveals a great deal about the condition of Springfield's blacks in the wake of the violent Fugitive Slave Law:

> They very much need encouragement and advice; and some of them are so alarmed that they tell me they cannot sleep on account of either themselves or their wives and children. I can only say I think I have been enabled to do something to revive their broken spirits. I want all my family to imagine themselves in the same dreadful condition.

Before he left home, Brown gave strict instruction to Mary and the children to "join in resisting any attempt that might be made" upon Timbucto. Slavemasters and their advocates were now treading on dangerous ground, Brown had told his family. "Their cup of iniquity is almost full." Their young friend and employee Cyrus was a fugitive, and they were not about to see him taken back into slavery. "We would *all* have defended him," Ruth recalled, even if they had to splash boiling hot water in the eyes of marshals and agents. However, Cyrus did not remain in North Elba, choosing instead to return to Springfield to help John Brown with his work.[1]

Only days before writing home to Mary, Brown had completed a document for a proposed self-defense organization in the black community called the "United States League of Gileadites," which he apparently hoped would be the first of many branches throughout the Northern black community. The document was headed "Words of Advice" and consisted of a lengthy preamble entitled "Union is Strength," followed by an "Agreement" and nine resolutions. Brown and black community leaders were clearly determined that no Henry Long incident would occur in Springfield. With the assistance of Thomas Thomas and the Zion Methodist Church, Brown rallied a small army, most of whom signed his handwritten document. The Gileadite name was derived from the biblical book of Judges, referring to a small but formidable army under the leadership of Gideon, an Israelite leader who liberated his nation from oppressive invaders.

The preamble and "Agreement" to "Words of Advice" both reflect John Brown's patriotism—his belief in America and its potential *apart* from the evil of slavery. He rejected the notion that abolitionists were not patriotic, and he never stopped emphasizing his belief in the American dream of his forefathers. But Brown presumed that his black allies should feel the same way: "As citizens of the United States of America, trusting in a Just and Merciful God, whose spirit and all-powerful aid we humbly implore," he wrote, "we will ever be true to the Flag of our beloved Country, always acting under it." Perhaps he had some reason to presume this since the Gileadites had not chosen to flee the country for Canada. But he would later demand the same patriotic loyalty from black allies who had found sanctuary in Canada. Of course, in general, John Brown insisted that his views prevail.

He also believed that whites were charmed by personal bravery, and therefore one black fighting for freedom "would arouse more sympathy throughout the nation" than would the passive suffering of many blacks. Brown told the Gileadites that they had white friends indeed, and would have more if they were "half as much in earnest to secure their dearest rights as they are to ape the follies and extravagances of their white neighbors, and to indulge in idle show, in ease, and in luxury." These hard, caustic words not only reflected his strong conservative bent but reiterated the same candid critique of Northern blacks as in "Sambo's Mistakes." Brown seems naive to have believed white Americans would admire blacks fighting other whites for their freedom. Most white Americans feared the arming of blacks and Native peoples, and racists and abolitionists alike preferred that blacks go unarmed.

Brown clearly unfolded the strategy of the organization in the heart of the "Union is Strength" preamble. Gileadites would be armed at all times, though concealing their weapons. They must be hostile toward treachery in their ranks, "understanding that all traitors must die, wherever caught and proven to be guilty." When intervening on behalf of a fugitive, the Gileadites were not to delay, and at the first blow, all were to attack, making "clean work" of fugitive-hunters and marshals. In their assault, the Gileadites were to move quietly and quickly in order to take the enemy by surprise and avoid drawing other enemies, "for they will be wholly unprepared with either equipments or matured plans—all with them will be confusion and terror." In crisis, Brown wrote, blacks could "safely calculate on a division of the whites," some coming to their side though many would oppose the liberation struggle. Brown's strategy required that the Gileadites be "firm, determined, and cool," not driven to desperation but forceful in showing their enemies that "those who live in wooden houses should not throw fire."

Brown advised them to hold up in the homes of whites who claimed to be their friends if their rescue party was pursued. Whites who "would flinch" could thereafter be disregarded. Fleeing to the homes of whites would also discourage harsh reprisals, since authorities valued white life and property and would not quickly wreak devastation as they would in the black community.

Absolute loyalty would have to be maintained, to the very last drop of blood. "Stand by one another, and by your friends . . . be hanged if you must, but tell no tales out of school. Make no confession." Brown understood that the nature of the Gileadite movement was revolutionary and subversive to the political order of the land, and could not afford compromise within its ranks. Fugitive slave trials could be interrupted by creating a "tumult in the court-room" by exploding small packets of gunpowder, while making good the liberation of the fugitive. If necessary, Brown wrote, a "lasso might possibly be applied to a slave-catcher for once with good effect"—which seems to suggest that the fugitive-hunters might also be hanged.

The rest of the document, including the "Agreement" and resolutions, largely pertained to organizational concerns, especially the obligation of the members to supply their own weapons. The organization would also develop a list of supportive persons in the black community, and explore the availability and quality of weapons. Seniors, children, females, and the "infirm" among the Gileadites would work in surveillance and communication. Temporary officers would serve until the Gileadites had faced their "first trial," after which an election would confirm the natural leaders emerging within the organization. Thomas Thomas served as the president *pro tem*, but since the Gileadites were never forced into action it appears no permanent officers were elected.

John Brown remained in Springfield until perhaps late February 1851. During that time he met with the Gileadites and invited Charles Sumner to visit Springfield and address the Gileadites and other abolitionists. Sumner, a politician who would later be physically assaulted for his strong stance against slavery in Washington, is said to have met with Brown and the Gileadites in the back room of Rufus Elmer's shoe store. Elmer's store was a frequent night time meeting place for Springfield's abolitionists. After speaking, Sumner told Brown that slavery was doomed, "but not in your day or mine." Without agreeing or disagreeing, Brown only raised his hand as if to make a vow, saying "I hope to die in the cause."[2]

Though about forty-four people signed the original Gileadite document, only about twenty-seven are known. One familiar name is that of

Cyrus, listed as Cyrus Thomas, who had trailed the Browns from Springfield to Timbucto in 1849. A few of the Gileadites, male and female, are known only by their professions, but others were prominent in the black community. Overall, the Gileadites worked as laborers, barbers, waiters, and cooks, but there were also machine operators and craftsmen in woodwork, carriage building, and even a tinsmith. Of the available names, the average age of male Gileadites was about thirty-five, the youngest being a twenty-one-year-old waiter named Charles Rollins. The Gileadites embraced the involvement of women, though the ages of only two of the four female Gileadites listed is known, both being under twenty years. One of them, Ann Johnson, seems to have joined the organization with her father. At least eleven of the sixteen males listed were married, and at least five had children. Based on the surviving names, six Gileadites were born in Maryland, four in Virginia, one in Alabama, and another in Washington, D.C. Other Gileadites were born in the North, particularly New York, Massachusetts, and Pennsylvania.

Among the most prominent Gileadites were Beverly C. Dowling, John N. Howard, William H. Montague, and William Green. Dowling and Howard were Thomas Thomas's "lieutenants" in the organization. Dowling operated an "eating saloon" in Springfield. His wife Ann was born in Maryland, and they had five children. Howard and his wife Mary were born in Virginia. Howard supported his wife and two children as sexton of South Church in Springfield. William Montague was not yet thirty years old when he joined the Gileadites, and is listed in the city directory as a professional hairdresser and barber, and recorded as owning real estate valued at $1,200. Montague was born in the nation's capitol, and his wife, Eliza, was born in Maryland, and they had four children and a foster child. Montague was also a trustee of Zion Methodist Church, where John Brown was in regular attendance. William Green was born in Maryland, and partnered in a painting business. He later wrote an autobiography published in 1853. Henry Johnson, a shoemaker and carriage-builder, was born in Maryland and joined the movement with his daughter Ann, the eldest of his five children. Ann Johnson, Jane Fowler, Eliza Green, and Jane Wicks were female Gileadites, though there were other women members. Whether or not there were white Gileadites is not clear, though some of the Gileadites had white relatives. The young Gileadite Jane Fowler was the daughter of Nancy Fowler, a white woman. So was Mary Madison, the wife of Gileadite James Madison, a woodworker from New York.

The Gileadites were workaday citizens of Springfield at the time when the Fugitive Slave Law was enacted. Prior to the Gileadite call, John Brown undoubtedly knew many of these black townspeople and recognized the Law's threat to them. The black community in Springfield was growing, but it was not so expansive that the capture and deportation of any one person would have occurred without creating trauma throughout the whole community. Whether or not Brown's document was aligned completely with the ideology of the fugitives and the black community is open to discussion. Nevertheless it was a crisis document that reflected the essential elements of a black-oriented abolitionist perspective, and certainly met the pressing need of the hour. Clearly the document was approved and signed by a significant number of Springfield's black community, and was no doubt appreciated by all. More importantly, the Gileadites did not remain a paper organization, but actively patrolled Springfield in the event of an attack on the fugitives in the community.

In June 1854, Anthony Burns of Boston was returned to slavery despite a great deal of protest and outrage, including a failed attempt to storm the courthouse and seize the victim. Burns was supported by the lawyer Richard Henry Dana, who once wandered onto the Brown farm in North Elba in 1849. A week after Burns's rendition, the black writer William Wells Brown visited Springfield. By this time, John Brown had relocated to Akron and the Gileadites were functioning under the leadership of Thomas Thomas and other *pro tem* officers. When the abolitionist writer reached town, he found that the Burns incident had created an atmosphere of "despair and revenge" among the blacks and their white sympathizers in Springfield.

Entering a black residential area, he could see by moonlight that "black sentinels were stationed at the corners of the streets and alleys." The writer and his companion were then escorted to a two-story home occupied by a number of black families. After being thoroughly examined, they were guided into the "hot room." Inside were women moving around an old stove, on which were heating large, steaming pots filled with a boiling brew of water, soap, and ashes, which the women called the "King of Pain." Brown spoke to one woman, a former slave in Virginia, whose face bore the scars of slavery, and who had been forced to leave her children behind when she escaped. She had no intention of being taken back into slavery. "I'll die first," she declared. Perhaps following a method prescribed by John Brown, these fugitives intended to fight off any attempt by agents to seize them, vowing to "scald their very hearts out." When the abolitionist writer asked if they could throw the boiling brew on their assailants without hurting each other, the woman replied: "Oh, yes, honey; we've been practicin' all day.' At this point "the whole company joined in a hearty laugh," Brown recalled, "which made the old building ring." The Gileadite guards laughed too, the kind of laughter "which showed very clearly that these blacks felt themselves masters of the situation." While waiting to catch a train back to Boston, William Wells Brown noted "some ten or fifteen blacks" in the vicinity, "all armed to the teeth and swearing vengeance upon the heads of any who would attempt to take them." He learned later that some fugitive-hunters had actually come to Springfield earlier in the day. But city authorities were so certain that they would be killed that they warned the agents to leave on the evening train to New York. John Brown would have been more than pleased.

The League of Gileadites functioned for several years, but declined by the later 1850s. Thomas Thomas left Springfield for the West in 1855, and this may have marked the decline of the organization. John Howard, one of Thomas's lieutenants, was "forced to sell his property at a nominal value and flee to Canada to keep his liberty" in 1857. Howard's decision to move suggests he lacked the network of support formerly provided by the Gileadites. He returned to Springfield at the outbreak of the Civil War. With the exception of individual Gileadites who carried the ideas of the movement to Canada, the organization was never expanded into a national effort as John Brown had hoped, nor does it seem to have outlasted the Fugitive Slave Law.[3] However, no fugitive was ever taken back into slavery from Springfield, and perhaps the reputation of the Gileadites outlasted the organization itself, serving the interests of the black community long after John Brown's departure.

If William Wells Brown was impressed by the League of Gileadites in Springfield, he and many other blacks were even more impressed by the bold resistance of a combined force of free blacks and fugitives in a skirmish often mislabeled "the Christiana Riot." In September 1851, a slavemaster named Edward Gorsuch, his son and other associates left Maryland for southeastern Pennsylvania for the rendition of four male fugitives, with the assistance of a federal marshal. The former slaves had found a haven in the home of William Parker, a fugitive from Maryland residing in the southeastern Pennsylvania town of Christiana. Parker was an activist and a veteran of other forceful efforts to protect fugitives. When the Gorsuch party arrived at Parker's home, they not only found the blacks armed and secure in Parker's house, but militantly determined to fight rather than be taken. With the support of local blacks, the Gorsuch party was beaten back, fleeing before the bold counterattack. The old master himself stubbornly fought, but was finally clubbed and slashed to death. Parker and the fugitives then fled to Canada and were never apprehended, and those arrested and charged with treason served only a few months in prison. William Wells Brown, who had visited Springfield's Gileadites in 1851, stopped at Christiana several years later to pay his respects at the battle site. He came away with the impression that "no master would ever come there again in pursuit of his fugitive slave."

John Brown's daughter Ruth, who had married a neighboring abolitionist named Henry Thompson in 1850, had her own thoughts on the so-called Christiana "riot." Writing to John Jr. in January 1852, Ruth observed that society used a different standard when it came to whites fighting for freedom. By this time, the United States was animated with excitement over the visit of Louis Kossuth, the Hungarian revolutionist. In the early 1850s, Kossuth had become an icon of republican virtue, locked in a desperate struggle for the freedom of his people against the superior forces of Austria and Russia. Ruth was irritated by the outpouring of praise afforded a foreign white liberator, while Parker and the other Christiana blacks engaged in a similar struggle at home were condemned. "Does it not realy [*sic*] look inconsistent for some of the toasts given to [Kossuth] on his arrival at New York[?] They say 'Who so acclaimed as he who strikes for Freedom.' Why should it not be said, 'Who so brave and noble as the heros of Christiana[?]'" Instead, Ruth concluded, the Christiana warriors were "cast out" for "nobly defending themselves."[4]

The intense interest and celebration that arose at the coming of Kossuth to North America was part and parcel with the general excitement over revolutionary events taking place across Europe in this period. Even John Brown was watching with expectation for the Sovereign design to unfold on a global scale. "The great excitement produced by the coming of Kossuth, and the last news of a new revolution in France, with the prospect that all Europe will soon again be in blaze seem to have taken all by surprise," Brown wrote to Mary late in December 1851. "I have only to say in regard to these things that I rejoice in them from the full belief that God is carrying out his Eternal purpose in them all." William Lloyd Garrison too lauded Kossuth, publishing a sonnet and welcoming tributes in *The Liberator*. To no surprise, black Americans also perceived a hopeful light emanating from Kossuth, and watched intently for the

Hungarian to show himself an ally. Frederick Douglass watched Kossuth too, documenting his visit to England on the front page of his newly renamed *Frederick Douglass' Paper*. If nothing else, the celebration of Kossuth provided abolitionists an opportunity to criticize his pro-slavery supporters in the United States. "A sympathizer with the oppressed at least ought not to be a tyrant himself," declared the report of the Massachusetts Anti-Slavery Society as early as January 1850.

After a controversial career in politics, Kossuth had great influence in Hungary as long as his nation was able to push back her Austrian oppressors. But Hungary was defeated when Russia intervened to assist Austria, and Kossuth was forced into flight. Supported by the United States, Kossuth first made his way to England, and finally crossed the Atlantic for a hero's welcome in December 1851. Unfortunately, he turned out to be a great disappointment, selfishly side-stepping the slavery issue in order to protect his own interests. Kossuth would only say that he hoped "every man who feels sympathy with the [anti-slavery] cause will be inclined to do something for it in a practical manner."

The Hungarian's self-serving expediency evoked the wrath of brilliant, fiery-tongued William Lloyd Garrison of Boston. Indeed, the controversial editor of *The Liberator* went after Kossuth with a ferocity that did great damage to his quest for support in the United States. Garrison "hammered Kossuth week after week," and finished off the deed with a pamphlet exposing the Hungarian as a self-seeking toady. To his discredit, Kossuth had unfortunately ignored his "natural constituency among the abolitionists" in order to please the pro-slavery establishment, even though the slaveholding element did not really back him in political terms. Kossuth ultimately left the country with only a fraction of the money he had hoped to receive on his tour, and entirely lost the support of abolitionists. Frederick Douglass wrote that Kossuth had bought the support of "the mass of the American people" at the expense of the abolitionists, "who are but applying the great principle of freedom which he professes to hold dear." The abolitionists of Massachusetts concluded with greater scorn. "Kossuth's visit to this country was a mistake; he has made it a crime."

The only abolitionist who seems not to have been overcome with disgust by the Kossuth affair was John Brown. Hearing of Douglass's remarks, he wrote a peculiarly optimistic letter that was then published in the Douglass paper. Though Kossuth was not a superior man to Dou-

glass, Brown wrote, he had somehow managed to hold the "true Philosopher's Stone"—suggesting that Douglass should at least appreciate Kossuth's minimal contribution.

> I think that, notwithstanding policy, prevents his opening all his batter-
> ies direct upon our *accursed* hypocrisy, aristocratic feeling, injustice,
> God-insulting, provoking ingratitude, and most abominable cruelty and
> oppression, he is doing more to instruct our young people and to indoc-
> trinate them in the *true* republican principle, than any man has done
> since the revolution.

Brown's approach was surprisingly conservative and, once more, apparently naive in his belief that white Americans would include blacks in
their enthusiasm for "republican principle." He also suggested that
blacks not lament too much about the disappointment of Kossuth because God was working in the situation. If the Almighty had removed one
potential leader, it was only to reveal another hero, waiting in the wings
of Providence:

> *I therefore rejoice, and will rejoice*, and let none of my colored friends
> "faint and grow weary in well-doing, *for in due time we shall reap* if we
> faint not." "The Lord our God shall raise up for a us a deliverer" in the
> very best possible time; and who shall pretend to prove that he is not
> *even now born*. Moses was born at the very time that the bitter cup of
> Egyptian bondage was pouring out to Israel to its very dregs.

Brown's messianic allusion, based on Deuteronomy 18 and the Exodus
story in the Bible, hinted that the liberator "Moses" was already on the
scene. Was Brown dropping hints about himself? By this time he had indeed taken definite steps forward in his self-perceived role as an instrument of Providence for the liberation of the slaves. Yet he may have entertained the notion of a coming black messiah—perhaps a dark Sparta-
cus, or another Nat Turner. Brown acknowledged that he was watching
and waiting for militant black leaders to arise, and it may be that he
merely saw himself as supporting their efforts the way the biblical warrior Joshua supported Moses. (Douglass published the letter unedited,
perhaps flattering himself that Brown was speaking about him.) "No! Let
no man's heart fail him," Brown concluded. "But let us resolutely trust in

God, and keep our *powder dry.*" Whomever God would choose as an instrument of deliverance, it would be God, not man, who would strike the actual blow to end slavery.[5]

The Reverend Jermain W. Loguen, a former fugitive distinguished by his underground railroad and abolitionist efforts, declared that the whole Kossuth affair only highlighted white American hypocrisy. "They are trying to make that great man Kossuth (and for ought I know succeed in making him believe) they are lovers of Liberty." Loguen had also made a name for himself by participating in the rescue of a fugitive in Syracuse, New York. In 1851, William Henry, known as "Jerry," was arrested, manacled, and beaten after nearly escaping from authorities. In response to the arrest, a group of abolitionists, including Loguen and Samuel Ringgold Ward, stormed the police station, overcame the officers, and took "Jerry" from his cell. Breaking his chains, they whisked him away to freedom in Ontario, Canada. As a result, proceedings began for the indictment of eighteen of the Syracuse raiders, including Loguen and Ward, who both then fled to Canada. But Loguen hated his exile, and returned on a pledge from New York's governor that he could stand trial with all guaranteed protection as an American citizen. Loguen was not indicted, but the experience enhanced his militance.

In August 1853, Loguen wrote to Douglass while awaiting trial, declaring that "I go for agitating, and agitating again. I believe that slavery has yet to be done away with, either by agitation or bloodshed." Though all things were in the hands of "the God of the oppressed," Loguen wrote, he still had "an old grey-headed mother" and siblings in slavery. Yet he preferred to "hear of them swimming in blood, and nobly contending for their rights, even at the cost of their own lives, than have them remain passive slaves all the rest of their days." Loguen concluded that he would rather die than return to slavery. "I feel ready to try titles at any time with the slaveholder, or his meaner lickspittles of the North. *Death is sweeter than slavery.*"

When John Brown read Loguen's letter in Douglass's paper, he was nearly euphoric. Scribbling off a hurried, excited response, Brown declared that Loguen's letter "has a certain music in it that so fills *my* ear, that I cannot well suppress the pleasure it affords." He was particularly charmed by Loguen's statement that he would "glory" in his upcoming trial. "Allow me to say hereafter, that shall be my music," Brown added. "This with me comes up to the full measure of a man."

I would a thousand times rather share with Loguen in his *glorying*, and his *suffering* too, than to receive all the honors that ever Millard Fillmore, Daniel Webster, and all other such like traitorous "lickspittles" could even dream of.

He was convinced that he had read the words of a leader that *even John Brown* would follow: "I go for agitating and agitating again in the true *Loguen style*."

Friend Douglass I have been waiting and watching with longing eyes for many years to see some full sized colored men leaping their full length above the surface of the water and I hope some day to see Loguen, and to give him such a shake of the hand, as will make his snap.[6]

From his "Sambo" essay to the League of Gileadites, and finally to this signal letter prompted by Loguen, John Brown showed his high hopes for black people—if only they would help themselves to a bloody portion of the struggle. Then surely he would stand with them and fight, even unto death.

# PART VI

# Enduring Hardness

I expect nothing but to "endure hardness," but I expect to effect a mighty conquest, even if it be like the last Victory of Samson.

—John Brown

# 16

## Ohio and Beyond

And he hath brought us into this place, and hath given us this land,
even a land that floweth with milk and honey.

—Deuteronomy 26:9

The demise of P&B was a great disappointment to Brown, but
probably more for personal reasons, both pride and the lost cause of the
wool growers. A man of great means with other enterprises unscathed,
partner Perkins incurred the real financial loss, as Brown put it, "with
philosophic calm." Not that Brown emerged from the failure with money,
or that the potential for further loss did not overshadow him. But when
he wrote to John Jr. that he and Perkins were having "trouble" with lawsuits amounting to $40,000, he was not writing in desperate dependence
upon Providence as he had a decade before. If they lost these cases, Brown
wrote, he would be left "nice and flat." But while he worked hard at selling leftover wool and collecting outstanding payments, he was privately
comforted by Perkins's sound demeanor and his interest in keeping their
association active beyond the grave of P&B. Litigation from wool growers, manufacturers, and disappointed banks kept Brown traveling in the
northeast for several more years and required working with various
lawyers in representing P&B's interests. Overall these lawsuits were irritating more than threatening, consuming time and energy he would have
preferred to devote to other pursuits. "There were all sorts of tangled
knots in the wool business," Stutler concluded of this frustrating period.
But history has tangled knots too. One of P&B's lawyers for a case in
Pittsburgh was Edwin M. Stanton, later to serve as Secretary of War in
the Lincoln administration.[1]

When he could return to North Elba, Brown busied himself with work,
such as helping the declining black colony by surveying, "or in tracing old
lost boundaries." Moving about the Adirondack wilderness charmed his

senses and "almost entirely diverted" his thinking "from its burdens." He wrote to his father Owen that he was frustrated by the prospect of trying to collect on P&B's accounts, and disappointed by the slow sale of remaining wools.

In March 1851, Brown moved his family back to Akron. Though his heart remained in Timbucto, it was necessary to return to Ohio in order to continue his work with Perkins. Whatever apprehensions he may have had about continuing with Perkins had been allayed when the two met in western Pennsylvania in April 1850. Perkins made it clear he had no intention of dissolving their partnership, and gave Brown "the fullest assurance of his undiminished confidence and personal regard." Their common denominator remained his great abilities as a shepherd, and Perkins's expressions of trust so warmed Brown that he wrote to John Jr. that he now felt "nerved to face" the ongoing lawsuits as long as "God continues me such a partner." While Perkins could not have taken the failure of P&B lightly, by 1851 he seemed more concerned that Brown come back to Ohio. A month before the Browns moved to Akron, Perkins showed up in Springfield, as John Brown wrote, seeming "anxious to have us go back to Akron, and wants me to go on with him."

However, John Jr., who had already moved back to Ohio with his wife Wealthy, had different feelings on the Perkins-Brown partnership. Writing in late 1850, John Jr. expressed concern because it had gotten back to him that Grace Perkins felt Brown ought to have born the losses of P&B instead of her husband. Consequently, John Jr. feared that Brown would be disgraced, abused, and reduced to "slavery of the soul" if he returned to work with Perkins. But Simon Perkins was not influenced by his wife's condescending attitude, and his only dissatisfaction seems to have been with Jason's work at the farm. Unlike his father, Jason did not give regular reports on the flock, and it bothered the mogul to have to come asking about his sheep. John Jr. changed his mind later, writing to his father that Perkins was not a money-grubber like his former partner, Heman Oviatt. In fact, he concluded that Perkins showed a "magnanimous spirit in an eminent degree." Rather than returning to Ohio in a downcast state, there seems to have been a good measure of optimism among the Browns, largely brought about by Perkins's renewed commitment. Jason and Owen continued working on another of Perkins's farms, and John Brown and family resumed their place on Mutton Hill in management of the notable Perkins flock. Though Brown reminded his family that "we really do not consider gain to be Godliness," he was hopeful that the continued partnership with Perkins would get them back on their feet. Probably with a half-smile, he privately encouraged his sons that "this is the place for [']weuns['] to get our money back."[2]

Yet John Brown had other concerns. His son Frederick, now in his early twenties, was sporadically set aside by illness and seizures. Frederick's condition became chronic in his teen years, though the contemporary diagnosis of "blood pressure on the brain" is probably meaningless in modern medical terms. As he entered young manhood, Frederick became sleepless, moody, and gluttonous in his eating habits, taking "wild" fits of "insanity." Brown consulted doctors and his letters from this period are riddled with remarks about Frederick's health status. These problems culminated in a "terrible operation for his breach" in 1854 that nearly killed him, Brown afterward nursing Frederick so intently that he never changed his clothes for two weeks. The nature of this "operation" is unclear, but an enemy of Brown claimed, perhaps with some authority, that Frederick had castrated himself.

Brown also lost a child while in Ohio. Mary Brown and Grace Perkins had both given birth to boys in April 1852, and their infants shortly became sick with measles. But the Brown baby could not recover before developing whooping cough. Four days before he died, Brown reported that the baby's sickness would probably cause him to "sink under his *increased* load." When he died, the Perkins family was shocked to hear that Brown had hastily built a coffin in the same room where Mary was convalescing, and that there would be no funeral service. Placing the little body inside the box, Brown nailed it shut, buried it in the yard, and "drove his oxen back and forth over the spot." The angel of death had come so often that all John Brown could do was wipe away any trace of his merciless presence. To make matters worse, the grieving parents became sick, Mary coughing up blood and Brown falling prey to "the fever and ague," a kind of malaria common at the time.

But Brown was mourning the living more than the dead. In 1852–53 there seem to have been religious tensions between John Brown, his sons, and Ruth Brown Thompson back in North Elba. Though his sons' agnosticism did not develop overnight, it had blossomed by the time Brown was settling in at the Perkins place. In a letter to Henry and Ruth in August 1852, he mentioned that John Jr. had not been in touch with him for "some months." Perhaps the father and son had fallen out over religious differences. "We are fixing a little for the State Fair," Brown wrote, "but whether any of us are preparing for *Heaven*; is very doubtful." Brown was too close to his namesake to hold a grudge, however, and soon assured him that his affections for his children were "too deep rooted to be alienated from them." Still, Brown wrote to his sons, he did not want to die until the "true God" forgave their denial [*sic*], and rejection Of him." He was "perfectly conscious" that their eyes were "blinded to the real truth, and minds prejudiced by Hearts unreconciled to their Maker and Judge." Quoting Isaiah the prophet, Brown concluded: "A deceived Heart hath turned them aside." Apparently Wealthy shared the unorthodox views of her husband, for her determined father-in-law noted that he was likewise praying for her and the rest of his children to have "Eyes to see."

In contrast, Brown vented his frustrations to his daughter Ruth as an ally in the faith: "Why will not my family endeavor to secure *his* favor, and to effect in the *one only* way a perfect reconciliation?" John Jr. probably withheld further expressions of disdain for evangelical faith in order to avoid disturbing his father. But a revival took place in North Elba in 1853, and Ruth wrote to her father and elder brother to report the good news, including the conversion of her husband Henry. Brown rejoiced, but with a measure of Calvinist reserve, expressing hope that "those seeming conversions may prove *genuine*." John Jr. reacted skeptically, questioning the tenets of orthodoxy and saying that revivals merely had a "freezing, contracting influence" on people. Declaring that true religion consisted of loving "our Infinite Father, and Mother, and universal love to the whole family of man," he also negated biblical authority, the divinity of Christ, and the notion of a future judgment. Ruth was appalled by her brother's heretical remarks, and penned a furious response: "You must have most deplorably forgotten the principles of your early education. . . . O sad and gloomy future. . . . Have you turned Un[i]versalist?"[3]

Ruth's letter showed a quality of theological understanding and an ability in the art of religious debate. On the other hand, her father was given to sheer bombardment in such discussions despite his extensive readings in the Bible and Reformed theology. John Jr.'s views invariably reached his father, who then wrote a long rejoinder consisting of ninety-four scripture quotations and several more allusions to biblical texts. John Jr. could hardly have responded to his father's tour-de-force "exhortation" because it was not much more than an unbroken flow of regurgitated biblical texts. The letter exemplifies Brown's vast knowledge and memorization of the Bible, and despite its clear warning against apostasy, it was overkill—as much an emotional reaction as an expression of sincere spiritual concern. Brown prefaced his scriptural onslaught by re-marking that Mary's sons had even gone further in rejecting orthodoxy than had John Jr., Jason, and Frederick. Apparently Watson, Salmon, and Oliver had told their father that the Bible was "all a fiction," whereas John Jr. seems to have limited his defiance to liberal revisions. Meanwhile, Frederick and Jason were toying with Spiritualism by consulting medi-ums, perhaps attempting to speak to their mother Dianthe beyond the grave. Frederick thought evangelical revivals were meaningless excite-ments that produced "more evil than good," believing they merely worked on human fear and emotion. John Brown probably agreed some-what with this criticism, though his Calvinism did not permit him to rule out the possibility of genuine works of grace and revival by the Holy Spirit. But he was concerned whether these works of grace were also pro-ducing good anti-slavery Christians:

> I am much rejoiced at the news of a religious kind in Ruth's letter; and would be still more rejoiced to learn that all the sects who bear the Christian name would have no more to do with that mother of all abom-inations—man-stealing. "If any man love not his brother whom he hath seen, how can he love God whom he hath not seen?" [I John 4:20]

Brown probably wrestled with his own emotions over the heterodoxy of his sons, sometimes feeling anger and resentment at their rebellion, then feeling compassionate and hopeful that they would return to the fold. Salmon remembered when one of his brothers asked Brown if he ever doubted the tenets of Christianity. "'No,' said Father, 'but I have doubted my own sincerity.' He was a candid man—truthful. He mourned nearly to the point of distraction because none of his boys shared his religious views."[4]

Another apostasy among the Brown boys was their dislike of the Adirondack lands. In 1852, John Jr. and Wealthy seem to have been con-templating a move to North Elba with its "pure air, pure water, glorious mountains, and invigorating climate." John Jr. had developed a case of "Essex fever," and seemed to think that the whole family might also be persuaded to relocate to the Adirondacks. Jason and Owen had tried in vain to persuade Perkins to hire John Jr. onto the farm they were keeping, but Perkins gave notice that he planned to sell the farm and did not want to do much more with it. Perkins's plans not only dashed the brothers' hopes, but cast a shadow over their own future in Ohio as well. Still,

Jason and Owen were dead set against their elder brother moving to the Adirondacks, and wrote to persuade him otherwise. "I hope you will not go to North Elba," Jason wrote, noting that farming in the Adirondacks meant living "7 months on the gain of 5 months."

> If you go to Essex, John, you will realise [*sic*] your dependance and the truth of Scripture where it says, "who can stand before his cold"? I am not writing this to make levity of Father[']s recommend[ation], nor of his feelings about Essex, but to give you the best reason I can for not going there to live.

Owen too felt that the whole prospect of going to North Elba had a "cold chilly wet look about it." North Elba was better suited to a colony of Norwegians, Jason concluded. "Father's New Palestine" was just too cold.

Of course the family remained united in support of militant abolitionism. Even Brown's born again son-in-law, Henry Thompson, saw an inherent flaw in the "moral suasion" doctrine of other abolitionists: "Their plan is to use . . . verry [*sic*] mild means: a plan which I think will do about as much good as it wold [*sic*] to try to pacify a raging Tiger with the promise of a good meal—by and by." Back in Ohio's Western Reserve, a militant spirit was becoming pervasive in the wake of the Fugitive Slave Law. It was a milestone of abolitionist success that Frederick Douglass was invited as the commencement speaker at Western Reserve College in July 1854—something that undoubtedly delighted the aged Owen Brown. Douglass trumpeted black manhood and the place of the "negro race" in the "human family," challenging the enemies of black people: "You cannot exterminate our race. The influence of Christianity, if not self interest, will not permit it. . . . The ten thousand horrors of Slavery have tried it, and it lifted up a smiling face amid it all." Douglass visited the Browns at Akron too, probably during this trip to Ohio. Another abolitionist visitor was Henry Highland Garnet, the fiery clergyman and underground railroad veteran. Salmon Brown remembered being a teenager when Garnet made a visit during the winter. Salmon was sympathetic to Garnet, and in his enthusiasm he unintentionally overheated the stove in the room where the black preacher was staying. Rather than being comfortably warmed, Garnet spent a miserable, sleepless night, sweating profusely before Salmon's monstrous fire. To punish him for his carelessness, Brown made his son carry Garnet's bag all the way to the train station "past staring neighbors and grinning school children."[5]

Besides managing the Perkins flock and traveling for court cases and wool sales, John Brown returned to underground railroad activities in Ohio. His efforts became more aggressive, possibly including forays into slave states and extended escorting of fugitives from Ohio into Michigan for transport to Canada. William Lambert, a leading underground railroad operator in Detroit, remembered Brown's energetic labors at this time. Lambert claimed that Brown brought more than two hundred fugitives to Detroit, "and that he had traveled everywhere in the South." Even granting some exaggeration, there is reason to believe that Brown's aggressiveness had begun to distinguish him. He would likely have been inclined to make daring efforts, given his growing hunger for a militant enterprise against slavery. Once, Lambert recalled, Brown was nearly killed while smuggling slaves underneath a wagon load of furniture. Detected by fugitive hunters while passing through Indiana, he had to flee, narrowly escaping under gunfire. An Ohio tradition has Brown coming up from Kentucky with a wagon full of furniture, suggesting that he used the same method to smuggle fugitives from slavery at other times. Lambert, who became a leading citizen in black Detroit, recalled Brown bringing a load of human "freight" in 1853, and fighting off two pursuers in the process. "He was indefatigable in these respects. He was always on time, and his personal courage tested a thousand times, was beyond dispute."

According to Lambert, Brown mastered the passwords, grips, and rituals that black leaders developed for security purposes. Because Detroit was a terminus on the underground railroad, black leaders there took special precaution to bring fugitives into the city by night in order to prepare them to cross over to Canada. They were understandably suspicious of white helpers, and put them through "severe tests," and "had one ritual for them alone and a chapter to test them in," Lambert said. One evening John Brown brought in about twenty fugitives, all of whom were tested, along with their guide. The test, preserved by Lambert, partly went:

Q: Cross?
A: Over.
Q: Have you ever been on the Railroad?
A: I have been a short distance.
Q: Where did you start from?
A: The depot.
Q: Where did you stop?

A: At a place called Safety.

Q: Have you a brother there? I think I know him.

A: I know you now. You traveled the road.

After the slender, smooth-shaven white man answered all the questions correctly the first time, Lambert asked knowingly if he was *the John Brown* he had heard about. "You are. I know it brother," he insisted. "Yes brother, I am John Brown." Though the two became friends, Lambert pointed out that Brown's dangerous experiences were familiar to others engaged in the same work.[6]

Brown's partnership with Perkins continued until 1854, allowing him further opportunity to see his brothers, sisters, and father Owen, now suffering the ailments of advanced age. The elder, perhaps out of spiritual concern to "be better prepared and more resigned" for death, had eased up on collecting rents and lost so much money as to jeopardize his estate. Trying to recover some of these losses marred his last few years with financial embarrassment, though he stubbornly refused to sell his land. But the elder Brown maintained a strong presence as patriarch, dispensing wisdom and counsel to his family. Writing to a nephew studying law, Owen urged caution since "it is easier to advocate the cause of the [*righteous*] than to vindicate the deeds of the wicked." Above all in importance was "[*Perseverance*] in that which is [*right*]." Nor was the old man's sense of humor bankrupt. Brown's daughter Sarah remembered the time her father and uncle Frederick got into an argument that quickly escalated into a shouting match. Suddenly old Owen hobbled out with his walking stick and leaned over, putting his hand to his ear. "What *is* it you have for to *say?*" the elder shouted. "Speak a little *louder*." John Brown and his brother laughed, and tensions eased.[7]

Though the Browns perceived an end to the work with Perkins by 1853, he extended the arrangement for another year, once more fervently expressing a desire to keep Brown in Akron. "He seems so pleasant and anxious to have me continue, that I cannot tear away from him," he wrote to John Jr. It was a good arrangement, Perkins carrying all the actual expenses of the operation and Brown overseeing the labor and management of the farm, and sharing taxes and insurance. Contrary to narratives that generalize the failure of P&B in representing Brown's partnership with Perkins, John Brown wound up his work with the Akron magnate on a positive and profitable note. Only after 1853–54, when he had obviously decided to move away from farming, was

"Dear Father." Owen Brown, the abolitionist patriarch, in later years. Owen sustained a close correspondence with his son throughout the years, and was especially concerned over his family's struggles in Kansas. *West Virginia State Archives.*

Perkins willing to release him. "We have great reason to be thankful that we have had so prosperous a year and have terminated our connection with Mr Perkins so comfortably, and on such friendly terms to all appearance," Brown wrote in early 1854. He would have immediately moved back to North Elba, except that he could not put all his business in order. Wool sales declined too, depriving him of extra cash he had planned on advancing to his son-in-law, Henry Thompson, who was building a house for him in North Elba. Instead, Brown rented some farms in the Akron area for an additional year, allowing himself enough

When the Browns returned to North Elba they moved into their own house, not quite finished at their arrival in 1855. The simple structure was built by Brown's son-in-law, Henry Thompson, who afterward accompanied him to Kansas. *Author's photograph, 1999.*

time and financial opportunity to make good his return to North Elba in the spring of 1855.

In the meantime, the Brown boys were making their own plans. John Jr. and Jason in particular were growing discontent in Ohio, and a recent drought had further persuaded them to look elsewhere to farm. They had attended a lecture in Akron by an editor from Lawrence, Kansas, who urged listeners to settle in the newly opened Kansas territory and make it a free state. "He [lauded] the country in glowing terms [and] told of fine soil and glorious climate and the opportunities that awaited the settlers who had courage to take up the fight," recalled Salmon Brown. The newspapers were filled with glowing accounts about the new Kansas and Nebraska territories, and John Jr. now caught the westward fever. The Browns also knew that their Aunt Florilla and Uncle Samuel Adair had already moved to Kansas as missionaries in a town called Osawatomie. John Brown saw the fraternal insurrection forming against his wishful plans to "have all my children settle within a few Miles of *each other*." But he knew "advising" his sons to make a "*forced* move" would have regretful results. By June 1854, he was yearning for North Elba, even putting off a counter-suggestion from John Jr. to move to the "Western lands" with them. Brown assured his son that he never saw North Elba "look half so inviting before," and could only wish his sons would follow "in that direction."

The single sons, Owen, Frederick, and Salmon, left for the Kansas territory in October 1854, taking their livestock as far as Illinois for the winter. John Jr. and Jason, both family men, lingered until the spring of 1855, traveling down the Ohio River with their families to St. Louis, Missouri. There they purchased tents, farming equipment, and other necessities. Boarding a steamer on the Missouri River, the Browns found themselves surrounded by Southerners, many of whom were crude pro-slavery people armed with revolvers and knives, also headed for Kansas. John Jr. remembered that during the trip, a young black man was strung up by his thumbs for having bumped into a white passenger. Meanwhile, John Brown and his family prepared to return to the Adirondacks, finally to settle amidst the omnipotence of the cold Canaan land.[8]

# 17

## "Kansas the Outpost"
### An Overview

For the land is full of bloody crimes, and the city is full
of violence.

—Ezekiel 7:23

The Kansas-Nebraska Act of 1854 opened up lands west of
Missouri, repealing the old Missouri Compromise by allowing the possible expansion of slavery into western territories. In theory, democracy
was to guide the process of attaining statehood, allowing the settlers to
decide by vote whether they would enter the Union in free or slave states.
In practice, the road to statehood for Kansas was a long, violent conflict
between pro-slavery and anti-slavery forces. Northern groups immediately began to raise funds and finance emigration of free-state settlers to
Kansas. Pro-slavery forces, especially in Missouri, viewed this aggressiveness with fear and loathing, and began to organize in order to counter the
free-state movement.

However, this was not entirely a battle between good and evil. Most
free-state settlers were anti-black too, Negrophobia being the main reason
they opposed the expansion of slavery into the new territories. The attitude expressed by one free-state settler was typical: "I don't want niggers
a' trampin' over my grave." Under the free-state Topeka movement, abolitionists like the Browns were a minority and exclusion of blacks was
overwhelmingly supported.[1] Neither were all Missourians in favor of the
illegal and murderous intrusion of southern groups into Kansas that began
in reaction to the Northern movement. Nevertheless, from the onset, leaders from Missouri and other parts of the South orchestrated invasion and
illegal voting in order to form a pro-slavery territorial government in
Kansas. Buttressed by strong pro-slavery sympathy in Washington, D.C.,

militant forces bullied free-state settlers, and armed Southerners poured across the border in an increasingly violent program of terrorism.

The story of the Kansas conflict centers around passionate advocates, not mild-mannered moderates. Senator David Atchison of Missouri personified the hell-bent hostility of militants determined to force slavery on Kansas regardless of the democratic process. These leaders suspected all free-state men of being abolitionists and thought Northern emigration to Kansas was nothing but the work of militant anti-slavery forces in New England. In a letter to a colleague in 1854, Atchison wrote:

> Now the men who are hired by the Boston Abolitionists to settle and abolitionise Kansas will not hesitate to steal our slaves. . . . We are organizing to meet their organization. We will be compelled to shoot, burn and hang, but the thing will be soon over.[2]

At first free-state leaders seem to have responded conservatively, vulnerable in their belief that American democracy would somehow vindicate their cause in Kansas. But pro-slavery forces and their "border ruffian" soldiers advocated a "Law and Order" platform that eventually pushed free-state people to extreme reactions.

Though the climate and soil of Kansas provided great potential for "slave crops" like tobacco and hemp, the move to Kansas was not popular among slaveholders. Going west seemed risky, giving greater opportunity to slaves to run away or be "stolen." In contrast, Northern emigration to Kansas was increasingly strong. Nevertheless, Atchison and his allies moved through the South to glean support, forming emigrant aid societies and publishing fervent calls to Kansas. "Unless you come quickly, and come by thousands, we are gone," went one appeal. "The elections once lost are lost forever." To support the militant Missouri faction, slavery strongholds like Alabama, Georgia, and South Carolina sent settlers to Kansas, and Jefferson Buford of Alabama led an expedition of three hundred men financed by the sale of slaves. While in the deep South, Buford masqueraded his effort as a nonviolent, Bible-toting movement, but he clearly intended to send armed men into the territory. With the support of the fraudulently elected territorial government, his men rode into Kansas with guns and banners, such as one declaring "The Supremacy of the White Race" and "Kansas the Outpost."[3]

John Brown's sons came into this setting at odds with free-state racism and pro-slavery militancy, but political necessity aligned them with the free-state movement. Yet from the beginning, the Browns neither apologized for their abolitionist convictions nor hid their own militancy. Perceived as a threat to the interests of the pro-slavery faction in Kansas, they were also resented by free-state people who thought them fanatical and troublesome.

As early as October 1854, armed forces from Missouri tried to invade and disrupt free-state settlements, and used brute force to stuff ballot boxes in the first territorial election in November. These violations were outrightly encouraged by pro-slavery leaders like Atchison of Missouri. Even though the free-state population had not yet swelled to a majority in the territory, the pro-slavery faction was determined to undermine any advance of abolitionism. Paramilitary vigilante groups were formed to patrol Missouri and Kansas territory in order to eliminate abolitionists and "nigger stealers." In the election of March 1854, pro-slavery thugs were intent on forcing another victory, since members of the Territorial Legislature were to be chosen. One thousand armed Missourians invaded Lawrence alone, terrorizing free-state settlers and stuffing ballot boxes to the extent that five-sixths of the vote was illegal.

In the summer of 1855, while John Brown was preparing to travel west, the pro-slavery "Bogus Legislature" subverted any chance for the free-state side to work within legal and governmental means. Despite the doctrine of "Popular Sovereignty" underlying the Kansas-Nebraska Act, democracy in the territory was completely undermined. Attempts by the territorial governor to counter the Legislature's movements were vetoed by pro-slavery judicial representatives in the territory, and President Franklin Pierce then removed the governor, replacing him with a pro-slavery official.[4]

Some free-state leaders promptly organized their own conventions during the summer and fall of 1855, only to form a compromise platform that tolerated slavery where it previously existed in the territory and outlawed the presence of free blacks. The militant Browns were displeased with the outcome, though anti-slavery whites generally followed the thinking of journalist Horace Greeley, who felt compromise was better than seeing "Slavery obtain a foothold" in Kansas. In October 1855, pro-slavery and free-state settlers had separate polls for the congressional election and sent their chosen officials to claim the territorial seat in Washington, D.C. The free-state representative was immediately dismissed, though controversy between the warring camps led to a congressional investigation and the de-seating of the pro-slavery representative too. Kansas was hopelessly divided between irreconcilable factions vying for control of the fledgling state.

Political conflict in Kansas was further exacerbated by a series of homicides committed by terrorists, such as one free-state man who was smashed in the face with a hatchet, and another who was shot and scalped, his killer afterward being acquitted by a pro-slavery jury. Other free-state men were threatened, abused, and driven from their homes by pro-slavery thugs. To be sure, free-state men here and there fought back, but there was yet no organized armed response to the marauding violence of Missouri terrorists and their allies in Kansas.

John Brown entered Kansas in October 1855, just in time to witness the heightening of violent attacks by pro-slavery terrorists culminating in the first siege of the free-state town of Lawrence in December 1855. During this time Brown received a captain's commission and charge of "The Liberty Guards," a group of nineteen free-state men, including four of his sons. However, a peace treaty was struck before any fighting broke out, and the Browns returned to their camp believing that their side had been maneuvered into withdrawing. Initially Brown reacted with animosity toward the treaty, having preferred to fight with "the enemies of God." He changed his mind afterward, believing that the outcome of the treaty would result in the dominance of the free-state cause.

To the contrary, in 1856 it became evident that enemy forces were still intent on making Kansas a slave state. Arrests of free-state men were renewed by a message to Congress from President Pierce declaring his support of the pro-slavery legislature and opposition to free-state efforts in Kansas. Pierce went further by denying aid to free-state forces and placing federal troops at the disposal of the pro-slavery territorial governor. Meanwhile, Brown and his sons conducted surveying expeditions on behalf of Indian peoples like the Ottawa, whose lands were being stolen by pro-slavery settlers.

To no surprise, the Browns became outspoken anti-slavery advocates in their vicinity, which irritated free-state conservatives as well as outright pro-slavery men. In April 1856, they were part of the first meeting in the territory where free-state men openly challenged President Pierce and the pro-slavery legislature. Participants issued resolutions repudiating the legislature as a government "forced upon us by a foreign vote" and promised to resist any attempt to enforce its laws. Brown and his sons then openly defied a pro-slavery district court the same month when warrants were issued for their arrest. Meanwhile John Jr.

had become captain of a volunteer brigade called the "Pottawatomie Rifles."[5]

In May 1856, pro-slavery forces again moved on Lawrence, this time finding it unprepared for conflict. After free-state leaders surrendered, the invaders made some arrests and began to sack the town. Printing presses were destroyed and buildings were burned while "border ruffians" vandalized and looted. The most significant loss was a hotel that served as the headquarters for free-state meetings. For a moment it appeared that the violent tyranny of the pro-slavery side would triumph in Kansas. However, instead of vanquishing their foes, their violence provided the free-state side a bitter inspiration to retaliate. "We had no friends but ourselves," recalled one free-state settler. "We took up the cudgel that they offered and we used it."

Immediately after the sacking of Lawrence, a number of pro-slavery advocates in the area of Osawatomie were brutally killed in apparent retaliation by free-state men. News of the carnage sent the pro-slavery community reeling in fear, and word traveled that the militant Browns were behind the killings. Many free-state people were also disturbed and frightened by the bloodletting. Despite their bitter contempt for Southern terrorists and the inevitability of a pro-slavery invasion, many free-state settlers remained conservative and given to compromise.

In June 1856, John Brown and other free-state men successfully engaged a pro-slavery force at the Battle of Black Jack, though John Jr. and Jason were elsewhere captured and held until later in the year. Violence intensified in the summer of 1856, and a real state of guerilla war now existed in the territory, with both free-state and pro-slavery men fighting and raiding. However, "for downright atrocities committed on individuals, the pro-slavery men were infinitely worse than the Free State."[6] Brown and his associates remained in the field throughout the summer of 1856, raiding pro-slavery camps and communities, finally returning to the Brown settlements at Osawatomie in August. On August 30, a large Southern force took the town by surprise, sacking and burning most of the community. Brown and others fought valiantly, but had to withdraw into the wilderness to escape.

In September 1856, a new territorial governor assumed office, ordering the disbandment of all militia and an end to guerilla warfare. The new governor brought a balanced policy and enforced peace in the territory. Without state-sanctioned force operating in their favor, pro-slavery leaders recognized that the political tide had turned against them in Kansas.

In 1855, John Brown left his family in New York State to assist his grown sons by fighting pro-slavery forces in the Kansas territory. Stress, sickness, wilderness life, and fighting took their toll on him, and thereafter he always looked older than his actual age. *Villard Collection, Columbia University Library.*

Northern emigrants were far greater in number than their Southern counterparts, and if the ballot box was to decide the destiny of the territory, it now seemed that Kansas would enter the Union as a free state. Sickly, wearied, and homeless, the Browns quit the territory, returning to Ohio. Now a wanted man with a price on his head, John Brown eventually returned to the States too, but with no intention of ceasing hostilities against slavery. Evading capture in Nebraska, he passed through Iowa and Illinois, reaching Ohio by Christmas 1856.

# 18

## Pottawatomie and the Fatherless

And my wrath shall wax hot, and I will kill you with the sword;
and your wives shall be widows, and your children fatherless.
—Exodus 22:24

The first of Owen Brown's children in Kansas was his daughter, Florilla, who went west with her husband, Samuel Adair, to serve as missionaries in the territory. Both graduates of Oberlin, the Adairs were abolitionists too. After serving over a decade in the pastorate, Samuel and Florilla came to Osawatomie, a new settlement about fifty miles southwest of Kansas City, in early 1855. From the onset the Adairs had found the "frontier Missourians" repulsive, noting how they extorted money from Northern emigrants. "They are generally among the most wicked and wretched of the human race that we meet with," Adair wrote to Owen Brown. Adair noted that Missourians had invaded the territory "by hundreds at the recent election and carried it all their own way." Indeed, a pro-slavery government had stolen its way into Kansas, prohibiting free-state men to hold office and threatening penalties to anyone who challenged them. Free-state settlers acquiesced without a fight, Adair wrote, but he hoped that affidavits sent to the governor would correct the injustice. They did not.[1]

Finally joining their single brothers, John Jr. and Jason arrived in the territory with their families in May 1855. Their journey had been difficult, not only because of outright Southern prejudice, but also because Jason and his wife Ellen lost their four-year-old son to cholera during the trip, leaving him buried in Missouri. In Kansas, the Browns' hopeful work was interrupted by rain, sickness, and depression—especially the grieving Jason and Ellen, who began to speak of returning to Ohio. Unable to complete their cabins, they lived in tents, struggling against sickness and the heavy rains that seeped through and drenched them and their possessions. Worse was the growing threat of intrusion by Missourians and the fraudulently elected pro-slavery government. The Browns were naturally inclined to involve themselves in political affairs, especially John Jr., who attended a free-state convention in September 1855. The Brown boys made no secret of their views in conversation with pro-slavery people. 'We are Free-state," they declared to a group of Missourians on horseback. "More than that, we are abolitionists." They were far different from most Northern settlers, whom Wealthy Brown considered "decidedly timorous."

Though he had wanted to return to the Adirondacks, John Brown was increasingly distracted by thoughts of going to Kansas. He began to wonder if he might do more by joining the struggle in Kansas than by returning to declining Timbucto. But if his desires had begun to shift, he still felt obligated to family and friends. In February 1854, Brown wrote to an associate that he had "undertaken to direct the opperations [*sic*] of a Surveying, and exploring party, to be employed in Kansas" for a couple of years. But the expression was more a flourish than a plan. Actually, the associate was holding some of his livestock, and Brown's apparent intent was to get him to either buy or sell them on his behalf. Still, by the summer of 1854 he wrote to John Jr. that, were it not for his commitment "to operate in another part of the field," he would leave for Kansas that fall. In September, he wrote to Ruth and Henry in North Elba, asking for their "advice and feeling in the matter," and for them to solicit the opinions of Lyman Eppes "and all the colored people" at Timbucto. He also wrote to abolitionists Gerrit Smith, Frederick Douglass, and James McCune Smith for their input. Brown's desire to go to Kansas was now evident, and he seems to have hoped that his family and associates would relieve him of his obligations, sending him off with their blessings. Instead, Gerrit Smith voted that Brown return to the Adirondacks, and probably Ruth and Henry, along with Eppes and others at Timbucto also preferred that he stay in New York. Besides, Brown had to care for an ailing wife and three daughters, the youngest having been born that September. Despite his desire to be at the center of the conflict, nothing short of a family crisis could justify John Brown going west.[2]

In late May 1855, John Jr. wrote a lengthy letter detailing life in Kansas, family concerns, and the political condition. Contrasting well-armed and organized pro-slavery thugs with the poorly armed and unorganized "friends of freedom," he lamented that free-state people showed "the most abject and cowardly spirit" before the "lawless bands of miscreants" from Missouri. Southerners had even organized to intimidate and terrorize free-state settlers, John Jr. wrote. The only "remedy" would be that free-state men "should *immediately, thoroughly* arm and *organize themselves* in military companies." This would require someone to "lead off in the matter," he concluded, if only they could obtain good firearms. Here was John Brown's cue.

The Brown boys were probably not surprised that their father obtained the weapons and delivered them to Kansas himself. They may even have been counting on it. Financed by abolitionist friends and associates, Brown set out for Kansas in the summer of 1855, escorted by his son-in-law Henry Thompson and joined en route by his strapping teenage son Oliver. Stopping in Ohio to see his family in August, he gleaned more money and weapons from strong anti-slavery associates in the Western Reserve. After their visit, Owen Brown noted that his son had "something of a warlike [*spirit*]. I think as much as [*necessary*] for [*defense*]," he wrote to the Adairs in Kansas. "I will hope nothing more." Owen anticipated that Kansas would be "the seat of war," but was very concerned that such a conflict would involve his family. He had probably discussed the likelihood of war in Kansas with his son John, expressing apprehension about him going into the territory with the intention of fighting. Over a month after Brown went west, the elder wrote him saying that he supported defensive measures but advised "[*guarding*] against [*offensive*] [*measures*], as the one sometimes runs into the other." Owen closed by warning his son: "See that ye fall not out by the way. Plant no seeds that [*bear*] bitter [*fruit*] and if any spring up attend to them before they take root."[3]

Brown traveled to Cleveland, Detroit, and Chicago, where he purchased a horse and wagon to carry an assortment of rifles, revolvers, ammunition, and swords. With Oliver and Henry Thompson, he made the slow trek from late August 1855, arriving in Kansas by early October. Along the way, Brown later wrote, they kept meeting bands of armed riders, many of them boasting of their violent exploits in Kansas against the "defenceless [*sic*] Free State men." He was disgusted at the delight they took in having killed the horses, mules, and livestock of the "d-d Abolitionists." Stopping in Waverly, Missouri, Brown located and exhumed the body of his grandson, bringing it along for Jason and Ellen in Kansas. At the Missouri River, the Brown party waited for a ferry, where an old Missourian tried to intimidate them when he surmised they were going to Kansas. "You won't live to get there," he said. John Brown replied, "We are prepared *not to die alone*," and his defiant look pierced the old Southerner like a sword.

When Brown finally arrived in Kansas, he found most of his family sickly and weak, their work neglected and settlements unfinished due to illness and the demands of free-state business. He went to work on getting the settlement and farming in order, helped settlers battle dangerous prairie fires, and then joined his sons in guarding a free-state election poll. The Browns went out "powerfully armed" but found no pro-slavery bullies. Afterward, Brown wrote home that he was optimistic about Missouri giving up on Kansas and the territory soon becoming a free state. "You are all very dear to me; and I humbly trust we may be kept and spared, to meet again on Earth," he wrote to his wife and children back in North Elba. "But if not, let us all endeavour [*sic*] earnestly to secure admission to that Eternal Home where will be no more bitter separations, 'where the wicked shall cease from troubling; and the weary be at rest.'"

An especially hard winter set in by late October, with "cutting cold Winds" that Brown felt were more harsh than any he had ever known. Writing to Mary, he assured her that despite her contempt for the "miserable Frosty region" of the Adirondacks, life in Kansas was "not altogether in Paradise." Still he wrote assuredly, "Slavery will soon die out here; and to God be the praise." In fact, in October and November 1855, free-state leaders had met in Topeka to prepare a constitution and an application to permit Kansas to the Union as a free state. In response, pro-slavery forces rallied, and by late November the territory seemed ready to explode in civil war.[4]

That fall, John Brown wrote to his father in Ohio expressing gratitude to God for the elder's longevity and health. "We really hope you may enjoy the few days at the close of your journey (as regards all things both spiritual and temporal) much more than any preceeding [*sic*] ones." But Owen's last days could hardly have been enjoyable, concerned as he was about his family's well-being in the troubled territory. Early in 1856, grandson Jason Brown wrote thanking Owen for his "many instances of generosity," and reporting that pro-slavery forces were still "comiting [*sic*] outrages near the Missouri line," including an attack upon an antislavery editor whose press was thrown into the river. Missionary son-in-law Adair wrote to him too, likewise reporting the troubled condition of Kansas, as in January 1856 when he wrote that the territorial governor and President Franklin Pierce were "siding with the Missourians." Free-state men were now on the alert to defend themselves, fearing they would be left to "contend with the desperadoes of Missouri and Slavery alone." Adair felt they were on the verge of facing a "bloody onslaught" from the pro-slavery faction. "Remember us at the Throne of Grace," he concluded with a prayer request.

Though John Brown was a man of prayer, he did not think piety precluded the use of force. He had gone to Kansas to fight, not pray for mercy. Even in several forays into Missouri to buy food and supplies, Brown took no discretion to conceal his position in the conflict. "*I always* (when asked) frankly avow myself a *Free State* man," he wrote to a relative. "For One I have no desire (all things considered) to have the Slave power cease from its acts of aggression," he likewise wrote to Mary in April 1856. "'Their foot shall slide in due time.'" Among his relatives in Kansas, Brown expressed the belief that war was imminent. "John . . . appears also anxious to have the crisis come so that if he lives through it he may soon return to his family again," Adair wrote to his worried father-in-law.

During his last months, Owen Brown corresponded often with his family in the Kansas territory, especially writing to John Brown and son-in-law Adair. Apprehensive that his children were in the midst of a most "eventfull [sic] location and an eventfull period of life and action," Owen declared, "we are very anctious [sic] about you all," and "may God give us more [strength] to bear with our ungodly Rulers." Adair acknowledged Owen's "deep interest," but the elder could hardly find comfort in kind words considering the worsening news from Kansas. "As for law here—every man to a great extent is his own law here. We greatly need wholesale law and a righteous government," Adair noted. "But as things are we may have bloody war before a government in Kansas is organized on a permanent basis." At the end of March 1856, Owen's health took a turn for the worst and he had such a hard time breathing at night that he felt "as though death was at the door." Writing to his son, Owen expressed a typical self-effacing humility, calling himself a "great sinner" and asking for prayers for the certainty of his salvation rather than "for the life of my body."[5]

In early February 1856, Oliver Brown—not quite seventeen years old—wrote home to his mother that "War again threatens Kansas and we expect every day to bee [sic] warned out to meet its call. All we have to say is god Speed the day." It was Oliver's opinion that of the thirty or forty thousand free-state men in the territory, only about two thousand would turn out to fight. The rest were "peace men, money lovers, fence riders [and] proslavery men." John Jr. wrote to Frederick Douglass that the illegitimate pro-slavery government in the territory was determined "either to compel us into slavish submission" or to "drive us into a forcible resistance. . . . Hourly are we moving in the midst of inflammable material which it needs but a spark to ignite." Heretofore, he concluded, free-state men had hoped to reform their enemies, hoping to "smother the flame, though it burned the kindly hand." But that policy was "fast drawing to a close," young John wrote. "The shadows of a night are now settling upon our pathway through which no gleam of morning is discernible, except through a struggle."

Though the Browns were speaking generally of the Kansas territory, they were keenly aware of the vulnerable state of Osawatomie. Named for its location at the convergence of the Osage River and Pottawatomie Creek, Osawatomie was a free-state community with pro-slavery neighbors in its vicinity. Founded by an agent of the Massachusetts Aid Society named O. C. Brown (no relation to John Brown), Osawatomie was equipped with good machinery, such as a grist saw mill, that attracted settlers. The young town also obtained a printing press, which pro-slavery forces felt was dangerous to their cause. With the largest voting precinct in the territory, Osawatomie became "the banner town for casting a full liberty vote."

O. C. Brown recalled that a plot was made by pro-slavery leaders to "depose" him and other free-state leaders. However, even though Osawatomie "was decidedly free-state," the settlers were also fearful of anti-slavery agitation and "conservative in action." Initially, pro-slavery forces overlooked Osawatomie, but as it began to develop into a potentially powerful and outspoken community, it became the target of resentment. One embittered enemy of Osawatomie was Allen Wilkinson, who had come to the territory as a free-state man but moved to the pro-slavery neighborhood at Dutch Henry's Crossing along the Pottawatomie Creek. Conservatives were especially put off by the Browns, such as a racist preacher named Martin White, who debated with John Brown over paying taxes to the territorial government. Brown responded that he was an "Abolitionist of the old stock—was dyed in the wool, and that Negroes were his brothers and equals—that he would rather see this Union dissolved and the country drenched in blood than to pay taxes to the amount of the one-hundredth part of a mill." According to O. C. Brown, some settlers in the Osawatomie vicinity began to act as spies and guides to the pro-slavery faction. "We were informed of this and began to understand that the sleeping tiger had an open eye for us."[6]

On May 8, 1856, John Brown awoke, perhaps thinking of his father in Ohio. Deciding to write "a few lines . . . notwithstanding my lack of interesting news," he described the "cold, backward and wet" climate, details about corn and cattle, and Frederick's recent spell of ill health. Brown wrote that he had done a little surveying for "an Indian tribe," undoubtedly knowing such news would please his father. "We are all very glad to get your letters," he concluded, signing the note, "Your affectionate Son." But even as Brown scrawled these words, his father was dying or dead. In fact, the Browns in Kansas had not heard of Owen's death even as late as May 16, when son-in-law Samuel Adair wrote another letter to the elder, this one filled with frightening news. Adair complained that most of the Alabamans and Georgians he had seen wandering around the territory were "hard cases. . . . Drunken, profane, wreckless [*sic*]." These Southerners were not staking claims, Adair wrote, but gathering in camps and "threatning [*sic*] to drive off free state men from their claims and take possession of them." The timid free-state settlers were greatly insecure, fearing arrest by the "bogus officials" of the pro-slavery regime. Worse was the growing desperation and bitterness that free-state people felt toward the territorial government for neglecting to bring pro-slavery terrorists to justice.

> Such a state of things as this maddens men, and throws them back upon their own resources for redress. And it is dreadful to see how all the evil passions rise and rage at the oft recital of these terrible outrages so near home. . . . O the deepth [*sic*] of revenge in the human heart when the powers that should execute justice not only connive at the wrong, but abet, and help it on. . . . May Heaven grant us deliverance soon.

News that pro-slavery forces were about to attack the free-state town of Lawrence had also spread like wildfire, but word of an attack on Osawatomie was also spreading. Reports were circulating that a company of armed Southerners were camping on some Indian lands nearby.

In the days immediately before his death, Owen Brown had been gloomy and sleepless because of reports coming from Kansas. Carriage rides and fresh air brought some relief, as did frequent visits from clergymen, prayer sessions, and readings from the Psalms. But his arms and legs had swelled, and it became difficult for him to breathe. If Owen dreaded death, however, it was only because he could not bear leaving the world without knowing of the safety of his family in Kansas. "His anxiety for his family was his principle theme," wrote John Brown's half-brother Jeremiah. Even in the midst of prayer his thoughts had drifted westward. When his daughter Sally came to sit with him, she observed that the elder could only lament in "deep solicitude" for Florilla and her husband, "and John [in] particular."[7]

Owen Brown's funeral took place on Sunday, May 9 (John Brown's fifty-sixth birthday), marking one of the largest congregations the community had seen, with guests and "friends from all quarters" coming to pay their last respects to the old abolitionist. After an exposition from the Scriptures and the reading of the eulogy, a "great concourse of relatives and friends" flowed in procession into the old Hudson cemetery. As a "most beautiful and Solemn hymn was sung at the grave," sons Frederick, Oliver, Jeremiah, and Edward lowered the coffin into a cement vault next to the grave of Owen's beloved Ruth. "He was buried in the Old Yard beside your Mother," wrote Jeremiah to his half-brother John Brown.[8]

Had Owen lived, he would have died a thousand deaths over the worsening conditions in southeastern Kansas. When it became clear that Buford's Southern forces were camped in the vicinity, John Brown decided to conduct surveillance by posing as a territorial surveyor. With his sons working as assistants, they ran a line through the Buford camp. Since government surveyors were typically pro-slavery appointees, they were assumed to be supportive of slavery in the territory. In conversing with Buford's men, Brown surmised that their presence was intended to support local pro-slavery settlers, some of whom were acting as their guides. It was clear they intended to strike at the free-state men in the area, especially the "damned abolitionists."

The Browns also noted a neighbor from the Pottawatomie Creek moving in the camp. James Doyle was a Tennessean who had come to Kansas with his family, supposedly to escape the "ruinous" influence of slave labor. In fact, he and his older sons had worked as plantation patrols in the South and maintained a strong pro-slavery stance. The Doyles collaborated with Missourians in watching for fugitives, always prepared to pursue them with their bloodhounds. Poorly educated and militant, they hated "Yankees" and were known to talk about cutting "their damned throats." Doyle and his sons spent a great deal of time in the Buford camp and provided information about their free-state neighbors. Once Henry

Owen Brown's gravestone, marking his death on May 8, 1856. He lived long enough to see abolitionism rise to preeminence, but not long enough to see his son John Brown become a nationally controversial figure in the struggle against slavery. *Author's photograph, 2000.*

Thompson, Brown's son-in-law, had occasion to meet and speak with the elder Doyle. When he declared that blacks "had neither sensibilities, sense, nor souls," Henry rebuked him. "Look here, old man. I know colored men that are as much smarter than you as you are smarter than that little dog." Doyle accused Henry of making "incendiary" remarks and threatened, "You will hear from it later." In the spring of 1856, Doyle swore out a warrant for Henry's arrest; however, a circuit-riding judge was too intimidated by the militant Browns to have the warrant executed.[9]

There were other enemies along the Pottawatomie Creek, just as there were signs that the pro-slavery faction was plotting against free-state men. One settler at a local store was handed a threatening note ordering free-state men living in the vicinity to "leave the Territory within 30 days or their throats will be cut." It was signed, "Law and Order." The store owner, a Polish Jew named Theodore Weiner, was already at odds with local pro-slavery men. When Weiner saw the threat, he told the settler, "We ought to cut [their] throats." Weiner and his partners, a Bohemian named Jacob Benjamin and an Austrian named Anshel "August" Bondi, were embittered by threatening visitations from pro-slavery neighbors and turned to the Browns for support. Though they were hardly pro-black (Weiner had lived in the South and owned slaves and Bondi admitted to having little sympathy for blacks), the immigrants had been alienated by the terrorism of the pro-slavery faction. Weiner had already gotten into a fight with William Sherman, a German-born neighbor who lived on the Pottawatomie Creek. Henry Thompson found the men brawling in Weiner's store—Sherman getting the worst of it at the end of an ax handle. Weiner's partner Bondi had originally gone to meet Sherman and his brother, "Dutch" Henry, hearing they were German immigrants. But when Sherman learned that Bondi was free-state, he threatened him to leave the area immediately.

The Sherman brothers had lived in the territory prior to its organization and owned a store and tavern that served as the unofficial headquarters of the local pro-slavery faction. Both men loathed the free-state movement and were distinguished in the community for engaging in shady business too. Some settlers considered Henry the "brains and head" of local pro-slavery men, and it was known that he was in communication with the Buford troops after they appeared in the spring of 1856. However, the leader among these opponents was Allen Wilkinson, the best educated among the pro-slavery men on the Pottawatomie. Wilkinson was considered a "worthless and dangerous man," a turncoat whose involvement in the pro-slavery territorial legislature seemed to harden him all the more in his hatred of the free-state cause. He had become "a very subservient tool" of the pro-slavery faction.[10]

When Lawrence was attacked in late May 1856, pro-slavery men on the Pottawatomie Creek seized the opportunity to terrorize free-state men. After the Browns and others left to aid the fallen town, Wilkinson, Doyle, and Sherman began to move throughout the free-state neighborhood issuing threats. With Weiner and Bondi absent, their partner Benjamin was threatened to leave in five days or be killed. Other free-state people were harassed and threatened, such as one man who was knocked down simply for having a copy of the *New York Tribune*. While some of this amounted to big-mouthing, the increasingly aggressive behavior of the pro-slavery men suggested an expectation of imminent triumph. A free-state settler named Wilbur West had employed Doyle early on, and consequently had a friendly rapport with the Tennessean. But around the time Lawrence was attacked, West chanced to meet Doyle on the road. While they conversed, Doyle paused and looked into his eyes "in a way that made a strong impression on me," he recalled. "'West, I may never see you again. And, if I do, it may be under different circumstances from this.'" West sensed that he wanted to say more, and later concluded Doyle was hinting that he was "in danger in the contemplated cleaning out of the free state settlers."

The time had come "when either one party or the other had to be subdued." It has long been maintained by Brown's critics that free-state men would not have left Osawatomie to defend Lawrence if they really believed their own community was in danger. But this rationale does not take into consideration that pro-slavery terrorism and thuggery in the Kansas territory had a strong element of the machismo. Women and children might be threatened, insulted, or even intimidated, but the real target was *free-state men*. Even after Osawatomie was sacked and burned by pro-slavery men in August 1856, Adair wrote to his sister-in-law that women and children "have heretofore been considered generally safe." Indeed, during the same invasion by "border ruffians," Florilla Brown Adair and other free-state women went unharmed while her husband and the rest of the free-state men fled for their lives. Conversely, when John Brown and other free-state men retaliated, they too followed the same code. Although some pro-slavery settlers were more bark than bite, free-state men had good reason to fear the collaboration of their pro-slavery neighbors with "border ruffians" and other thugs.[11]

Furthermore, according to Adair, John Brown did not want to go to the aid of Lawrence without reliable information, probably because of the threat looming over the Pottawatomie free-state settlement. When they did go out—only to learn their help was too little and too late—Brown and others concluded it was time to respond to local threats with violent action. "We expect to be butchered—every free state settler in our region," declared one of Brown's associates. Jason Brown recalled hearing his father conferring in the camp with other free-state men:

Now something *must* be done. We have got to defend our families and our neighbors as best we can. Something *is going to be done now*. We must show by actual work that there are two sides to this thing and that they cannot go on without impunity."

The killings that followed have often been presented as a manifestation of John Brown's private hatred and paranoia, as if the bloody actions were his alone, or forced through others acting under his irresistible influence. In fact, even though Brown clearly exerted leadership and authority over his men, they were volunteers who each held equally strong political and/or moral views. He held no spell over those who joined him, and those who did not join him were either too meek or fearful of retaliation. John Brown facilitated the deadly venture but should neither be credited nor blamed as if the bloody work was his private accomplishment. Brown came to Kansas to fight pro-slavery men, not settle. His distinct abolitionist views and a theology untouched by pacifism inclined him to respond militantly, while other free-state men hoped for compromise and feared retaliation. But Brown's reasons for striking along the Pottawatomie were also personal and familial. Genuine concern for his family's safety, no doubt exacerbated by recent news of his father's death, probably added a measure of desperation to his response. For John Brown, a dear but distant light had gone out in Hudson, only adding to the darkness along the Pottawatomie Creek.

The primary weapons of the Pottawatomie killers were swords donated by an Ohio abolitionist and carried to Kansas by Brown in 1855. The short broadswords were straight and double-edged, and honed to sharpness prior to the attack. Designed for cuts rather than thrusts, the weapons were hollow and loaded with quick silver. When held upright, the quick silver dropped to the hilt, but slid upward to the point in striking motion so as to increase the force of the blow. With swords sheathed in darkness, Brown and his companions—sons Owen, Frederick, Oliver, Salmon, and son-in-law, Henry Thompson—were joined by the warlike Theodore Weiner and another free-state man named Townsley, whose role was to convey the killers in his wagon.

The first to be seized were Doyle and his two sons, William and Drury, who were also active in the "Law and Order" faction. Sparing a third teenage son at the pleading of his mother, Brown marched the Doyles into the darkness, where Owen and Salmon were waiting. Fierce, heavy blows sliced through upraised arms, and the awful blades split their skulls almost to the neck. Doyle's bloodhounds and bulldogs, trained for slave-hunting, also lay mutilated in the yard. As the Doyles were led out to their deaths, Mahala Doyle, crying and terrified, shrieked at her husband, "I told you what you were going to get." Wilkinson's wife pleaded for her husband, but he was likewise escorted out of the house in his stocking feet and forced into deadly shadows. Weiner and Thompson hacked him to death. The same men escorted William Sherman down to the Pottawatomie Creek, falling on him with heavy blades. Blood and brain matter tainted the flowing water, but gradually washed away. Probably to signal the men to regroup, Brown fired a single pistol shot into old man Doyle's corpse. The somber leader had raised no sword, and the only shot he fired was into the head of a dead man. "There shall be no more such work as that," Owen said after he and the other killers washed their bloody swords in Pottawatomie Creek.[12]

By the time Brown finally saw his son Jason, the news of the killings had already reached the camp. He had stayed behind, but had sharpened the swords for his father without knowing they were to be used on unarmed men. Jason confronted him immediately, asking if it was true that his party had killed Sherman, Wilkinson, and the Doyles. Brown answered, "I did not do it, but I approved of it." Disgusted, Jason said, "I think it was an uncalled for, wicked act." "God is my judge," Brown declared. "It was absolutely necessary as a measure of self-defense, and for the defense of others." Seeing the hurt in his son's eyes, the fatherless father appealed, "The people of Kansas will yet justify my course." But gentle Jason, who would not so much as eat a hunted quail after seeing it struggle for its life, turned away from his father. Nearly three decades later Jason Brown told an interviewer that if he had understood more of his father's purpose, he would have put a sharper edge on the swords.[13]

In the years immediately following John Brown's death, few spoke of the killings, and many denied his involvement altogether. In the latter part of the nineteenth century, when Reconstruction was abandoned and black people were betrayed into the hands of their former masters, the tide turned against Brown too. Writers with personal and political vendettas arose, successfully diminishing Brown by capitalizing on his role in the Pottawatomie killings.[14] Later historians prepared self-serving narratives portraying the Pottawatomie killings as ideological murders, or outrightly accusing Brown of being a vicious killer and brigand. With some notable exceptions, more recent writers have generally been influenced by the cynical, distorted interpretation that has become the mainstay of American writing on the Pottawatomie killings. Even though writers may claim objectivity in evaluating Brown's role in the incident, he is often implicitly condemned within the framework of their narratives.

Brown's devoted son-in-law, Henry Thompson, lived many years after participating in the Pottawatomie killings. When questioned about the incident, it was characteristic of the elderly Thompson to insist that the violent attack was "a necessary and righteous act." Once his granddaughter asked how he and the others could kill as they did at Pottawatomie, and Thompson nearly cried out that it was "the best act that was ever done in Kansas." The granddaughter persisted, saying she was not seeking a justification, but wanted to know how "*such* men could do it." His eyes flushed with tears, the old man replied: "We were *just the ones* to do it." Rather than presuming to ask if John Brown could justify committing such an evil, unwarranted act, perhaps a fundamentally different question is needed to frame the Pottawatomie killings. *What kind of circumstances* would drive exceptionally moral and religious people like the Browns to such desperate measures?[15]

# PART VII

# I Will Raise a Storm

I may be hung but I will not be shot. But what I will do is this: I will raise a storm in the country that will not be stayed so long as there is a slave on its soil.

—John Brown

# 19

## "The Language of Providence"

To open the eyes of the blind, to bring out the prisoners from the prison, and them that sit in darkness out of the prison.
—Isaiah 42:7

Frederick Brown was murdered in August 1856, and his father refused to avenge the crime. Brown and Martin White, Frederick's killer, had argued vehemently in 1856 over the taxing of Osawatomie by the pro-slavery territorial government. White, allegedly a minister, loathed blacks and turned against the free-state side in opposition to Kansas becoming "a free Negro State." White later justified killing Frederick by falsely charging that the Browns had raided his homestead and shot into a house full of women and children. But White probably killed Frederick out of sheer malice while acting as guide for Buford's army. When John Brown saw the body of his son, he brushed away his tears, saying that Frederick had always been "a sufferer" but now his troubles were over. He quashed any notion of revenge by associates and family members. "If I thought I had one bit of the spirit of revenge, I would never lift my hand," he said after the killing. "I do not make war on slaveholders even when I fight them, but on slavery." When associate James Hanway mentioned his son's killer, Brown likewise declared: "People mistake my objects. I would not hurt one hair of his head. I would not go one inch to take his life; I do not harbor the feelings of revenge. *I act from a principle*. My aim and object is to restore human rights." One report says that Brown's only feeling for Martin White was the expressed hope "that he repented."

However, the loss of a son only steeled his determination to destroy slavery. He told associate James Blunt that for twenty years "he had been possessed of an earnest and firm conviction that his mission here on earth was to be the instrument, in the hands of a divine Providence," for the

239

liberation of slaves. Associates and fellow soldiers remembered Brown as a "deeply religious" man who observed the Protestant Sabbath, asked the blessing of God at mealtime, and never tolerated profanity in the camp. As he once did as an employer, Brown encouraged the men in his camp to engage in moral discourses and debates, and was fond of singing songs around the campfire. When he met a youth with a violin, Brown asked him to play "a certain hymn"—undoubtedly "Blow Ye the Trumpet"— in exchange for his own personal hymnal. John Brown's nightly devotionals caught the attention of one free-state soldier, who later sneaked a look into his Bible, observing that markings and notes covered its pages. Of course, he was seen "as an unusual man," not only because of his pious habits and considerate attitude, but because he "treated Negroes on exactly the same footing as white men."[1]

Beyond the immediate concerns of Kansas, the territory had proven a doorway into a life of political activity. The year 1857 was one of new associates and plans, largely spent in pursuit of financial support from free-state sympathizers back East. Most notable in regard to Brown's ongoing work were "the Secret Six," who gave Brown political and financial support leading to the Harper's Ferry raid. Franklin B. Sanborn was a young scholar and educator who was serving as the secretary of the Massachusetts State Kansas Committee (MSKC) when Brown met him, and subsequently introduced him to others. George L. Stearns, a prosperous business man, was likewise attracted to Brown and became one of his major financial supporters. He served as the MSKC chairman following abolitionist Samuel G. Howe, another one of the Six. Howe was a physician who had once enlisted in support of the Greek revolution, and was later distinguished for his work with the blind. Brown also attracted two clergymen, neither of whom were evangelical. Thomas W. Higginson was pastor of a Unitarian congregation in Worcester, Massachusetts and a protege of the controversial and brilliant pastor, Theodore Parker. Parker is closely identified with the transcendentalist movement, which broke from the traditional Congregational Unitarianism so pervasive in New England. Parker maintained that Christianity rested on universal truths that are discerned by intuition, not Scripture or the person of Christ. Parker's Christianity was essentially a moral religion reflective of the oneness of the deity, and was therefore naturally inclined to practical application in reform work and abolitionism. Theologically speaking, Brown could not have disagreed more with Unitarian transcendentalism, particularly in its rejection of the authority of scripture and the divinity of Jesus Christ. Yet Brown had heard Parker in the early 1850s and "admired his piety and morality," though "severely disapproving his theology." John Jr. recalled that he and his father had gone to hear Parker speak, and even though Brown "did not consider Mr. Parker's theology as sound, he was wonderfully taken up with the discourse and from that time on had a liking for Mr. Parker which constantly increased during the remainder of his life." Another vital supporter of Brown was Gerrit Smith, the wealthy New York real estate tycoon who had contributed the Adirondack lands for black settlement in the 1840s. Like Brown, Smith enjoyed an especially good rapport with black leaders, including Frederick Douglass.

Brown met with many prominent New England citizens, from literati to politicians and various anti-slavery figures, including members of "The Club" in Springfield, some of whom he had known from his days in Massachusetts. Brown was interviewed by officers of the National Kansas Committee in New York City, addressed the Joint Committee on Federal Relations of the Massachusetts Legislature, and dined with authors Henry D. Thoreau and Ralph Waldo Emerson. There was also a notable meeting with William Lloyd Garrison, which occasioned an impromptu debate lasting much of the evening. Garrison respected Brown's devotion to the anti-slavery cause but resented his dependence on "carnal weapons," while Brown had no patience for men of words only, let alone pacifists. The two champions of abolition quoted and counter-quoted biblical texts, though their debate was probably far more complex than an "Old Testament versus New Testament" contest. Garrison's long-term and noteworthy contributions notwithstanding, Brown's sentiments about Garrisonian pacifism were probably confirmed by an encounter with the man himself.

Garrison was likewise unimpressed, though this would hardly have mattered to Brown, who never doubted his calling as an instrument for the destruction of slavery. When her father first went to Kansas, Sarah Brown recalled, he met with Henry Ward Beecher, the famous abolitionist preacher from Brooklyn, New York. When he became strong in his demands for support, the celebrated preacher bluntly refused, cutting him off with the declaration, "*I am Beecher.*" Brown never forgot this snub to God's anointed. Emerging from the Kansas wars and popularly known as "Osawatomie Brown," he occasioned to meet Beecher once more during a train ride. "This time Beecher was effusive in his feelings for Kansas" in the presence of the celebrated hero. But even though Brown was seeking support for his efforts, he put off Beecher flatly. "*He* was *Brown*," Sarah concluded.[2]

While touring for financial support, Brown was invited to speak before some children in a one-room schoolhouse in Torrington, Connecticut, the place of his birth. Slender and grayish, Brown seemed tall to one student, who remembered the guest lecturing on the cultures and peoples of Africa, and the great harm done to the continent by slavery. Brown spoke further on the nature of slavery in the United States, and concluded by asking for a show of hands from students who would "use your influence, whatever it may be, against this great curse" when they became adults. Though all the students held up their hands Brown was not satisfied. "Now I want those who are quite sure that they will not forget it, who will promise to use their time and influence toward resisting this great evil, to rise." When two boys stood, he put his hands on their heads and pronounced a blessing of commission:

> Now may my Father in heaven, who is your Father, and who is the Father of the African; and Christ, who is my Master and Savior, and your Master and Savior, and the Master and Savior of the African; and the Holy Spirit, which gives me strength and comfort when I need it, and will give you strength and comfort when you need it, and that gives strength and comfort to the African, enable you to keep this resolution which you have now taken.

While in Connecticut, Brown also appeared at an event sponsored by local Republican supporters in Canton, who made a $75 donation to the Kansas cause. Then he met with Charles Blair, the foreman of the Colins Company Ax Factory in Colinsville, Connecticut. Blair was contracted to make one thousand pikes, each one a "sharp pointed two sided blade about ten inches long," mounted on "a strong handle" a foot longer than the typical pitchfork handle. Due to financial difficulties, however, it took Brown over a year before he could afford to have the order completed. At the time, he explained that the pikes were for free-state settlers in Kansas, but he really wanted them for the black army he envisioned. Oliver Brown, who had gone East to find work, heard about the project, and wrote home that "Mr. Blair is now at work making 1,000 Kansas butter knifes [*sic*] for Father."

Ever since Brown's departure from Kansas, relatives had expressed concern over his operations. Jeremiah Brown wrote to Adair in Kansas that he feared "Capt[.] Brown has got the war spirrit [*sic*] so strong that he will carry the thing farther than is best[,] but we hope not." Adair had an even better idea of how far Brown would "carry the thing." Around the time Brown was in Connecticut contracting pike production, Adair wrote to Jeremiah that he still held strictly to fighting in self-defense, and felt that in most cases, even self-defense was "inexpedient." As to John Brown's intention of "provoking an attack, or carrying the 'war into Africa,' as the saying is, I differ decidedly." Adair was pleased that some of Brown's sons had decided to refrain from further warfare. When things seemed to be coming to a positive conclusion in Kansas, Adair was even more pleased that "Bro. John's preparations for war" would not likely be needed. However, when Brown heard from Mary that his sons had decided to "learn, and practice war no more," he was no doubt displeased. He wrote to his wife that he did not love fighting any more than they did. "Still I think there may be *possibly* in their day that which is more to be dreaded: if such things *do not now exist.*"[3]

Brown's success at gaining financial assistance was measured and frustrating to him. Though George Stearns and Gerrit Smith proved generous and faithful supporters, his endeavors did not bring the results he had imagined. As a result he prepared a written appeal, "Old Browns *Farewell*," in which he recounted his family's suffering and sacrifices in Kansas, and lamented that the wealthy and "'*Heaven exalted*' people" of New England had not provided him "even the necessary supplies, for a common soldier." Brown felt that his writings stirred up some response, and he wrote to a relative in April 1857 that he had "some hope of succeeding" as a consequence. Overall, he enjoyed moderate success, returning to Kansas that summer the "master of considerable supplies." However, a good part of promised support was not made available, and the money he had received was consumed by the expenditures, wages, and other expenses required to gather fighters in Kansas. Brown also struggled with "the ague" sickness, lingering at Tabor, Iowa (a strong abolitionist Quaker community) until late in 1857. Meanwhile, things were quiet in Kansas, free-state settlers were in the majority, and now it seemed the fate of the territory depended on politics, not warfare. Brown's attention had turned toward another field of operation against slavery, though this was not evident in 1857. But when he reached Kansas in November, he began to recruit men for an effort against pro-slavery forces. Ordered to leave for Iowa, they were informed that "Capt[.] Brown's ultimate destination was the State of Virginia." While leaving them to winter in the anti-slavery stronghold of Springdale, Iowa, Brown again made his way eastward.

He had also recruited a British abolitionist named Hugh Forbes as a drill master for the small army he was assembling. Forbes had fought in the Italian independence movement under Garibaldi and seemed an ideal associate for Brown's endeavor. However, Forbes clashed with Brown, questioned his plans, and then grew impatient and distrustful of his supporters back East. Inflamed by the disruption of his salary, Forbes abandoned the effort and proceeded to work Brown's eastern supporters and their associates for money by whining, accusing, and finally threatening to expose Brown's plans. In the end, Forbes proved treacherous and exploitative, and his twists and turns caused most of the Six to force a postponement on Brown.[4]

In early 1858, Brown traveled to Ohio, then up to Rochester, New York, where he stayed at the home of Frederick Douglass. Sequestered there from late January until mid-February, Brown carried on correspondence (sometimes using his Kansas pseudonym, Nelson Hawkins), talked endlessly with Douglass about his plans, and enlisted young Charles Douglass to carry his correspondence back and forth from the mail. Brown wrote to John Jr. that Douglass "seemed to appreciate my theories, and my labours." He also received correspondence from the Reverend James Gloucester of Brooklyn, New York, a prosperous African American and a firm supporter. Gloucester wrote to Brown that despite his personal admiration, he feared the masses of black people were too impulsive and troubled to support the effort. "I only note it as it may form a part of the history of your undertakings and that it may not damp[en] ardor," Gloucester concluded.

But Brown did not waver in his belief that blacks would respond in support of his militant anti-slavery effort. Indeed, his main effort while at Douglass's was the composition of his *Provisional Constitution and Ordinances for the People of the United States*. The document was comprised of forty-eight articles outlining the government of a guerilla state he intended to plant in the South. According to the preamble, slavery was a "most barbarous, unprovoked, and unjustifiable War" upon black people. Brown intended his document to represent the interests of "Oppressed People" and "all other people degraded" by slavery and injustice. The mountain-based community he envisioned would consist of members of "the Proscribed and oppressed races of the United States" and their "minor children." The constitution's first twenty-one articles pertain to political structure, which Brown modeled on the three branches of the U.S. government. However, his intention was not a permanent nation, but "an instrument for the government of a nation of liberated slaves by 'amendment and reform' of the government of the United States."

Douglass had first heard of the plan during a visit with the Browns in Springfield in the late 1840s. Brown had long considered the Allegheny Mountains, which stretched from the North to the South, as the basis of his plan. It was his intention to take a small brigade of trained men into the mountains, where they could easily hide in "natural forts" and defend themselves. Spreading through the mountains in squads of five, Brown's brigades would deplete Southern communities by inducing "the slaves to join them, seeking and selecting the most restless and daring." In this manner, Brown envisioned building an army of "one hundred hardy men" to be drilled and trained as freedom-fighters. In turn, these men would run off slaves in large numbers, sending some northward on the underground railroad while the heartiest remained to fight. Brown believed the least bloody way of undermining slavery was to destroy "the money value of slave property," and he hoped to destabilize counties, then states, until the evil institution collapsed. Consequently, a "regularly constituted government" was needed to "avoid anarchy and confusion."

The *Provisional Constitution* reflects a great deal of consideration and analysis indicative of Brown's indefatigable commitment to the anti-slavery effort. The idea of arming fugitive slaves with pikes and establishing a guerrilla community devoted to destabilizing slavery suggests Brown's awareness of various historical and contemporary dissenting communities, especially the West Indian "maroons" and other self-liberated societies. But his conception of radical community also reflected the fundamental principles of Puritan life, as illustrated by his emphasis on family, school, and church as an integral part of the state (Article LVII), just as they had been in the Western Reserve. Brown thus included a strong moral code against "Irregularities," such as profane and filthy language, indecent conduct, drunkenness, fighting, and fornication (Article XL). Brown's own conservative bent is reflected in a prohibition against "Needless Waste" of property, livestock, and resources (Article XXXV). As a community in struggle, his envisioned state would prohibit concealed weapons and laziness, and capital punishment would be administered for treachery and rape of prisoners (Articles XXXVII, XXXVIII, and XXXIX). A declaration of loyalty to the United States and its flag was also inserted as a defense against the inevitable charge of treason

(Article XLVI). Finally, with himself in mind, Brown created the office of Commander-in-Chief as separate from the President. The Commander-in-Chief would serve a three-year term after being selected by all three branches of the government, have total direction of military affairs, and access to a "safety fund" with the approval of the Secretary of War (Articles VII, XXIX, and XXX).[5]

Douglass wrote that Brown's entire stay at his home in Rochester was consumed by preparation of the *Provisional Constitution*. "It was the first thing in the morning and the last thing at night, till I confess it began to be something of a bore to me," the famous abolitionist recalled.

With his constitution completed, Brown went to Peterboro, New York, where he stayed with his supporter, Gerrit Smith. He had hoped to rally Higginson and other members of the Six, but only Sanborn came in from Massachusetts, coincidentally pleased to meet his old classmate, Edwin Morton, who was working as the Smith children's tutor. Brown felt warmly received by the Peterboro mogul, and wrote to John Jr. that the Smiths

> are ready to go in for a share in the *whole trade*. I will say (in the language of another) in regard to this most encouraging fact: "*My soul doth magnify the Lord.*" I seem to be almost "marvelously helped": *and to his name be the praise.*

To Mary and the children, he similarly wrote that the Smiths "go *all* lengths with me." Brown presented his *Provisional Constitution* to Smith, Morton, and Sanborn, which the latter remembered as "an amazing proposition—desperate in character, wholly inadequate in its provision of means, and of most uncertain result." Sanborn, Smith, and Morton listened and raised objections, but Brown countered them by appeals to divine purpose: "If God be for us, who can be against us." Ultimately, Smith and Sanborn agreed that they were obligated to support Brown lest he be left entirely alone, knowing his determination to act regardless. Edwin Morton recalled that during Brown's visit they strolled the countryside in deep conversation about the sovereignty of God and the condemnation of sinners. Unlike Higginson and Parker back in New England, Morton agreed with Brown that "a perfectly just and good God" could decree "the final and utter perdition and eternal condemnation of some souls" without self-contradiction. Morton remembered that Brown would pause during their walk, delightfully looking back at their foot-prints in the snow. Years later Morton related Brown's fondness for foot-prints to his "trusting reliance" on "the constant, instant Presence of an overruling Providence." Several weeks before, Brown had written to Mary expressing his desire to see her and the children, reminding her that "the great work of my life" had been guided by "the unseen Hand" of God. Even in the ups and downs of "great encouragements: and discour-agements," he heard a voice calling him to persevere. "On the whole," Brown later wrote, "the language of Providence to me would certainly seem to say [']try on.[']"

While at the Smith mansion Brown also met the elderly abolitionist, Charles Stuart, who was also a close friend of evangelist Charles Finney. In younger days, Stuart had served in the British East India Company, and was afterward a major proponent of West Indian emancipation. While Smith and Sanborn conferred, Brown and Stuart enjoyed a theological *tête-à-tête*—Brown undoubtedly holding forth the orthodox Calvinist po-sition. Yet this was a friendly episode, since Stuart had supported Brown at the onset of his Kansas endeavor. Furthermore, Brown likely shared Stuart's conviction that God had shown "great patience" with white peo-ple, restraining his wrath from "breaking up the earth beneath our feet, and dashing us all into sudden hell." Both probably agreed too that God's patience was running out. Brown would also have found Stuart's knowl-edge of the black Canadian population of great interest. He had worked among black refugees at Amherstburg on the Detroit River, and later set-tled near the Georgian Bay of Lake Huron and served as secretary of the Anti-Slavery Society of Canada.[6] Stuart was probably informed of Brown's plans to shortly convene a convention in the very heart of the black Canadian refuge.

Canada had a black community from the time of the Revolutionary war, but they had little interaction with the black expatriate communities that began to appear in the 1820s. That white Canadians accepted the steady flow of black Americans was not so much due to philanthropy as to "an ambivalent anti-Americanism." Furthermore, black settlers chose Canada by default, not wanting to repatriate to Africa, South America, or the Caribbean. Nor did black Americans settle in the Canadian inte-rior, but preferred a more familiar soil and climate. African Americans were thus attracted to places like St. Catharines near the Niagara River, Windsor and Amherstburg opposite Detroit, Michigan, and the long peninsula that reached southward against Lake Erie nearly to the latitude of New York City. Though blacks found freedom in Canada, they were not really treated as equals by whites except in legal terms—a mediocre step up from life in the Northern United States.

John Brown first's visit to Canada in 1858 lasted from April 8–24, during which time he visited St. Catharines, Canada West, and Ingersoll, Ontario. Brown entered the country from Rochester, accompanied by abolitionist Jermain Loguen, who also introduced him to Harriet Tubman. Brown was delighted to meet Tubman, whom he nicknamed "the General." After shaking Tubman's hand enthusiastically, he conferred with her about his intention to establish a community in the mountains of Virginia and gather fugitives. Brown not only hoped to enlist her assistance, but to rely upon her as his Canadian agent. After she agreed, Brown showed his admiration by referring to her as a manly leader. "Harriet Tubman hooked on his whole team at once," he wrote to John Jr. "He (Harriet) is the most of a man, naturally, that I ever met with."[7]

On April 15, 1858, the *Oxford Herald* of Ingersoll advertised that "Captain 'Osawatomie' John Brown of Kansas" was to speak on conditions in Kansas at the Wesleyan Church. Afterward he traveled on the Great Western Railroad to Chatham, Ontario, the city which thereafter became the center of his Canadian activities. In 1858, Chatham was "a muddy, busy little market town of perhaps 4,000 people," more than one-third fugitives from American slavery. With other black settlements in its vicinity, here was the largest number of blacks in Canada concentrated within a fifty-mile radius. Chatham was a major terminus of the underground railroad and its black population was concentrated in one section. Black Chatham buzzed with the business of town and country, including a large self-improvement association. It was also the new home of the *Provincial Freeman*, a black-owned publication recently transplanted from Toronto.

Brown made his initial Chatham contacts by visiting the office of the *Provincial Freeman*, where he had informal conversations with various black community leaders. When publisher Isaac Shadd expressed concern over the risks involved in Brown's proposed raid, the old man retorted: "Risk? When God is with me and I am doing God's work, what can touch me? I have letters of marque from the Almighty to destroy the accursed institution of slavery by whatever means He may place in my hands. I am God's instrument." Brown also sought out the black nationalist leader, Martin Delany. Delany was a physician, scholar, and an advocate of repatriation to Africa. He had previously been associated with Frederick Douglass's newspaper, but the two leaders had come to different conclusions

John Brown wore a long beard as a disguise following his activities in Kansas, but had it trimmed down at the time of the raid. It is the bearded Brown that is often pictured in texts and cinema, as in this portrait. *West Virginia State Archives.*

about the future of blacks in the United States. Brown probably also knew about Delany's book, *The Condition, Elevation, Emigration, and Destiny of the Colored People of the United States, Politically Considered* (1852). While the leader was absent from home, Brown appeared at his door, looking to Catherine Delany like "one of the old prophets." Still a wanted man, Brown had let his beard grow long and thick as a disguise. He had aged hard in the Kansas struggle too, and his graying hair, care-worn face, stooping posture, and white beard made him look quite elderly.

When they finally met, the plan that Brown shared with Delany varied from the one he had shared with Harriet Tubman. No mention was made of Virginia, though Brown did speak of the Subterranean Passage Way and plans for an impenetrable fortress. Barring defect in Delany's recollection, Brown was either indecisive or deliberately misrepresenting his intentions to safeguard his plans. Furthermore, he seems to have been stressed, perhaps put off by a lack of enthusiasm or confidence in his plans among associates. Slavery had made cowards of Americans, Brown declared. "The whites are afraid of each other, and the blacks are afraid of the whites. You can effect nothing among such people." He even disdained the need for money, declaring that his real need was for men. "Men are afraid of identification with me, though they favor my measures. They are cowards, sir! Cowards!"

Brown left Canada in late April to gather his men at Springdale, Iowa and bring them back to Chatham. He had issued invitations to abolitionists and black leaders for "a quiet convention" on May 8 and 10, 1858. Copies of his *Provisional Constitution* were to be prepared by a black printer for distribution. Though invited, neither Frederick Douglass nor Gerrit Smith attended, and the only whites involved were Brown's men, including his son Owen. About thirty-five black men from the vicinity also attended, including clergymen, doctors, businessmen, farmers, laborers, and newspapermen.[8]

John Brown was the driving spirit of the "quiet convention" at Chatham, and the Canadian attenders could hardly have taken primary ownership of the event. Notwithstanding their respect and admiration, the black leaders had to count the cost of involving themselves in a plan that was largely fueled by one man's moral outrage and self-conception as an instrument of God. But the Chatham convention was not a self-serving façade, nor were the attenders manipulated. The black attenders were quite supportive, and when an anti-Brown clergyman closed the doors of his church to their meetings, the Chatham participants quickly found another convention site.

The Chatham convention was originally intended to precede the raid only by a short time, and the adoption of Brown's *Provisional Constitution* and election of officials were revolutionary acts with real implications for slavery. When the nature of Brown's work was revealed to the attenders, it was recognized that Americans would consider it treason. But "when they got ready to sign, every man was anxious to have his name at the head, and a crowd stood about the desk to grasp the pen." Yet some of the black attenders objected to Brown's loyalty to the flag of a slave nation, while others entertained serious doubts about the reliability of fugitives in the effort. These differences aside, his plan was supported and commitments were made for the raising of companies of soldiers from the black communities in Chatham, Ingersoll, and Buxton. However, the treachery of Hugh Forbes not only led to a postponement of the raid for over a year, but also interrupted the rhythm of cooperation that Brown had attained among black expatriates in 1858. Given the apparent liabilities of his plan, Brown badly needed immediacy if he was going to make inroads toward extensive involvement by blacks from Canada.

James Monroe Jones, the son of fugitive slaves and a graduate of Oberlin College, recalled Brown's frequent visits to his gunsmith shop in Chatham during May 1858. While Brown characteristically paced the floor with hands clasped behind his back, the two debated over strategy. Jones declared Brown's proposed raid an "utterly hopeless" venture, saying that it would only waste the few good whites on their side. At this remark, Brown stopped and blurted out: "Did not my Master, Jesus Christ, come down from heaven and sacrifice Himself upon the altar for the salvation of the race? And should I, a worm, not worthy to crawl under his feet, refuse to sacrifice myself?" Jones said that he never doubted Brown's sanity. But he believed that he came to discern that *only* the deaths of white men would arouse the people of the North from their stupor of indifference toward slavery. "If that was his real object," Jones concluded, "the event that followed justified his plans."[9]

# 20

## "This Spark of Fire"

But thou shalt say unto them, This is a nation that obeyed not the voice of the Lord their God, nor receiveth correction: truth is perished, and is cut off from their mouth.

—Jeremiah 7:28

John Brown was changing, but it was not merely the maturity of years that showed. Others saw the change, like William Phillips, author of a popular free-state book, *The Conquest of Kansas* (1856). After having met Brown twice previously, Phillips met him again in Kansas for the last time in 1859. Despite his obvious physical change—stooped shoulders and a worn look accented by graying hair and a long white beard, Brown himself seemed different to the writer. "There was in the expression of his face something even more dignified than usual," Phillips recalled. "His eye was brighter, and the absorbing and consuming thoughts that were within him seemed to be growing out all over him." Brown had gone to Kansas after news reached Canada that Hugh Forbes had indeed leaked information about his plans for the raid. His trip west was a diversion intended to throw off suspicion by discrediting the traitor's claims. Meeting Phillips at Lawrence, he spoke candidly about slavery's evil history and his belief that even if it was stopped in Kansas, the pro-slavery faction would not relent. Brown correctly predicted that the South would secede from the Union in 1860 if the Republicans won the presidential election. He also declared that pro-slavery leaders in Washington were already positioning the government's resources to the advantage of the South in the event of war. "For my part," he said, "I drew my sword in Kansas when they attacked us, and I will never sheathe it until the war is over." Like most conservative free-state people, Phillips had an unstudied view of national leadership, which Brown chided. "You forget the fearful wrongs that are carried on in the name of government and law." Nor did Phillips believe his contention that enslaved blacks would rise up and fight if given an opportunity. "You have not studied them right," Brown lectured, "and you have not studied them long enough. Human nature is the same everywhere." When Phillips continued to differ, the old man responded, "The world is very pleasant to you, but when your household gods are broken as mine have been, you will see all this more clearly." Phillips became offended and rose to leave, and Brown grabbed his hands and looked into his face with tearful eyes. "No, we must not part thus," he appealed. "I wanted to see you and tell you how it appeared to me. With the help of God I will do what I believe to be best." At that, he kissed Phillips like a son and released him. He never saw Brown again, but always believed this last meeting was the most important, and had the most "peculiar historical significance."

Years, tears, and self-discovery guided by a sincere religious faith had begun to transform John Brown. His critics notwithstanding, he had done more than brood over slavery for thirty years. "Many a night," Mary Brown said later, her husband "had lain awake and prayed" about his role in Providence. Not that he thought his actions divinely inspired, but he did believe that even his failures "would be overruled by Providence for the best." His visage showed an open tenderness emerging from his stoic demeanor—quite in contrast to the tendency of the Browns to be a "people of deep feelings, but of undemonstrative habits." Furthermore, Brown had come to personify a unique blend of radical abolitionism and conservative theology. As his liberal ally Higginson concluded, Brown's "theology was Puritan, like his practice." He had always felt strongly about slavery, and all along his passionate expressions against the institution were vivid. But the last few years of his life were entirely devoted to anti-slavery endeavors, and "the whole power of his mind had been given to one subject."

Brown had blended contemplation with struggle, as recalled by the Iowa Quakers and spiritualists who watched him withdraw morning and evening every day to pray alone and meditate on the Bible. "He had the love which casts out fear," recalled one associate. Rather than violence and revenge, they recognized in him a "common concern to forward the freedom of the slaves," and felt confident "in Brown as a man of integrity, kindliness, sincerity, and spirituality." He often declared that he would fight no war "unless it was a war of liberty" and that he regarded "human life as precious." He told another Iowa associate: "I make no war on man. Against the system I will offer my blood. North and South are both guilty—the North for its introduction, the South for its continuation. It is most abhorrent, most abhorrent!"

To the critic and indifferent observer, John Brown was indeed a fanatic, but to those who shared his hatred of slavery and love for humanity, he had evolved into a "crusader with one dominating idea. He talked only of religion and the evils of slavery." Of course, he was not the only one who recognized the complexity of guilt and compromise that forced whites toward civil war and blacks to a sense of hopelessness. Gerrit Smith wrote that slavery had so "debauched" white society that blacks had come to the conclusion "that no resource is left to them but in God and insurrections."[1]

Brown too was looking to God for a chance to strike at slavery. Traveling under the pseudonym Shubel Morgan ("Shubel" is a biblical Hebrew name meaning "captive of God"), he waited throughout the rest of 1858 until Providence seemed to open a door of opportunity late in the year. In mid-December, one of his men was approached by a slave from Missouri whose entire family was about to be split up and sold at an estate auction. Brown recognized opportunity in the problem and "hailed it as heaven-sent." With his men divided in two parties, he entered Missouri and forcefully removed a total of eleven slaves, including a pregnant woman. Though displeased that one of the slaveholders was killed while attempting to draw his weapon, Brown did not hesitate to sack the slaveholders' homes. "He believed that a state of war existed and that it was proper to despoil the enemy," wrote one of his men. "None of this property ever went for his own enrichment. . . . He refused to recognize all laws protecting slave property and considered wealth created by slaves as just spoil."

When they reached the home of an ally in Kansas, John Brown introduced the fugitives to his host, "waving his hat around the circle of smiling blacks. 'Allow me to introduce to you *a part* of my family,'" he said. "'Observe that I have carried the war into Africa.'" Of course, many free-state conservatives were displeased with his Missouri foray, especially those who feared reprisals for the intrusion. Brown responded defensively in an open letter to the *New York Tribune* entitled "Old Brown's Parallels," in which he compared his liberation of eleven slaves from Missouri with a murderous attack on eleven "quiet citizens" of a free-state settlement that had taken place in 1858. He expressed disdain and amazement that "All Pro-Slavery, conservative Free-State, and doughface men, and

Administration tools" could be so "filled with holy horror" by his efforts. Brown would probably have felt even more justified if he had known that the slaveholder who had been killed was a veteran of raids in free-state neighborhoods. According to one of the liberated blacks, he had been involved in "all manner of devilment."

After sequestering the fugitives in Kansas for several weeks, Brown led them out in the dead of winter with wagons and provisions provided by free-state supporters. Passing slowly and painfully through frigid Iowa, they had to evade lawmen and federal marshals. Once he even put a Colt's revolver in the hand of one of the woman fugitives. "Now, you use that the first chance you get," Brown ordered. Despite several close calls, the party never had to fight, and found greater support as they moved eastward. To no surprise, Brown held tight reins in the camp too, and even when it came to cooking he insisted on having his way—something that annoyed fugitive Jane Harper, who repeatedly clashed with the old man over food preparation. The former slaves could not help but appreciate and admire their friend Brown, but they found him a strange hero. "He was a very quiet man," Sam Harper recalled. "Awful quiet. He never laughed. . . . as solemn as a graveyard."

With the assistance of anti-slavery associates, the fugitives and their escorts traveled by railroad boxcar from West Liberty, Iowa to Chicago. Private investigator Allen Pinkerton then arranged for their transport to Detroit, where they could cross over into Canada. One supporter remembered that many of the blacks had scars on their backs. He never forgot one of the fugitives wiping the tears from her eyes and saying, "I be better over in Can'da."

John Brown did not make the final crossing with the fugitives from the United States to the land of freedom. Standing on the wharf, he waited with them for a ferry to arrive—a tiny smile forming on his lips as he observed the revelry of some of the fugitives. "You'd better quit your fooling and take up your book," the old man admonished. When the ferry finally sailed across the cold waters, he watched quietly, quoting a biblical character who had waited many years to hold the infant messiah in his arms. "Lord, now lettest thy servant depart in peace, for my eyes have seen thy salvation." During the trying sojourn, the pregnant fugitive had given birth to a boy and named him John Brown.[2]

This bold foray and victorious trek across eleven hundred miles while evading agents and spies won Brown great notoriety. Both the President and the governor of Missouri offered rewards for his capture, and his critics found great reason to declare him a thief and bandit. Typically, Northern conservatives were more disturbed that he had seized slaveholders' livestock than they were about the evil of black enslavement. One such critic pushed Brown to the point of disgust when they met at a Cleveland restaurant. When the man demanded that he make a biblical justification for taking Missouri horses, the old man's "eyes flashed, his brow contracted," and he pounded his knife so hard that dishware and utensils bounced everywhere. "Upon what principle?" Brown shouted. "Upon the same upon which Moses spoiled the Egyptians!" Typically, the man thought Brown a fanatic, but abolitionist supporters in the East were thrilled by his success. The admiring Sanborn thus wrote to Higginson: "He has begun the work in earnest. . . . I am glad of what he has done, and earnestly hope he will not fall into the hands of [the United States] or [Missouri.] If he does not, I think we may look for great results from this spark of fire."

Before leaving Detroit, Brown went to hear his old friend Frederick Douglass speak at City Hall, and afterward joined him in a meeting of black leaders at the home of William Webb, a business man in the city. Among the men present were participants of the Chatham convention, including Brown's old underground railroad associate William Lambert, and Isaac Shadd of the *Provincial Freeman*. As Brown shared his renewed intention to conduct a raid in Virginia, he was probably not surprised that some in attendance were underwhelmed. George de Baptiste, a farmer, business man, and head of a vigilance committee in Detroit, wanted to set explosives in various white churches throughout the South—something Brown thought unacceptable, as did most of the others. Yet the old man was not offended by the disinterest of de Baptiste as much as he was by opposition from Douglass, who seems to have openly called into question the plans for the raid. Douglass later denied this conflict, though in the long run he proved a great disappointment to his friend.[3]

By the summer of 1859, Brown had moved to the vicinity of Harper's Ferry, Virginia, where he rented a farm in nearby Maryland. Known in the community as Isaac Smith, he established his presence and reputation as a godly businessman with interests in mining and cattle. Brown continued to wear a beard, but had it trimmed quite short. His rented farmhouse was headquarters to the small army he assembled over the following weeks. Much to Brown's disappointment, his wife Mary refused to come down from North Elba and assist in housekeeping. Instead, teenagers Annie Brown and Martha, Oliver's wife, came down to keep the appearance of a normal household. With additional men arriving at the house, however, keeping up normal appearances was difficult—especially with the presence of black men, all of whom had to be brought in during the night. For the most part, the men were concealed during the daytime, only coming out to romp and exercise in darkness.

When Brown passed through Ohio for the last time, he borrowed a copy of *The Life of Jehudi Ashmun* (1835) from John Jr. and took it with him to Maryland. Written by the hand of the American Colonization Society, the book chronicled Ashmun's role in leading blacks from Baltimore, Maryland, to Liberia, West Africa in 1822. Brown would hardly have agreed with the author's contention that blacks were better off as slaves in a Christian land than as pagans in Africa. However, he was clearly concerned about the nature of the black society he intended to establish in the mountains of the South. His *Provisional Constitution* reflects a concern for social order and moral bearing, and Brown probably agreed with Ashmun's conviction that "*an African Colony, in order to answer any benevolent design, must have for its basis the promotion of the Christian Religion.*" Brown too was likely inspired by the description of Ashmun's success among the black colonists in Liberia, and probably hoped for a similar achievement:

> He had infused much of his own spirit into the minds of the settlers; and while he saw intelligence, industry, fortitude, and enterprise springing up vigorously around him, he saw also testified in the gratitude beaming from many eyes, a conviction that, under Providence, these virtues had been reared and fostered by the discipline of his hand, and the energy of his example.

His earliest efforts on behalf of blacks, from "Sambo's Mistakes" to his presence at Timbucto, were always bound up with the idea of being a paternal Christian model and providing the help, training, and spiritual context that would encourage the oppressed to nurture a positive society. He might be accused of paternalism were he like many elitist white abolitionists, but what he prescribed for blacks was no different than the social and religious strictures he prescribed for all his men and children too. Osborne P. Anderson, one of the several blacks to follow Brown to Harper's Ferry, recalled him as a "patriarch leader" whose home and organization had become "an Anti-Slavery family . . . wherein no hateful prejudice dared intrude its ugly self."

Anderson, a Pennsylvanian by birth, was the only black raider to come directly from the Chatham convention the year before. A local tradition has it that Isaac Shadd, publisher of the *Provincial Freeman*, told his associates that blacks ought to have some part in Brown's plan in case he succeeded in setting up "the kingdom of God in the south." To avoid finding themselves in a "mighty uncomfortable" place, it was decided to draw lots—the fateful lot falling to journeyman printer Osborne Anderson. However, Anderson was hardly drafted against his will. He had been an active supporter of Brown's effort in Canada, and had even been elected to serve as congressman under the *Provisional Constitution*.[4]

A small representation of Brown's Kansas warriors had gone to Chatham too, but he lost touch with some of them during the Forbes hiatus. Not counting Brown's son Owen, seven of the Harper's Ferry raiders had served in Kansas in the free-state cause. Several others met Brown in his Iowa sojourn among abolitionist Quakers, and others followed Brown's sons Watson and Oliver from New York to Virginia. Besides Brown, only two of the raiders were over thirty years old, and the youngest was barely twenty. The group included three sets of brothers (including Brown's sons), and an uncle and his nephew. Brown was not the only husband and father among them, there being six married men, four of whom had children (including Oliver Brown, whose wife gave birth after his death).

Though some of the black raiders may have been evangelical Christians, none of the whites shared the faith of their leader, including Owen, Oliver, and Watson Brown. Still, the old man saw to it that the fashion of the farmhouse was distinctly Christian, and the raiders were called to daily Bible reading and prayer—Brown's invocations always replete with "strong appeals to God for the deliverance of the slave." Despite his personal beliefs, however, he also demonstrated a great deal of religious tolerance, and encouraged his little army to freely debate and discuss religious matters. "He only asked his men to do what they knew to be right." Indeed, Brown demonstrated that he was a strong advocate of free thought and "the fullest expression of opinion from his men," even when his own views were severely criticized. "It was evidence of self-sustaining power," Anderson wrote.

In addition to Osborne Anderson (who was called "Chatham Anderson" to distinguish him from another raider with the same last name), the little army included four other blacks. John Copeland Jr. and Lewis Leary were Oberlinites attracted to the cause by Brown's successful Missouri raid, and were themselves anti-slavery activists. Both freemen, Leary had fled his native North Carolina for preaching liberation to slaves, and Copeland was involved in a successful effort to interrupt a slave rendition in Oberlin, Ohio. Dangerfield Newby, forty-four years old, was also the oldest raider. The son of a Scotsman and his slave, Newby was freed by his father and was working in Southern Ohio as a blacksmith when he met John Brown. His anti-slavery commitment notwithstanding, Newby joined the raiders to liberate his enslaved family in Virginia. Newby's wife was corresponding with him from the land of bondage, and he shared some of her pleading words with the rest of the raiders:

> It is said Master is in want of money. If so, I know not what time he may sell me, and then all my bright hopes of the future are blasted, for there has been one bright hope to cheer me in all my troubles, that is to be with you, for if I thought I should never see you this earth would have no charms for me.

"Emperor" Shields Green, was the only fugitive from slavery among Brown's men. Green had escaped from South Carolina after the death of his wife, leaving a small son behind. He had participated in a fugitive slave "riot" in Harrisburg, Pennsylvania and declared his willingness to die on behalf of "liberty for myself and my race" because "blows from an overseer's lash cut into my soul." Green joined the raid through association with Frederick Douglass, and was living in Rochester, New York when he first met John Brown.[5]

According to Douglass, Green had already decided to join Brown's effort by the summer of 1859, when they traveled together to a secret meeting with the old man and his Secretary of War, John Kagi. Sequestered in a quarry near Chambersburg, Pennsylvania, the four conferred at length about Brown's plans for the raid. Douglass wrote that he strongly protested when he heard that Brown now intended to attack the armory at Harper's Ferry, and dismissed the effort as a "perfect steel-trap." He wrote that Brown tried to persuade him otherwise, appealing to his role in a special work. "When I strike the bees will begin to swarm, and I shall want you to help hive them." But the orator demurred further and the meeting ended with separation, Douglass being amazed when Green decided to stay with Brown. "Here we separated," he wrote, "they to go to Harper's Ferry, I to Rochester."

However, the Douglass-Green episode is not without its cloudy aspects, especially regarding the abolitionist's well-crafted version prepared many years later. Despite their warm camaraderie for over a decade prior to the raid, perhaps Douglass's enthusiasm for Brown's efforts had waned by early 1859, when he seems to have clashed with the old man during the Detroit meeting. Though Douglass denied that conflict, he later portrayed himself as having serious questions about Brown's plans as early as the 1840s. It is unclear to what extent he ever supported Brown's plans in those days, though it is likely that Douglass was never sold on the plan as much as he was on the man himself. It is no surprise, then, that Douglass backed away from Brown at the threshold of the conflict.

Yet there is reason to believe that he had made some sort of commitment to support Brown early on in their relationship. Despite Salmon Brown's bitter and digressive outlook in old age, there is probably substance to his claim that Douglass "had always promised to go with Father when he should strike in the South." During the Springfield years, the Douglass and Brown families had become quite close, Salmon recalled, even to the point of baby-sitting the Douglass children. Annie, who would have been no more than six at that time, insisted that she remembered Douglass in Springfield promising her father to "go with you even unto death." Annie claimed that after the disappointing meeting at the quarry in the summer of 1859, she reminded her father of Douglass's earlier promise. Astonished that she recalled the incident, the old man agreed, saying, "These were his very words." Brown's devoted son-in-law Henry Thompson showed scorn and contempt at the question of the abolitionist's devotion, declaring, "*Fred Douglass backed out.*" Even gentle Sarah, who grew up in the shadows and stories of her mother's troubled sojourn, would simply say her father "expected" Douglass to join him. The resentment toward his alleged abandonment was so strong in the family that it endured among Brown's descendants into the 1970s.

On the other hand, Brown supposedly had Douglass on a list of unreliable supporters, and John Jr. (who did field work in advance of the raid) said that he had no knowledge "as to how far Douglass had committed himself to the undertaking." Douglass always acknowledged his unwillingness to participate in the "rash and wild" Harper's Ferry raid. But unlike Brown, who believed himself worth more to the cause dead than alive, perhaps Douglass—a celebrated figure in 1859—thought it best for his career not to throw himself headlong into his friend's "steel-trap." Posterity may be happy for his decision, whatever the real chemistry of its content. One visitor to Brown's jail cell after the raid remembered the old man expressing some sense of lost opportunity and attributing it to "the famous Mr. Frederick Douglass." The visitor recalled that Brown then "shut his mouth in a way that made me know that he thought no good of Fred Douglass." Still, John Brown could hardly have been justified to blame him for the failure of the raid, and it may be that the witness against Douglass was tainted with personal resentments and prejudice. Neither Salmon, John Jr., nor Henry Thompson chose to go to Harper's Ferry either, so their criticisms seem all the more unfair. Yet we are left to wonder to what extent Douglass styled his autobiography to smooth over the rough edges of history. "It may be the mist will never be cleared away respecting this actor in the drama," John Jr. concluded in 1885.[6]

Though posing as businessman Isaac Smith, Brown was quite sincere in his involvement in religious activities throughout the summer and early fall of 1859. During this time he often visited Chambersburg, Pennsylvania, where his weapons—clandestinely shipped by freight on the Cumberland Valley Railroad—were received and then forwarded to Maryland by wagon. John Kagi was also stationed in Chambersburg, and he used Mary Ritner's boarding house in town as headquarters because she was an abolitionist. During visits to Chambersburg, Brown probably visited the black church in the Wolftown section, and he was also known to have done some lay preaching at the Falling Spring Presbyterian Church. He also developed a friendly rapport with William S. Heaton, an Episcopalian missionary who directed services in Chambersburg as well as mission work in Mont Alto, Pennsylvania. Brown preferred to attend services at the Emmanuel Chapel, a small country church at Mont Alto, probably because it exposed him to fewer people. As Isaac Smith, he won Heaton's trust as an active parishioner who collected offerings, taught Sunday School, and—according to one local tradition—even established a Sunday School for black children while encouraging local blacks to become involved in the congregation. Brown apparently received Holy Communion not long before the raid, and another account says that when he left the chapel a woman prophet confronted him, predicting that his involvement with slaves would lead to his doom if he crossed into the South. Local legend speaks of a "mulatto woman" with whom Brown conferred, a "dark Huguenot girl and religious exhorter," and although her activities are exaggerated, there is probably some truth to the story. Perhaps the young black woman had knowledge of Brown

Prior to the raid in 1859, John Brown frequently attended services at Emmanuel Chapel in Mont Alto, Pa., but people knew him as "Isaac Smith." It is said that Brown organized a Sunday School for black children here. *Author's photograph, 1996.*

and his mission and, after having a disturbing dream, felt it necessary to warn him when he left Emmanuel Chapel for the last time.

If Brown was warned by dreams that his mission was in danger, this was not the first time. Before he and his sons started for Maryland, Owen had a disturbing dream and finally decided to share it. "Father," he said, "I dreamed last night that I saw you on a scaffold with a great concourse around the scaffold, about to be hung." The old man looked rather sober, but said nothing. In contrast, after they rented the Maryland farmhouse and brought Annie and Martha there to set up housekeeping, Brown thought he had a good sign of success. As Annie recalled, her father was not superstitious nor given to seeking after signs, but one incident took place that seemed to him almost classic biblical imagery. Brown and Annie were sitting together one afternoon when they heard the fluttering and twittering of two wrens at the door. When they went out to see the frantic birds, they found a snake had crawled nearby and was poised to strike at the young in their nest. Brown killed the snake, and later asked his daughter if she thought it was an omen of impending success in fighting on behalf of the slaves.

Perhaps John Brown was better at reading Providence then omens. Nor did he realize that someone far more adept at dreams and visions had been repeatedly haunted by a dream about him too. In her dream, Harriet Tubman saw a "wilderness sort of place, all full of rocks and bushes," and a serpent raise its head among the rocks. The serpent became the head of an old man with a long, white beard, gazing at her "wishful like," as if he was going to speak to her. Suddenly "two other heads rose up beside him, younger than he," and as she wondered what they wanted with her, "a great crowd of men rushed in and struck down the younger heads, and then the head of the old man, still looking at her so 'wishful.'" Only after she heard the news from Virginia, did Harriet Tubman finally understand the dream. John Brown's raid on Harper's Ferry had failed, and among the dead raiders were his sons Oliver and Watson. Brown had misread the meaning of the serpent as representing the evil of slavery, while Tubman intuitively understood the serpent in different biblical symbolism. Like the Savior with whom she later compared John Brown, the fiery serpent lifted up in the wilderness was a sign of salvation in death. "As Moses lifted up the serpent in the wilderness, even so must the Son of man be lifted up."[7]

# 21

## "My Public Murder"

> But if ye had known what this meaneth, I will have mercy, and not sacrifice, ye would not have condemned the guiltless.
> —Matthew 12:7

The twenty-one-man "Provisional Army of the United States" seized Harper's Ferry late Sunday night, October 16, 1859. The element of surprise enabled Brown to seize key positions as well as the armory, though it was essential that the raiders strike and withdraw quickly if they were to initiate Brown's mountain-based program. The raiders likewise enjoyed initial success in attracting slaves from Virginia and Maryland. Despite the short-term nature of recruitment in the vicinity, there were between twenty and thirty slaves directly involved at the height of the takeover in the early morning hours of October 17. But Brown lingered far too long, and by late morning local militia had seized the bridge and blocked all means of escape. By delaying he also lost most of the slaves he had come to liberate. When they saw the tide of battle turning against Brown's men, they astutely "slipped back and joined their masters." The old man had counted on the fact that the Harper's Ferry armory, the only government arms production site in the South, was not under military supervision. But he was not informed by his spy about the trained local militia, and was somehow put off by the exploding mayhem and the armed response of the townsmen. "I could not help thinking that at times he appeared somewhat puzzled," recalled raider Osborne Anderson. By noon on Monday it was too late for escape, and now it was simply a question of holding off the enemy for as long as possible.[1]

Early Tuesday morning, October 18, a company of U.S. Marines, led by Col. Robert E. Lee, offered terms of surrender to Brown, now holed up in the engine house with a few of his men and some leading citizens he had taken hostage. When he refused to surrender, the Marines stormed

The Engine House at Harper's Ferry, where Brown and a few of his raiders made their last stand on October 18, 1859. *Photograph by Paulo Freire, 2000.*

the building with orders to kill Brown's men with bayonets, but not to harm the valuable black chattel unless they resisted. Expecting to be killed immediately, Brown urged the slaves fighting at his side to move away from him. Though one Marine was killed, the white raiders were easily overcome and ruthlessly bayoneted. Brown, who refrained from firing, was then attacked by a Marine who was somehow unable to inflict mortal wounds with his bayonet, and was likewise ill-suited with a costume sword instead of a combat saber. The Marine lunged hard but despite the force of his blow, his sword bent and doubled, perhaps striking Brown's belt buckle. Frustrated by his inability to kill the old man, he rained blows on his head with the sword's hilt until Brown fell unconscious. A Northern journalist afterward saw Brown's blood and strands of his gray hair smeared on the white-washed brick wall of the engine house. But John Brown lived, and the South would regret it.

When the struggle was finally over, ten of Brown's raiders were dead, including his sons and two brothers of his son-in-law, Henry Thompson. Of these ten, two were murdered outright by townsmen. Seven raiders escaped but two were caught and later executed along with four captive raiders. The bodies of the black raiders and slaves (along with one white mistaken for a "mulatto") were horribly desecrated by the townspeople and then stuffed into containers. As a final show of contempt, the corpses were alternately layered according to color—the body of Oliver Brown being laid in Dangerfield Newby's arms in a mock embrace. Not long after interment, students from the Winchester Medical School dug up the graves and stole some of the corpses for dissection. Watson Brown's body was made into a grotesque anatomical exhibit, highly prized by the Southern school. The bodies of the black raiders were not treated as well. Family and friends back in Ohio begged in vain for the body of John Copeland, but the students would not surrender their prey, and the remains were sliced and dissembled under the pretense of science.[2]

When John Brown regained consciousness, he was lying in the yard outside of the Harper's Ferry engine house. Manacled to another prisoner, he was weak and bloodied, and his eyes swollen from head wounds. Brown was immediately subjected to interrogation and questions from reporters after being carried into the office of the Master Armorer. Besides Robert E. Lee and J. E. B. Stuart, future leaders in the army of southern secession, prominent Virginia leaders were present, including Governor Henry Wise and Senator J. M. Mason, who would later lead a congressional investigation of the raid. But bystanders, militiamen, and curious onlookers also entered and spoke to Brown. Soon the old man was engulfed in a sea of questions:

*"Do you consider this a religious movement?"*
"It is, in my opinion, the greatest service man can render to God."
*"Do you consider yourself an instrument in the hands of Providence?"*
"I do."
*"Upon what principle do you justify your acts?"*
"Upon the Golden Rule. I pity the poor in bondage that have none to help them: that is why I am here; not to gratify any personal animosity, revenge, or vindictive spirit. It is my sympathy with the oppressed and the wronged, that are as good as you and as precious in the sight of God."

Brown was asked if he had anything else to say. Knowing his remarks would be reported by journalists, the old man prophesied:

I wish to say, furthermore, that you had better—all you people of the South—prepare yourselves for a settlement of this question, that must come up for settlement sooner than you are prepared for it. The sooner you are prepared the better. You may dispose of me very easily—I am nearly disposed of now; but this question is still to be settled—this negro question I mean; the end of that is not yet.

*"Brown, suppose you had every nigger in the United States, what would you do with them?"*

"Set them free."

*"I think you are fanatical."*

"And I think you are fanatical. 'Whom the gods would destroy, they first make mad,' and you are mad."

While John Brown lay on the floor of the armory office, the Reverend George Sigler entered the room. Sigler was a Church of God pastor who traveled a regular circuit preaching in the vicinity of Brown's Maryland farmhouse. The minister had known Brown as Isaac Smith, remembering him as a "grey bearded and grey headed man" who attended services and showed himself "an interested, attentive hearer." Sigler had previously heard that Smith had received "mysterious looking loads of heavy boxes," but thought nothing of such rumors until the raid. Now Sigler realized that Isaac Smith was indeed John Brown, the "wounded[,] bloody prisoner." A Roman Catholic priest also entered, perhaps hoping to minister to him in his suffering. Though bloody and bruised, Brown reared up his head and cut him off before he could speak. "Go out of here—I don't want you about me—go out!" The priest, probably a local clergyman, bowed gravely and withdrew. John Brown the Protestant saint had no time for Roman Catholic priests, especially priests who interceded for slavemasters.

On October 21, Brown and the surviving raiders were taken from Harper's Ferry to Charlestown, where they were jailed. As he lay on his bed, George Leech and Norval Wilson, two Methodist clergymen, entered to visit. When Wilson proposed they pray together, Brown's eyes flashed. "Mr. Wilson, *do you believe in slavery?*" The minister tried to evade Brown's question.

"This is a great and glorious government!"

"But Mr. Wilson, I'd like to have a categorized answer—*yes or no. Do you believe in slavery?*"

When Wilson said he believed in slavery "under the present circumstances," Brown responded bluntly: "Then, Mr. Wilson, I do not want your prayers. I do not want prayers of any man that believes in slavery." Wilson's partner also visited with the black raider Copeland, finding him educated and "well up in the controversy as to slavery." Speaking of his dead comrades, Copeland declared to the pastor: "Mr. Leech, this is but the beginning of the matter. They died for a great principle that will not die."

After being examined on October 25, Brown was indicted for conspiring with blacks to produce insurrection, for treason in the Commonwealth of Virginia, and for murder. It was more than revealing that the pro-slavery interests, who tried so hard to deny that Brown obtained support from the slaves, could not hide evidence to the contrary in their indictment. In the second count, eleven male slaves were listed from two nearby plantations alone. Yet this hardly accounted for all the slaves involved, both from Virginia and Maryland. (Nor was it explained how a man from the State of New York could be charged with treason by a state he had invaded.) Brown's trial was pushed through and he was found guilty in less than a week. On November 2, he heard the verdict and sentence of death, and made his statement to the court.

Denying that he had any intention of murder, treason, slave rebellion, or insurrection, Brown insisted that all he had intended to do was "free the slaves," and to "have made a clean thing of that matter" similar to his Missouri raid at the end of 1858. Brown has been attacked by scholars as deliberately misrepresenting his purposes, but for him the line between "freeing the slaves" and "insurrection" was moral and biblical, not political. Obviously pro-slavery society would tolerate no distinction between freeing their slaves and starting an insurrection. Yet Brown's point was no less sound. Had he been a murderer and terrorist as many presume today, the Harper's Ferry incident would have had an entirely different result, much to the disadvantage of the community. Certainly a terrorist would not be charged by his own men with erring "in favor of the families of his prisoners," as was John Brown. Of course, Brown's critics also overlook the fact that chattel slavery in the United States was actually institutionalized terrorism and state-sanctioned race war. When they are further reminded that many women and children were killed in the Nat Turner revolt of 1831, for instance, perhaps the difference between Brown's plan and "insurrection" will finally be appreciated.[3]

The bruised old man continued his remarks, pointing out that had he "interfered in behalf of the rich" and politically privileged, he would have been approved and his act considered "worthy of reward rather than punishment." Appealing to the courtroom Bible, Brown both cited and alluded to several New Testament scriptures acknowledging his duty on behalf of God's "despised poor," and concluded:

A Virginia politician named Alexander Boteler witnessed the
defeat and arrest of Brown and his men, and later observed
him during his trial. Boteler sketched Brown prior to this
1860 sketch, which accurately recalls Brown's features, including his trimmed beard. *West Virginia State Archives.*

Now, if it is necessary that I should forfeit my life for the furtherance of the ends of justice, and mingle my blood further with the blood of my children and with the blood of millions in this slave country whose rights are disregarded by wicked, cruel, and unjust enactments, I submit; so let it be done!

As he undoubtedly saw it, Providence had delivered him over to his enemies while enabling him to survive a ruthless assault. As if to make a mockery of the mortal forces opposing him, Providence had also placed him in a pulpit elevated above the entire nation. There were forty days from his first newspaper interview on October 22 until December 2, the day of his execution, and he used them well.

Speaking to journalists, Brown reiterated his belief that he had failed at Harper's Ferry largely because of a "feeling of humanity" toward his hostages. Neither did he act out of vengeance or personal hatred. "I merely abominate your *false priorities*, and the barbarous enactments you have been from time to time driven to pass in order to sustain that false position," he wrote in answer to a reporter's written questions. "I feel no shame on account of my doom. Jesus of Nazareth was doomed in like manner. Why should not I be?" To a question about his political party affiliation, Brown wrote that he belonged to "God's party (I think)." Another question was whether he believed in equality between whites and blacks. "Yes, God forbid I should doubt it; further than is occasioned by their dreadfully unfortunate circumstances." As to what he would do with liberated blacks, Brown wrote that he would do "precisely as I would do with other men—do them justice as God requires." Another journalist visited him after his wounds had begun to heal and found him heavily chained but showing "the utmost gentleness and tranquility," even though his visitors were at times abusive and hostile.

One witness who saw Brown frequently during his incarceration was a young guard named William Fellows, who remembered him as kindly but reserved, and thought he "liked to show his stoicism." When Brown was refused a letter from his wife one day, Fellows recalled, he nearly lost his composure but then caught himself, "closed his mouth, put his hands into his pocket and walked back inside his cell." As the weeks passed, the young guard developed admiration for the old man, especially because "he was hated and disliked everywhere in that locality," but never showed anger when abusive remarks were made to him. Brown used his time astutely, writing or answering letters and was "generally buried in thought or serious reading." He would "gaze into vacancy for hours" after reading letters from home. Fellows recalled him reading history books about the French Revolution, ancient Rome, and a biography of the Haitian liberator, Toussaint L'Ouverture. Fellows said that Brown classed the black warrior as a world hero, adding that Brown told him "he had read all the literature he could find about L'Ouverture for a dozen years."

Above all, Brown often prayed and pored over the Bible for hours, carefully marking passages pertaining to slavery, justice, and righteousness with his pen, or folding page corners to mark whole books, such as the epistles of Paul. As Brown likely intended, the marked passages suggested a statement about the purpose and beliefs underlying his raid. When he made a gift of the Bible to one of the jail staff, he was probably hoping the selected texts would continue to speak for him after his execution. John Brown would have been pleased to know that many of the passages he had marked were listed in the *New York Illustrated News* only one week after his death.[4]

Throughout his last weeks, Brown wrote many letters to family, associates, and strangers who had written to him expressing support. He received far more mail than he could answer and was literally writing responses almost to the time of his execution. However, he did not see all the letters written to him, not only because some were too late, but because his mail was increasingly screened by Andrew Hunter, special prosecutor for the State of Virginia. Hunter withheld letters with extreme expressions as well as letters deemed eccentric or bizarre. For instance, a woman from Rochester, New York, wrote a peculiar letter advising Brown to don white robes for the gallows and even attempted to script his last words. The screed from a Kentucky writer was also withheld, Hunter considering it improper in its sarcasm and vindictive celebration of Brown's impending execution. Some letters from him were published in newspapers, heightening the North's perception of the old man as a martyr and intensifying resentment against the South. But the most important letters were naturally those flowing between Brown and his family.

His first letter to Mary and children after his arrest was written on October 31, in which he informed them of the deaths of Oliver, Watson, and the Thompson brothers, and his own wounded condition. Brown admonished his family with scriptural quotes and allusions, telling them he was "quite cheerful in the assurance that God reigns; and will overrule all for his glory." Typically, he encouraged them to remember the poor and oppressed. However he held the letter until the end of his trial, after which he added a postscript: "Yesterday Nov 2d I was sentenced to be hanged on 2 Decem [*sic*] next. Do not grieve on my account. I am still quite cheerful." Writing to Mary about a week later, Brown updated her on his recovery, his cheerful nature, and his belief that his impending execution, his "testimony for God and humanity," would "do vastly more toward advancing the cause I have earnestly endeavored to promote, than all I have done in my life before." Harkening to the deaths of Christ, the prophets, and apostles, Brown scrawled praises to God and reminded his wife and family to remember "the crushed millions" without comfort. He also admonished her against coming to Virginia, not only to avoid undertaking great expense but the heightening pain of their separation. "Oh, Mary!" Brown wrote, "do not come, but patiently wait for the meeting of those who love God and their fellow-men, where no separation must follow." Wishing his family the "purifying and sustaining influence of the Christian religion," Brown added:

> I cannot remember a night so dark as to have hindered the coming day, nor a storm so furious and dreadful as to prevent the return of warm sunshine and a cloudless sky. But, beloved ones, do remember that this is not your rest—that in this world you have no abiding place or continuing city.

Determined to see her husband nevertheless, Mary Brown set out for Virginia, stopping in Boston where she found "cordial friends" and "was received with great sympathy." By the time he heard about her trip, Mary had reached Philadelphia. At Brown's urging, his lawyer promptly telegraphed Mary's abolitionist hosts in Philadelphia to detain her: "Mr. Brown says [']for God's sake don't let Mrs. Brown come.[']" Brown then wrote, asking her to comply and assuring her that

> the sacrifises [*sic*] *you* and I, have been called to make in behalf of *the cause we love*[,] *the cause of God*; and *of humanity*: do not seem to me as at all too great. . . . I can recover all the lost capital occasioned by that disaster; by only hanging a few moments by the neck; and feel quite determined to make the utmost possible out of a defeat.

But now he decided he wanted Mary to come, though only to gather his remains and those of Oliver and Watson. About a week later, Brown changed his mind again, writing that she could come and see him if she could handle "the trials and the shock," and the certain insult she would face from Southerners. "*Do consider the matter well* before you make the *plunge*," Brown urged.

Besides family members, he received letters from various clergymen in the North, including some he did not know. To a pastor in Ohio, Brown wrote assuring that he was "not a stranger to the way of salvation by Christ" and had indeed almost become a minister himself, except that "God had another work for me to do." His only regret was that he had no "ministers of Christ here," because all the clergy he met were either slaveholders or advocates of slavery. "I cannot abide them," Brown concluded. "My knees will not bend in prayer with them while their hands are stained with the blood of souls." Indeed, he could not help but remember his youthful ministerial studies after receiving a letter from his old teacher, H. L. Vaill in Connecticut. The elder wrote a reflective, sentimental letter, concluding: "Be of good cheer, then, my brother; and living or dying, all will be well." Brown responded cheerfully, declaring that "Christ, the great Captain of liberty as well as of salvation . . . saw fit to take from me a sword of steel after I had carried it for a time; but he has put another in my hand ('the sword of the Spirit;')." Brown was also deeply moved by a letter from a Pennsylvania clergyman from the Calvinist Covenanters, a group known for their abolitionist views and strong conviction that Jesus Christ should be declared king of the United States. The clergyman wrote warmly, challenging Brown to examine his motives even at death, and assuring him that he had been raised up "to a high, commanding eminence, where every word you utter reaches the furthest corner of this great country." Brown wrote a glowing letter in return. "Dear Covenanter. . . . I am greatly obliged for this your visit to my prison. It really seemed to impart new strength to my soul."[5]

Letters poured into Virginia from his children, siblings and relatives, old and new friends, former associates, Quakers, clergymen, black women's associations, old people, even children ("Good by till we meet in heaven. I am a little boy and this is the First letter I ever wrote"). A spiritualist from Buffalo wrote, asking Brown to look him up after he was hanged, and even provided him with the home address of a suitable medium in New York City. Brown wrote to many people, perhaps more letters than have survived and emerged from the dust of history. "I am weeping for *joy*: and *gratitude*," he wrote to his half-sisters. "I get many *very kind* and *comforting* letters that I cannot possibly reply to. Wish I had time and strength to answer all." John Brown had finally lit a fire that would spread and consume slavery in earnest, and he felt its mounting flame and knew there were growing numbers ready to bless that fire. He merely needed to die.

"I am waiting the hour of my public murder with great composure of mind, and cheerfulness," he wrote to Mary and the family on November 30. He assured them that their sacrifices on behalf of God and humanity would not be wasted because a *"Just, and holy God*: rules not only the affairs of *this world*; but of all worlds." Their "seeming *disaster*" would "ultimately result in the most *glorious success.*" The rest of his long letter is full of admonitions to follow the Christian faith and remain devoted to the Bible. "Oh be determined at once to give your whole hearts to God; and let *nothing* shake; or *alter*; that resolution." Here was John Brown, shortly to die, returning to the theme and text of his life, and reminding his skeptical sons that he firmly held to the "Divine inspiration of the Bible." So strongly did he believe in the Scriptures that his last will required the purchase of at least twenty Bibles for his children and grandchildren.

Had Brown been an unprincipled criminal or a contemptible terrorist, he would not have troubled the religious establishment of North and South. While Northern clergy with anti-slavery sympathies responded favorably to him (as evidenced in the letters he received), many Northern religious publications ignored the Harper's Ferry incident in keeping with their standard disinterest in political concerns. Those that did observe Brown were geared to compromise, urging "reason and sanity" so as not to offend the South. In varying degrees, the Northern religious press feared and blamed John Brown rather than acknowledge the inevitable rending of the nation over slavery. One would not be surprised that Southern clergymen condemned him, but it did seem that he exercised a peculiar power over them, as if his moral integrity was an inherent challenge. Perhaps this was why Brown's jail cell was frequented by uninvited Southern clergymen, all of them seeking to pray with him—and if not convert him, at least win some tender word of concession. When a young Episcopalian priest asked his jailer if he could come and offer the old man "spiritual advice," Brown "civilly" agreed. "Then let him come," he told the jailer, "and I will pray for him, but he cannot pray for me."

As his last day neared, the Charlestown sheriff received a package in the mail from Frances Keeyes of Alexandria, Virginia. Keeyes had not only knitted a special rope for Brown's noose, but paid the postage too. Charlestown's mayor made a security proclamation, ordering citizens to remain indoors and stay away from the jail in the event of an emergency. The town and its environs were tense, some fearing invasion and rescue attempts by Northern abolitionists, but more so the explosion of a slave revolt. Bold talk among abolitionists about a rescue plan proved empty, nor would Brown have cooperated anyway. However apprehension over the reaction of blacks was realistic.

Interestingly, Brown expressed apprehension that he and his men would be blamed for fires that had been set in the "immediate neighborhood," though the fires were the work of local blacks in reaction to Brown's conviction. "The barns of all of the jurors of John Brown's trial were burned—a time honored signal of revolution that went unanswered" by slaves outside the vicinity. Indeed, on the day of Brown's execution, the farm of a notably ruthless slaveholder killed at Harper's Ferry was burned, and his livestock poisoned by slaves. Slaves in Maryland stopped a westbound train, carrying the rebellion into a different county, and five were arrested after trying to organize a horse-and-carriage "stampede" to freedom.

Notwithstanding the claims of Brown's critics, he knew that in the immediate vicinity of Harper's Ferry there was a relatively small number of slaves, the entire black population alone being no more than 150 adults. Brown intended his movement to spread and grow, and in the long run the slaves seem to have reflected something of the process he assumed. The 1860 Census of Jefferson County and four surrounding Virginia counties reveals that a "mass movement of self-liberation" actually took place after the raid—the highest number of fugitives coming from Jefferson County, following "the path of the hostage foray" during the raid. As fires burned and fear of slave rebellion haunted local whites, Brown was probably concerned about harsh white reprisals of the kind that followed the Nat Turner revolt in 1831. Perhaps to ward off the fear of a black uprising, he engaged in a bit of revisionist work, dashing off a note to the state prosecutor in which he made sure to refer to "the slaves we took *about the Ferry*." He seems to have hoped that by claiming that the slaves in the raid were actually "taken" by force, white people's fear would be allayed and black people spared their wrath and retribution.[6]

Meanwhile, Mary Brown was staying at the home of abolitionist Lucretia Mott in Philadelphia, where she wrote to her children:

I am here . . . where I expect to stay untill [*sic*] your dear father is disposed of. O what a terrible thought. . . . I cant [*sic*] tell you the sympathy that is felt and the good that it is likely to do for the poor slave yet[.] I hope that we shant forget "those that are in bonds as being bound with them" but be more firm and active than ever.

From North Elba, Ruth Brown Thompson wrote tenderly to her father:

Your kind instruction will never be forgotten by me. I cannot tell you how *I long to see you.* . . . And now *my dear Father*, if I am never permitted to see your *dear face again* in this world, I trust I shall meet you in that world where sorrow and parting never can come.

But mail moved slowly from the Adirondacks, and Ruth's loving letter failed to reach John Brown before the day of his death. Accordingly, Mary prepared herself for the worst, while being observed by a journalist preparing a piece for the *National Anti-Slavery Standard*. The writer thus described Mary Brown as "brave without insensibility, tender without weakness," and noted her teary composure at the mention of her two lost sons. Mary told the interviewer that her husband was "in advance of his years" and a "deep thinker like his father." He had "high regard" for religion and was especially fond of Puritan books. Above all, Mary concluded, her husband's Christianity was practical, and love for God was to be shown by good will to men."

Accompanied by some abolitionist associates from Philadelphia on December 1, Mary was given a military escort to the Charlestown jail. When she entered her husband's cell, the couple embraced in silence, Mary resting her head on his chest, her arms hugging his neck.

"My dear husband, it is a hard fate."

"We must all bear it in the best manner we can. I believe it is all for the best," Brown responded.

"Our poor children; God help them."

"Tell them their father died without a single regret for the course he has pursued—that he is satisfied that he is right in the eye of God and of all just men." Sharing a last meal together provided by the jailer, John and Mary Brown discussed his will, the education of their daughters, and her future. When it came time for her to depart, he pleaded that Mary be permitted to stay the night. But much to his obvious displeasure, Governor

THE LAST SUPPER   JOHN BROWN AND HIS WIFE IN THE PARLOR OF MR. AVIS.   FROM A SKETCH BY OUR OWN ARTIST

On December 1, 1859, Brown finally saw his wife Mary, though for the last time. An artist captured their final meal together in the jailer's residence. *West Virginia State Archives.*

Wise had made strict orders that Mary return to her hotel in Harper's Ferry to await his body the next day.

Brown's concern over his wife's safety and comfort in the South was well-grounded. Contrary to the propaganda issued about the courteous treatment she received on her dismal journey, she and her companions felt the contempt of the community. Indeed, while she and her escort walked through the streets of Harper's Ferry, shots were fired over their heads. After Mary left him, Brown penned a note to her: "Today is my last day upon Earth. Tomorrow I shall see God. I have no fear, I am not afraid to die. And I can say the words of our blessed Saviour: 'Father, forgive them: they know not what they do.'"

The next morning, as Mary Brown sat weeping and holding hands with her companions at Harper's Ferry, her husband was preparing to see

God. After prayer, Brown read letters from his daughters, wiping away tears and then regaining his composure before taking care of some final duties. After completing a revision of his will, he gave his books to the guards, his watch to the jailer, and then briefly bid farewell to the other prisoners. "God bless you, my dear men . . . may we meet in heaven." Emerging from the jail, the old man realized the streets were dense with militia. "I had no idea Governor Wise considered my execution so important," he said as he climbed into a wagon and sat on his coffin. But the town was fearful, and slavemasters would not breathe freely for some time, even after his death. Some, perhaps many, local slave-owners had also taken precautions that no uprising would occur. On the day of Brown's hanging, slaves were whipped and then tied up until their masters thought it safe to release them.

The old man's last ride was only a few minutes long, ending in a vast open area where the gallows waited, strung with a Southern rope and surrounded by militia. "I see him as he places his foot on the first step," wrote a journalist for the Baltimore *Daily Exchange*. "No bravado, but a calm mien and exquisite poise. Step after step he takes, as though he were ascending the stairs . . . to a chamber in which he was to rest."[7]

# A Saint's Rest

Fill ye up then the measure of your fathers.

—Matthew 23:32

John Brown's body was controversial too. To no surprise, some of his enemies in the South did not even want his remains sent home. A doctor in Virginia wrote to Governor Wise suggesting it be withheld for dissection in order to further degrade Brown. This would discourage "many another scoundrel" rather than tempt them "to vanity" by a triumphal funeral procession "through the Eastern states." Another doctor wrote to Governor Wise offering to embalm the body for "half the profits," and donate the balance of his fee to "the good Old Dominion, for the expense she has been put to by the old Ragamuffin . . . and be a warning to future generations." Even Mary Brown's escort, Hector Tyndale, was not sure Brown's body would be handed over to them until he forced his spiteful hosts to open the coffin. Apparently it was "rumored" in their hearing that the body was "thrown out on a dung-heap and a 'dead nigger' put in his coffin."

"I do not think it right," complained a knowledgeable abolitionist, "that the country should be assured that Mrs. Brown and her friends were treated while in Virginia with becoming gallantry and courtesy. For certainly it was not so." After Tyndale stubbornly insisted that he inspect the coffin for the widow, Mary received her husband's remains and escorted them northward to Philadelphia, where a viewing was held for abolitionist friends. When the coffin was opened, they found the corpse's ear stuffed with cotton to stop the flow "produced by that mode of death," and removed it. The blood-soaked cotton was then distributed among the abolitionists as a keepsake, one of whom then shared it with her housekeeper. The next day, the black woman returned part of the bloody cotton to her employer—now shaped into a cross and surrounded with green laurel leaves, and set in a glass-covered walnut frame.

The body was secretly delivered to an undertaker in New York City, where it was then discretely prepared for burial. Upon closer inspection it was discovered that the noose had not been removed from the scarred neck of the corpse—a final tribute from the Old Dominion. The body was afterward placed in a fine black walnut coffin, and finally began the journey home. It was said that the northbound train bearing Brown's coffin passed many cities without stopping, "so intense was the excitement and fear of an insurrection among the colored people." When the coffin and its escorts finally reached North Elba, the grieving Browns prepared for a memorial service attended by the likes of orator Wendell Phillips and abolitionist J. Miller McKim. But when the Reverend Joshua Young of Burlington, Vermont, arrived in North Elba, he found no other clergy present at the Brown home. Young, who was asked to preside over the funeral, was a Unitarian minister. But this was perhaps fitting, not only because of the scarcity of evangelical abolitionist clergymen, but because Brown would probably have preferred to pray with Young in his jail cell than with the several pro-slavery clergy who had courted him in his last days.

The funeral service began with the singing of Brown's favorite hymn, "Blow ye the trumpet," by his friend Lyman Eppes and his three children. Then everyone joined in the singing, though Young recalled that "the plaintive voices of the deeply-moved Negroes" were heard above the rest. Annie Brown recalled not knowing many of the people who had come "from long distances," and nearly half of the attenders were black. After Phillips spoke, the family opened the coffin "and gazed for the last time upon the face of the dead," recalled Salmon Brown. "He looked as though sleeping, the features being natural as could be." The coffin was carried in procession to the grave, near the great rock outside the house where Brown once sat to read the Bible and study the majesty of creation. As the coffin was lowered, Young repeated the words of St. Paul: "I have fought the good fight, I have finished my course, I have kept the faith. Henceforth there is laid up for me a crown of righteousness which the Lord, the righteous Judge, shall give me at that day." For his efforts in support of the Browns, Young returned to the harsh criticism and condemnation of his conservative congregation—opposition which shortly led to his resignation.[1]

After Brown's execution, the address of a Canadian black named Harvey Jackson was circulated, lauding the raid on Harper's Ferry as a "bold

The gravestone of John Brown originally marked the grave of his paternal grand-father, Captain John Brown, who died during the Revolutionary War. In 1857, Brown retrieved the gravestone from Connecticut when it was replaced with a newer stone. He described it as an "old fashioned granite Grave Stone," and he valued it as a "relic" of his family's history. Indeed, Brown speculated that by 1956 it would "be a great curiosity" if preserved. It did become a point of inter-est, but only because it was used to mark the graves of John Brown and his son, Oliver, who was killed at Harper's Ferry in 1859. *Author's photograph, 1999.*

and heroic" effort to end slavery. Even though many considered it futile and wild, Jackson said, it would ultimately "be productive of much good." Declaring Brown and his men "brave, undaunted" heroes, he urged blacks to provide financial support for the widows and children of the Harper's Ferry raiders. "I know you will assist. Coming ages will appreciate Capt. Brown's worth, his greatness of soul." This Canadian voice was but a shadow in the light of Brown's visits in 1858, not to mention the scant support Brown seems to have received from Northern blacks.

W. E. B. Du Bois suggested that one reason for the blunted response from free and fugitive blacks was that Brown was looking for "picked leaders"—not mere soldiers. He wanted prominent black leadership that could guide and—if need be—control an expanding population of fugitives in the dynamic circumstances he hoped to initiate in the South. The absence of Harriet Tubman, due to illness, was indeed "a grave loss to the cause." (Might she have put much needed fire *under Brown* at Harper's Ferry?) Frederick Douglass had withdrawn his enthusiasm if not his support after twice questioning Brown's plans. As "the first great national Negro leader," his iron-and-clay alliance with John Brown in 1859 undoubtedly dissuaded other black leaders. Like Douglass, their "trust was not in Brown's paperwork" or ostensible military prowess, but "in the man." Other black leaders may have had mixed feelings about working with whites, like the activist physician, James McCune Smith. Smith was the hub of a circle of leaders who were far more critical of whites, and far less inclined to collaborate with them. Though a confidant of John Brown, Smith ultimately disappointed the old man, either by yielding information to the devious Forbes, or simply by turning away from him in favor of an all-black movement. There are other varied reasons, such as Brown's excessive secrecy and the frustrating hiatus in 1858–59 that resulted from the Forbes betrayal, during which he lost touch with white and black volunteers. Many Northern black leaders were ministers, orators, and scholars—not likely candidates for a guerilla operation. Others were psychologically and emotionally unprepared to risk going back into "the eagle's claw," as Shields Green called the Slave South. Finally, Brown's support was tenuous and his followers few. It was far more preferable for fugitives and freemen to return to the South with the power of the government behind them, as many did several years later, marching in the Union army.

On December 2, 1859, Abraham Lincoln spoke in Atchison, Kansas, in a Methodist Church. Since this was also the day of Brown's execution, it was inevitable that his name would be invoked, and Lincoln was thus asked what he thought of the controversial abolitionist. "He was hanged and he deserved it," Lincoln said assuredly. "I don't know much about Brown's history in Kansas. . . . John Brown violated the laws of his country, and Governor Wise did right in hanging him." This remark brought hearty applause from the pro-slavery men in the audience, one of whom afterward declared of Lincoln, "He's no Republican." In fact, Lincoln and the Republicans would not so easily disassociate themselves from John Brown. In death he had become like the beheaded John the Baptist to King Herod, and his spirit seemed now to prevail over flesh and blood. Within two years, Lincoln won the White House and lost the South, and all hell had broken loose, just as John Brown had prophesied. On the day they led the old man out to die, he produced a final document in his handwriting. Scrawled on a small piece of paper were the words:

> I John Brown am now quite *certain* that the crimes of this *guilty, land*: *will* never be purged away; but with Blood. I had *as I now think*: vainly flattered myself that without *very much* bloodshed; it might be done.

Brown has all too often been accused of sparking the flames of the Civil War, though in fact he was more a warning of what was to come.

Toward the end of the Civil War, John Brown's old Adirondack associate Willis Hodges made an investigative tour of Virginia to look into the treatment of ex-slaves by the Union army. When he visited Princess Anne County, he happened to stay at a plantation formerly owned by Henry Wise, the Virginia governor who had been so instrumental in executing Brown in 1859. The Wise family had fled from their secluded plantation when Norfolk fell to the Union army in 1862, and the property was being used by religious groups to house and educate former slaves. Hodges was well aware of the significance of the home, but was overwhelmed when he found that the missionary teachers had a portrait of Brown hanging in what was formerly the Wise family's parlor. "Before me hangs the picture of my old friend John Brown upon the nail which his murderer's looking glass once hung," Hodges excitedly wrote home.

"How wonderful is the change! How plain one can see the hand of God in this strange work!" Indeed, it seemed a stroke of Providence to him, and as he thought of his old friend, the black man walked along the river in the moonlight, finally falling to his knees under a wild chestnut tree. And turning eastward, Willis Hodges "prayed to Him who created the heavens and the earth."[2]

# Notes

ENC     Edwin N. Cotter Jr., John Brown scholar and documentarian

ENC/tr  Transcript by Edwin N. Cotter Jr.

FBA     Florilla Brown, younger half-sister of John Brown, and daughter of Owen Brown and Sally Root Brown; she married the Reverend Samuel L. Adair

FBS     Franklin B. Sanborn, associate and biographer of John Brown

FCCH    *Records of the Free Congregational Church of Hudson; Organized October 7th* A.D. *1842*, in the Hudson Library and Historical Society, Hudson, Ohio

FrB     Frederick Brown, son of Owen Brown and brother of John Brown

FrB2    Frederick Brown, son of John and Dianthe Brown

GEE     John Brown Collection of the Reverend Clarence S. Gee, Hudson Library and Historical Society, Hudson, Ohio

GLC     The Gilder Lehrman Collection of John Brown autographs, in the Morgan Library, New York, New York

GLS     George Luther Stearns, associate and supporter of John Brown

HLAGO   Lora Case, *Hudson of Long Ago: Progress of Hudson During the Past Century Personal Reminiscences of an Aged Pioneer* (1897; rpt. The Hudson Library and Historical Society, Hudson, Ohio, 1963), in Brown Papers; Pamphlets folder, Box 21, OGV (*which see*)

JaB     Jason Brown, son of John and Dianthe Brown

HT      Henry Thompson, husband of Ruth Brown Thompson and son-in-law of John Brown

JB      John Brown

JBA     John Brown's autobiographical sketch in letter to Henry L. Stearns, July 15, 1857. Photocopy of original in GEE (*which see*)

JB-ELS  Eric Ledell Smith, "John Brown in Crawford County: the Making of a Radical Abolitionist." Pennsylvania Historical and Museum Commission, Harrisburg, Pennsylvania, 2001

JBJr    John Brown Jr., son of John and Dianthe Brown

JBOOK    Letter book transcribed by Clarence S. Gee, in GEE (*which see*)

JBR    *A John Brown Reader.* Louis Ruchames, ed. New York: Abelard and Schuman, 1959

JB-STUT    Boyd B. Stutler's *John Brown*, an incomplete, undated, and unpublished manuscript consisting of chapters 1–5, in the Brown-Gee Collection, Series II, Box 11, GEE (*which see*)

JB-WAH    Letters from John Brown to Willis A. Hodges, 1848–49, reprinted in the *Evening Post* [New York], December 20, 1859

JB2    John Brown, Jr. Papers, Microfilm edition (MIC 50), in OHS (*which see*)

JeB    Jeremiah Brown, half-brother of John Brown

KM    Katherine Mayo, journalist, researcher, and interviewer for Oswald G. Villard, her notes being found in OGV (*which see*)

KM/tr    Transcript by Katherine Mayo

KSHS    Collections of the Kansas State Historical Society, Topeka, Kansas. Thus:

     AD/KSHS    The Samuel Lyle and Florella [*sic*} Brown Adair Family Collection, Microfilm version

     BR/KSHS    The John Brown Collection, Microfilm version

LLJB    Franklin B. Sanborn, *The Life and Letters of John Brown, Liberator of Kansas, and Martyr of Virginia.* Boston, 1885; rpt. New York: Negro Universities Press, 1969

MB    Mary A. Brown, second wife of John Brown

MBD    Martha Brown Davis, daughter of Owen Brown and half-sister of John Brown

NYPL    Various collections from the Rare Books and Manuscript Department of the New York Public Library, New York, New York. Thus:

     NYPL/KOHNS    The Lee Kohns Memorial Collection

     NYPL/ANTHONY    The Alfred Anthony Collection

| | |
|---|---|
| OB | Owen Brown, father of John Brown |
| OB2 | Owen Brown, son of John and Dianthe Brown |
| OBA–1841 | "Owen Brown's Autobiography," a brief sketch written on November 10, 1841. Transcribed by Clarence S. Gee, in GEE (*which see*) |
| OBA–1850 | "Owen Brown's Autobiography as written to his daughter, Marian Brown Hand ca. 1850," transcribed by Clarence S. Gee, in GEE (*which see*) |
| OGV | The John Brown Collection of Oswald Garrison Villard, in the Rare Books and Manuscripts Division of the Columbia University Library, New York, New York |
| OHS | Various documents pertaining to John Brown in the Ohio Historical Society, Columbus, Ohio |
| OliB | Oliver Brown son of John and Mary Brown |
| P&B | Specifically, the wool commission house established in Springfield, Massachusetts, by Simon Perkins and John Brown, lasting from about 1846–49 |
| RBT | Ruth Brown Thompson, daughter of John Brown and Dianthe Brown |
| SA | Reverend Samuel L. Adair, husband of Florilla Brown, daughter of Owen Brown |
| SA-GEE | Typewritten transcriptions of the letters of Samuel L. Adair in Folder 28, Gray Box 1, GEE (*which see*) |
| SaB | Salmon Brown, son of John and Mary Brown |
| SBH | Sally Brown Hand, daughter of Owen Brown and half-sister of John Brown |
| SP | Simon Perkins of Akron, Ohio, a business partner of John Brown |
| STUT-GEE | Correspondence of Boyd B. Stutler with Clarence S. Gee, Microfilm, Hudson Library and Historical Society, Hudson, Ohio |
| STUT-MICRO | John Brown Collection of Boyd B. Stutler, West Virginia State Archives, microfilm version in the Ohio Historical Society collection, Columbus, Ohio |

STUT-WEB     John Brown/Boyd B. Stutler Collection Database of the West Virginia State Archives at http://129.71.134.132/imlsintro.html

TLV     Author's interview with Thomas L. Vince, archivist and historian of the Western Reserve Academy, Hudson, Ohio, March 16, 2000

TPTL     Stephen B. Oates, *To Purge This Land With Blood: A Biography of John Brown*. New York: Harper and Row, 1970

TRANS     Transcript

TWH     Thomas Wentworth Higginson, Unitarian clergyman and abolitionist who served as one of John Brown's "Secret Six"

URIS     *The Underground Railroad in Springfield, Massachusetts*. Kathryne Burns, ed. Springfield, Massachusetts: Springfield Bicentennial Committee, 1976

VFHF     Osborne P. Anderson, *A Voice From Harper's Ferry: A Narrative of Events at Harper's Ferry*. Boston: Printed for the Author, 1861

WH     Willis A. Hodges, abolitionist associate of John Brown and publisher of *The Ram's Horn*

WHB     Wealthy Hotchkiss Brown, wife of John Brown Jr.

NOTES TO INTRODUCTION

1. "Verbatim Report of the Questioning of Old Brown by Senator Mason, Congressman Vallandigham, and Others," *New York Herald* (Oct. 21, 1859), 1.

2. Stan Cohen, *John Brown "The Thundering Voice of Jehovah": A Pictorial Heritage* (Missoula, Mont.: Pictorial Histories, 1999), 152–53; quoted in John G. Nicolay, *A Short Life of Abraham Lincoln* (New York: Century, 1903), 135.

3. Or consider this opening statement by a prominent historian: "John Brown is one of the most vexing figures in American history." The question one would ask in response would be "Vexing to whom?" Certainly not black people. See the introduction by William S. McFeely in the new edition of Benjamin Quarles, *Allies for Freedom* (New York: DaCapo Press, 2001), v.

4. Malcolm X, *By Any Means Necessary: Speeches, Interviews and a Letter*, George Breitman, ed. (New York: Pathfinder Press, 1970, 1985), 81–82. Speech

before the Organization of Afro-American Unity, July 5, 1964, New York City. On "Santa Fe Trail," see Cohen, *John Brown*, 133–37.

5. Stephen B. Oates, *To Purge This Land with Blood: A Biography of John Brown* (New York: Harper and Row, 1970), 6 and 22. Hereinafter, *TPTL*.

6. E. Harris Harbison, "The Marks of a Christian Historian," in *God, History, and Historians: Modern Christian Views of History*, C. T. McIntire, ed. (New York: Oxford University Press, 1977), 355.

7. James Redpath, Brown's first biographer, dedicated his 1860 publication to those chiefly responsible for glorifying John Brown, declaring that it was Phillips, Emerson, and Thoreau "who, when the mob shouted, 'Madman!' said, 'Saint!'" Redpath quotes each to this effect, especially Emerson, who outrightly called John Brown a saint prior to his execution, and declared his "gallows glorious like the Cross." See James Redpath, *The Public Life of John Brown* (Boston, 1860); Brown's supporter and scholarly defender wrote: "Such was the man . . . who was selected by God, and knew himself to be so chosen, to overthrow the bulwark of oppression in America." Franklin B. Sanborn, *The Life and Letters of John Brown, Liberator of Kansas, and Martyr of Virginia* (Boston, 1885; rpt. New York: Negro Universities Press, 1969), 121. Hereinafter, *LLJB*.

8. C. G. Thorne, Jr., "Saints," *The New International Dictionary of the Christian Church*, J. D. Douglas, ed. (Grand Rapids, Mich.: Zondervan, 1981), 872. Hereinafter, *DCC*; After Brown's death, Harriet Tubman visited a home and found there the famous bust of John Brown by the sculptor Brackett, which Brown modeled before his execution. Overwhelmed by the stone likeness, the hero of the underground railroad declared: "It was not John Brown that died at Charlestown. It was Christ—it was the Saviour of our people." Earl Conrad, *Harriet Tubman* (New York: Paul S. Eriksson, 1943, 1969), 143.

9. William Roscoe Thayer in *Atlantic Monthly*, November 1918, reprinted in "The November Almanac," *Atlantic Monthly* (November 1993), 30; "Verbatim Report of the Questioning of Old Brown."

PART I

Epigraph: JB to RBT, August 10, 1852, in *LLJB*, 151.

NOTES TO CHAPTER 1

1. Slave auction broadside, February 12, 1859 [New Orleans, Louisiana], in John Brown Collection, "Holographs and Photostats," Item #20, Clarence S. Gee Papers, Hudson Library and Historical Society, Hudson, Ohio. Hereinafter, *GEE*.

2. *TPTL*, 234–35.

3. Bertram Wyatt-Brown, *Lewis Tappan and the Evangelical War Against Slavery* (New York: Atheneum, 1971), 180–81.

4. For an example of Christ's illustration of slavery, see Luke 17:7–10; David Brion Davis, *The Problem of Slavery in Western Culture* (Ithaca, N.Y.: Cornell University Press, 1966, 1970), 60 and 61; Peter J. Parish, *Slavery, History and Historians* (New York: Harper and Row, 1989), 31 and 28.

5. Mayer adds: "We are, in this area, unable to face reality, and so accept the versions of our history that are tacitly premised on the assumption that the pre–Civil War Negro was not quite a human being. . . . If there is any single cause, more than any other, that may be blamed for this deficiency, it is the anaesthesia of conscience that is peddled under the deceptive label 'American History.'" Howard N. Mayer, "John Brown and the Souls of White Folk," *Crisis* (May 1962), 267; R. Washington to Andrew Hunter, November 18, 1859, in "John Brown Letters," *Virginia Magazine of History* (October 1902), 172; Though Malcolm X probably repeated this remark often in speeches, it is best known within a speech he gave in Detroit, Michigan, in March, 1964, entitled "The Ballot or the Bullet."

6. Leon F. Litwack, *North of Slavery: The Negro in the Free States, 1790–1860* (Chicago: University of Chicago Press, 1961), 15, 64–65, 75–76, 79.

7. "Abolitionism in America," *New York Quarterly* (October 1854) [New York: James G. Reed, 1855], 324; "Negroland and the Negroes," *Harper's New Monthly Magazine* (July 1856), 162; See chapters 3 and 5 of Litwack, *North of Slavery.*

8. Parish, *Slavery, History and Historians*, 22–23, 129–30; Litwack, *North of Slavery*, 67, 69–70; Litwack, *North of Slavery*, 97, 99–101; Michael A. Bellesiles, *Arming America: The Origins of a National Gun Culture* (New York: Alfred A. Knopf, 2000), 368.

9. Frederick Norton, "Negro Slavery in Connecticut," *Connecticut Magazine* (June 1899), 328; Janice Law Trecker, *Preachers, Rebels, and Traders: Connecticut 1818–1865* (Chester, Conn.: Pequot Press, 1975), 34; Litwack, *North of Slavery*, 123–31; Eugene H. Berwanger, *The Frontier Against Slavery: Western Anti-Negro Prejudice and the Slavery Extension Controversy* (Urbana: University of Illinois Press, 1967), 18–20, 30.

10. Berwanger, *Frontier Against Slavery*, 23–39, 140; Thomas W. Higginson, "Cheerful Yesterdays," *Atlantic Monthly* (June 1897), 780.


NOTES TO CHAPTER 2

1. Letter of CSG to Mrs. [Eleanor] Schapiro [probably November 1961], in Gray Box 5, GEE.

2. BBS to CSG, April 10, 1952, STUT-GEE. John Brown's descent from Peter Brown of the Mayflower was never questioned until Oswald Garrison Villard presumed to have settled the question in his self-proclaimed unbiased biography of Brown (1910). Villard introduced authoritative declarations that the claim was

false, and that Peter Brown died in 1633 without a male heir to carry his name. This conclusion angered John Brown's surviving children, such as Annie Brown Adams, who complained that "Mr. Villard is rather hard on us, to not allow us any ancestors to be proud of." Despite his reliance on the official pronouncement of New England genealogical authorities, Villard's conclusions were also questioned by Boyd Stutler, the most rigorous Brown documentarian heretofore: "The Mayflower Descendants' quarrel with the Brown family is of long standing. I have gone over the evidence several times and believe there is no good reason for rejecting Peter Brown. But some one of the New England Brahmins denied him; the others followed suit." Stutler found that Peter Brown did leave a male heir from an overlooked second marriage, and thus *could* be traced to John Brown the abolitionist, though this male heir is not identified in any official record as bearing the name Peter Brown. See Oswald G. Villard, *John Brown: A Biography 1800–1859* (Garden City, N.Y.: Doubleday, 1910, 1929), 10, 591, n. 6; ABA to FBS, December 8, 1910, Box 2, Brown Family/Annie Brown Adams folder, Kohns/NYPL; BBS to CSG, April 15, 1932, in STUT-GEE; Boyd B. Stutler, *John Brown* (an incomplete, unpublished, and undated manuscript), 3–4, in Series II, Box 11, GEE. Hereinafter, *JB-STUT*; Frederick Humphrey, *The Humphrey Family in America* (New York: Humphrey Print, 1883), 301, n., photocopy in Gray Box 5, GEE.

3. Humphrey, *The Humphrey Family*, 302, see note, second paragraph; CSG/tr, "Owen Brown's Autobiography as written to his daughter, Marian Brown Hand ca. 1850," in GEE. Hereinafter, OBA–1850; ABA to FBS, December 8, 1910, Box 2, Brown Family/Annie Brown Adams, NYPL/KOHNS. Annie Brown claimed the original Mills' name was Von Huysen Muysen, and complained that Villard had given her mother's ancestors "an entirely new name" in his biography. In his *John Brown*, Villard says that the Mills' name was Wouter van der Meulen (see p. 15). This is perhaps so, but Villard does not cite his source for this statement. See KM's note, "Annie Brown to Hinton on JB's descent," in J.B.'s Ancestry folder, Box 3, Oswald Garrison Villard Papers, Columbia University. Hereinafter, OGV.

4. Biographer Oates does not understand Owen's phrase, "I was under some conviction[s] of sin," which he mistakes for a veiled reference to a particular act of shame—"he never explained clearly what he meant," Oates concludes. Owen was not speaking of a particular sin, but rather consciousness of a state of unworthiness before the holiness of God, which the evangelical Puritans held as prerequisite to Christian salvation. Oates misunderstands the Puritans' religion, certainly believing their "fear of the Lord" a religion of dread and terror. Fear of divine discipline and judgment were real aspects of Puritan theology, but they were always viewed in the context of a God whose unconditional love for the elect has no limit. Thus, when Oates adds, "Afraid that God had damned him, he returned to West Simsbury and sought out the Reverend Hallock for counsel," he is not only reading the chronology of events in Owen's story incorrectly, but he is also

infusing the narrative with a fear that Owen never expressed. See *TPTL*, 5, and *LLJB*, 4–11.

5. OBA–1850; CSG, "The Browns," p. 3, in Series II, Box 1, Frederick Brown folder, GEE; Owen Brown's Last Will and Testament, October 29, 1855, in Gray Box 5, GEE; CSG, "Lydia Brown Crothers Reminiscences," June 12, 1928, Gray Box 5, GEE; CSG, "Two Autobiographical Letters of Owen Brown," August 19, 1974, accompanying OBA–1841 and OBA–1850, GEE; Levi Blakeslee's daughter told an interviewer that Owen had adopted her father "because he thought they would have none of their own." KM's interview with Amelia Blakeslee Hobart, December 1908, in JB Prior to 1859–Ohio Interviews folder, Box 5, in OGV; CSG/tr, "Owen Brown's Autobiography, 1841," GEE. Hereinafter, OBA–1841; Eleanor Schapiro to CSG, October 31, 1961, Gray Box 5, GEE.

6. OBA–1950; OBA–1841; George Marsden, "Samuel Hopkins," *DCC*, 482–83; Owen Brown's untitled autobiographical sketch of his abolitionist development, in *LLJB*, 10–11. We must rely on Sanborn's 1850 date of this account, since the document was apparently passed into his hands from the Brown family at the same time he received Owen's 1850 autobiographical sketch (pp. 4–11), and both are so heavily edited that the flavor of Owen's writing is all but removed. If both documents were written in 1850, then the relationship of the two is probably strengthened. Oates did not distinguish the two sources (see *TPTL*, 364, ch. 1, n. 1). In 1961, Clarence Gee obtained the original manuscript of the 1850 autobiography, producing a complete transcription, though without Owen's abolitionist material as published by Sanborn.

7. OBA–1851; CSG's notes on Edward Brown's *The Wadsworth Memorial* (p. 231), 3, in Series II, Box 1, Judge Frederick Brown, GEE; Gerald W. McFarland, *A Scattered People: An American Family Moves West* (New York: Pantheon Books, 1985), 43–44, 69–71; James F. Caccamo, *The Story of Hudson Ohio* (Hudson, Ohio: Friends of Hudson Library, 1995), 1–4; Grace Goulder, "Hudson Prepares for Five Anniversaries," *Plain Dealer Sunday Magazine* (Cleveland, Ohio), June 7, 1936, 7, in GEE; OBA–1850. In order to maintain Owen Brown's writing style, emended words are bracketed and italicized in the text but preserved in quotation marks in the endnotes. Thus, emendation of "seport."

8. Goulder, "Hudson Prepares for Five Anniversaries"; J. B. Holm, "John Brown Was Resident of Kent; 100th Anniversary of Harper's Ferry Is Today," *Record-Courier* (Ravenna-Kent, Ohio), October 16, 1959, 9, in GEE; OBA–1850. Emendations of "there," "injery," "seamed," and "quarel"; McFarland, *A Scattered People*, 72.

9. Howard Clark to CSG, January 23, 1962, in Gray Box 5, GEE; Howard Clark to CSG, February 5, 1962, in Gray Box 5, GEE; McFarland, *A Scattered People*, 73–74, 115; Author's interview with Thomas L. Vince, Archivist and Historian of the Western Reserve Academy, Hudson, Ohio, March 16, 2000. Hereinafter, TLV; OBA–1850; OBA–1841. Emendation of "dieing."

10. OBA–1850. Emendations of "beleave," "injery," and "Famely"; CSG/tr, OB to FB, March 22, 1838, in Series II, Box 1, Florilla Brown, GEE; OBA–1850. Emendations of "two," "Famely," and "sattisfaction"; KM's interview with Salmon Brown, October 11–13, 1908, Salmon Brown folder, Box 6, OGV; OB to Frederick Baldwin, October 20, 1820, in GEE; John Botzum, "Looking Back," *Times-Press* (Akron, Ohio), December 1929, in Gray Box 5, GEE.

11. CSG's notes from "Reminiscences of Hudson, Ohio," a supplement to the *Independent* (Hudson, Ohio), ca. 1899, 47–49, in Gray Box 5, GEE; McFarland, *A Scattered People*, 73–74, 76; "Excerpts from the material sent in by N. B. Hobard, Greenwich, Conn.," in J.B. Anecdotes folder, Box 3, OGV; Goulder, "Hudson Prepares for Five Anniversaries"; *JB-STUT*, 10; TLV; "Preliminary Organization." Excerpts from Frederick C. Waite, *Western Reserve University: The Hudson Era* (Cleveland, Ohio: Western Reserve University Press, 1943), (pp. 44–45) in C. D. Russell to CSG, September 10, 1957, in Owen Brown file, Gray Box 5, GEE; Gerald W. McFarland, "Squire Owen Brown of Hudson, Ohio," *Brown Family News and Genealogical Society* (April 1993), 4.

12. Ellen D. Larned, "New Connecticut, or Western Reserve," *Connecticut Quarterly* (January–March 1897), 88–89; OBA–1841. Emendation of "don." See similar expressions in OBA–1850; CSG, "Two Autobiographical Letters of Owen Brown."

13. CSG/tr, OB to FB, March 22, 1838, in Florilla Brown folder, Series II, Box 1, GEE. Emendation of "richous," "murrmering," and "sinfullness."

14. CSG/tr, OB to JB, September 30, 1855, in Gray Box 5, GEE. Emendations of "chuse," "Imbasaders," "imatated," and "apostels."

15. McFarland, *A Scattered People*, 6; OB to FB, June 5, 1837, Series II, Box 1, Florilla Brown folder, GEE. Emendation of "coald"; OB to FB, July 21, 1837, Series II, Box 1, Florilla Brown folder, GEE. Emendation of "spirritual"; OBA–1850.

NOTES TO CHAPTER 3

1. An interview with Charles S. S. Griffing, originally published as "John Brown's Men; An Old Associate of Theirs in the Anti-Slavery Movement Relates Some New Facts About Them," *Cincinnati Enquirer* (June 18, 1879), in Louis Filler, "John Brown in Ohio: An Interview with Charles S. S. Griffing," *Ohio Archaeological and Historical Quarterly* (April 1949): 217–18; the incident is also verified by John Brown Jr. in a letter to Franklin B. Sanborn, January 8, 1884, #MS04-0043 A-D, STUT-WEB; see also Grace Goulder, "John Brown Reunion; Clan (Without Browns) Gathers in Kent and Exchanges Legends of the Abolitionist," *Cleveland Plain Dealer* (August 10, 1958), GEE. According to BBS, the most reliable account is that of Griffing, who was apparently an eyewitness.

2. Franklin B. Sanborn, "Captain John Brown" (a speech made at the Concord School, Concord, Massachusetts, March, 1857). Handwritten manuscript in Boyd B. Stutler Collection, West Virginia State Archives, Microfilm Copy (MIC 49) in the Ohio Historical Society Collection, Reel 2. Hereinafter, STUT-MICRO.

3. Sydney E. Ahlstrom, *A Religious History of the American People* (New Haven, Conn.: Yale University Press, 1972, 1979), 124–25, 128–29, 135; Robert T. Handy, *A Christian America: Protestant Hopes and Historical Realities* (New York: Oxford University Press, 1971), 12; H. Richard Niebuhr, *The Kingdom of God in America* (Middletown, Conn.: Wesleyan University Press, 1937, 1988), 51, 56.

4. Handy, *A Christian America*, 29; Alec R. Vidler, *The Church in an Age of Revolution* (New York: Penguin Press, 1961, 1976), 239; Ahlstrom, *A Religious History*, 148, 401, 416–17; Williston Walker, *A History of the Christian Church* (New York: Charles Scribner's Sons, 1918, 1970), 507.

5. Ahlstrom, *A Religious History*, 387, 417, 423–25, 432–44; Niebuhr, *The Kingdom of God in America*, 150; Handy, *A Christian America*, 28–29, 33.

6. Earl F. Cairns, "The Plan of Union," *DCC*, 787; Wyatt-Brown, *Lewis Tappan*, 48–49, 320; Vidler, *The Church in an Age of Revolution*, 239; Ahlstrom, *A Religious History*, 455–57, 468–69; CSG to BBS, April 19, 1952, 2; CSG to BBS, September 30, 1952, 2. Correspondence of CSG to BBS, Microfilm in the Hudson Library and Historical Society, Hudson, Ohio. Hereinafter, STUT-GEE.

7. Ahlstrom, *A Religious History*, 464–69; Martin E. Marty, *Righteous Empire: The Protestant Experience in America* (New York: Dial Press, 1970), 64.

8. Andrew E. Murray, *Presbyterians and the Negro: A History* (Philadelphia: Presbyterian Historical Society, 1966),82, 89–94; Dwight L. Dumond, *Anti-slavery Origins of the Civil War in the United States* (Ann Arbor: University of Michigan Press, 1959, 1964), 21–34; Louis Filler, *The Crusade Against Slavery 1830–1860* (New York: Harper Torchbooks, 1963), 32–33; Benjamin B. Warfield, *Perfectionism*, Samuel G. Craig, ed. (Philadelphia: Presbyterian and Reformed Publishing, 1958, 1980), 16–19, 23–27, 36–39, 57–58; Ahlstrom, *A Religious History*, 461.

9. Merton L. Dillon, *Elijah P. Lovejoy, Abolitionist Editor* (Urbana: University of Illinois Press, 1961), 28, 32, 39–41, 159–70, 178; Wyatt-Brown, *Lewis Tappan*, 311; Murray, *Presbyterians and the Negro*, 99, 102.

10. Thomas W. Higginson, "Gabriel's Defeat," *Atlantic Monthly* (September 1862), 343. An extensive study of the ongoing nature of slave rebellion is found in Herbert Aptheker, *American Negro Slave Revolts* (New York: International, 1943, 1987).

11. Higginson, "Gabriel's Defeat," 341; Vincent Harding, *There Is a River: The Black Struggle for Freedom in America* (New York: Vintage, 1981), 55–57, 70; Aptheker, *American Negro Slave Revolts*, 219–23; David Roberton, *Denmark*

*Vesey* (New York: Vintage, 1999), 41–71; Thomas W. Higginson, "Denmark Vesey," *Atlantic Monthly* (June 1861), 728–44.

12. Aptheker, *American Negro Slave Revolts*, 293–324; Thomas W. Higginson, "Nat Turner's Insurrection," *Atlantic Monthly* (August 1861), 173–87; Herbert Aptheker, *Nat Turner's Slave Rebellion* (New York: Grove Press/Humanities Press, 1966, 1968), 33–56; Stephen B. Oates, *The Fires of Jubilee: Nat Turner's Fierce Rebellion* (New York: Harper and Row, 1976), 69–143. Also see Tony Horwitz, "Untrue Confessions," *New Yorker* (December 13, 1999), 80–89.

13. Henry Mayer, *All on Fire: William Lloyd Garrison and the Abolition of Slavery* (New York: St. Martin's Griffin, 1998), 120–21, 123–24, 131, 135, 137, 224–25, 249–51.

14. David Walker, *Appeal to the Coloured Citizens of the World, but In Particular, and Very Expressly, To Those of the United States of America* (1830 version), James Turner, ed. (Baltimore: Black Classics Press, 1993), 12–13; Benjamin Quarles, *Black Abolitionists* (New York: Oxford University Press, 1969, 1970), 16–17; Harding, *There Is a River*, 85–93; Mayer, *All on Fire*, 83–84, 108 and n., 644.

15. Litwack, *North of Slavery*, 244–46; Benjamin Quarles, *Allies for Freedom: Blacks and John Brown* (New York: Oxford University Press, 1974), 67 and 209, n. 10 and 11; Frederick Douglass to "My Dear [William C.] Nell," in February 5, 1848, in "Editorial Correspondence," *North Star* (February 11, 1848), 2.

Part II

Epigraph: JB to FBS, May 14, 1858, in LLJB, 457.

Notes to Chapter 4

1. For articles on the Brown home in Torrington, see William H. Vary, "John Brown in Springfield," *Union* [Springfield, Mass.], (May 1927), CVHM; "Connecticut Neglects Memory of John Brown," anonymous clipping, ca. 1920, CVHM; John Brown's Local History; Told by Men Who Remember Him," *Republican* [Springfield, Mass.] (May 13, 1900), in T.C.B. Newell Scrapbook, Vol. 5, 263–64, CVHM; "The House in Which John Brown Was Born Still Stands in Torrington, Conn.," undated clipping, ca. 1900, from a Cleveland, Ohio, newspaper, in Birthplace folder, Box 3, OGV; Pasted newspaper clipping, "John Brown's Birthplace Burns," [June 20], 1918, in Birthplace folder, Box 3, OGV; [Dwight C. Kilbourn], The John Brown Association, Torrington, Conn. (October 1910), in Birthplace folder, Box 3, OGV; John Brown's autobiographical sketch in letter from John Brown to Henry L. Stearns, July 15, 1857, photocopy of original in Box 1, GEE. Hereinafter, JBA.

2. JBA; KM's interview with JaB, December 28, 1908, in Jason Brown folder, Box 2, OGV; SaB to Anna Heacock, May 11, 1913, in Box 2, John Brown Family Histories and Biographies, Salmon Brown folder, GEE; JBJr quoted in Eleanor Atkinson, "The Soul of John Brown: Recollections of the Great Abolitionist by his Son," *American Magazine* (October 1909), 636, in Box 21, OGV.

3. Larned, "New Connecticut, or Western Reserve,"89, 96; *JB-STUT*, 8; Marion L. Starkey, *The Congregational Way: The Role of the Pilgrims and their Heirs in Shaping America* (Garden City, N.Y.: Doubleday, 1966), 172; *Records of the Congregational Church in Hudson; Organized September 4, 1802, Transcribed August, 1820*, an exact transcription by Jeffrey A. Mills and John J. Fedak, Columbus, Ohio (February–May 1986), in the Hudson Library and Historical Society, Hudson, Ohio. Hereinafter, CCH.

4. Thomas Vince in *Hudson: A Survey of Historic Buildings in an Ohio Town* (Kent, Ohio: Kent State University Press, 1989), 10; Helen S. Waterhouse, "John Brown Called 'Early Kasch Edition,'" *Beacon-Journal* [Akron, Ohio] (January 17, 1920), Gray Box 6, GEE; *JB-STUT*, 11; KM's interview with Robert W. Thompson, December 20, 1908, in JB Prior to 1859–Ohio Interviews folder, Box 5, OGV; KM's notes, "Early pronouncements of Hostility to Slavery by J.B. Testimony of Emily E. Metcalf, in Historical Papers, Hudson, Ohio," September 4, 1902, 28, Early Days folder, Box 3, OGV; OBA–1841. Emendation of "Gaul"; as to Ruth Brown's well-worn gravestone, Hudson historian Thomas Vince suggests that it more likely read "delightful child" than "dutiful child," as is usually stated. Compare McFarland, *A Scattered People*, 259, n. 26, with *HLAGO*; KM's interview with Amelia Hobart, daughter of Levi Blakeslee, December 1908, in JB Prior to 1859–Ohio Interviews folder, Box 5, OGV; JBJr to FBS, January 8, 1884, #MS04-0043 A-D, STUT-WEB; "John Brown notes," beneath "Random Recollections," #RP08-0103 A-O, STUT-WEB; *HLAGO*, 48–49; JBA.

5. Mary Brown told a reporter for an abolitionist publication that her father-in-law had always had his family recite the Catechism, but that John Brown had chosen not to continue the practice in his own home. See KM's notes from "Mrs. Brown and Her Family," *National Anti-Slavery Standard* (November 28, 1859), in Mrs. Brown and Family folder, Box 6, OGV. It is possible that another Puritan catechism was used by the Brown family, or that the *Westminster Larger Catechism* was used, though the latter is far more expansive. Regardless, the theological characteristics varied little between Reformed catechisms. See *Reformed Confessions Harmonized*, Joel R. Beeke and Sinclair B. Ferguson, eds. (Grand Rapids, Mich.: Baker Books, 1999), vii, xii–xiii, and the various questions and answers of the *Westminster Shorter Catechism*; *Savoy Declaration of 1586*, available from the Center for Reformed Theology and Apologetics [document on-line], at http://www.reformed.org/documents/Index.html; Colin Buchanan, "Catechisms," *DCC*, 199–200.

6. The *Savoy Declaration* "became more or less the standard in New England Congregationalism." Brian G. Armstrong, "Savoy Declaration," *DCC*, 880. Thus perhaps the Browns followed the *Savoy Declaration*—at least until they came to Hudson, where it seems the church was already using the *Westminster Confession*.

7. "Mrs. Brown and Her Family," in Mrs. Brown and Family folder, Box 6, OGV; TRANS, FBS to TWH, March 21, 1858, in Higginson Collection folder, Box 9, OGV; Letter of Mrs. [Mary] L. Stearns to T. C. Richards, May 8, 1900, in "One Hundredth Anniversary of John Brown's Birth Celebrated," *Register* [Torrington, Conn.], May 10, 1900, in Sanborn Scrapbook, Reel 5, STUT-MICRO; *TPTL*, 191–92; Jeffrey Rossbach, *Ambivalent Conspirators: John Brown, the Secret Six, and a Theory of Slave Violence* (Philadelphia: University of Pennsylvania Press, 1982), 122–23.

8. JBA. Emendations of "verry," "habbit," "inteligent," "deffinite"; GLS to JB, April 18, 1857, in CSG's notes on JBA, November 6, 1969, Box 1, GEE.

9. Ross Miller, "Autobiography as Fact and Fiction: Franklin, Adams, Malcolm X," *Centennial Review* (Summer 1972), 221–22, 230–32; Atkinson, "The Soul of John Brown," 634; George B. Delamater, "John Brown of Civil War Fame Was a Pioneer Resident of Titusville Section of Crawford" (reprint of an 1888 memoir), *Enterprise-News* [Cambridge Springs, Pa.] Historical Edition (November 12, 1931), 2, in Gray Box 4, GEE.

10. BBS suggests that the youth may have been a slave on loan to the landlord in the story—"a transient who had been lodged . . . while the master went about his business." However, he is open to the possibility that the story was something of a moral tale. See *JB-STUT*, 21; Benjamin Quarles is curiously doubtful, writing that the slave story "could have been an example of almost total recall . . . , but this story could equally be an example of sentiment playing a trick on memory. It reads like a wishful reconstruction, however well-intentioned and honestly held." Quarles, *Allies for Freedom*, 16; CSG writes: "Something probably took place and it made a deep impression upon him. No slaves would be permitted in the territory he visited, yet there may have been a colored lad where he remained over night, and the lad may have been abused. Years later, when so much had taken place, he may have 'colored' the tale a bit." CSG to BBS, October 25, 1954, 1, STUT-GEE.

NOTES TO CHAPTER 5

1. Mary Land, "John Brown's Ohio Environment," *Ohio Archaeological and Historical Quarterly* (January 1948), 28, 29, 36; Lora Case, *Hudson of Long Ago: Progress of Hudson during the Past Century Personal Reminiscences of an Aged Pioneer* (1897; rpt. Hudson, Ohio: Hudson Library and Historical Society, 1963), in Brown Papers; Pamphlets folder, Box 21, OGV. Hereinafter, *HLAGO*;

Quarles, *Allies for Freedom*, 17; Boyd B. Stutler, "John Brown and the Masonic Order" (manuscript), 2, #RP08-0066 A-L, STUT-WEB.

2. JBA; McFarland, *A Scattered People*, 76; *HLAGO*,50–51; CSG to BBS, September 30, 1952, 2, STUT-GEE; CCH, 7, 9.

3. *The Savoy Declaration of 1586*, Chapter 26, "Of the Church," No. 5; *The Westminster Confession* has no comparable statement, though the *Westminster Larger Catechism of 1648* includes a statement that could be interpreted to please post-millennialists. See the answer to Question #191, *Reformed Confessions Harmonized*, 181.

4. Richard Kyle, *The Last Days Are Here Again: A History of the End Times* (Grand Rapids, Mich.: Baker Books, 1998), 80–81; Kerry A. Trask, *In the Pursuit of Shadows: Massachusetts Millennialism and the Seven Years War* (New York: Garland, 1989), 209, 218–19; Nathan O. Hatch, "The Origins of Civil Millennialism in America," in *Reckoning with the Past: Historical Essays on American Evangelicalism from the Institute for the Study of American Evangelicals*, D. G. Hart, ed. (Grand Rapids, Mich.: Baker Books, 1995), 87; James H. Moorhead, "Searching for the Millennium in America," *Princeton Seminary Bulletin* VII (2) (1987), 30; JB to H. L. Vaill, November 15, 1859, in *A John Brown Reader*, Louis Ruchames, ed. (New York: Abelard-Schuman, 1959), 135–36. Hereinafter, *JBR*.

5. CCH, 40, 8; compare Article XXVIII (4), Answer to Question #95, and Answer to Question #166, respectively, in *Reformed Confessions Harmonized*, 217.

6. KM's notes from letter of ABA to Richard Hinton [no date given], Hinton Papers, KSHS, in J.B.'s Ancestry folder, Box 3, OGV; JBA; *JB-STUT*, 13–16; TLV; Will M. Clemens, "John Brown, The American Reformer," *Peterson Magazine* (January 1898), 22–23. Clemens confuses details, however, placing the Brown boys at Morris before going to Plainfield, while Stutler errs in placing the story of John's discipline of Salmon at the Plainfield academy; Letter of J. H. Vaill to FBS, April 11, 1885, Reel 2, BR/KSHS; quoted in James Redpath, *The Public Life of Capt. John Brown* (Boston: Thayer and Eldridge, 1860), 353. Also see KM's notes from L. W. Bacon, "John Brown Invasion," *Independent*, November 1859, in J.B. Hudson, Franklin, and Kent folder, Box 4, OGV.

7. TRANS, JB to OB2 et al., May 18, 1858, in L. R. Witherell, "Old John Brown," *Davenport Gazette* [Davenport, Iowa] (February 27, 1878), in Letters through 1859 folder, Box 5, OGV.

8. Author's telephone interview with ENC, April 12, 2001; See "Environment, 1815," and "Agriculture, 1816," in James Trager, *The People's Chronology* (Henry Holt, 1996), on *Microsoft Bookshelf 98*; "Tambora," *Microsoft Encarta 98* Encyclopedia.

9. See list of baptisms in CCH; CSG's notes, "Brown Genealogy," Gray Box 5, GEE; *Hudson: A Survey of Historic Buildings*, 10, 147; KM's interview with Amelia Hobart, daughter of Levi Blakeslee, December 1908, in JB Prior to

1859–Ohio Interviews folder, Box 5, OGV; SaB to Anna Heacock, May 11, 1913, in Box 2, John Brown Family Histories and Biographies, Salmon Brown folder, GEE; Letters from BBS to Stephen B. Oates, June 6 and 15, 1968, #RP09-0106 A-C, STUT-WEB; KM's interview with John Whedon, son of Benjamin Whedon, December 20, 1908, in JB Prior to 1859–Ohio Interviews folder, Box 5, OGV; KM's interview with Mrs. Porter Hall [*sic*], stepdaughter of OB through his third wife, Lucy Hinsdale, December 22, 1908, in JB Prior to 1859–Ohio Interviews folder, Box 5, OGV; *JB-STUT*, 22.

10. CCH, 12, 13, 42, 43. The Hudson Congregational Church was joined to the Grand River Presbytery informally in 1815, and then officially in 1819. It later became the Portage Presbytery; *HLAGO;* Grace Goulder, "The Brown Boyhood Years," *Cleveland Plain Dealer* (May 3, 1959), Scrapbook 10, Reel 7, STUT-MICRO; KM's interview with Charles Lusk, nephew of Dianthe Brown, December 21, 1908, in JB Prior to 1859–Ohio Interviews folder, Box 5, OGV; Clemens, "John Brown, The American Reformer," 24; Villard, *John Brown*, 18; Charles Wesley, "Blow Ye the Trumpet" (1750), Selection #445 from *The Congregational Hymn Book for the Service of the Sanctuary* (Boston: John P. Jewett, 1857); Atkinson, "The Soul of John Brown," 635.

NOTES TO CHAPTER 6

1. BBS to Stephen B. Oates, June 6, 1968, #RP09-0106 A-C, STUT-WEB; *Hudson: A Survey of Historic Buildings*, 27, 147; Notes of Dr. George A. Miller on Hudson Masons, October 5, 1935, in Gray Box 3, Miscellany, GEE; Boyd B. Stutler, "John Brown of Osawatomie—His Record as a Mason," *Wisconsin Freemason* (October 1955), 6–7, Box 11, GEE; BBS to CSG, February 7, 1954, 1, STUT-GEE; *LLJB*, 34–35. There is some confusion of events in the story of the fleeing fugitive couple with the previous account of the frightened fugitive whom John Brown found hiding by hearing his throbbing heart. John Jr. attributes a similar outcome to the story of the couple, but it is possible he conflated the two incidents, having been too young to remember both in great detail; tanning details from "Leather," *Microsoft® Encarta® Encyclopedia 99* © 1993–1998 Microsoft Corporation; lists for birthdates of John Brown's children found in *LLJB*, 35, and for Owen Brown, see CSG's notes, "Brown Genealogy," Gray Box 5, GEE.

2. KM's notes from interview with Amelia Hobart, daughter of Levi Blakeslee, December 1908, in JB Prior to 1859–Ohio Interviews folder, Box 5, OGV; Goulder, "The Brown Boyhood Years"; Annie Brown Adams—daughter of John Brown's second wife, Mary Ann Day—claimed that Dianthe threw baby John Jr. into the fireplace, and that her father had snatched the infant out of the flames immediately, so that no harm came to him. Annie's remarks in later life cannot be accepted without close scrutiny, especially in family matters, since there seems to have been tension between the children of John Brown's wives. See KM's interview with ABA, October 2 and 3, 1908, in J.B. Harshness to His Wife Di-

anthe folder, Box 4, OGV; *JB-STUT*, 26; KM's interview with Mrs. Henry Pettengill [*sic*], Lusk family relative, December 20, 1908, in J.B.'s Harshness to His Wife Dianthe folder, Box 4, OGV; WHB to KM, January 24, 1909, in Mr. and Mrs. John Brown, Jr. folder, Box 6, OGV; KM's interview with Robert W. Thompson, relative of the Lusk family, December 20, 1908, in JB Prior to 1859–Ohio Interviews folder, Box 5, OGV; KM's interview with Benjamin K. Waite, December 26 and 27, 1908, in JB Prior to 1859–Ohio Interviews folder, Box 5, OGV; KM's interview with Charles Lusk, nephew of Milton Lusk, December 21, 1908, in JB Prior to 1859–Ohio Interviews folder, Box 5, OGV.

3. TLV; OBA–1850; McFarland, "Squire Owen Brown," 11; John Brown purchased his tract from unsettled "donation lands" originally set aside by the state for veterans of the Revolutionary struggle. *JB-STUT*, 31–32; William R. Lingo, *The Pennsylvania Career of John Brown* (Corry, Pa.: Journal, 1926), 10–11; Ernest C. Miller, *John Brown: Pennsylvania Citizen* (Warren: Penn State Press, 1952), 3–5, 8–9; Salmon Brown, "My Father, John Brown," *Outlook* (January 25, 1913), 217, in Box 6, Salmon Brown folder, OGV; JBA.

4. George B. Delamater, "John Brown of Civil War Fame," *Enterprise-News* [Cambridge Springs, Pa. Historical Edition], (November 12, 1931), 2, in Gray Box 4, GEE; Miller, *John Brown: Pennsylvania Citizen*, 4–5; Edward Erf, "An Abolitionist," *Pittsburg[h] Post* (May 28, 1899), J.B. in Pennsylvania folder, Box 4, OGV; KM's interview with Alfred Hawkes, January 2, 1909, in J.B. in Pennsylvania folder, Box 4, OGV; Boyd B. Stutler, "John Brown—The Pennsylvania Farmer," *Service Magazine* (September–October 1930), 13, in Gray Box 4, GEE; *TPTL*, 30–32; Villard, *John Brown*, 49; JB to FrB, November 21, 1834, in "Words of John Brown," *Old South Leaflets* No. 84, Letters through 1854 file, Box 4, OGV; Alice Edison, "Grandson of Great Abolitionist Recalls Days of Slave Smuggling," *Akron Sunday Times* (August 1, 1926), D3.

5. Letter of Esther Lucetta Brittain Molthrop in "Friend of John Brown Tells of Abolitionist," *Record Herald* [Chicago] (January 5, 1909), in J.B. in Pennsylvania folder, Box 4, OGV; Jason Brown quoted in "Pottawatomie," *Journal* [Lawrence, Kansas] (February 12, 1880), in Jason Brown folder, Box 2, OGV; Clemens, "John Brown, The American Reformer," 108. Jason provided the information for the "Indian story" in both accounts, but I prefer John Brown's words in the 1880 version, since the older account retains what seems to be an authentically blunt warning typical of Brown; the later version seems a bit stylized, with Brown holding his rifle and threatening to shoot the first man who leveled a gun at a "peaceable Indian"; TRANS, James Foreman to James Redpath, December 28, 1859, in Reel 2, STUT-MICRO; Richard Baxter, *The Saints' Everlasting Rest* (1650, rpt. New York: American Tract Society, ca. 1840), 21, 23–24, 212–13, 214, and 238.

6. BBS/tr, JBJr to FBS, February 26, 1883, in Green Box 4, GEE; *LLJB*, 39; the story of the calf skin thief took place in Hudson prior to the Browns coming

to Pennsylvania, though the same strict moral procedure was typical of Brown's business leadership in Pennsylvania and elsewhere. TRANS, James Foreman to James Redpath, December 28, 1859, Reel 2, STUT-MICRO; CSG's notes, "Extracts from an Address on John Brown Delivered at Meadville, Pa., by George Delamater," Box 4, GEE; "Friend of John Brown Tells of Abolitionist"; KM's interview with Charles Lusk, nephew of Dianthe Lusk, December 21, 1908, in JB Prior to 1859–Ohio Interviews folder, Box 5, OGV; Atkinson, "The Soul of John Brown"; Lou V. Chapin, "The Last Days of Old John Brown," *Overland Monthly* (April 1899), 325, in Box 21, OGV.

7. Atkinson, "The Soul of John Brown"; KM's interviews with JaB, December 13 and 14, and 28, 1908, Jason Brown folder, Box 2, OGV; Ruth's pussy-willow story in Chapin, "The Last Days of Old John Brown"; JaB's accident account is found in two sources: Edison, "Grandson of Great Abolitionist," D3, and KM's notes on interview with daughter-in-law of JaB, December 28, 1908, "J.B. anecdotes," in J.B. Anecdotes folder, Box 3, OGV; *JBA*. Emendations of "verry" and "habbit"; Baxter, *The Saints' Everlasting Rest*, 238–39; "John Brown's Old Home," newspaper clipping incompletely cited, ca. May 1903, in Connelley Scrapbook, Reel 4/5?, STUT-MICRO.

8. For birth dates of John and Dianthe's children, as well as note of Salmon's death, see *LLJB*, 35 and 26, respectively. Martha, another child of Owen and Sally, died in 1826. Also see Richard O. Boyer, *The Legend of John Brown: A Biography and a History* (New York: Alfred A. Knopf, 1973), 248. Stutler says that even though the second Frederick was born before the first Frederick died, the second "was still unnamed when his brother died." This does not change the point, since John and Dianthe deliberately refrained from naming the second child so that the first Frederick's "name, if not his place, was immediately filled by naming another son Frederick." See *JB-STUT*, 40; KM's interview with JaB, December 28, 1908, in Jason Brown folder, Box 2, OGV; CSG/tr, JB to OB, August 11, 1832, in John Brown letter book, GEE. Hereinafter, JBOOK; Lingo, *The Pennsylvania Career of John Brown*, 27; Walter Jack, "Famed Leader Lived in Ohio—N.W. Pennsylvania Area," *Jefferson Gazette* [Jefferson, Ohio] (July 5, 1949), 4, in GEE; BBS/tr, JB to Seth Thompson, August 13, 1831, JBOOK; KM's handwritten note, "Holmes Papers," in J.B.'s Harshness to His Wife Dianthe folder, Box 4, OGV.

PART III

Epigraph: JB in diary of Henry D. Thoreau, in F. B. Sanborn, *Recollections of Seventy Years, Vol. 1* (Boston: Gorham Press, 1909), 112.

NOTES TO CHAPTER 7

1. Boyd B. Stutler, "John Brown: Postmaster," *American Philatelist* (March 1953), 443–45. Brown served as postmaster from January 7, 1828 until May 27,

1835. See F. H. Hitchcock, Postmaster General, to Oswald G. Villard, August 9, 1909, in J.B. in Pennsylvania folder, Box 4, OGV. Some writers have suggested that John Brown gave the name of Randolph township when he became postmaster, but more recent research by Eric Ledell Smith has shown that Randolph township was already so named when Brown arrived for his first visit in 1825. Eric Ledell Smith, "John Brown in Crawford County: the Making of a Radical Abolitionist," 1 (Pennsylvania Historical and Museum Commission, Harrisburg, Pa., 2001). Hereinafter, JB-ELS; "John Brown's Old Home," newspaper clipping incompletely cited, ca. May 1903, in Connelley Scrapbook, Reel 4/5?, STUT-MICRO; Lingo, *The Pennsylvania Career of John Brown*, 12; "Friend of John Brown Tells of Abolitionist"; KM's interview with Alfred Hawkes, January 2, 1909, in J.B. in Pennsylvania folder, Box 4, OGV; John Duncan, "John Brown in Pennsylvania," *Western Pennsylvania Historical Magazine* 2 (4) (1928), 51; *JB-STUT*, 33.

2. BBS/tr, James Foreman to James Redpath, December 28, 1859, in Reel 2, STUT-MICRO; Boyer, *The Legend of John Brown*, 250–51; *JB-STUT*, 41–42; Ernest C. Miller, *John Brown: Pennsylvania Citizen* (Warren: Penn State Press, 1952), 8; Lingo, *The Pennsylvania Career of John Brown*, 14; KM's interview notes, "Talks with Miss Sarah Brown," September 16 and 20, 1908, in Miss Sarah Brown folder, Box 6, OGV. Also see M.H.F., " A Brave Life," *Atlantic Monthly* (October 1885), 360–67.

3. KM's note, "Holmes Papers," in J.B.'s Harshness to His Wife Dianthe folder, Box 4, OGV; KM's interview with Fanny Dean, January 2, 1909, in JB in Cleveland . . . Thence folder, Box 4, OGV; KM's interview with Eunicia Fobes, January 6, 1909, in J.B. in Cleveland . . . Thence folder, Box 4, OGV; KM's notes on letter from RBT to WHB, March 10, 1850, in JB Early Days in Charlestown Jail folder, Box 4, OGV; BBS/tr, James Foreman to James Redpath, December 28, 1859, in Reel 2, STUT-MICRO; KM's interview with WHB, November 30–December 3, 1908, in Mr. and Mrs. John Brown Jr. folder, Box 6, OGV; "John Brown's Old Home"; JB-ELS, 9; There were six Delamater children, born between 1821 and 1832. CSG's notes from Mary Ann Bidwell Higby, *The First Hundred Years of Townville and Vicinity* (1924), 64–67, in Gray Box 4, GEE; KM's notes on interview with JBJr in "His Goal," *Cleveland Press* (May 3, 1895), in Mr. and Mrs. John Brown Jr. folder, Box 6, OGV; Miller, *John Brown: Pennsylvania Citizen*, 5; Boyer, *The Legend of John Brown*, 134.

4. KM's notes from transcript of an address on John Brown by George B. Delamater, delivered at Meadville, Pa. [undated], in JB in Pennsylvania; the Delamater Narrative folder, Box 4, OGV. Hereinafter, DELNAR. Also see CSG's notes on the same, in Gray Box 3, GEE; BBS/tr, James Foreman to James Redpath, December 28, 1859, in Reel 2, STUT-MICRO; Atkinson, "The Soul of John Brown," 635; CSG/tr, "Owen Brown on Intemperance" (ca. 1850), in Gray Box 5, Owen Brown folder, GEE. Emendations of "whorlepools" and "distruction";

Brown, "My Father, John Brown"; KM's notes from E.A.D., "Reminiscences of John Brown," in J.B. in Pennsylvania, Box 4, OGV. In late 1850, John Brown directed his sons to send two bottles of cherry wine to his lawyers in New York, concluding: "We can effect something to purpose by producing unadulterated domestic wines. They will command great prices." See JB to sons and daughters, December 4, 1850, in *LLJB*, 78 and note 1 (original in Box 1, Folder 5, JB2).

5. JB-ELS, 2–4,6; *LLJB*, 37; Richard J. Hinton, *John Brown and His Men* (New York: Funk and Wagnalls, 1894), 24; DELNAR; BBS/tr, James Foreman to James Redpath, December 28, 1859, Reel 2, STUT-MICRO; Darrel Bigham, "Unitarianism," *DCC*, 995–96; a question of dates arises within the chronology presented here. The "articles of faith" written by Brown for his new church are no longer available despite scholarly references dating them at January 11, 1832. The earliest source for this date is a newspaper article by George Delamater in 1888, which was probably Villard's source (p. 25). BBS accepted the given date (*JB-STUT*, 38–39). If Brown's church was planted in early 1832, it is unlikely that three-year-old Ruth would have been baptized at "a neighbor's house" since her father's young congregation met on site at the Brown settlement. Furthermore, she recalled that (1) both her "father and mother" were present, probably meaning Dianthe, not Mary Brown; and (2) she was baptized by a minister, as expected, except that Brown's church did not have a minister available at the onset. This matter could be clarified were primary documents for the church available. Since Brown did not join the Unitarian Church in Meadville after leaving the Meadville Bible Society, his daughter Ruth was probably baptized at the latter church, prior to Dianthe's death. The only extant document from Brown's church is a September 1833 letter of recommendation in his hand. I suggest the following summary: Brown and family were in the Guys Mills Church from about 1826 to 1827; the Meadville Bible Society from 1827 to the end of 1832, and separated, possibly over race prejudice, and formed another church in early 1833. Of course, this conclusion is open to correction and revision with further research. I am indebted to Eric Smith for sharing his critical research on John Brown in western Pennsylvania. I differ only in my belief that Brown was not affiliated with the Unitarian Congregational Church. See JB-ELS, 2–3, n. 6.

6. Erf, "An Abolitionist"; DELNAR; BBS/tr, James Foreman to James Redpath, December 28, 1859, Reel 2, STUT-MICRO; Boyer, *The Legend of John Brown*, 135, n. 50, 588; Robert G. Clouse, "Arminianism," *DCC*, 70; *LLJB*, 33.

7. JB-ELS, 3–6, 9–10; *LLJB*, 37; "John Brown's Old Home"; CSG/tr, JBJr, "John Brown at Home; Some Incidents Showing His Natural Kindness of Manner," *Akron Beacon* (January 12, 1881), Box 2, John Brown Family Histories/John Brown Jr. folder, GEE.

8. KM's interview notes, "Talks with Miss Sarah Brown," September 16 and 20, 1908, in Miss Sarah Brown folder, Box 6, OGV; Boyd B. Stutler, "John Brown

and the Masonic Order" (an unpublished manuscript), 3–5, #RP08-0066 A-L, STUT-WEB. Also see Boyd B. Stutler, "John Brown and the Masonic Order," *Ohio History* (January 1962), 24–32; JB to OB, June 12, 1830, OHS. Also see photocopy in Box 11, GEE.

9. Stutler, "John Brown and the Masonic Order," 5. Also see Miller, *John Brown Pennsylvania Citizen*, 9–12; JB to OB, June 12, 1830. Emendation of "evenig"; The Anderton affidavit and the Masons' rebuttal were published in the *Crawford Messenger*, April 29, 1830 and May 20, 1830, respectively. See BBS/tr of both in Box 11, GEE; JB-ELS, 8–9; DELNAR.

NOTES TO CHAPTER 8

1. *JB-STUT*, 50; Brown, "My Father, John Brown"; BBS to CSG, August 2, 1952, 1, STUT-GEE.

2. Excerpt from letter of Marvin Kent to David Utter, November 29, 1883, in BBS to CSG, September 28, 1952, Gray Box 6, GEE.

3. KM's interview with E. O. Randall, grandson of Heman Oviatt, December 26, 1908, in JB Prior to 1859–Ohio Interviews folder, Box 5, OGV; Kent to Utter, November 29, 1883; J. B. Holm, "John Brown Was Resident of Kent; 100th Anniversary of Harper's Ferry Is Today," *Record-Courier* [Ravenna-Kent, Ohio] (October 16, 1959), 9.

4. CSG/tr, JB to Zenas Kent, April 24, 1835, JBOOK; *TPTL*, 33, 34, 36; *JB-STUT*, 45–46, 47–48; excerpt of letter from SaB to William E. Connelley, November 6, 1913, in BBS to CSG, May 1, 1954, 2, STUT-GEE; Marvin Kent quoted in letter from Dudley Weaver to BBS, August 12, 1952, #RP05-0042 A-I, STUT-WEB; KM's interview with Meliam Stewart Kent, December 23 and 24, 1908, in JB in Hudson, Franklin, and Kent folder, Box 4, OGV; CSG/tr, JB to H. J. Huidekoper, July 5, 1838, JBOOK; "John Brown, of Harper's Ferry," unsigned 1906 article [Akron *Beacon?*], in J.B. in Hudson, Franklin, Akron, and Kent folder, Box 4, OGV; Holm, "John Brown Was Resident of Kent"; Clemens, "John Brown, The American Reformer"; "John Brown Had Faith in Kent, O," *Plain Dealer* [Cleveland, Ohio] (July 6, 1926), Scrapbook 9, Reel 7, STUT-MICRO; TLV; "Andrew Jackson; Specie Circular," Microsoft® Encarta® Encyclopedia 99© 1993–1998 Microsoft Corporation.

5. *JB-STUT*, 54; KM's interview with Mrs. Porter Hall [*sic*], Owen Brown's stepdaughter from his third marriage to Lucy Hinsdale, December 22, 1908, in JB Prior to 1859–Ohio Interviews folder, Box 5, OGV; KM's interview with Benjamin K. Waite, December 26 and 27, 1908, in JB Prior to 1859–Ohio Interviews folder, Box 5, OGV; *LLJB*, 41 and 34, n.1; Land, "John Brown's Ohio Environment," 32; McFarland, *A Scattered People*, 108–09; excerpt from material sent by N. B. Hobart to Oswald G. Villard, no date, in J.B. Anecdotes folder, Box 3, OGV;

KM's interview with John Whedon, son of Benjamin Whedon, December 20, 1908, in J.B. Prior to 1859–Ohio Interviews folder, Box 5, OGV; *HLAGO*, 27.

6. McFarland, *A Scattered People*, 109–13; Wyatt-Brown, *Lewis Tappan*, 47; Land, "John Brown's Ohio Environment," 30–32; *HLAGO*; Dr. George Miller's notes on Hudson Masons, October 5, 1935, in Gray Box 3, Miscellany, GEE; Waite, *Western Reserve University: The Hudson Era*, 166–68.

7. *JB-STUT*, 50, 54–58; by the end of 1839, Brown had only paid part of his taxes. See CSG/tr, JB to Frederick Haymaker, December 4, 1839, in JBOOK; JB to MB, June 12, 1839, *JBR*, 44–45; JB to MB, June 19, 1839, *JBR*, 45; Ian Sellers, "Philip Doddridge," *DCC*, 306; in an article describing Mary Brown shortly before her husband's death, she listed Doddridge's work as one of John Brown's favorite books. See KM's notes on "Mrs. Brown and Her Family," *National Anti-Slavery Standard* (December 3, 1859), in Mrs. John Brown and Family folder, Box 6, OGV; Philip Doddridge, *Rise and Progress of Religion in the Soul* (ca. 1740; rpt. New York: American Tract Society, 1849), 373–84.

8. *JB-STUT*, 55–56, 58–61; JB to George Kellogg, August 27, 1839, *JBR*, 46; JB to MB, February 6, 1839, NYHS. Also see CSG/tr in JBOOK; "Former Land Surveyor Hanged at Charlestown, Virginia–December 2, 1859," *Empire State Surveyor* [Lockport, N.Y.] (March–April 1969), 3–5, in Box 1, GEE; Robert S. Fletcher, "John Brown and Oberlin," *Oberlin Alumni Magazine* (reprint of February 1932 edition), New Materials folder, Box 19, OGV.

9. M. H. F., "A Brave Life," 362; JB to MB, December 5, 1838, *JBR*, 44; Brown, "My Father, John Brown"; John Jr. claimed that after the incident at the Franklin Mills Church, the leadership retaliated by cutting them off from membership. But the church records contradict John Jr.'s recollections. After the incident, during the year the Browns spent back in Hudson, they were actually "received into fellowship." John Brown's membership in the Hudson church somehow remained intact until 1842, after which he transferred his membership to the Congregational Church in Richfield, Ohio. John Jr. probably dramatized the incident in order to justify his own eventual abandonment of the church. Beyond the visit of the scolding deacons, the greater portion of the congregation probably viewed the Browns as fanatical but well-meaning. It may have been the Browns who eventually soured on the congregation, finally withdrawing from the church. The Franklin Mills Church record has no date or explanation of the Browns' removal from their records. Nevertheless, the church pew incident is undoubtable and collaborated by John Jr.'s younger sister, Ruth. Compare RBT and JBJr's recollections in *LLJB*, 37 and 52–53; *JB-STUT*, 50–52; letter from M. B. Spelman, clerk, to CSG, March 30, 1954, in Box 11, GEE; CSG's notes, "John Brown—Church and Religion," Box 11, GEE.

N O T E S   T O   C H A P T E R   9

1. *LLJB*, 53; Handy, *A Christian America*, 60; KM's notes from letter of JBJr, reprinted as "Old John Brown," *Topeka Capital*, December 22, 1883, in J.B. in Hudson, Franklin, and Kent folder, Box 4, OGV.

2. KM's interview with Charles Lusk, nephew of Brown's first wife, Dianthe, December 21, 1908, in JB Prior to 1859–Ohio Interviews folder, Box 5, OGV; "Sketch Map of Hudson Township" by F. C. Waite, December 27, 1908, in Box 4, OGV; Lusk's recollection in *LLJB*, 34; Goulder, "The Brown Boyhood Years"; KM's interview with Benjamin K. Waite, December 26 and 27, 1908, in JB Prior to 1859–Ohio Interviews folder, Box 5, OGV; Bernard A. Weisberger, "When the Hereafter Was Now," *American Heritage* (October 1997), 16–18; KM's interview with Robert W. Thompson, a Lusk relative, December 20, 1908, in JB Prior to 1859–Ohio Interviews folder, Box 5, OGV.

3. For a thorough study of the Oberlin theology and the doctrines of Finney and his associate, Asa Mahan, see Warfield, *Perfectionism*; BBS's notes on Robert Fletcher, *History of Oberlin College* (1943), in BBS to CSG, February 28, 1952, STUT-GEE; Sally Brown to FB, March 13–14, 1837, Folder 1, Box 1, AD/KSHS; OB to FB, June 5, 1837, Florilla Brown folder, Series II, Box 1, GEE; OB to FB, July 21, 1837, Florilla Brown folder, Series II, Box 1, GEE.

4. OB to FB, October 14, 1837, Folder 1, Box 1, AD/KSHS. Emendations of "profectionism," "formely," "any bodys," "two," "ment," "baptisam," "disolving," and "erors."

5. OB to FB, June 25, 1838, Folder 1, Box 1, AD/KSHS; OB to FB, July 12, 1838, Folder 1, Box 1, AD/KSHS; Wendell P. Garrison, "The Preludes of Harper's Ferry, Part 1: John Brown, Practical Shepherd," *Andover Review* (December 1890) reprint, Box 9, OGV; Mayer, *All on Fire*, 237–38; *TPTL*, 41–42; Clemens, "John Brown, the American Reformer," 26–27; CSG to BBS, September 22, 1958, STUT-GEE. Three testimonies concerning John Brown's vow survive—that of Emily Metcalf, Lora Case, and Frederick Brown. While all three agree that Brown made a vow to oppose slavery, Metcalf and Case report the vow almost identically, and I have chosen to use their version/s in this chapter. Edward Brown's recollection has Brown saying: "Here before God, in the presence of these witnesses, from this time, I consecrate my life to the destruction of slavery." See KM's notes, "Early pronouncements of Hostility to Slavery by J.B.," from testimony of Emily E. Metcalf, Historical Papers, Hudson, Ohio, September 4, 1902, in J. B. early days folder, Box 3, OGV; Edward Brown's recollection is in *JBR*, 179–80; and Lora Case's version is quoted in KM's notes from Charles H. Small, "The Last Letter of John Brown," *New England Magazine* (July 1899), in J.B. Jail Letters 1859 folder, Box 5, OGV.

6. OB to FB, June 13 and 25, 1838, in Folder 1, Box 1, AD/KSHS. Emendations of "injoyment," "allways," "famely," "unfaithfull," "unfaithfullness," and

"faithfull"; the number of loved ones John Brown lost includes the death of his father in 1856, a son murdered in Kansas the same year, and two more sons killed during the Harper's Ferry raid in 1859.

7. OB to FB, October 14, 1837, Folder 1, Box 1, AD/KSHS. Emendation of "injoy"; Martha Brown to Florilla Brown, February 26, 1838, Folder 1, Box 1, AD/KSHS; Brown, "My Father, John Brown"; JB to Theodore Parker, February 24, 1858, in *LLJB*, flyleaf at p. 444; also see Sanborn, "John Brown and His Friends," *Atlantic Monthly* (July 1872), 54; excerpt of letter from James H. Cox to Charles B. Storrs, April 23, 1832, in letter from Thomas L. Vince to author, April 3, 2000; CSG to BBS, January 22, 1953, STUT-GEE; TLV; "Between January 1834 and December 1837, *Niles' Register* reported thirty-one anti-abolition and racial incidents throughout the nation." Leonard R. Richards, *"Gentlemen of Property and Standing": Anti-Abolition Mobs in Jacksonian America* (New York: Oxford University Press, 1970), 156–57; *LLJB*, 138, n. 1; Atkinson, "The Soul of John Brown," 636; Letter of JBJr in F. B. Sanborn, "John Brown's Family Compact," *Nation* (December 25, 1890), 500; John Brown's prayer posture: note the reminiscence of the daughter of his "adopted" brother, Levi Blakeslee: "He always stood, in family prayers. His prayers were short and comprehensive." KM's interview with Amelia Blakeslee Hobart, December 1908, in JB Prior to 1859–Ohio Interviews folder, Box 5, OGV.

8. *JB-STUT*, 56, 63–69; JB to George Kellogg, November 15, 1841, Reel 1, STUT-MICRO; Villard, *John Brown*, 37–39; KM's notes from JBJr to the *Exponent*, reprinted as "Old John Brown"; *TPTL*, 37–39; JB to Amos Chamberlain, April 27, 1841, in Autographs folder, Box 1, OGV; KM's interview with Henry and Daniel Myers, December 11, 1908, in JB Prior to 1859–Ohio Interviews folder, Box 5, OGV; "Inventory and appraisement of the necessary and kitchen furniture and other articles and necessaries set off and allowed to John Brown of the Township of Richfield in the County of Summit and State of Ohio, who has been duly declared a bankrupt," September 28, 1842, Reel 1, STUT-MICRO; also see KM's handwritten notes, "Certified Inventory," in J. B. in Hudson, Franklin, Akron, and Kent folder, Box 4, OGV; JB to the New England Woolen Company, October 17, 1842, *JBR*, 49; JB to Heman Oviatt, October 29, 1842, *JBR*, 50; Clemens, "John Brown, the American Reformer," 27–28.

9. "He *looked* like a *meat-ax*, didn't he?" KM's interview with SaB, October 11–13, 1908, in Salmon Brown folder, Box 6, OGV; *HLAGO*; KM's interview with E. O. Randall, grandson of Heman Oviatt, December 26, 1908, in JB Prior to 1859–Ohio Interviews folder, Box 5, OGV; A signed agreement between JB, Heman Oviatt, and Orson M. Oviatt, January 3, 1842, #MS01-0012 AB, STUT-WEB; CSG's notes from an article in *Community News* [West Richfield, Ohio] (August 1955), Box 11, GEE; JB to JBJr, with attached from JaB to JBJr, September 25, 1843, *JBR*, 50; Tappan quoted in Wyatt-Brown, *Lewis Tappan*, 305.

Part IV

Epigraph: JB to OB2, May 21, 1858, #MS 02-0025, STUT-WEB.

Notes to Chapter 10

1. Salmon Brown, "Personal Recollections of My Father, John Brown," *Evening Telegraph* [Portland, Oregon] (October 20, 1906), in Salmon Brown folder, Box 6, OGV; SaB to Anna Heacock, May 11, 1913, in John Brown Family Histories and Biographies folder, Box 2, GEE; KM's interview notes, "Talks with Miss Sarah Brown," September 16 and 20, 1908, in Miss Sarah Brown folder, Box 6, OGV; KM's interview with Salmon Brown, October 11–13, 1908, in Salmon Brown folder, Box 6, OGV; Boyer, *The Legend of John Brown*, 237 and 342; CSG/tr, "Statement of Annie Brown," November 1866, in Chicago Historical Society, in John Brown Family Histories and Biographies, Annie Brown Letters folder, Box 2, GEE; KM's interview with JaB, December 13 and 14, 1908, in Jason Brown folder, Box 2, OGV; Villard, *John Brown*, 20.

2. KM's interview with Anna Perkins, December 12, 1908, in JB in Hudson, Franklin, and Kent folder, Box 4, OGV; KM's interview with SaB, October 11–13, 1908, in Salmon Brown folder, Box 6, OGV; Boyer, *The Legend of John Brown*, 239; CSG/tr, JBJr, "John Brown at Home; Some Incidents Showing His Natural Kindness of Manner"; KM's interview with WHB, November 30–December 3, 1908, in Mr. and Mrs. John Brown Jr. folder, Box 6, OGV; Brown, "My Father, John Brown"; also see same article in *JBR*, 183; Brown, "Personal Recollections of My Father, John Brown."

3. *HLAGO*; according to *HCC*, William and Sally Dawes of McConnelsville, Ohio, joined on January 12, 1834. It is not clear how long Dawes remained a member; CSG to BBS, April 19, 1952, 2, STUT-GEE; transcription of an edited letter from Owen Brown to "Brethren," April 24, 1837, in *Report of the Ohio Anti-Slavery Society* (April 27, 1837), #MS05-0003 AB, STUT-WEB; *Records of the Free Congregational Church of Hudson, Organized October 7th* A.D. *1842*, 2, in Hudson Library and Historical Society, Hudson, Ohio. Hereinafter, FCCH.

4. FCCH, 4–5, 9–10; Niebuhr, *The Kingdom of God in America*, 156, 158; the "Free Church" structure was dedicated on December 12, 1843. According to a son of one of the founders, the church was built between 1842 and 1843, but an authority on Hudson architecture says the building is "an 1841 Greek Revival-style" structure, originally one floor. FCCH, 28; Compare KM's interview with Ransom Sanford, December 20, 1908, in J.B. Prior to 1859–Ohio Interviews folder, Box 5, OGV, and *Hudson: A Survey of Historic Buildings*, 258; notes from secretary's office, Oberlin College, on Owen Brown's role as Trustee, Owen Brown 1st folder, Box 6, OGV; according to McFarland, Owen may also have

been alienated from Oberlin by the outcome of the western Virginia land grant survey, in which the school opted to sell the land instead of providing John Brown the 1,000-acre tract they had earlier agreed upon in exchange for his surveying work. See McFarland, *A Scattered People*, 116.

5. FCCH. Also see CSG, "John Brown and His Church Relations" (notes), in Box 11, GEE; JB to JBJr, January 18, 1841, Folder 1, Box 1, JB2; KM's notes from interview in F[ranklin] B. S[anborn], "John Brown Jr.," *Cleveland Leader* (April 1879), John Brown scrapbook #9, KSHS, in Mr. and Mrs. John Brown Jr. folder, Box 6, OGV; *JB-STUT*, 70–71; Atkinson, "The Soul of John Brown," 636; Brown, "Personal Recollections of My Father, John Brown"; JB to JBJr, January 11, 1844, Folder 1, Box 1, JB2.

6. TRANS, SaB to FBS, September 10, 1909, in F. B. Sanborn folder 2, Box 16, OGV; "The Perkins Company's Woolen Factory," *Summit Beacon* [Akron, Ohio] (June 6, 1849), 3; *JB-STUT*, 73, 77; JB to JBJr, January 11, 1844.

7. *JB-STUT*, 73–74; Thrity Umrigar, "Abolitionist Made Akron His Home; John Brown Rented from Col. Simon Perkins, Jr.," *Akron Beacon Journal* (September 10, 2000); KM's interview with Anna Perkins, December 12, 1908, in J.B. in Hudson, Franklin, and Kent folder, Box 4, OGV; KM's interview with George Perkins, December 12, 1908, in J.B. in Hudson, Franklin, and Kent folder, Box 4, OGV; KM's interview notes, "Talks with Miss Sarah Brown," September 16–20, 1908, in Miss Sarah Brown folder, Box 6, OGV; Alexis de Tocqueville quoted in Bellesiles, *Arming America*, 317; Fred Lockley, "John Brown's Son Talks about His Father," *American Magazine* (May 10, 1919), 59.

8. See FBS's notes from an interview with Simon Perkins Jr., May 29, 1878, in *LLJB*, 57–58 and n. 1, 57; John Brown (Perkins and Brown) to Thomas Noble, December 27, 1845, #MS01-0017 AB, STUT-WEB; Jack, "Famed Leader Lived in Ohio–N.W. Pennsylvania Area," in GEE; *JB-STUT*, 74; letter from Samuel Lawrence to Simon Perkins, July 22, 1844, in M. B. Bateham, "Fine Sheep and Wool," *Ohio Cultivator* [Columbus, Ohio] (September 1, 1846), 134.

NOTES TO CHAPTER 11

1. *JB-STUT*, 77–78, 36–37; Perkins and Brown [JB] to M. B. Bateham, editor, *Ohio Cultivator* (January 15, 1847), 12.

2. The first exclusive meeting of wool growers took place in August 1846, in Springfield, Mass., but had little result except to determine the need for information for the February 1847 convention in Steubenville, Ohio. See *JB-STUT*, 82; JB to M. B. Bateham, editor, March 1846, in *Ohio Cultivator* (April 1846), 59–60; Brown, "Personal Recollections of My Father, John Brown"; see comments of M. B. Bateham in "Fine Sheep and Wool," *Ohio Cultivator* (September 1, 1846), 134; KM's transcription of "Wool Growers' Meeting at Steubenville, O, February 10, 1847," *Cleveland Weekly Herald* (March 17, 1847), in J.B. in Springfield, Box 4, OGV.

3. Boyd B. Stutler, "A Few Suggested Corrections for a New Edition of *John Brown: A Biography,*" 2, under letter from BBS to Oswald G. Villard, March 22, 1943, #RP13-0053 A-H, STUT-WEB; Doddridge, *The Rise and Progress of Religion in the Soul,* 16–17; TRANS, James D. Ladd to George D. Cook, January 6, 1901, Folder 6, Box 2, JB2, also reprinted in "The Immortal John Brown; His Wool Meeting at Steubenville," *Herald-Star* [Steubenville, Ohio] (June 13, 1904), in Connelley Scrapbook, Reel 4, STUT-MICRO; KM's interview with SaB, October 11–13, 1908, in Salmon Brown folder, Box 6, OGV. Emendation of "finical."

4. BBS to Henry D. Brown, May 18, 1953, #RP04-0103 A-E, STUT-WEB; Robert G. Clouse, "Alexander Campbell," *DCC,* 1841; Frank S. Mead and Samuel S. Hill, *Handbook of Denominations in the United States* (Nashville, Tenn.: Abingdon Press, 1951, 1995), 95–96; KM's notes, "Talks with Miss Sarah Brown," September 16–20, 1908, in Miss Sarah Brown folder, Box 6, OGV; "(CIRCULAR.) TO WOOL GROWERS," March 16, 1846, Reel 1, STUT-MICRO; "To Wool Growers," *Ohio Cultivator* (April 15, 1846), 59–60; note that here "P&B" specifically refers to the Springfield wool commission house, in contrast with "Perkins and Brown," which refers to the general partnership between Simon Perkins and John Brown that preceded the Springfield operation and continued several years after its demise.

5. *JB-STUT,* 78–81; Simon Perkins quoted in *LLJB,* 57; JB to JBJr, March 24, 1846, in *LLJB,* 62; JB to SP, December 16, 1846, Reel 1, STUT-MICRO; Salmon Brown said that Perkins lost everything when he backed the Hudson, Akron, Zanesville railroad line. A similar financial disaster befell Harvey Baldwin of Hudson, Ohio, who was the son-in-law of founder David Hudson. Baldwin and other prominent Hudsonians lost money in railroad ventures. Thomas Vince aptly concludes that all too often, "John Brown is not viewed in relation to his peers and contemporaries. Nobody points a finger at Baldwin. There were hundreds of lawsuits due to this failure. Yet the Hudsons are not dismissed as failures." See TRANS, SaB to FBS, September 10, 1909, in F. B. Sanborn folder, Box 16, OGV; TLV.

6. "Where Old John Brown Sold Wool in Springfield," *Boston Globe* (October 25, 1908), in Connelley Scrapbook, Reel 4, STUT-MICRO; CSG/tr, Albert H. Hardy, "John Brown as a Merchant," *Springfield Republican* (July 2, 1889?), in GEE; *JB-STUT,* 79; JB to SP, December 16, 1846, Reel 1, STUT-MICRO.

7. *JB-STUT,* 85; JB to OB, April 2, 1847, Reel 1, STUT-MICRO; JB to MB, November 8, 1846 and November 29, 1846, in *JBR,* 56 and 57; JB to OB, December 10, 1846, in *LLJB,* 21–22.

## NOTES TO CHAPTER 12

1. Michael H. Frisch, *Town into City: Springfield, Massachusetts, and the Meaning of Community, 1840–1880* (Cambridge: Harvard University Press, 1972), 32–54; Joseph Carvalho III, *Black Families in Hampden County,*

*Massachusetts 1650–1855* (Westfield: Institute for Massachusetts Studies, 1984), 16. Hereinafter, *BFHC*; *The Underground Railroad in Springfield, Massachusetts*, Kathryne Burns, ed. (Springfield, Mass.: Springfield Bicentennial Committee, 1976), 1. Hereinafter, *URIS*; Letter of Frederick Douglass to [William C.] Nell, February 5, 1848, in "Editorial Correspondence," *North Star* (February 11, 1848), 2; Frederick Douglass to Richard J. Hinton, January 17, 1892, in Richard J. Hinton file, Box 10, OGV.

2. Springfield, Mass. newspaper clipping, "James H. Osgood Dead; His Memory of John Brown," November 4, 1914, in the Genealogical and Local History Library of the Connecticut Valley Historical Museum of the Springfield Museums, Springfield, Massachusetts. Hereinafter, *CVHM*; *URIS*, 3–8; "Underground Railroad in Massachusetts," *Journal of the American Antiquarian Society* (April 1935), 90–92, CVHM; Quarles, *Allies for Freedom*, 18–19; "During one troublous year, Osgood had as many as 51 fugitives living at the parsonage." See "Underground Rail Road and John Brown's Activities," *Republican* [Springfield, Mass.] (July 4, 1909), in Joseph K. Newell Scrapbook, 167, CVHM; "'Underground Railway' Station of Slavery Days to Be Auctioned," *Springfield Daily Republican* (July 15, 1926), CVHM; "John Brown's Local History; Told by Men Who Remember Him," *Republican* [Springfield, Mass.] (May 13, 1900), in J.C.B. Newell Scrapbook, Vol. 5, 263–64, CVHM; CSG/tr, Hardy, "John Brown as a Merchant"; *JB-STUT*, 84; Brown, "My Father, John Brown," 217.

3. Harry A. Wright, "John Brown in Springfield," *New England Magazine* (May 1894), 272; F. B. Sanborn, "John Brown in Massachusetts," *Atlantic Monthly* (April 1872), 422; *LLJB*, 133; "Where Old John Brown Sold Wool in Springfield," *Boston Globe* (October 25, 1908), in Connelley Scrapbook, Reel 4, STUT-MICRO; Clemens, "John Brown, The American Reformer," 28; CSG's extracts from letter of Reuben Chapman to Richard Hinton, November 15, 1859, in J. B. Springfield folder, Box 4, OGV.

4. "Thomas Thomas's Retirement; From the Famous Eating-House," *The Republican* (January 8, 1893), John C. B. Newell Scrapbook, Vol. 1, 493, CVHM; "Death of Thomas Thomas; Who Long Kept the Restaurant," *Republican* (March 10, 1894), CVHM; *URIS*, 8; *BFHC*, 17; F. B. Sanborn, *Memoirs of John Brown, Written for Reverend Samuel Orcutt's History of Torrington, Ct.* (Concord, Mass.: January, 1878), 22. Sanborn erroneously reports that Thomas was a fugitive slave; Hardy, "John Brown as a Merchant."

5. KM's notes from article, "John Brown's Local History," *Springfield Sunday Republican* (May 13, 1900), in J.B. in Springfield folder, Box 4, OGV; William H. Vary, "John Brown in Springfield" (ca. 1927), *The Union* [Springfield, Mass.], CVHM; Hardy, "John Brown as a Merchant"; Redpath, *The Public Life of Capt. John Brown*, 54; Boyer, *The Legend of John Brown*, 452–53; "Bits of History; John Brown Said His Will Power Kept Him Warm," undated newspaper clipping from Springfield, Massachusetts newspaper, CVHM; Spring-

field, Mass. newspaper clipping, "James H. Osgood Dead; His Memory of John Brown."

6. KM's transcript of letter from Watson Brown to OB, February 1848," attached to SaB to OB, February 23, 1848, in Watson Brown folder, Box 6, OGV; JBJr to FBS, March 27, 1885, Reel 2, STUT-MICRO; Hardy, "John Brown as a Merchant"; Wright, "John Brown in Springfield," 272–74; ABA to editor, *Springfield Republican* (June 6, 1908), in GEE; KM's interview with Amelia Hobart, December 1908, in JB Prior to 1859–Ohio Interviews folder, Box 5, OGV; Atkinson, "The Soul of John Brown," 637–38; Naomi T. Cummings, Sylvia G. Humphrey et al., *The History of St. John's Congregational Church, Springfield, Massachusetts, 1844–1962* (Springfield: St. John's Congregational Church History Committee, 1962), 19–20; Frederick Douglass to [William C.] Nell, February 5, 1848, in "Editorial Correspondence," *North Star* (February 11, 1848), 2; *Life and Times of Frederick Douglass*, 278–81. In his autobiography, Douglass seems to have erred in saying his dinner with the Browns took place in 1847 (p. 282), even though Brown was supposed to have met him in Springfield on May 15, 1847. But if Douglass dined with Brown that day, it was not with Mary and the children, who did not move to Springfield until mid-July 1847. Since there is no evidence that Douglass was back in Springfield for the rest of 1847, and since the Browns moved to a number of places in Springfield before settling on Hastings Street, it could not have been any earlier than his visit in February 1848 that Douglass enjoyed Mary Brown's good home cooking, as recounted in his autobiography. Since Douglass visited Springfield twice more in 1848—according to *The North Star*, on October 29 and November 18—his dinner with the Browns might just as well have been on one of these dates. See Benjamin Quarles, *Frederick Douglass* (New York: DeCapo Press, 1997), 170, n. 2. Compare JB to JBJr, May 15, 1847, NYPL/KOHNS ("I am in hourly expectation of a visit from Fred Douglas [*sic*]"), JB to JBJr, July 9, 1847, and JB to RBT, September 1, 1847, *LLJB*, 144–45, which give a sense of the details of the move and setting up house in Springfield; CSG/tr, "Statement of Annie Brown," November 1866, from manuscript in Chicago Historical Society, John Brown Family Histories and Biographies, Annie Brown Letters folder, in Box 2, GEE; *HLAGO*.

7. Jo Ann Webb, "From obscurity, an African American photographer's life comes into focus," *Smithsonian Institution Research Report* 97 (Summer 1999), 3; Hinton, *John Brown and His Men*, 27; *Life and Times of Frederick Douglass*, 277, 278–79; "Subterranean Pass Way": compare *TPTL*, 64, where it is suggested that "SPW" represented Brown's own scheme, and Quarles, *Allies for Freedom*, 18, who says: "In Springfield one branch of the underground railroad had a name of its own, the Subterranean Passage Way"; JB to JBJr, May 15, 1847, in NYPL/KOHNS; After his primary education with the Brown children, George Delamater studied at Oberlin College, then studied law and was admitted to the bar in 1847. Later in life he was a publisher and manufacturer. CSG's notes on

George B. Delamater (1821–1907) from *History of Crawford County, Pennsylvania*, Box 4, GEE; JB to JBJr, April 24, 1848, Folder 1, Box 1, JB2.

8. Willard B. Gatewood Jr., *Free Man of Color: The Autobiography of Willis Augustus Hodges* (Knoxville: University of Tennessee Press, 1982), xli–xlii, 76–78; *The Ram's Horn* (Vol. 1:43) (November 5, 1847) microfilm version (Washington, D.C.: Library of Congress Photoduplication Service, 1947); no copy of "Sambo's Mistakes" in *The Ram's Horn* is extant, though a copy (actually an early form of carbon copy, or letterpress book) in Brown's hand was found among his papers after the Harper's Ferry raid, and is today held by the Maryland Historical Society, Baltimore. I quote from the version found in Villard, *John Brown*, 659–61; KM's notes on letter from ABA to Richard Hinton, February 15, 1893, Hinton Papers, KSHS, in J.B. Anecdotes folder, Box 3, OGV; Jane Rhodes, *Mary Ann Shadd Cary: The Black Press and Protest in the Nineteenth Century* (Bloomington: Indiana University Press, 1998), 22; Quarles, *Allies for Freedom*, 21; W. E. B. DuBois, *John Brown* (New York: International Publishers, 1909), 99–100; Redpath, *The Public Life of Capt. John Brown*, 59.

9. KM's handwritten copy of letter from JB to Joshua R. Giddings, June 22, 1848, in JB Letters Through 1854 folder, Box 4, OGV. Also see *JBR*, 65–66; KM's handwritten copy of letter from John Brown to Joshua R. Giddings, September 7, 1848, in JB Letters Before 1854 folder, Box 4, OGV; Land, "John Brown's Ohio Environment," 33–35; Quarles, *Black Abolitionists*, 225; Harding, *There Is a River*, 112–13; Filler, *The Crusade Against Slavery*, 164–65; Mary Kay Ricks, "Escape on the Pearl," *Washington Post* (August 12, 1998), H 01; JB to JBJr, April 24, 1848, Folder 1, Box 1, JB2; JB to OB, January 10, 1849, OHS.

PART V

Epigraph: JB to JBJr et al., December 4, 1850, in Folder 5, Box 1, JB2.

NOTES TO CHAPTER 13

1. JBJr to FBS, March 27, 1885, Reel 2, STUT-MICRO; newspaper clipping, Lester A. Walton, "Harlem Negroes Honor Cane of John Brown" (December 8, 1929), Stutler Scrapbook, Reel 6, STUT-MICRO; *BFHC*, 124; "Thomas Thomas's Retirement; From the Famous Eating-House;" "Death of Thomas Thomas; Who Long Kept the Restaurant." When recounting Brown's later life, Thomas sometimes conflated events in his narration, but his recollection of Brown's Springfield years seems reliable; William H. Vary, "John Brown in Springfield," *Union* [Springfield, Mass.](ca. 1927), CVHM; *LLJB*, 64–65. Emphasis in the text; much has been made of a letter from industrialist Aaron Erickson to Gov. Henry Wise of Virginia after Brown's raid. Erickson recounted meeting Brown a decade earlier, describing him as naive, deluded, and insane—though

only in the context of his wool affairs. Of course Erickson represented the manufacturers and was fundamentally hostile toward P&B at the time. However, in 1859 Erickson was writing on behalf of "duty and humanity"—clearly hoping to save Brown from the death penalty by proving him insane. Though Erickson recognized that Brown was not a good businessman, by his own admission he was dishonest with Brown at the time they met, and his diminution of P&B's wool grading process likewise discredits his witness. See TRANS, Aaron Erickson to Henry A. Wise, November 8, 1859, in Tatham Papers folder, Box 17, OGV. In contrast, see *TPTL*, 57 and 372, n. 10.

2. BBS to CSG, August 16, 1957, 2, STUT-GEE.

3. BBS to CSG, April 4, 1953, 1, STUT-GEE; TRANS, JB to SP, March 17, 1848, in Letters through 1854 folder, Box 4, OGV; *JB-STUT*, 85; JBJr to FBS, March 17, 1885, #MS04-0050 A-D, STUT-WEB, and Reel 2, STUT-MICRO; Atkinson, "The Soul of John Brown," 637–38.

4. *LLJB*, 96–97; Atkinson, "The Soul of John Brown," 638; ENC/tr, "Gerrit Smith's Liberality," *Plattsburgh Republican* (October 10, 1846), in Folder 1, Green Box 4, GEE; John R. McKivigan, "The Frederick Douglass-Gerrit Smith Friendship and Political Abolitionism in the 1850s," in *Frederick Douglass: New Literary and Historical Essays*, Eric J. Sundquist, ed. (Cambridge: Cambridge University Press, 1995), 207–08, 212–14; Gatewood, *Free Man of Color*, xliii and xliv, n. 74; W[illis] A. H[odges], "The Smith Lands Again," *The Ram's Horn* (November 5, 1847), 2; *Proceedings of the National Convention of Colored People and Their Friends Held in Troy, N.Y., on the 6th, 7th, 8th, and 9th October, 1847* (Troy, N.Y.: J. C. Kirkland, 1847, reprinted in *Minutes of the Proceedings of the National Negro Conventions 1830–1864*, Howard H. Bell, ed. (New York: Arno Press, 1969).

5. Gatewood, *Free Man of Color*, xlv–xlvi; "Gerrit Smith's Land," J[ermaine] W. Loguen to James M. Smith, March 16, 1848, *North Star* (March 24, 1848), 2; Undated letter from JB, in "Movements of the Grantees of the City of Troy," *North Star* (November 10, 1848), 3; *Proceedings of the National Convention of Colored People . . . October, 1847*.

6. JB to WH, October 28, 1848, in "John Brown in Essex County," *Evening Post* [New York] (December 20, 1859), 1. Hereinafter, JB-WAH; Gatewood, *Free Man of Color*, xliii; ENC to CSG, March 14, 1970 and July 5, 1971, in Folder 1, Green Box 4, GEE; "Gerrit Smith's Land," *North Star* (December 8, 1848) 2–3; SaB to editor, "Wildest Scheme Father Ever Had—Salmon Brown On North Elba Venture," *Adirondack Enterprise* [Saranac Lake, N.Y.] (1913), Sanborn Scrapbook, Reel 5, STUT-MICRO; Edwin Cotter [Jr.], "The History of John Brown of North Elba," *Lake Placid News* (May 5, 2000), 9; excerpt from T. Addison Richard, *The Romance of American Landscape* (New York, 1854), 236, in note from Warder H. Cabury to CSG, June 4, 1964, in Folder 1, Green Box 4, GEE.

7. BBS's notes from letter of James McCune Smith to Gerrit Smith, February 6, 1850, annotated in the Calendar of the Gerrit Smith Papers, Syracuse University Library, General Correspondence, Vol. 1 (1819–46), #RP09-0095, STUT-WEB; "Census Notes," New York State Census, 1855, #RP09-0090 A-D, STUT-WEB; letter from Lyman E. Eppes, July 12, 1854, *Frederick Douglass' Paper* (July 21, 1854), 3; JB to WH, January 22, 1849, GLC 6615, in the Gilder Lehrman Collection, The Morgan Library, New York. Hereinafter, GLC. Also in JB-WAH; JB to WH, May 7, 1849, JB-WAH; JB to WH, May 22, 1849, Collector Code 0000, Accession #00A-00, Manuscript Society Information Exchange Database, Department of Archives and Manuscripts, University Libraries, Arizona State University, Tempe. Also in JB-WAH.

8. RBT to James H. Holmes, March 30, 1897, in Box 17, Tatham Papers, OGV; interview with marble worker B. A. Barrett in anonymous newspaper clipping, hand-dated as 1897, in J.B. Funeral and Burial folder, Box 3, OGV; Thomas W. Higginson, "Cheerful Yesterdays," *Atlantic Monthly* (May 1897), 675; Edwin Cotter, "A Visit to the Doctor—150 Years Ago," *Lake Placid News* [Lake Placid, N.Y.] (August 13, 1999); Edwin Cotter Jr., "John Brown in the Adirondacks," *Adirondack Life* (Summer 1972), 9; [Hattie Thomas?], "The John Brown Rocking Chair," a handwritten statement, ca. 1894, CVHM; TRANS, JB to SP, May 24, 1849, in Letters through 1854 file, Box 4, OGV; CSG/tr, Elizabeth Porter Gould, "John Brown at North Elba," *Outlook* (November 21, 1896), in North Elba file, Green Box 4, GEE; CSG, "The Browns at North Elba" (study notes), folder 14, Green Box 4, GEE; *LLJB*, 100; BBS to ENC, February 1, 1966, #RP03-0102 A-D, STUT-WEB; Atkinson, "The Soul of John Brown," 638; ENC, "Information taken from records in Courthouse at Elizabethtown, N.Y.," #RP09-0094, STUT-WEB; ENC to BBS, January 27, 1966, #RP03-0102 A-D, STUT-WEB; CSG, "Notes on Lot 95, North Elba, Home of John Brown," Folder 10, Green Box 4, GEE; CSG/tr, "Indenture Gerrit and Ann C. Smith to JB et al., November 9, 1849, from Essex County Record, Book GG, 265, in Folder 10, File 1, Green Box 4, GEE.

9. JB to OB, January 10, 1849, OHS; "John Brown in Essex County," *Evening Post* [New York] (December 20, 1859), 1; Typewritten transcript of anonymous article, "The John Brown Day at Lake Placid; Memories of the Adirondack Forest," STUT-MICRO; RBT in *LLJB*, 101; Quarles, *Allies for Freedom*, 24–25; Anonymous clipping, December 2, 1859, in JB Letters before 1854 folder, Box 4, OGV; Brown, "Wildest Scheme Father Ever Had—Salmon Brown on North Elba Venture"; CSG/tr, Gould, "John Brown at North Elba"; ENC to BBS, December 13, 1965, #RP03-0096 A-I, STUT-WEB.

10. Unlike other writings from John Brown quoted in this book, I have edited his notes for this sermon in order to provide a more flowing sense of

the message rather than an exact reproduction of Brown's tedious, overly punctuated document. See "Notes for a sermon, not dated," Reel 1, STUT-MICRO.

11. JaB and OB2 to JBJr and FrB, February 15, 1853, Folder 1, Box 2, JB2; Mary Lee, "John Brown Rests amid the Mountains," *New York Times Magazine* (October 20, 1929), 23; JB to JBJr, JaB, and FrB, December 4, 1850, Folder 5, Box 1, JB2.

NOTES TO CHAPTER 14

1. Richard H. Dana Jr., "How We Met John Brown: A Letter from R. H. Dana, Jr.," *Atlantic Monthly* (July 1871), 3–9. Also see RBT's recollections in *LLJB*, 101–02; ENC, "Census Notes," New York State Census, 1855, #RP09-0090 A-D, STUT-WEB; KM's notes on interview with Lyman Epps in "John Brown," *New York Tribune* (October 1886), John Brown Scrapbook #10, in J.H. Holmes folder, Box 10, OGV; handwritten note, "Biographical Information on Lyman Epps," MS06-0065 A-B, STUT-WEB; Lee, "John Brown Rests amid the Mountains," 6–7; TRANS, anonymous 1886 article, "John Brown in the Adirondacks," File 14, Folder 1, Green Box 4, GEE.

2. Letter from JB to SP, April 7, 1849, OHS; CSG/tr, JB to SP, May 1, 1849 [in Ms. E.5.1, Pt. 1, p. 2, Thomas W. Higginson Collection, Boston Public Library, Boston, Mass.]; Edward Morris, "John Brown, Wool Merchant," *Republican* [Springfield, Mass.] (August 1908), CVHM; *URIS*, 14. Some unauthorized wools were accidentally shipped to England and Brown did not realize this until he was in Europe. These may account for some of the ill–prepared wools that he later complained about in reporting to the wool growers. See CSG/tr, JB to SP, October 29, 1849, in JBOOK; KM/tr, JB to SP, May 24 and July 27, 1849, in JB Letters through 1854 folder, Box 4, OGV; *JB-STUT*, 88–90; handwritten family copy, dated September 24, 1849, of JB to JBJr, August 31, 1849, Folder 2, Box 1, JB2; based on 1849 European hotel bills from Brown family, in JB Letters through 1854 folder, Box 4, OGV; JB to JBJr, August 29, 1849, in *LLJB*, 72; Thomas Thomas to JBJr, August 15, 1849, Folder 2, Box 1, JB2; see *LLJB*, 70–73 for a summary of events and letters pertaining to Brown's European venture. There is no doubt that Brown was constantly thinking about military movements against slavery while on tour in Europe. But Sanborn imputes too much strategy and study to the tour, when it probably did little more than fuel Brown's imagination.

3. Cotter, "A Visit to the Doctor—150 Years Ago"; CSG/tr, JBJr to JB, September 18, 1849, in Folder 3, Box 8, GEE; CSG's notes, "Dr. David Ruggles' Water-Cure Establishment," based on entry in *History of the Negro in Medicine, International Library of Negro Life and History* (p. 24), in Folder 3, Box 8, GEE;

CSG/tr, MB to JBJr, November 8, 1849, Folder 3, Box 8, GEE. According to biographer Margaret Washington, Sojourner Truth was at Ruggles's "Water Cure" in the fall of 1849. Author's interview with Margaret Washington, May 10, 2001, New York City. I am grateful to Prof. Washington for the insight she provided on Ruggles and the poor health he suffered as a consequence of the racist abuse he faced as an activist. Note also that Ruggles "was jailed several times because of his frank criticism of the police who collaborated with slave hunters." Given what we know of the ongoing problem of constabulary racist violence, we can assume that Ruggles was not simply jailed but physically abused. See *The Life and Writings of Frederick Douglass*, Vol. 5, Philip S. Foner, ed. (New York: International, 1975), 524, n. 7; Thomas Thomas to JBJr, September 4, 1849, Folder 2, Box 1, JB2; Mayer, *All on Fire*, 305; "Northampton Water Cure," *North Star* (March 3, 1848), 3; Excerpt from MB to JBJr, September 25, 1849, in CSG's notes, "Mary A. Brown, a patient at David Ruggles' Water-Cure 1849," Folder 3, Box 8, GEE; JB to JBJr, November 9, 1849, Folder 3, Box 1, JB2; CSG/tr, JB to MB, December 22, 1849, in JBOOK.

4. FCCH, 40–52; Grace Goulder, "Grace Goulder's Ohio," *Plain Dealer* [Cleveland, Ohio] (August 24, 1952); OB to JBJr, December 2, 1850, Folder 5, Box 1, JB2.

5. Perkins and Brown circular, "Springfield, Mass.," Folder 3, Box 1, JB2; JB to JBJr, April 12, 1850, Folder 4, Box 1, JB2; CSG/tr, JB to MB, September 4, 1850, in JBOOK; RBT to JB, April 10, 1850, Reel 1, BR/KSHS; Gatewood, *Free Man of Color*, xlviii; Text of the Fugitive Slave Law in *The Underground Railroad: A Record of Facts, Authentic Narratives, Letters, Etc.*, William Still, ed. (Philadelphia, Pa.: People's Publishing, 1871), 343–48; CSG/tr, JB to MB, November 28, 1849, in JBOOK; CSG/tr, JB to MB, December 31, 1850, in JBOOK.

Notes to Chapter 15

1. T. S. Nash, "Personal Recollections of John Brown," *Essex County Republican* [*Keeseville, NY*], April 27, 1900, within letter of T. S. Nash, Osakis, Minnesota, to *The New Voice*, Chicago, Illinois, May 21, 1900, in J.B. Funeral and Burial folder, Box 3, OGV; W. U. Hensel, *The Christiana Riot and The Treason Trials of 1851: An Historical Sketch* (Lancaster, Pa.: New Era Printing, 1911), 5–11; "American Slavery Lecture No. VII, January 12, 1851," in *The Life and Writings of Frederick Douglass*, Vol. 5., 170–71, and 525, n. 10; *Springfield Republican*, October 15, 1850, quoted in *URIS, 2; BFHC*, 86–87. During the Civil War, Mars served as chaplain in a "colored brigade" stationed in North Carolina; "In and about Springfield; Colored Man's Varied Life," *Republican* [Springfield, Mass.] (December 10, 1896), 10, CVHM; JB to MB, January 17, 1851, in *LLJB*, 132; RBT quoted in Villard, *John Brown*, 75.

2. The biblical references for the Gileadite story are Judges 7:3 and 20:8. The

oldest published version of the Gileadite document is found in an 1870 article by abolitionist writer William Wells Brown. Brown seems to have transcribed the text directly from John Brown's original manuscript, retaining more of the author's script style than Franklin B. Sanborn, who also used the original manuscript for his 1883 publication. Since Sanborn took great liberties in editing and splicing Brown's documents in general, I preferred William Wells Brown's transcript. However, Brown omitted the Gileadite signatures while Sanborn retained many of them. The original document has been misplaced on the shelf of history, though hopefully not for good. Compare William Wells Brown, "John Brown and the Fugitive Slave Law," *Independent* [New York] (March 10, 1870), in J. B. in Springfield folder, Box 4, OGV; and *LLJB*, 124–27. One essential source refers to Thomas Thomas as having had "lieutenants" in the Gileadite movement. See entry for B. C. Dowling in *BFHC*, 48; "Historical Sketches of Springfield, No. 65," *Republican* [Springfield, Mass.] (March 29, 1953), CVHM; *URIS*, 4.

3. My study of the Gileadites of Springfield is based on the list provided in Sanborn's transcription, *LLJB*, 127, and a complementary list found in [Harry Andrew Wright], "John Brown's Fugitives; How They Hid in Springfield," *Republican* [Springfield, Ma.] (June 17, 1909), 13, in Box 4, J.B. in Springfield folder, OGV. I have checked the composite of information from these sources against *BFHC*, which is essential for studying black Springfield at the time of John Brown. As to aged Gileadites, Sanborn's transcript includes the name of John Strong, who appears in *BFHC* (nicknamed "Jack") as having lived in Monson and having married in 1806. If this is the same John Strong of the Gileadites, he was probably one of the older members of the organization, and would have been relied upon to do surveillance and relay information; William Green's slave narrative makes no mention of Brown but shares his assessment that the Fugitive Slave Law had ultimately "done a great deal of good" by increasing anti-slavery militancy. See *Narrative of Events in the Life of William Green (Formerly a Slave), Written by Himself* (Springfield [Mass.]: L. M. Guernsey, 1853), 9; Quarles, *Black Abolitionists*, 207–09; Brown, "John Brown and the Fugitive Slave Law"; see entry for John N. Howard in *BFHC*, 72; According to one Canadian researcher, there were a number of Gileadites in western Canada when John Brown visited that region in 1858, including one who met with Brown in Chatham, Ontario. James C. Hamilton, "John Brown in Canada," *Canadian Magazine* (December 1894), 126–27.

4. Thomas Whitson, "William Parker, The Hero of the Christiana Riot," *Lancaster County Historical Society*, Vol. 1 (1896–97), 32–34; Hensel, *The Christiana Riot*, 28–45, 100–24; Quarles, *Black Abolitionists*, 211–13; RBT to JBJr, under letter of Henry Thompson to same, January 14, 1852, Box 1, Folder 7, JB2.

5. CSG/tr, JB to MB, December 22, 1851, JBOOK; "Arrival of Kossuth in England," *Frederick Douglass' Paper* (November 20, 1851), 1; "Hungarian Sympathizers," *18th Annual Report of the Massachusetts Anti-Slavery Society* (rpt.

Westport, Conn.: Negro Universities Press, 1970), 49–51; Mayer, *All on Fire*, 416–17; "Lajos Kossuth," *Microsoft Encarta 98 Encyclopedia*; "Address of the Coloured People to Kossuth"; "Kossuth's Reply," *National Anti-Slavery Standard* (December 18, 1851), 3; "Kossuth and American Slavery," *Frederick Douglass' Paper* (December 15, 1851), 2; "Louis Kossuth," *20th Annual Report of the Massachusetts Anti-Slavery Society*, January 28, 1852 (rpt. Westport, Conn.: Negro Universities Press, 1970), 65–68; JB to Frederick Douglass, December 15, 1851, in *Frederick Douglass' Paper* (December 25, 1851), 3.

6. Letter from J[ermain] W. Loguen to Frederick Douglass, December 18, 1851, in *Frederick Douglass' Paper* (January 8, 1852), 2; Quarles, *Black Abolitionists*, 209–10; Letter of J[ermain] W. Loguen to Frederick Douglass, August 5, 1853, *Frederick Douglass' Paper* (August 12, 1853), 3; JB to Frederick Douglass, August 18, 1853, *Frederick Douglass' Paper* (August 26, 1853), 3.

PART VI

Epigraph: JB to FBS, February 24, 1858, in *LLJB*, at 445.

Notes to Chapter 16

1. *JB-STUT*, 90; JB to JBJr, November 4, 1850, Folder 5, Box 1, JB2; Villard, *John Brown*, 64–66; see letter of JB to "Messrs Loomis and Stanton," April 18, 1851, JBOOK. Also see CSG to BBS, February 28, 1953, and BBS to CSG, March 4, 1953, STUT-GEE.

2. JB to JBJr et al., December 4, 1850, Folder 5, Box 1, JB2; OB to JBJr, December 2, 1850, Folder 5, Box 1, JB2; the Browns left North Elba for Ohio in late March. See JB to JBJr, March 24, 1851, Folder 6, Box 1, JB2; JB to JBJr, April 12, 1850, Folder 4, Box 1, JB2; KM/tr, JB to MB, February 21, 1851, in Letters before 1854 folder, Box 4, OGV; JBJr to JB, December 1, 1850, Folder 5, Box 1, JB2; JBJr to JB, July 1, 1851, Folder 6, Box 1, JB2; KM/tr, JB to OB, May 23, 1850, in JB Letters before 1854 folder, Box 4, OGV; JaB to JBJr, September 26, 1852, Folder 7, Box 1, JB2.

3. Frederick's condition: *LLJB*, 202, Boyer, *The Legend of John Brown*, 455–56, CSG to BBS, February 28, 1953, BBS to CSG, March 4, 1953, and BBS to GEE, March 8, 1953, STUT-GEE; JB to JBJr, May 14, 1852, Folder 7, Box 1, JB2; KM's interview with Anna Perkins, December 12, 1908, in JB in Hudson, Franklin, and Kent folder, Box 4, OGV; JB to JBJr, July 20, 1852, *LLJB*, 150; KM/tr, JB to HT and RBT, July 20, 1852, in JB Letters before 1854 folder, Box 4, OGV; JB to JBJr, August 6, 1852, JBOOK; JB to RBT, August 10, 1852, in *LLJB*, 151; JB to JBJr and WHB, February 21, 1853, Folder 1, Box 2, JB2; RBT to JBJr, April 18, 1853, Folder 1, Box 2, JB2.

4. JB to JBJr, August 26 and September 23, 1853, #MS01-044 A-G, STUT-WEB. Also see *LLJB*, 45–51; FB2 to JBJr, May 25, 1853, Folder 1, Box 2, JB2;

JaB to JBJr and WHB, January 23, 1854, Folder 2, Box 2, JB2; JB to HT and RBT, June 30, 1853, *JBR*, 81; KM's interview with SaB, October 11–13, 1908, in JB Anecdotes, Box 3, OGV.

5. JBJr to HT and RBT, September 12, 1852, OHS; JaB to JBJr and WHB, February 8, 1853, Folder 1, Box 2, JB2; JaB and OB2 to JBJr and FrB2, February 15, 1853, Folder 1, Box 2, JB2; JaB to JBJr, March 13, 1853, Folder 1, Box 2, JB2; HT to JBJr and WHB, February 1, 1853, Folder 1, Box 2, JB2; "Frederick Douglass—Western Reserve College," *Frederick Douglass' Paper* (August 4, 1854), 3; KM's interview with George Perkins, December 12, 1908, in JB in Hudson, Franklin, and Kent folder, Box 4, OGV; Brown, "Personal Recollections of My Father, John Brown."

6. "50 Years a Detroiter—William Lambert" (April 29, 1890), clipping in Burton Collection; "Recollections of William Lambert, Negro," undated clipping, Scrapbook 1, Burton Collection, 19. All cited in BBS, "Research notes: John Brown in Detroit," #RP02-0193, STUT-WEB; Katherine DuPre Lumpkin, "'The General Plan Was Freedom': A Negro Secret Order on the Underground Railroad," *Phylon* [Atlanta University] (Vol. XXVIII) 1 (1967): 63–77; KM's notes on "Detroit Letter to *Cincinnati Commercial Gazette*" (February 5, 1886), John Brown Scrap Book #11, KSHS, in J.B. in Hudson, Franklin, and Kent folder, Box 4, OGV; W. A. Weygandt, "East Cleveland and John Brown," *Plain Dealer* [Cleveland, Ohio] (December 3, 1927); "Freedom's Railway; Reminiscences of the Brave Old Days of the Famous Underground Line," *Detroit Tribune* (January 17, 1886). Transcribed by Abdul-M Aquil for (and reprinted by) the Detroit Public Library, Burton Historical Collection.

7. OB to JB, December 4, 1849, Reel 1, BR/KSHS; JeB to SA, August 18, 1856, Folder 9, Box 3, AD/KSHS; OB to Frederick Brown, December 16, 1852, OB General, Box 1, Series II, GEE. Emendations of "ritious," "Persaverance," and "wright"; KM, "Talks with Miss Sarah Brown," September 16 and 20, 1908, in Miss Sarah Brown folder, Box 6, OGV.

8. JB to JBJr and WHB, February 21, 1853, Folder 1, Box 2, JB2; JB to JBJr, February 24, 1854, Folder 2, Box 2, JB2; JB to JBJr, April 3, 1854, Folder 2, Box 2, JB2; SaB, manuscript (1913), #MS05-0023 A-J, STUT-WEB; JBJr,"Recollections of Early Days in Kansas," Folder 6, Box 2, JB2; JB to JBJr, June 26, 1854, Folder 2, Box 2, JB2.

NOTES TO CHAPTER 17

1. Berwanger, *The Frontier Against Slavery*, 110–12.

2. Melton A. McLaurin, *Celia, A Slave* (New York: Avon Books, 1991), 63–64; BBS/tr, David R. Atchison to Jefferson Davis, September 24, 1854, Reel 3, STUT-MICRO.

3. Elmer L. Clarke, "Southern Interest in Territorial Kansas, 1854–58,"

*Collections of the Kansas State Historical Society* XV (1919–22), 358–63, 391; Franklin B. Sanborn, "Guess-Work History," intended for *Outlook*, Reel 3, BR/KSHS; W. L. Fleming, "The Buford Expedition to Kansas," *American Historical Review* (October 1900), 38–48.

4. William E. Connelley, *John Brown* (Topeka: Crane, 1900), 57–59; Villard, *John Brown*, 94–100; McLaurin, *Celia, A Slave*, 73.

5. Villard, *John Brown*, 101–35; Connelley, *John Brown*, 58; *TPTL*, 109, 119–21.

6. Connelley, *John Brown*, 139–41; KM's interview with A. H. Case, August 16, 1908, in Kansas Interviews folder, Box 11, OGV; *TPTL*, 126–37; Villard, *John Brown*, 189–215.

NOTES TO CHAPTER 18

1. "Samuel Lyle and Florella [*sic*] Brown Adair Family Collection," Collection #161 Description (Topeka: Kansas State Historical Society), 1–2; CSG/tr, SA to OB, April 28, 1855, in S. L. Adair Letters folder, Box 11, Series II, Brown-Gee Collection, GEE; CSG/tr, SA to OB, April 6, 1855, in S. L. Adair Letters, Folder 28, Gray Box 1, GEE. Hereinafter, SA-GEE; *TPTL*, 100–06.

2. Villard, *John Brown*, 84; KM's interview with WHB, November 30–December 3, 1908, in Mr. and Mrs. John Brown, Jr. folder, Box 6, OGV; JB to HT and RBT, September 30, 1854, in *JBR*, 86; JB to JBJr, August 21, 1854, in *LLJB*, 191; see JB to HT and RBT, February 13, 1855, in *LLJB*, 192, where he is encouraged by a good report from Adair in Kansas, and TRANS, JB to John Cook, February 13, 1854, in J.B. Letters before 1854, Box 4, OGV. JB writes that since "the most of a *Cattle man of my Boys*"— probably Frederick—was going to Kansas, his cows should be sold. Historians have misconstrued these letters as showing an early change in Brown's plans in favor of Kansas. Actually it seems Brown was more concerned to get cash for his family's return to North Elba. See *TPTL*, 86; Villard, *John Brown*, 84.

3. JBJr to JB, May 20, 1855, DREER; OB to SA, August 8, 1855, Folder 11, Box 3, AD/KSHS. Emendations of "spiret," "necessary," and "defence"; OB to JB, September 30, 1855, Reel 1, BR/KSHS. Emendations of "garding," "offencive," "bair," and "fruite."

4. Villard, *John Brown*, 87–88; JB to OB, October 19, 1855, Holograph file, Box 1, GEE; JB to MB, October 13–14, 1855, Reel 1, BR/KSHS; JB to MB, November 2, 1855, Reel 1, BR/KSHS.

5. CSG/tr, JB to OB, October 21, 1855 (under October 19, 1855), Gray Box 1, Folder 5, GEE; CSG/tr, JaB to OB, January 23, 1856, Gray Box 1, Folder 15, GEE; SA to OB, January 31, 1856, SA-GEE; JB to Orson Day, February 21, 1856 and JB to MB, April 7, 1856, Reel 1, BR/KSHS. In the latter JB quotes Deuteron-

omy 32:35; OB to SA, #MS05-0012, STUT-WEB; SA to OB, March 4, 1856, SA-GEE; SA to OB, March 26, 1856, SA-GEE; OB to JB, March 27, 1856, Reel 1, BR/KSHS.

6. TRANS, OliB to MB, February 4, 1856, in Oliver and Martha Brown folder, Box 6, OGV; Letter of JBJr, *Frederick Douglass' Paper* (April 4, 1856), #MS04-0081, STUT-WEB; KM's notes from anonymous article, "Early Reminiscences," Miami County Scrapbook, KSHS, in James Hanway folder, Box 9, OGV; KM's notes from O. C. Brown, "Pioneer Life in Kansas, 1854–1861," O. C. Brown papers, KSHS, in O. C. Brown folder, Box 6, OGV; KM's notes on Martin White's speech before the Territorial House of Representatives (late 1856 or early 1857), in Reverend Martin White folder, Box 18, OGV.

7. JB to OB, May 8, 1856, Gray Box 1, Folder 5, GEE; SA to OB, May 16, 1856, SA-GEE; JeB to JB et al., May 14, 1856, Folder 9, Box 3, AD/KSHS; SBH to SA and FBA, May 1856, Folder 4, Box 4, AD/KSHS. This letter reports the death of Owen Brown but is incorrectly dated May 6, two days prior to his death. Internal evidence suggests the letter may have been written over a week after Owen's death.

8. Descriptions of Owen Brown's last days and funeral: JeB to JB et al., May 14, 1856, Folder 9, Box 3, AD/KSHS; SBH to SA and FBA, May 1856, Folder 4, Box 4, AD/KSHS; SBH to FBA [late May 1856], Folder 4, Box 4, AD/KSHS; MBD to SA and FBA, June 8, 1856, Folder 1, Box 4, AD/KSHS; We know that the Browns in Kansas had received word of Owen's death either on or before May 19 because Florilla wrote a letter to her sister Sally on that date, inquiring of more details concerning her father's death and burial. See above, SBH to FBA [late May 1856].

9. Despite variations in detail, there is ample testimony that John Brown and his sons infiltrated the Buford camp by posing as surveyors and ascertained that they expected to conduct some action against free-state men in Osawatomie. See SaB to J. Holmes, January 28, 1903, in Salmon Brown folder, Box 6, OGV; TRANS, Narrative of E. A. Coleman, Folder 2, Box 3, JB2; TRANS, JBJr, "Recollections of Early Days in Kansas," Folder 6, Box 2, JB2; SaB's handwritten statement, November 17, 1911, Reel 2, STUT-MICRO; and KM's interview with Henry Thompson, August 22 and September 1, 1908, Henry and Ruth Thompson folder, Box 17, OGV; Description of William Doyle and sons: recollections of settlers John Shore and John Manes in FBS, "The Early Days of Kansas, 1854–1861," *The Proceedings of the Massachusetts Historical Society* (May 1908), 471, 473–74; KM's interview with Henry Thompson, August 22 and September 1, 1908, in Henry and Ruth Thompson folder, Box 17, OGV.

10. Narrative by S. J. Shively, December 1, 1903, Reel 2, BR/KSHS; Leon Huhner, "Some Jewish Associates of John Brown," *Magazine of History with Notes and Queries* (September 1908): 143–51, in Brown Papers; Pamphlets folder, Box 21, OGV; KM's notes from "Statement of Horace Haskell Day, Oct.

10, 1894," from Holmes's Diary, in J. H. Holmes folder, Box 10, OGV; "Fought Over Again: Veterans of Battle of Blackjack Recall the Day; One is John Brown's Son," *Morning Oregonian* (September 3, 1903), in August Bondi folder, Box 2, OGV; Martin Litvin, *The Journey* (Galesburg, Ill.: Galesburg Historical Society, 1981), 132; August Bondi, "With John Brown in Kansas," *Transactions of the Kansas State Historical Society* 1903–04 (Topeka: Clark, State Printer, 1904): 275–89. According to Bondi, Weiner had owned a 4,000-acre property in Shreveport, La. and was a former slave owner. See "Fought Over Again" and KM's notes, "Memoir of Bondi from the Kansas State Hist. Society, A. Bondi Papers," in August Bondi folder, Box 2, OGV; *TPTL*, 97–98; Sanborn, "The Early Days of Kansas," 471; TRANS of W. Connelley's interview with Montgomery Shore, June 4, 1892, Reel 2, BR/KSHS.

11. Brown's foremost biographer writes: "The evidence that open hostility existed between the proslavery and free-state factions on the Pottawatomie and that the Wilkinson-Sherman-Doyle faction flung threats and insults at their free-state rivals seems quite convincing." *TPTL*, 382, n. 24; handwritten statement of Wilbur D. West, November 8, 1894, witnessed by James H. Holmes, in Pottawatomie folder, Box 14, OGV; KM's notes from Holmes's interview with Wilbur Dennis West, Holmes' Diary, in Pottawatomie folder, Box 14, OGV; reiterating Villard (p. 178), Oates reasons that if the free-state men in Osawatomie "regarded the local proslavery faction as a truly dangerous threat, they would never have left their families and the older free-state settlers and marched off on a mission that could well keep them away for days, perhaps weeks" (*TPTL*, 126); SA to SBH, September 15, 1956, SA-GEE.

12. SA to OB, May 16, 1856, SA-GEE; KM's interview with JaB, December 13–14, 1908, Jason Brown folder, Box 2, OGV. Unfortunately, Oates proposes the notion of John Brown holding some wizard-like "spell" on his sons and the others who joined him in the Pottawatomie killings. The myth of John Brown's "spell" is the only way to explain the event without acknowledging the fact that free-state men along the Pottawatomie had an evidential and experiential basis for believing themselves in danger; swords: see Luke Parsons to J. Hays Beach, March 23, 1913, Reel 3, BR/KSHS; Pottawatomie killings: *TPTL*, 132–37; Villard, *John Brown*, 153–67; KM's interview with JaB, December 13–14, 1908; SaB to FBS, November 17, 1911, Reel 2, STUT-MICRO; SaB to William E. Connelley, May 28, 1913, Reel 2, STUT-MICRO; KM's interview with Henry Thompson, August 22 and September 1, 1908, in Henry and Ruth Thompson folder, Box 17, OGV.

13. Statement by JaB to F. G. Adams, April 2, 1884, in Frederick Brown folder, Box 2, OGV; JaB quoted in "Pottawatomie," *Journal* [Lawrence, Kan.] (February 12, 1880), in Jason Brown folder, Box 2, OGV; KM's interview with JaB, December 28, 1908, in Jason Brown folder, Box 2, OGV.

14. The foremost attack on JB in the later nineteenth century came from his former Kansas ally, G. W. Brown, *Reminiscences of Old Brown: Thrilling Incidents of Border Life in Kansas* (Rockford, Ill.: Abraham Smith, 1880), and David N. Utter, "John Brown of Osawatomie," *North American Review* (November 1883), 435–46.

15. KM's interview with Henry Thompson and Mary E. Thompson, August 22 and September 1, 1908, in Henry and Ruth Thompson folder, Box 17, OGV. Emphasis by KM. In order to discredit Brown further, his critics allege that the Pottawatomie killings brought about civil war in Kansas. Pro-slavery reprisals were probably exacerbated as a result of the killings, but given the political intentions of the territorial regime (and the terrorists assisting them), the acceleration of attacks upon free-state men was inevitable. Pro-slavery terrorism had flourished with no interference from Washington D.C. as long as free-state settlers were essentially nonviolent. When the free-state side finally resorted to counter-terrorism, not only were pro-slavery thugs effectively challenged, but the federal government was obligated to enforce the democratic process. See Mary Grant statement no. 9, in KM's "Opinions' on the killings," in Pottawatomie folder, Box 14, OGV; KM/tr, John Shimmons, "Pottawatomie Provoked Retaliation?" *Daily Journal* [Lawrence, Kan.] (December 4, 1859), in Pottawatomie folder, Box 14, OGV; and TRANS, John Brown Jr., "John Brown of Osawatomie—A History, Not an Apology," *Cleveland Leader* (November 29, 1883), in Mr. and Mrs. John Brown Jr. folder, Box 6, OGV.

PART VII

Epigraph: JB in Delamater, "John Brown of Civil War Fame Was a Pioneer Resident of Titusville Section of Crawford," 3.

NOTES TO CHAPTER 19

1. KM's notes from letter of Martin White, January 14, 1860, in *Standard* [Bates Co., Missouri], in Reverend Martin White folder, Box 18, OGV; CSG/tr, E. P. Gould, "John Brown at North Elba," *Outlook* (November 21, 1896), in N. Elba folder, Green Box 4, GEE; Villard, *John Brown*, 357; Anonymous note, "Holmes Dear," in Frederick Brown folder, Box 2, OGV; KM's notes, James Hanway to Richard Hinton, December 5, 1859, in J. Hanway folder, Box 9, OGV; handwritten document by James G. Blunt, Reel 2, BR/KSHS; TRANS, Edward Bridgman, "The Battle of Osawatomie," May 25, 1910, Reel 3, BR/KSHS; Samuel LePage, "Memories of John Brown of Osawatomie," *Current History* (June 1928), 429; Edward P. Bridgman and Luke F. Parsons, *With John Brown in Kansas: The Battle of Osawatomie* (Madison, Wis.: Davidson, 1915), 5; TRANS, Luke F. Parsons, "John Brown," April 21, 1913, Reel 3, BR/KSHS.

2. Rossbach, *Ambivalent Conspirators*, 15–17, 21–22, 26–28, 56–58, and 91–93; George Marsden, "Theodore Parker," *DCC*, 748–49; Villard, *John Brown*, 271–72; KM's notes from John W. Chadwick, *Theodore Parker: Preacher and Reformer* (Boston: Houghton, Mifflin, 1900), in Theodore Parker folder, Box 14, OGV; "Many Bought Rifles Here for John Brown," *Republican* [Springfield, Mass.] (April 14, 1943), CVHM; JBJr to FBS, March 27, 1885, Reel 2, STUT-MICRO; Brown and Garrison met in the home of Theodore Parker in January 1857, but the only recollection comes from Garrison's sons. Theologically speaking, neither man would have limited a biblical defense to one testament. The real difference between them was a matter of interpretation, not text. See Villard, *John Brown*, 271–72; Mayer, *All on Fire*, 475; KM, "Talks with Miss Sarah Brown," September 16 and 20, 1908, in Miss Sarah Brown folder, Box 6, OGV.

3. TRANS, "General" Carrington, "The Boy's Promise," for *The Christian Register*, in Anecdotes folder, Box 3, OGV; Letter of Walter Brown to Dwight Kilbourn, May 2, 1900, in "One Hundredth Anniversary of John Brown's Birth Celebrated," *Register* [Torrington, Conn.] (May 10, 1900, in Sanborn Scrapbook, Reel 5, STUT-MICRO; George Sigler, "A Brief History of My Life and Labors" (ca. 1890). Courtesy of Natalie and Richard Smith; KM/tr, OliB to MB et al., May 16, [1857], in Oliver Brown and Martha His Wife folder, Box 6, OGV; JeB to SA, December 7, 1856, Folder 9, Box 3, AD/KSHS; SA to JeB, March 12, 1857, SA-GEE; SA to JeB, June 26, 1857, SA-GEE; JB to MB, March 31, 1857, *JBR*, 103.

4. Villard, *John Brown*, 288–309. It should be noted that the quiet that prevailed in Kansas in 1857 was hardly the end of problems, and the pro-slavery element continued to struggle to subvert the democratic process in the territory. Violent episodes occurred especially on the border of Missouri, and even with a majority opposed to slavery, Kansas was not admitted to the Union as a free state until 1861; JB to Heman Humphrey, April 18, 1857, JBOOK; *TPTL*, 200–01, 211–12, 217–18.

5. JB to TWH, February 2, 1858, JBOOK; Charles Douglass to Oswald Villard, July 27, 1908, in Frederick Douglass folder, Box 7, OGV; Quarles, *Frederick Douglass*, 173; JB to JBJr, February 4, 1858, Folder 3, Box 2, JB2; James Gloucester to JB, February 19, 1858, OHS; John Brown, *Provisional Constitution and Ordinances for the People of the United States*. Preface by Boyd Stutler (Weston, Mass.: M&S Press, 1969). See page 6 for Stutler's analysis; *Life and Times of Frederick Douglass*, 279–81; according to Martin Delany, when Brown presented the Provisional Constitution to him in Chatham, he referred to the Mormons and Native Americans as examples. According to TWH, Brown also "explained" to him and others the notion of emulating "the Maroons of Jamaica and Surinam." See Frank A. Rollin [Frances E. Rollin Whipper], *Life and Public Services of Martin R. Delany* (Boston: Lee and Shepard, 1883; rpt. New York: Arno Press/New York Times, 1969), 89; and Higginson, "Cheerful Yesterdays," 673.

6. *Life and Times of Frederick Douglass*, 319–21; JB to JBJr, Februrary 20, 1858, Folder 3, Box 2, JB2; JB to MB et al., February 24, 1858, in OHS; F[ranklin] B. Sanborn, *Recollections of Seventy Years,* Vol. 1 (Boston: The Gorham Press, 1909), 145–47; Edwin Morton quoted in letter of FBS, "The John Brown Anniversary," *Republican* [Springfield, Mass.] (May 10, 1900), in J.B. Anecdotes folder, Box 3, OGV; JB to MB et al., January 30, 1858, *JBR*, 109–10; JB to MB, March 2, 1858, OHS; *TPTL*, 230–32; "Charles Stuart (1783–1865)," in "Tales of the Early Republic," http://www.earlyrepublic.net/BIOG-S.htm; Fred Landon to BBS, December 12, 1951, #RP07-0064 A-G, STUT-WEB.

7. Robin W. Winks, *The Blacks in Canada: A History* (Montreal: McGill-Queen's University Press, 1971), 144, 149, 155, 218, 251, 270; James C. Hamilton, "John Brown in Canada," *Canadian Magazine* (December 1894), 125; Frank P. Stearns, "John Brown and His Eastern Friends," *New England Magazine* (July 1910), 116–17; Conrad, *Harriet Tubman*, 115–16; JB to JBJr, April 8, 1858, in *LLJB*, 452. While Brown's reference to Tubman in masculine terms would be offensive today, nineteenth-century abolitionists generally equated the "masculine ideal" with black strength and self-determination. Early womanists like Mary Ann Shadd Cary and Maria Stewart also evoked "masculinity as the ultimate symbol of black power and authority" while opposing gender discrimination. See Rhodes, *Mary Ann Shadd Cary*, 63.

8. "John Brown Advertisement," #RP02-0183 AB, STUT-WEB; Victor Lauriston, "House, Historical Site," *Daily News* [Chatham, Ontario] (November 12, 1932), in Stutler Scrapbook 10, Reel 7, STUT-MICRO; Quarles, *Allies for Freedom*, 43; Rhodes, *Mary Ann Shadd Cary*, 129–31; Victor Lauriston, "Samson in the Temple," *Canadian Magazine* (June 1932), 9–10; Quarles, *Black Abolitionists*, 215; Rollin, *Life and Public Services of Martin R. Delany*, 85–86; Hamilton, "John Brown in Canada," 125; Victor Lauriston, "When Chatham Made History," *Chatham Daily News* (May 8, 1958), and J. W. Mustard, "Kentiana: John Brown, Abolitionist," *Chatham Daily News* (May 5, 1923), in Stutler Scrapbook 10, Reel 7, STUT-MICRO.

9. Note the problematic assessment of the convention attenders by Nicolay and Hay, Abraham Lincoln's secretaries, who referred to them as Brown's "adventurers, mostly boys in years and waifs in society," or black "spectators" enthralled by Brown's "rhapsodical talk." Quoted in Stanley J. Smith, "Chatham Area Residents Backed John Brown in Move to End Slavery," *Free Press* [London, Ontario] (May 10, 1958), in Stutler Scrapbook 10, Reel 7, STUT-MICRO; TRANS, Charles W. Moffett quoted in "John Brown: A Reunion of His Surviving Associates," *Topeka Capital* (October 24, 1882), #RP02-0228, STUT-WEB; TRANS, James M. Jones quoted in *Cleveland Herald* (ca. 1880), in Stutler Scrapbook 5, Reel 7, STUT-MICRO; for accounts of the Chatham convention, see DuBois, *John Brown*, 253–72; Hinton, *John Brown and His Men*, 170–90; *TPTL*, 243–47; and Villard, *John Brown*, 329–38. Minutes from the convention

proceedings were published in Osborne P. Anderson, *A Voice from Harper's Ferry: A Narrative of Events at Harper's Ferry* (Boston, 1861), 10–13. Hereinafter, *VFHF*.

## NOTES TO CHAPTER 20

1. William P. Phillips, "Three Interviews with Old John Brown," *Atlantic Monthly* (December 1879), 740, 743–44; M.H.F., "A Brave Life," *Atlantic Monthly* (October 1885), 362; FBS, "The Virginia Campaign of John Brown," *Atlantic Monthly* (March 1875), 329; Alfred L. Donaldson, *A History of the Adirondacks Vol. 2* (New York: Century, 1921), 12; Thomas W. Higginson, *Contemporaries* (Boston: Houghton, Mifflin, 1899), 238; Elza Maxson quoted in Jeanette Mather Lord, "John Brown—They Had a Concern," *West Virginia History* (April 1959), 171–73; Ransom L. Harris, "John Brown and His Followers in Iowa," *Midland Monthly* (October 1894), 266; Gerrit Smith quoted in FBS, "The Virginia Campaign of John Brown," Part IV (May 1875), 599.

2. Villard, *John Brown*, 367–90; *TPTL*, 261–68; TRANS, Statement by Luke F. Parsons to J. H. Beach, April 21, 1913, Reel 3, BR/KSHS; JB to *New York Tribune*, January [7,] 1859, in *JBR*, 114–15; "Rescue of Missouri Slaves as told by James Townsend," Reel 2, BR/KSHS; "Testimony of George B. Gill," in George Gill folder, Box 8, OGV; Hamilton, "John Brown in Canada," 123; KM's notes from "Mrs. John Brown," *Chicago Times* (September 1, 1882), in J.B. Slave Raid folder, Box 5, OGV; Harris, "John Brown and His Followers in Iowa," 265; Quarles, *Allies for Freedom*, 59–60.

3. KM's notes from "Recollections of John Brown," *Capital* [Topeka, Kan.] (July 21, 1882), in J.B. Slave Raid folder, Box 5, OGV; TRANS, FBS to TWH, January 19, 1859, in Higginson Collection folder, Box 9, OGV; Quarles, *Allies for Freedom*, 60–61; BBS's notes on Richard J. Hinton, "John Brown and His Men," *Leslie's Popular Monthly* (June 1889), #RP02-0190 and -0193, STUT-WEB.

4. TRANS, "Statement of Annie Brown," November 1866, Brown Family Histories, Annie Brown Letters folder, Box 2, GEE; BBS to Dudley Weaver, April 5, 1954, #RP05-0039 A-D, STUT-WEB; Villard, *John Brown*, 401; J. H. Galbraith, "When John Brown Left Ohio for the Last Time," *Columbus Dispatch* (August 13, 1933); Ralph R. Gurley, *Life of Jehudi Ashmun* (James C. Dunn, 1835; rpt. New York: Negro Universities Press, 1969), 62, 64, 252; Anderson, *A Voice from Harper's Ferry*, 23–24; Lauriston, "House, Historical Site";Smith, "Chatham Area Residents Backed John Brown in Move to End Slavery."

5. Frederick Lloyd, "John Brown Among the Pedee Quakers," *Annals of Iowa* (April 1866), 668; *VFHF*, 24–25; detailed descriptions of Brown's men and their sequestered lifestyle prior to the raid in *TPTL*, 274–89; Barclay Coppoc to AB[A], January 13, 1860, in Edwin and Barclay Coppoc folder, Box 7, OGV; Villard, *John Brown*, 403–25 and 678–87; see John Copeland folder, Box 7, OGV; Lewis Leary folder, Box 12, OGV; KM's interview with Charley Garlick, January 2,

1909, in J.B. in Cleveland . . . Thence folder, Box 4, OGV; KM/tr, Watson Brown to Isabel Brown, undated, in Watson Brown folder, Box 6, OGV; KM/tr, Harriet Newby to Dangerfield Newby, August 16, 1859, in Dangerfield Newby folder, Box 13, OGV. Edited by author; KM's notes from *Reminiscences of Lucy N. Colman* (Buffalo, N.Y.: H. L. Grier, 1891), 86, in Shields Green folder, Box 8, OGV; KM's notes from *Cleveland Weekly Plain Dealer* (October 19, 1859), in Shields Green folder, Box 8, OGV; Hamilton, "John Brown in Canada," 131; Quarles, *Allies for Freedom*, 85 and 211, n. [57] and 58.

6. Douglass, *Life and Times of Frederick Douglass*, 322–25; KM's interview with SaB, October 11–13, 1908, in Frederick Douglass folder, Box 7, OGV; KM's interview with ABA, October 2 and 3, 1908, in Frederick Douglass folder, Box 7, OGV; KM, "Talks with Miss Sarah Brown," September 16 and 20, 1908, in Miss Sarah Brown folder, Box 6, OGV; KM's interview with HT, August 22 and September 1, 1908, in Henry and Ruth Thompson folder, Box 17, OGV; Jean Libby to author, March 15, 2001, concerning her interview with Brown descendant, Beatrice Keesey in December 1976; Quarles, *Allies for Freedom*, 78–79, 210, n. 37 and 38; KM's notes from "Owen Brown's Story of taking Shields Green to Kennedy Farm," in Oliver Brown and Martha His Wife folder, Box 6, OGV; Letter from FD, October 31, 1859, *Rochester Democrat?*, Sanborn Scrapbook, Reel 5, STUT-MICRO; KM/tr, speech of Mrs. Thomas Russell [*sic*], January 11, 1908, in Judge Thomas Russell folder, Box 15, OGV; JBJr to FBS, April 21, 1885, Box 4, NYPL/ANTHONY.

7. William Parker Neal, "History of Emmanuel Chapel," Marjory Blubaugh, ed., unpublished essay, Mont Alto, Pennsylvania, 1970; E. V. Collins, "The Episcopal Church in the Cumberland Valley," *Kittochtinny Historical Papers* (VI), 65–66; Virginia Ott Stake, *John Brown in Chambersburg* (Chambersburg, Pa.: Franklin County Heritage, 1977), 16–17, 65–66; "John Brown's Kin May Meet at Harper's Ferry," *Kansas City Star* (August 29, 1930), in Stutler Scrapbook 3, Reel 6, STUT-MICRO; "John Brown Changed Slavery Issue from Cold to Hot War," *Capitol News* [Harrisburg, Pa.] (July 17, 1950); KM's interview with JaB, December 28, 1908, in Jason Brown folder, Box 2, OGV; *LLJB*, 531; Stearns, "John Brown and His Eastern Friends," 117; the closing biblical text cited is John 3:14, King James Version. Also see Numbers 21:4–9.

NOTES TO CHAPTER 21

1. Jean Libby, "The Harper's Ferry Slave Insurrection—1859" (mss. 1985), 1–7, 32; "TRANS, "Conversation with [C.P. Tidd]," February 10, 1860, in TWH Collection (No. 167: Vol. 2), Boston Public Library, in Higginson Collection folder, Box 9, OGV. Unfortunately, narratives about the raid have often been influenced by pro-slavery versions that minimize or altogether deny the involvement of local slaves in the raid. Osborne Anderson, one of the few raiders to escape, demonstrates that Brown was well-received by slaves in Virginia and Maryland,

and took offense at the claim that the slaves had been uninvolved. See *VFHF*, 59–62. Two examples of pro-slavery propaganda about slave involvement are Alexander Boteler, "Recollections of the John Brown Raid by a Virginian Who Witnessed the Fight," *Century* (July 1883), 401; and Rayburn S. Moore, "John Brown's Raid at Harper's Ferry: An Eyewitness Account by Charles White" [November 10, 1859], *Virginia Magazine of History and Biography* (October 1959), 389–91; Alfred M. Barbour to Roger A. Pryor, April 2, 1860, *Pennsylvania Magazine of History and Biography* (1918), 175–76. For narratives about the Harper's Ferry raid, see *TPTL*, 290–309; FBS, "The Virginia Campaign of John Brown" *Atlantic Monthly* (January–May 1875); Villard, *John Brown*, 426–66; and William C. Everhart and Arthur L. Sullivan, *John Brown's Raid* (National Park Service History Series. Washington, D.C.: Office of Publications, National Park Service, 1974).

2. FBS, "Notes and Comments II," *North American Review* (January 1886), 115–16; Jean Libby, "The Slaves Who Fought with John Brown" (mss., September 1988), 22, 28–31; Willard C. Gompf, "John Brown's Raid by One Who Saw It," *New York Times* (October 13, 1929), 12XX; John E. Daingerfield, "John Brown at Harper's Ferry," *Century* (June 1885), 265–67; Israel Green, "The Capture of John Brown," *North American Review* (December 1885), 564–69; Murat Halstead, "The Tragedy of John Brown," *Independent* [New York] (December 1, 1898), 1545. Brown had "three sword-stabs in his body, and one sabre-cut over the heart." See *The Life, Trial and Execution of Captain John Brown* (New York: Robert M. De Witt, 1859), 58. Elsewhere Brown distinguished the wounds as "sabre cuts on my head and bayonet stabs in different parts of my body." See *JBR*, 124; "Scientific" mutilation of blacks was a common act of political terrorism in the South, and was certainly evident in the response to the black raiders. Libby, "The Slaves Who Fought with John Brown," 29–31; and Libby, "The Harpers Ferry Slave Insurrection—1859," 38–39; "John Brown and Oberlin," *Oberlin Alumni Magazine* (February 1932 reprint), in articles folder, Box 19, OGV.

3. "John Brown's Raid; Related by a Kentucky Gunsmith Who Was Master Armorer at Harper's Ferry," *Courier-Journal* [Lexington, Ky.], no date, in the Gunther Collection folder, Box 8, OGV; *JBR*, 121, 124–26; TRANS, George Sigler, "A Brief History of My Life and Labors" (ca. 1890), 8–9. Also see George Sigler to Daniel Breneman, June 15, 1912, in Folder 10, Box 3, AD/KSHS; Boteler, "Recollections of the John Brown Raid," 411; KM's notes from memoir of George Leech, Methodist Episcopal Church, Baltimore Conference, in JB First Days in Charlestown Jail folder, Box 4, OGV; *The Life, Trial and Execution of Captain John Brown*, 59–60. One scholar contends that Brown "reinvented" himself by revising the intention of the raid, and had "no respect for Southern property or for the lives of slaveowners." However, he trusts Villard's problematic interpre-

tation as well as presuming that slavemasters' rights over their chattel transcended human rights. Steven Lubet, "John Brown's Trial" (mss., 2000), 18; *VFHF*, 61. Osborne Anderson gently criticized Brown for allowing humanitarian "sympathies" to cloud his thinking at a critical hour in the raid. Yet Anderson later suggested that Brown had elevated "Insurrection" in a "progressive" manner (p. 8), not just strategically, but in an intelligent respect for freedom.

4. *JBR*, 126; See KM's "JB's Jail Schedule," in JB First Days in Charlestown Jail folder, Box 4, OGV; and "Jail Chronology," in JB in Charlestown Jail folder, Box 4, OGV; KM's notes from interview with JB in *Baltimore American and Commercial Advertiser*, October 24, 1859; and KM's notes on interview question sheet for the *Independent Democrat*, and JB's answers, November 22, 1859, both in JB First Days in Charlestown Jail folder, Box 4, OGV; KM's notes from anonymous article, "A Visit to John Brown," November 1859, in Francis J. Garrison folder, Box 8, OGV; William Fellows, "Saw John Brown Hanged," *New York Sun* (February 13, 1898), 2.

5. S.A.B. to JB, no date, in W. W. Scott (ed.), "The John Brown Letters," *Virginia Historical Magazine* (April 1903), 387–89; and "P.C.W." to JB, October 31, 1859, in "The John Brown Letters" (October 1902), 164; Boyd B. Stutler, "John Brown's Lost Carpet Bag," *Manuscripts* (Summer 1959), 3–5; JB to MB et al., October 31, 1859, in *JBR*, 128–29; JB to MB et al., November 8, 1859, in *JBR*, 132–33; JB to MB, November 10, 1859, in JB Jail Letters 1859 folder, Box 5, OGV; KM's notes from letters from TWH to J. Miller McKim, November 5, 10, and 12, 1859, in Meetings of Sympathy and Repudiation in the North folder, Box 12, OGV; JB to MB, November 16, 1859, in *JBR*, 137–38; JB to James W. McFarland, November 23, 1859, in *JBR*, 145–46; H. L. Vaill to JB, November 8, 1859, in *Echoes of Harper's Ferry*, James Redpath, ed. (Boston: Thayer and Eldridge, 1860), 388–89; JB to H. L. Vaill, November 15, 1859, in Redpath, *The Public Life of Captain John Brown*, 354–55; A. M. M[illigan] to JB, November 23, 1859, in *Echoes*, 395–96; JB to A. M. Milligan, November 29, 1859, in *LLJB*, 610.

6. "Little Boy" to JB, November 27, 1859, in *Echoes of Harper's Ferry*, 403; Charles Partridge to JB, November 21, 1859, in *Echoes of Harper's Ferry*, 393–94; JB to "Mary" [Sally Marian Hand] and Martha [Davis], November 27, 1859, in *JBR*, 153; JB to MB et al., November 30, 1859, in *JBR*, 156–58; CSG, "John Brown's Religion," Box 11, GEE; William S. Rollins, "The Northeastern Religious Press and John Brown," *Ohio Archaeological and Historical Quarterly* (April 1952), 128–45; Scott, "The John Brown Letters" (April 1902), 394–95; KM's notes on Mayor Thomas Green's proclamation, November 23, 1859, in J.B. Execution folder, Box 3, OGV; KM's notes from "Maker of the Rope that Hanged John Brown," *Muscatine Daily Journal* (December 9, 1859), in JB Execution folder, Box 3, OGV; JB to MB, November 21, 1859, in *JBR*, 141; Jean Libby et

al., *John Brown Mysteries* (Missoula, Mont.: Pictorial Histories, 1999), 19 and n., and 25; JB to Andrew Hunter, November 22, 1859, in *JBR*, 144. This insight into JB's attempt to "cover up to save lives" is found in Libby, "The Slaves Who Fought with John Brown," 25.

7. MB to "Dear Children," November 28, 1859, Reel 1, BR/KSHS; RBT to JB, November 27, 1859, in *Meeting of the Massachusetts Historical Society* (February 1908): 330–31, in Gov. Henry Wise folder, Box 18, OGV; KM's notes on "Mrs. Brown and Her Family," *National Anti-Slavery Standard* (December 3, 1859), in Mrs. John Brown and Family folder, Box 6, OGV; KM's notes from anonymous article, "John Brown's Execution; Full Details by Eye Witness," in Francis J. Garrison folder, Box 8, OGV; Villard, *John Brown*, 550; Rebecca Hemphill to Oswald G. Villard, February 26, 1908, in JB Funeral and Burial folder, Box 3, OGV; Fragment from JB to MB, December 1, 1859, quoted in undated article in *San Francisco Chronicle*, in JB Jail Letters 1859 folder, Box 5, OGV; KM's notes from J. M. McKim to MB, December 2, [1860], in J.B. Early Days in Charlestown Jail folder, Box 4, OGV; Fellows, "Saw John Brown Hanged"; KM's interview with ABA, October 2 and 3, 1908, in Annie Brown Adams folder, Box 1, OGV; Charles A. Jellison, "The Martyrdom of John Brown," *Journal of West Virginia History* (18:4).

Notes to the Epilogue

1. TRANS, Lewis Sayre to Henry Wise, November 30, 1859, in Tatham Papers folder, Box 17, OGV; KM's note, "Dreer #114," in JB Funeral and Burial folder, Box 3, OGV; James T. Mitchell to Oswald G. Villard, November 27, 1907, in JB Funeral and Burial folder, Box 3, OGV; KM's notes, J. M. Ashley to J. Miller McKim, December 14, 1859, in Meetings of Sympathy and Repudiation in the North folder, Box 12, OGV; anonymous article, "Tilton as He Is Now," in JB Funeral and Burial folder, Box 3, OGV; KM's note on cotton cross, in J.B. Funeral and Burial folder, Box 3, OGV; Cotter, "John Brown in the Adirondacks," 11; Chapin, "The Last Days of Old John Brown," 331; Henry J. Kilbourn, "When John Brown's Body Came Home: Events that Hastened the Civil War," *Congregationalist and Christian World* (1910?), in Funeral and Burial folder, Box 3, OGV; Mary Lee, "John Brown Rests amid the Mountains," *New York Times Magazine* (October 20, 1929), 23; ABA to MBD, August 13, 1897, in folder 7, Box 3, AD/KSHS; Brown, "Personal Recollections of My Father, John Brown"; Anonymous article, "John Brown's Funeral Sermon," in JB Funeral and Burial folder, Box 3, OGV.

2. Stanley J. Smith, "Writer Seeks Clues to Activities of John Brown in Western Ontario," *Free Press* [London, Ontario, Canada] (July 7, 1956), in Stutler Scrapbook 10, Reel 7, STUT-MICRO; Du Bois, *John Brown*, 267, 293, 295, 345–46; Quarles, *Allies for Freedom*, 51, 53, 72–75; Hinton, *John Brown and His Men*, 162–63. "McCune Smith was a distinguished colored doctor, Scotland

educated, whom JB came to view with distrust later." BBS to CSG, February 11, 1952, 2, STUT-GEE; KM's notes, "Owen Brown's Story of Taking Shields Green to Kennedy Farm," in Oliver Brown and Martha His Wife folder, Box 6, OGV, there is some reason to believe that John Brown was also expecting more help, black and white, at Harper's Ferry, and is perhaps an unspoken reason why he overstayed. Canadian researcher Stanley Smith believed a force of blacks were turned back at Detroit because Brown had already moved on Harper's Ferry. See BBS to Fred Landon, October 18, 1956, #RP07-0082 A-F, STUT-WEB. Another source requiring critical examination claims Brown had definite interaction with armed blacks in Philadelphia regarding the raid, but their involvement was thwarted by indiscretion, much to Brown's dismay. See *Autobiography of Dr. William Henry Johnson* (Albany, N.Y.: Argus, 1900), 194–96. Though offering nothing to back it up, another writer claims reinforcements disappointed Brown at Harper's Ferry, leaving him confused and stubbornly clinging to his position. See Robert Shackleton Jr., "What Support Did John Brown Rely Upon?" *Magazine of American History* (April 1893), 351; "Lincoln in Kansas: Some Reminiscences of an Atchison Man Who Entertained Him in 1859," *Topeka Capital*, Connelley Scrapbook, Reel 4, STUT-MICRO; Cohen, *John Brown: "The Thundering Voice of Jehovah,"* 111; Gatewood, *Free Man of Color*, lvi.

# Selected Bibliography

Articles: Primary to the Study

Atkinson, Eleanor. "The Soul of John Brown: Recollections of the Great Abolitionist by His Son." *American Magazine* (October 1909): 633–43.

Bondi, August. "With John Brown in Kansas." *Transactions of the Kansas State
Historical Society* (1903–04): 275–89.

Brown, John. "Preparing Wool for Market." *Ohio Cultivator* [Columbus, Ohio]
(March 1, 1847): 34–35.

Brown, John Jr. "John Brown at Home; Some Incidents Showing His Natural
Kindness of Manner." *Akron Beacon* (January 12, 1881).

Brown, Salmon. "Personal Recollections of My Father, John Brown." *Evening
Telegraph* [Portland, Oregon] (October 20, 1906).

———. "My Father, John Brown." *Outlook* (January 25, 1913): 212–17.

———. "John Brown and Sons in Kansas Territory" (ca. 1918). *Indiana Magazine of History* (June 1935): 142–50.

Brown, William Wells. "John Brown and the Fugitive Slave Law." *The Independent* [New York](March 10, 1870).

Chapin, Lou V. "The Last Days of Old John Brown." *Overland Monthly* (April
1899): 322–32.

Cotter, Edwin Jr. "John Brown in the Adirondacks." *Adirondack Life* (Summer
1972): 8–12.

———. "A Visit to the Doctor—150 Years Ago." *Lake Placid News* [Lake Placid,
N.Y.] (August 13, 1999).

———. "The History of John Brown of North Elba." *Lake Placid News* (May 5,
2000): 9.

Daingerfield, John E. "John Brown at Harper's Ferry." *Century* (June 1885):
265–67.

Dana, Richard H., Jr., "How We Met John Brown." *Atlantic Monthly* (July
1871): 3–9.

Delamater, George B. "John Brown of Civil War Fame Was a Pioneer Resident of
Titusville Section of Crawford" (reprint of an 1888 memoir). *Enterprise-News*
[Cambridge Springs, Pa.] Historical Edition (November 12, 1931): 2.

Edison, Alice. "Grandson of Great Abolitionist Recalls Days of Slave Smuggling." *Akron Sunday Times* (August 1, 1926): D3.

Erf, Edward. "An Abolitionist." *Pittsburgh Post* (May 28, 1899).

Featherstonaugh, Thomas. "The Final Burial of the Followers of John Brown." *New England Magazine* (April 1901): 128–34.

Fellows, William. "Saw John Brown Hanged." *New York Sun* (February 13, 1898): 2.

Filler, Louis. "John Brown in Ohio: An Interview with Charles S. Griffing." *Ohio Archaeological and Historical Quarterly* (April 1949): 213–18.

Fletcher, Robert S. "John Brown and Oberlin." *Oberlin Alumni Magazine* (February 1932).

Gompf, Willard C. "John Brown's Raid by One Who Saw It." *New York Times* (October 13, 1929): 12XX.

Goulder, Grace. "John Brown Reunion; Clan Without Browns Gathers in Kent and Exchanges Legends of the Abolitionist." *Cleveland Plain Dealer* (August 10, 1958).

———. "The Brown Boyhood Years in Austere Hudson Molded Crusader against Slavery." *Cleveland Plain Dealer* (May 3, 1959).

Halstead, Murat. "The Tragedy of John Brown." *Independent* [New York] (December 1, 1898): 1543–48.

Hamilton, James C. "John Brown in Canada." *Canadian Magazine* (December 1894): 119–40.

Harlow, Ralph V. "Gerrit Smith and the John Brown Raid." *American Historical Review* (October 1932): 32–60.

Harris, Ransom L. "John Brown and His Followers in Iowa." *Midland Monthly* (October 1894): 262–68.

Higginson, Thomas W. "Cheerful Yesterdays." *Atlantic Monthly* (June 1897): 665–78.

Holm, J. B. "John Brown Was Resident of Kent; 100th Anniversary of Harper's Ferry Is Today." *Record-Courier* [Ravenna-Kent, Ohio] (October 16, 1959): 9.

Jack, Walter. "Famed Leader Lived in Ohio—N.W. Pennsylvania Area." *Jefferson Gazette* [Jefferson, Ohio] (July 5, 1949): 4.

"John Brown in Essex County." *Evening Post* [New York] (December 20, 1859): 1.

Ladd, James D. "The Immortal John Brown; His Wool Meeting at Steubenville." *Herald-Star* [Steubenville, Ohio] (June 13, 1904).

Land, Mary. "John Brown's Ohio Environment." *Ohio Archaeological and Historical Quarterly* (January 1948): 24–47.

Landon, Fred. "From Chatham to Harper's Ferry." *Canadian Magazine* [Toronto, Ontario] (October 1919): 441–48.

Lauriston, Victor. "Samson in the Temple." *Canadian Magazine* (June 1932): 9, 40–41.

Lee, Mary. "John Brown Rests amid the Mountains." *New York Times Magazine* (October 20, 1929): 23.

Lockley, Fred. "John Brown's Son Talks about His Father." *American Magazine* (May 10, 1919): 49–50.

Macy Smith, Narcissa. "Reminiscences of John Brown." *Midland Monthly* [Des Moines, Iowa] (September 1895): 231–36.

Mayo, Katherine. "John Brown's Raid 50 Years Ago." *New York Post* (October 16, 1909).

———. "Brown in Hiding and in Jail." *New York Post* (October 23, 1909).

———. "In an Angry City to Visit Brown." *New York Post* (October 30, 1909).

McFarland, Gerald W. "Squire Owen Brown of Hudson, Ohio." *Brown Family News and Genealogical Society* (April 1993): 1–4, 11.

Meyer, Howard N. "John Brown—and the Souls of White Folk." *Crisis* [New York] (May 1962): 265–70.

M. H. F. "A Brave Life." *Atlantic Monthly* (October 1885): 360–67.

"Owen Brown's Escape from Harper's Ferry." *Atlantic Monthly* (March 1874): 342–65.

Phillips, William P. "Three Interviews with Old John Brown." *Atlantic Monthly* (December 1879): 738–44.

Porter Gould, Elizabeth. "John Brown at North Elba." *Outlook* (November 21, 1896).

Sanborn, Franklin B. "John Brown in Massachusetts." *Atlantic Monthly* (April 1872): 420–33.

———. "John Brown and His Friends." *Atlantic Monthly* (July 1872): 50–61.

———. "The Virginia Campaign of John Brown" [five-part series]. *Atlantic Monthly* (January–May 1875): 16–24; 224–33; 323–31; 453–65; 591–600.

———. "John Brown's Family Compact." *Nation* (December 25, 1890): 500.

Scott, W. W. (ed.) "The John Brown Letters." *Virginia Historical Magazine* (April, July, and October 1902; January and April 1903): 385–95; 273–82; 161–76; 17–32; 383–89.

Stearns, Frank P. "John Brown and His Eastern Friends." *New England Magazine* (July 1910): 589–99.

Stutler, Boyd B. "John Brown's Last Visit to Western Virginia." *West Virginia Review* (April 1926): 228–29, 240–41.

———. "John Brown's Letter." *West Virginia History* [Charleston, W. Va.](October 1947): 1–25.

———. "John Brown Postmaster." *American Philatelist* (March 1953): 443–49.

———. "John Brown's Letters and Documents: A Scholarly Survey." *Manuscripts* (Fall 1954): 4–12.

———. "John Brown of Osawatomie—His Record as a Mason." *Wisconsin Freemason* (October 1955): 6–10.

———. "John Brown's Lost Carpet Bag." *Manuscripts* (Summer 1959): 2–7.

———. "John Brown and the Masonic Order." *Ohio History* (January 1962): 24–32.

Umrigar, Thrity. "Abolitionist Made Akron His Home; John Brown Rented from Col. Simon Perkins, Jr." *Akron Beacon Journal* (September 10, 2000).

Wright, Harry A. "John Brown in Springfield." *New England Magazine* (May 1894): 272–81.

———. "John Brown's Fugitives; How They Hid in Springfield." *Republican* [Springfield, Ma.] (June 17, 1909).

Articles: Background to the Study

Butler Jones, Katherine. "They Called It Timbucto." *Orion: People and Nature* (Winter 1998): 27–33.

DuPre Lumpkin, Katherine. "'The General Plan Was Freedom': A Negro Secret Order on the Underground Railroad." *Phylon* [Atlanta University] (Vol. XXVIII) 1 (1967): 63–77.

Fleming, W. L. "The Buford Expedition to Kansas." *American Historical Review* (October 1900): 38–48.

Hatch, Nathan O. "The Origins of Civil Millennialism in America," in *Reckoning with the Past: Historical Essays on American Evangelicalism from the Institute for the Study of American Evangelicals.* D. G. Hart, ed. Grand Rapids, Mich.: Baker Books, 1995).

Huhner, Leon. "Some Jewish Associates of John Brown." *Magazine of History with Notes and Queries* (September 1908): 143–51.

Larned, Ellen D. "New Connecticut, or Western Reserve." *Connecticut Quarterly* (January–March 1897): 88–99.

McKivigan, John R. "The Frederick Douglass-Gerrit Smith Friendship and Political Abolitionism in the 1850s," in *Frederick Douglass: New Literary and Historical Essays.* Eric J. Sundquist, ed. Cambridge: Cambridge University Press, 1995.

Moorhead, James H. "Searching for the Millennium in America." *Princeton Seminary Bulletin* VII (2)(1987): 17–33.

Ricks, Mary Kay. "Escape on the Pearl." *Washington Post* (August 12, 1998), H 01.

Webb, Jo Ann. "From Obscurity, an African American Photographer's Life Comes into Focus." *Smithsonian Institution Research Report* 97 (Summer 1999): 3.

## Books: Primary to the Study

Anderson, Osborne P. *A Voice from Harper's Ferry: A Narrative of Events at Harper's Ferry.* Boston, 1861.

Boyer, Richard O. *The Legend of John Brown: A Biography and a History.* New York: Alfred A. Knopf, 1973.

Bridgman, Edward P., and Luke F. Parsons. *With John Brown in Kansas: The Battle of Osawatomie.* Madison, Wis.: Davidson, 1915.

Brown, John. *Provisional Constitution and Ordinances for the People of the United States.* Boyd Stutler, ed. Weston, Mass.: M&S Press, 1969.

Case, Lora. *Hudson of Long Ago: Progress of Hudson during the Past Century Personal Reminiscences of an Aged Pioneer* (1897). Hudson, Ohio: Hudson Library and Historical Society, 1963.

Cohen, Stan. *John Brown "The Thundering Voice of Jehovah": A Pictorial Heritage.* Missoula, Mont.: Pictorial Histories, 1999.

Connelley, William E. *John Brown.* Topeka: Crane, 1900.

Cox, Clinton. *Fiery Vision. The Life and Death of John Brown.* New York: Scholastic Press, 1997.

Douglass, Frederick. *Life and Times of Frederick Douglass, Written by Himself.* Hartford, Conn.: Park, 1881; facsimile edition, Secaucus, N.J.: Citadel Press, 1983.

Du Bois, W. E. B. *John Brown.* New York: International, 1909, 1962.

[Everhart, William C., and Arthur L. Sullivan.] *John Brown's Raid.* National Park Service History Series. Washington, D. C.: Office of Publications, National Park Service, 1974.

Featherstonaugh, Thomas. *John Brown's Men: The Lives of Those Killed at Harper's Ferry.* Harrisburg, Pa.: Harrisburg Publishing, 1899.

Finkelman, Paul (ed.) *His Soul Goes Marching On: Responses to John Brown and the Harpers Ferry Raid.* Charlottesville: University Press of Virginia, 1995.

Fried, Albert. *John Brown's Journey: Notes and Reflections on His America and Mine.* Garden City, N.Y.: Anchor Press/Doubleday, 1978.

Hinton, Richard J. *John Brown and His Men.* New York: Funk and Wagnalls, 1894.

Humphrey, Frederick. *The Humphrey Family in America.* New York: Humphrey Print, 1883.

Lampson, Edward C. *John Brown and Ashtabula County.* Jefferson, Ohio: Jefferson Gazette, 1955.

Libby, Jean. *Black Voices from Harpers Ferry.* Palo Alto, Calif.: Published by Author, 1979.

Libby, Jean, et al. *John Brown Mysteries.* Missoula, Mont.: Pictorial Histories, 1999.

Lingo, William R. *The Pennsylvania Career of John Brown*. Corry, Pa.: Journal, 1926.

McFarland, Gerald W. *A Scattered People: An American Family Moves West*. New York: Pantheon Books, 1985.

Miller, Ernest C. *John Brown: Pennsylvania Citizen*. Warren: Penn State Press, 1952.

Oates, Stephen B. *To Purge This Land with Blood: A Biography of John Brown*. New York: Harper and Row, 1970.

————. *Our Fiery Trial: Abraham Lincoln, John Brown, and the Civil War Era*. Amherst: University of Massachusetts Press, 1979.

Ott Stake, Virginia. *John Brown in Chambersburg*. Chambersburg, Pa.: Franklin County Heritage, 1977.

Quarles, Benjamin. *Allies for Freedom: Blacks and John Brown*. New York: Oxford University Press, 1974.

Redpath, James. *The Public Life of John Brown*. Boston: Thayer and Eldridge, 1860.

————. *Echoes of Harper's Ferry*. Boston: Thayer and Eldridge, 1860.

Richman, Irving B. *John Brown among the Quakers and Other Sketches*. Des Moines: Historical Department of Iowa, 1904.

Rossbach, Jeffrey. *Ambivalent Conspirators: John Brown, the Secret Six, and a Theory of Slave Violence*. Philadelphia: University of Pennsylvania Press, 1982.

Ruchames, Louis (ed.) *A John Brown Reader*. New York: Abelard- Schuman, 1959.

Sanborn, Franklin B. *Memoirs of John Brown, Written for Reverend Samuel Orcutt's History of Torrington, Ct*. Concord, Mass.: January, 1878.

————. *The Life and Letters of John Brown, Liberator of Kansas, and Martyr of Virginia*. Boston, 1885; rpt. New York: Negro Universities Press, 1969.

————. *Recollections of Seventy Years, Vol. 1*. Boston: Gorham Press, 1909.

Scott, John A., and Robert A. Scott. *John Brown of Harper's Ferry*. New York: Facts on File Publications, 1988.

Stavis, Barrie. *John Brown: The Sword and the Word*. New York: A. S. Barnes, 1970.

Stutler, Boyd B. *John Brown*. An incomplete, unpublished manuscript in the John Brown Collection of the Reverend Clarence S. Gee. Hudson, Ohio: Hudson Library and Historical Society.

Villard, Oswald G. *John Brown: A Biography 1800–1859*. New York: Doubleday, Inc., 1910, 1929.

Waite, Frederick C. *Western Reserve University: The Hudson Era*. Cleveland, Ohio: Western Reserve University Press, 1943.

BOOKS: BACKGROUND TO THE STUDY

Ahlstrom, Sydney E. *A Religious History of the American People.* New Haven, Conn.: Yale University Press, 1972, 1979.

Aptheker, Herbert. *American Negro Slave Revolts.* New York: International, 1943, 1987.

———. *Nat Turner's Slave Rebellion.* New York: Grove Press/Humanities Press, 1966, 1968.

Baxter, Richard. *The Saints' Everlasting Rest* (1650). Rpt. New York: American Tract Society, ca. 1840.

Beeke, Joel R., and Sinclair B. Ferguson (ed.) *Reformed Confessions Harmonized.* Grand Rapids, Mich.: Baker Books, 1999.

Bell, Howard H. (ed.) *Proceedings of the National Convention of Colored People and Their Friends Held in Troy, N.Y., on the 6th, 7th, 8th, and 9th October, 1847.* Troy, N.Y.: J. C. Kirkland, 1847, rpt. in *Minutes of the Proceedings of the National Negro Conventions 1830–1864.* New York: Arno Press, 1969.

Bellesiles, Michael A. *Arming America: The Origins of a National Gun Culture.* New York: Alfred A. Knopf, 2000.

Berwanger, Eugene H. *The Frontier against Slavery: Western Anti- Negro Prejudice and the Slavery Extension Controversy.* Urbana: University of Illinois Press, 1967.

Blassingame, John W. *The Slave Community: Plantation Life in the Antebellum South.* New York: Oxford University Press, 1972, 1977.

Caccamo, James F. *The Story of Hudson Ohio.* Hudson, Ohio: Friends of Hudson Library, 1995.

Carvalho, Joseph, III. *Black Families in Hampden County, Massachusetts 1650–1855.* Westfield: Institute for Massachusetts Studies, 1984.

Conrad, Earl. *Harriet Tubman.* New York: Paul S. Eriksson, 1943, 1969.

Cummings, Naomi T., Sylvia G. Humphrey, et al. *The History of St. John's Congregational Church, Springfield, Massachusetts, 1844–1962.* Springfield: St. John's Congregational Church History Committee, 1962.

Davis, David Brion. *The Problem of Slavery in Western Culture.* Ithaca, N.Y.: Cornell University Press, 1966, 1970.

Dillon, Merton L. *Elijah P. Lovejoy, Abolitionist Editor.* Urbana: University of Illinois Press, 1961.

Doddridge, Philip. *Rise and Progress of Religion in the Soul* (ca. 1740). Rpt. New York: American Tract Society, 1849.

Dumond, Dwight L. *Anti-slavery Origins of the Civil War in the United States.* Ann Arbor: University of Michigan Press, 1959, 1964.

Filler, Louis. *The Crusade Against Slavery 1830–1860.* New York: Harper Torchbooks, 1960.

Foner, Philip S. (ed.) *The Life and Writings of Frederick Douglass*. New York: International, 1952, 1975.

Frisch, Michael H. *Town into City: Springfield, Massachusetts, and the Meaning of Community, 1840–1880*. Cambridge: Harvard University Press, 1972.

Gatewood, Willard B. Jr. *Free Man of Color: The Autobiography of Willis Augustus Hodges*. Knoxville: University of Tennessee Press, 1982.

Handy, Robert T. *A Christian America: Protestant Hopes and Historical Realities*. New York: Oxford University Press, 1971.

Harding, Vincent. *There Is a River: The Black Struggle for Freedom in America*. New York: Vintage, 1981.

*Hudson: A Survey of Historic Buildings in an Ohio Town*. Kent, Ohio: Kent State University Press, 1989.

Kyle, Richard. *The Last Days Are Here Again: A History of the End Times*. Grand Rapids, Mich.: Baker Books, 1998.

Langston, John M. *From the Virginia Plantation to the National Capitol*. Hartford, Conn.: American Publishing, 1894; rpt. New York: Kraus Reprint, 1969.

Libby, Jean (ed.) *From Slavery to Salvation: The Autobiography of Reverend Thomas W. Henry of the A.M.E. Church*. Jackson: University Press of Mississippi, 1994.

Litvin, Martin. *The Journey*. Galesburg, Ill.: Galesburg Historical Society, 1981.

Litwack, Leon F. *North of Slavery: The Negro in the Free States, 1790–1860*. Chicago: University of Chicago Press, 1961.

———. *Been in the Storm So Long: The Aftermath of Slavery*. New York: Alfred A. Knopf, 1979.

Locke, Mary Stoughton. *Anti-Slavery in America from the Introduction of African Slaves to the Prohibition of the Slave Trade 1619–1808*. Gloucester, Mass.: Peter Smith, 1965.

Marty, Martin E. *Righteous Empire: The Protestant Experience in America*. New York: Dial Press, 1970.

Mayer, Henry. *All on Fire: William Lloyd Garrison and the Abolition of Slavery*. New York: St. Martin's Griffin, 1998.

McLaurin, Melton A. *Celia, A Slave*. New York: Avon Books, 1991.

Murray, Andrew E. *Presbyterians and the Negro: A History*. Philadelphia: Presbyterian Historical Society, 1966.

Niebuhr, H. Richard. *The Kingdom of God in America*. Middletown, Conn.: Wesleyan University Press, 1937, 1988.

Oates, Stephen B. *The Fires of Jubilee: Nat Turner's Fierce Rebellion*. New York: Harper and Row, 1976.

Parish, Peter J. *Slavery, History and Historians*. New York: Harper and Row, 1989.

Phillips, William. *The Conquest of Kansas by Missouri and Her Allies*. Boston: Phillips, Sampson, 1856.

Quarles, Benjamin. *Black Abolitionists*. New York: Oxford University Press, 1969, 1970.

———. *Frederick Douglass*. New York: DeCapo Press, 1997.

Rhodes, Jane. *Mary Ann Shadd Cary: The Black Press and Protest in the Nineteenth Century*. Bloomington: Indiana University Press, 1998.

Richards, Leonard R. *"Gentlemen of Property and Standing": Anti-Abolition Mobs in Jacksonian America*. New York: Oxford University Press, 1970.

Roberton, David. *Denmark Vesey*. New York: Vintage, 1999.

*The Life, Trial, and Execution of Captain John Brown*. New York: Robert M. De Witt, 1859.

*The Underground Railroad in Springfield, Massachusetts*. Kathryne Burns, ed. Springfield, Mass.: Springfield Bicentennial Committee, 1976.

Robinson, Gwendolyn, and John W. Robinson. *Seek the Truth: A Story of Chatham's Black Community*. Chatham, Ontario: Robinson and Robinson, 1989.

Rollin, Frank A. [Frances E. Rollin Whipper] *Life and Public Services of Martin R. Delany*. Boston: Lee and Shepard, 1883; rpt. New York: Arno Press/New York Times, 1969.

Trask, Kerry A. *In the Pursuit of Shadows: Massachusetts Millennialism and the Seven Years War*. New York: Garland, 1989.

Walker, David. *Appeal to the Coloured Citizens of the World, but In Particular, and Very Expressly, To Those of the United States of America*. James Turner, ed. Baltimore: Black Classics, 1993.

Warfield, Benjamin B. *Perfectionism*. Samuel G. Craig, ed. Philadelphia: Presbyterian and Reformed, 1958, 1980.

Winks, Robin W. *The Blacks in Canada: A History*. Montreal: McGill-Queen's University Press, 1971.

Wyatt-Brown, Bertram. *Lewis Tappan and the Evangelical War against Slavery*. New York: Atheneum, 1971.

## Scholarly Manuscripts

Libby, Jean. "The Harper's Ferry Slave Insurrection—1859." Manuscript, 1985.

———. "The Slaves Who Fought with John Brown." Manuscript, Sept. 1988.

Smith, Eric Ledell. "John Brown in Crawford County: The Making of a Radical Abolitionist." Harrisburg: Pennsylvania Historical and Museum Commission, 2001. Published under the same title in *Journal of Erie Studies* (Fall 2001): 41–54.

## Primary Documents

Correspondence of Boyd B. Stutler and Clarence S. Gee, Hudson Library and Historical Society, Hudson, Ohio.

George Sigler, "A Brief History of My Life and Labors" (ca. 1890). Transcript courtesy of Natalie and Richard Smith.

"Owen Brown's Autobiography." November 10, 1841. Transcribed by Clarence S. Gee, in the Hudson Library and Historical Society, Hudson, Ohio.

"Owen Brown's Autobiography as written to his daughter, Marian Brown Hand ca. 1850." Transcribed by Clarence S. Gee, in the Hudson Library and Historical Society, Hudson, Ohio.

*Records of the Congregational Church in Hudson; Organized September 4, 1802, Transcribed August, 1820.* Transcribed by Jeffrey A. Mills and John J. Fedak, Columbus, Ohio (February–May 1986), in the Hudson Library and Historical Society, Hudson, Ohio.

*Records of the Free Congregational Church of Hudson; Organized October 7th A.D. 1842,* in the Hudson Library and Historical Society, Hudson, Ohio.

INTERVIEWS

Thomas Vince, Archivist and Historian of the Western Reserve Academy, Hudson, Ohio, March 16, 2000.

Margaret Washington, Professor of History, Cornell University, in New York City, May 10, 2001.

# Index

# About the Author

Louis A. DeCaro, Jr., is an ordained minister and author of *On the Side of My People: A Religious Life of Malcolm X* and *Malcolm and the Cross: The Nation of Islam, Malcolm X, and Christianity,* both available from NYU Press. He also coedited *Signs of Hope in the City* with Robert Carle, and is a contributor to *New York Glory: Religion in the City,* edited by Tony Carnes and Anna Karpathakis, also available from NYU Press. He holds graduate degrees from Westminster Seminary and New York University.